THE EARLY POSTGLACIAL SETTLEMENT
OF NORTHERN EUROPE

NEW APPROACHES IN ARCHAEOLOGY
General Editor: Colin Renfrew
Professor of Archaeology in the University of Southampton

The Spatial Organisation of Culture   *Ian Hodder*
Ecology and Economy in Neolithic Eastern Europe   *Paul Dolukhanov*

The Early Postglacial Settlement of Northern Europe

An Ecological Perspective

Edited by Paul Mellars

Senior Lecturer in Prehistory
University of Sheffield

University of Pittsburgh Press

Published in Great Britain 1978 by Gerald Duckworth & Co. Ltd
Published in the U.S.A. 1979 by the University of Pittsburgh Press, Pittsburgh, Pa.
15260

Library of Congress Catalog Card Number 78-63264
ISBN 0-8229-1137-X

Photoset in Great Britain by Specialised Offset Services Limited, Liverpool
and printed by Page Bros (Norwich) Ltd., Norwich

Contents

Preface

In common with most areas of prehistory, research into the earlier stages of postglacial occupation in northern Europe has advanced at an impressive – almost alarming – rate during the past decade. To a large extent this progress reflects simply the rapid expansion in the scope and intensity of the research being carried out in different areas, with a corresponding increase in the total quantity of data available for all kinds of archaeological 'reconstruction' – chronological, 'cultural', economic, and so forth. Equally significant, however, are the radical changes which have taken place in the general aims and orientation of archaeological research in these areas, and the impact of these changes on some of the more traditional ideas concerning the behaviour of 'Mesolithic' communities, and the role which these communities played in the development of European prehistory as a whole.

The aim of the fourteen papers presented in this volume is to provide a review of the progress made in both these directions. From the papers contributed by Peter Woodman on the Irish Mesolithic, and those by Noel Broadbent and Svein Indrelid on the Scandinavian material, for example, it will be apparent that research carried out over the past five to ten years has necessitated a complete re-appraisal of our ideas regarding the earliest stages of postglacial colonisation and settlement in these areas. Even in a relatively well surveyed area such as northern England it will be clear from the study by Roger Jacobi that a firm outline of the detailed patterns of Mesolithic occupation is only just beginning to emerge.

Other papers in the volume illustrate how the application of new theoretical approaches and new methods of analysis can provide fresh insight into the economic and social patterns of Mesolithic communities, and the complex ways in which these aspects of human behaviour were articulated with particular elements in the natural environment. The application of various forms of spatial analysis to archaeological data, for example, is explored in detail in the papers by

Bailey, Mellars and Reinhardt and Whallon, and is implicit in the approaches adopted by several other contributors; these studies illustrate how different approaches to spatial and locational analysis can be used to throw light on a wide range of human behaviour, from the overall distribution of settlement and economic activities in different ecological zones to the detailed organisation of human activities within the confines of the individual occupation site.

A totally different approach to economic and social analysis is that adopted in the paper by Douglas Price, in which data on the distribution and seasonal fluctuations in food resources is used as a basis for constructing an explicit 'simulation model' for the subsistence and settlement strategies of Mesolithic communities. In a similar vein Jan Bay-Petersen shows how a combination of ecological studies and detailed faunal analysis can be used to challenge some of the more orthodox ideas about the patterns of man-animal relationships in the European Mesolithic, while the paper by Christopher Meiklejohn examines the more general question of human population growth during early postglacial times, and the ways in which demographic changes may have been related to changes in both economic and residential patterns associated with the transition from late-glacial to postglacial conditions. Clearly, no collection of this kind can hope to be comprehensive; nevertheless it is hoped that the various studies presented here will provide a reasonably balanced survey of the major advances which have been made in studies of the north European Mesolithic during the past decade, and indicate some of the lines along which research is likely to proceed in the future.

The original stimulus to collect together this series of papers was provided by a three-day conference on the Mesolithic in north-west Europe organised by the Prehistoric Society, and held at the University of London in April 1976. Several papers originally presented at this conference, and subsequently revised by the authors, are included here. The remaining papers were written at the special request of the editor in order to increase the geographical and theoretical scope of the volume.

The success of the original Prehistoric Society conference owed a great deal to the help and encouragement of the President of the Society, Professor John Evans, and to the conference secretaries, Mr James Dyer and Dr John Greeves. Kindly acting as Chairmen for the various sessions at the conference were Professor Evans, Professor Frank Mitchell and Professor Grahame Clark. Professor Clark's own introduction to the conference, which sets our present approach to the European Mesolithic firmly within its historical context, serves as the introductory essay to the present volume.

The task of editing the complete collection of papers for publication was made much easier by the assistance of Christine Williams, while many of the maps and diagrams were redrawn by Susan Vaughan. I would also like to express my thanks to Professor Colin Renfrew for his advice and guidance at several stages during the editing of the volume.

Department of Prehistory and Archaeology,   Paul Mellars
University of Sheffield.
May 1978

B

List of Contributors

G.N. Bailey – Department of Archaeology, University of Cambridge.

Jan Bay-Petersen – Institut for Forhistorisk Arkaeologi, University of Aarhus.

Noel D. Broadbent – Institute for North European Archaeology, University of Uppsala.

Grahame Clark – Peterhouse, Cambridge.

Svein Indrelid – Historisk Museum, University of Bergen.

Roger M. Jacobi – 27 Sandy Lodge Road, Moor Park, Rickmansworth, Hertfordshire.

Christopher Meiklejohn – Department of Anthropology, University of Winnipeg.

Paul Mellars – Department of Prehistory and Archaeology, University of Sheffield.

T. Douglas Price – Department of Anthropology, University of Wisconsin (Madison).

Sally C. Reinhardt – 212 Forest Hills Lane, Gastonia, North Carolina.

Stig Welinder – University Museum of National Antiquities, University of Oslo.

Robert Whallon Jr. – Museum of Anthropology, University of Michigan (Ann Arbor).

Peter C. Woodman – Ulster Museum, Belfast.

Marek Zvelebil – Department of Archaeology, University of Cambridge.

1

Neothermal orientations

Grahame Clark

The ambiguity of my title is more apparent than real. If we are concerned with the way the prehistoric inhabitants of temperate Europe reorientated their lives in the context of environmental change, the way they adapted their economy, their technology and their society to the manifold changes implied by the onset of Neothermal climate, the contraction of ice-sheets, the spread of forests and so on, we must at the same time orientate our thoughts – hopefully reorientate our thoughts – about the role these people played in European prehistory.

I do not wish to dwell at length or in detail on the history of European prehistory, but I must make the point that our attitudes to the prehistory of the Neothermal have been largely distorted by the attitudes of our predecessors. If one compares the situation in the northern hemisphere in the Old and New Worlds, it is evident that there is a certain disadvantage in living in the continent that invented prehistory, just as there is in living in the country that invented the Industrial Revolution: one has to put up with the aftermath of crude and often uncouth beginnings. Above all, we in Britain have had to live with the consequences of Sir John Lubbock, the Victorian evolutionists and their Marxist aftermaths. During the formative days of prehistory the definition of the Palaeolithic and Neolithic Stone Ages appeared to mark a palpable advance. Why then am I implying that some of the consequences were unhappy? It is understandable, but nonetheless unfortunate, that the distinction should have been over-emphasised – the point had to be made and made emphatically – and we must remember the context of Lubbock's book, *Prehistoric Times* (1865). It appeared within six years of the publication of Darwin's *On the Origin of Species by means of Natural Selection* (1859) – that is, in the first flush of applying the doctrine of evolution to human affairs. Again Lubbock was writing as a young man (31), and at a time when the finds of Lartet and Christy were coming fresh from the Dordogne caves and contrasting mightily and palpably with the fortuitous revelation a decade earlier of the Swiss lake dwellings.

Perhaps it was not so surprising that G. de Mortillet's *Musée Préhistorique* (1881), the first great systematisation of the French sequence (issued within seven years of Lubbock's first definition of the Palaeolithic/Neolithic dichotomy: c.f. Mortillet ·1872) should have incorporated the, to us, preposterous doctrine of the hiatus between the cave sequence and the Robenhausian.

I have described the hiatus theory as preposterous. Hugo Obermaier, writing in the immediately succeeding generation (1924), put the matter more mildly by objecting that 'it would be strange indeed if man should have deserted [the continent of Europe] at the very moment when its climatic conditions were becoming increasingly favourable'. This did not prevent the dogma (it was hardly advanced as a hypothesis) being fiercely held at the time. When Allen Brown ventured to write *On the Continuity of the Palaeolithic and Neolithic periods* (1893) and suggested the term Mesolithic to designate 'those objects in stone which neither belong to the drift period nor to that of polished stone', a designation which had already been proposed by Westropp (1872: 102-4) before the hiatus theory had been enunciated and one which comprehended a much more extended range of time than present usage, he was heavily jumped upon by Boyd Dawkins. As is so often the case the convert was more convinced than the originator. Dawkins emphasised the environmental as well as the cultural differences: in addition to the 'great gulf' in cultural terms there was 'a zoological break of the first magnitude' between the Palaeolithic and the Neolithic and, on an insular note, he recalled that Britain had become an island during this interval. He (rightly) dismissed the surface industries quoted by Brown as 'waifs and strays ... worthless for the purpose of archaeological classifications', and correctly discounted the primitive appearance of material from the flint mines. Dawkins concluded his furious broadside by stating that 'the progress of discovery has not yet bridged over the abyss separating the Palaeolithic age of the Pleistocene period from the Neolithic age of the Prehistoric period in any part of the world' (1894: 251). He was prepared to admit that there must somewhere have been continuity, though 'probably not in Europe', but emphasised that 'the intermediate stages by which he passed from the Palaeolithic to the Neolithic stage of civilisation still remain to be discovered'.

I have referred to the hiatus theory, not because there is any danger of its being revived, but because I believe it can be shown to have warped much of our thinking. When it was discovered that the early postglacial period was far from empty (I refer to the Azilian and Tardenoisian levels in cave sequences but above all to the successively earlier Stone Age industries brought to light in south Scandinavia) this did not change attitudes overnight. Mesolithic finds tended to be depreciated as mere gap-fillers, not as providing evidence for ongoing continuity or even as restoring, so to say, the seamless garment of prehistory. They were neither fish nor fowl. They represented a decline from the period of cave art and failed to anticipate the imagined lake villages of the Robenhausian, still less the megaliths of western and northern Europe. It seemed happily symbolic that the new age should be represented by microliths, whose diminutive size neatly suggested their historical insignificance.

In the first Presidential Address to the Prehistoric Society in 1935, Professor V. Gordon Childe was studious in avoiding any reference to the Mesolithic. 'What,' he asked, 'is to become of the hallowed terms Palaeolithic, Neolithic, Bronze Age, Iron Age? I would suggest that the classification Old Stone Age, New Stone Age, Bronze Age and Iron Age draws attention to real revolutions that affected all departments of human life' (1935a: 7). Childe was clearly not unaware of the existence of archaeological material intermediate in age between the Palaeolithic and Neolithic: a few years earlier, the first chapter of *The Dawn of European Civilization* (1927) had, after all, been entitled 'The Transitional Cultures'. On the opening page he admitted that the Palaeolithic and Neolithic could no longer be regarded as epochs 'standing over against one another sharply contrasted and separated by an impassable gulf. The Neolithic arts were not suddenly introduced complete and fully developed into an empty continent as our forefathers imagined. A whole series of intermediate stages have come to light to fill the old hiatus.' Yet it was clear that Childe was still captivated by the Palaeolithic/Neolithic dichotomy. For him the newly-found cultures of early Neothermal Europe did no more than fill an awkward temporal gap. On page 20 he wrote in so many words: 'Though the Epipalaeolithic cultures do fill a gap of time and prove the continuous occupation of parts of Europe from the Old Stone Age, they do not in any real sense constitute points of transition from the Palaeolithic to the Neolithic cultures.'

Childe preferred the term 'Epipalaeolithic' to 'Mesolithic' because he chose to regard the newly-found material as mere survivals of no real historical interest. After discounting the notion of indigenous domestication in Europe or of Palaeolithic pottery, he concluded that 'the contribution of the former age to European culture is negligible. The hiatus is only recreated. The traditional position may then be retained'. In *The Dawn*, as in *The Prehistory of Scotland* (1935b) he went through the motions of describing Epipalaeolithic finds, but relegated everything of importance to later prehistory as the outcome of diffusion from outside. So, for Childe, the only interest of the early Neothermal in temperate Europe was the evidence it provided for the adaptation of surviving hunter-fishers to environmental change – notably the onset of temperate forests. In passing, this adaptation was surely of significance not merely to the Mesolithic population, but also to its successors. In temperate Europe it was Mesolithic man who came to terms with the Neothermal environment, and for the first time sought out its resources. The subsistence and technology of the Neolithic, and indeed of later stages of European prehistory, rested on this foundation. For Childe, though, the Neolithic way of life on which subsequent history rested was seen as the outcome of a revolution – the 'Neolithic Revolution' – which was conceived of as taking place outside Europe. European society was thought of as the product of transformation by impulses from the most ancient east. If there had been no hiatus in settlement in Europe, then according to this view there might just as well have been. The Mesolithic phase of settlement was of so little relevance to the main course of prehistory.

What of the Russians? Here we can see very plainly the link between ideology and terminology. To begin with they followed the same antique model of mid-Victorian evolutionism followed by Childe. For thirty years or more after the Revolution attitudes were determined by the obligatory use of a book by Engels entitled *The Origin of the Family, Private Property and the State*, first published in 1884, a work itself based, as Michael Thompson has pointed out, on Lewis H. Morgan's *Ancient Society* (1877), and on Karl Marx's notes thereon. Prehistory had a special fascination in Soviet eyes because primitive society was held to have been classless, exemplifying communism in all its pristine pre-class and pre-civilised glory. As such, the findings of prehistorians took on something of the character of a sacred writ, or rather they could do so if the findings were correct. And correctness in a totalitarian society is what its leaders find most conducive to perpetuating their ideology and consequently their power. So careful guidance was needed. During N.Y. Marr's directorship of the Russian (State) Academy of History of Material Culture (1930-4), prehistory was divided into five periods equated with supposed stages in social evolution, rather than based on the classification of material data:

Primitive Herd (Lower Palaeolithic)
Primitive Community (Upper Palaeolithic)
Matriarchal Class Society (Neolithic)
Patriarchal Class Society (Bronze Age)
The period of break-up of tribal society (Iron Age) immediately
    preceding the emergence of the State

Note the clean break between the Upper Palaeolithic and the Neolithic: such a system presupposed a quantum jump, and for 'the transformation of the Primitive Community into the Matriarchal Clan Society' read Childe's 'Neolithic Revolution'.

The effect of Hitler's assault, like that of Napoleon's, was to stimulate patriotic feelings in Russia. One form taken by the upsurge of Russian patriotism was the revision, indeed the destruction, of Marrism, reviewed by Michael Thompson in his foreword to the Penguin edition of Mongait's *Archaeology in the U.S.S.R.* (1961). Stalin, in his *Marxism and the Problems of Philology* (1950), denounced Marr as non-Marxist. Marr's name was expunged from the title of the Institute and in 1951 leading archaeologists rushed to contribute to a book entitled *Against the Vulgarisation of Marxism in Archaeology* in which the errors of 'vulgar sociology' were denounced as leading to 'the decolourisation of the historical process'. What was needed was the replacement of abstractions by concrete archaeology and the enrichment of prehistory by taking less account of theory and more of national and racial variations. In other words prehistory was to help build a consciousness of Russian history. But it is of the essence of any national or regional history that it should be continuous and that, so far as possible, its course should be explicable in terms of indigenous development.

As Mongait expressed it in his book: 'Marr's followers [had] fitted the data of material sources to ready-made, prepared schemes. Works were published in which it was asserted that, as a result of a leap, by means of a miraculous transformation, one people changed into another ...' (1959: 57). In the same way, one could no longer explain the change from the Palaeolithic to the Neolithic in terms of a single leap. It is significant that in his book Mongait envisaged (p. 85) that 'the transition to a new historical epoch ... gradually took shape in the postglacial age'. The fact that he gave only 23 lines out of 429 pages to this transition he explained by the simple statement that 'much less is known in the world about the Mesolithic than about the other periods of the Stone Age'.

Since then, Mesolithic studies have undergone a rapid growth in the Soviet Union, from the east Baltic to the Caspian. Already in 1966 a whole volume of *Materialy i issledovaniya po Arkheologii S.S.S.R.* was consecrated to twenty-two studies on Mesolithic topics, under the editorship of N.N. Gurina. With a wholesome logic, V.M. Masson's map of Mesolithic sites in south-west Asia includes not merely Natufian but also some of those grotesquely designated 'Pre-Pottery Neolithic' in some western literature. As if to underline the point, the aceramic artefacts of flint, stone, antler and bone from sites like Jarmo, Palegawra, Djeitun, Eynan, Jericho or El Khiam, could be lost in early Neothermal assemblages over a large part of Europe.

Our colleagues in the New World were spared both the hiatus and the Mesolithic because they were equally spared the Palaeolithic and the Neolithic. There never has been any doubt that New World prehistory was continuous. In plotting its history our American colleagues have been helped immensely by radiocarbon dating. Indeed it may not be generally known that it was Willard Libby's belief in the remote antiquity of man in the New World (a belief still largely unfounded) that spurred him on to investigate the potential for dating purposes of the precise measurement of residual radiocarbon. It so happens that one of the classic applications of radiocarbon dating relates to our main theme, the continuity of prehistory. I refer to the investigations in the Tehuacan valley of central Mexico, sponsored by the Peabody Foundation for Archaeology, and directed by Richard S. MacNeish. Although subject to revision and supplementation by subsequent research, the volumes edited by Douglas S. Byers (1967) remain of particular therapeutic value to prehistorians trained in the broken-backed European tradition. Here the arid environment has preserved a stratigraphic sequence of plant remains in cultural contexts which provides invaluable clues to the changing pattern of man/plant relationships throughout almost the entire Neothermal period. Here we can see fossils of the key process saluted by Childe as the 'Neolithic Revolution'. In fact, this proved to have been gradual and protracted, though at critical points giving rise to decisive changes in the nature of the adjustment between human societies and their parent ecosystems. Indeed, one might go further and emphasise how much we have to learn from New World prehistory, not merely in relation to originative foci, but also and no less to an understanding of the twin processes of slow expansion depending on the need for genetic adaptation, and that of independent cultural developments in territories with differing ecologies.

Nearer home it has been not the least of the services rendered by the British Academy's Major Research Project on The Early History of Agriculture, under the direction of Eric Higgs, to treat the relationship between man and the animals and plants on which he depends as an ongoing, continuous one (Higgs 1972, 1975). To mention only one example, the study of transhumance, which after all is based on the simple biological fact that men predate herbivores which in turn go where the food is to be found at different times of the year, has yielded its best insights by being pursued across the period divisions of prehistory. We learn not merely about 'Palaeolithic' or 'Mesolithic' man, but also about the men of later prehistoric and indeed historical times. Such themes as Sangmeister's beaker reflux movements or the Hallstatt migrations into south-west Europe, inferred from correspondencies in pots or metal forms, may often be illuminated in the same terms as the distribution and location of early Stone Age sites.

What is perhaps not so well understood is that the continuities revealed in economic life exist also, and in some ways more significantly, at a conceptual level, at least for the forty thousand years or so since the final emergence of *Homo sapiens sapiens* with the physical attributes of modern man, including his brain and nervous system. The notion that man suddenly acquired a new dimension, the possibility of becoming civilised, at the moment he started to grow wheat, barley, rice or beans as controlled crops, is as absurd as the contemporary fallacies which attempt to equate consumption with well-being.

The fact that cave art is twice as old as the oldest cultivated crops is familiar enough. Herbert Read was not trying to be funny when he wrote: 'Some of the painters of Greek vases, some of the medieval illuminators of manuscripts, the great painters of the Renaissance, certain painters of the nineteenth century – all of these have perhaps reached the level of aesthetic quality present in the cave paintings of Lascaux or Altamira, but they have not exceeded that original standard' (1951: 12). Alexander Marshack (1972) is beginning to show with the aid of microphotography that the makers of this art were also practising a form of notation which in some instances appears to relate to the passage of the moon. Again, detailed observation of still living peoples, who, to judge from their material equipment and the fact that they subsisted by hunting and foraging, would in archaeological terms be judged Mesolithic or even Palaeolithic, has shown that they enjoyed a rich conceptual and ceremonial life, richer in many respects than that of most members of modern metropolitan communities. What may not always be realised is that such people engaged in an activity we are often prone to associate exclusively with communities whose economies were based on agriculture – namely the construction of monuments. Naturally, when the size of the day-to-day community was rarely more than fifteen or twenty persons a limit was set on the nature and scale of monumental constructions. That such were nevertheless made may be illustrated by the stone constructions made by the Australian aborigines in different parts of the continent. Although, as might be expected, the stones used in these were small by comparison with monuments set up in more populous societies, the structures are often quite extensive. The curvilinear alignment terminating in a spiral at one end observed by Richard Gould at Lake Moore, Western Australia, for instance, was over 200 feet long and made up of some 437 stone slabs, most of which stood about two feet high (Fig. 1). The *bora* grounds, where initiation rites involving circular dancing were being carried out in parts of Australia into the nineteenth century, were frequently enclosed by low earth banks (Howitt 1904: 593). Where there were two circles, as at Samford site, west of Brisbane, these might be connected by a straight avenue. No less evocative to a British archaeologist were the funerary mounds and their associated earthworks noted by early observers in New South Wales. That shown in my illustration (Fig. 2) was recorded by John Oxley when exploring the Lachlan river in 1817. The mound stood like the tump of a disc barrow in the midst of a flat area defined by a pennanular bank.The arc-shaped banks opposite the gap were interpreted by Oxley as seats for the spectators at the funerary rites (Oxley 1820). Analogies could be multiplied; for instance, the carvings made on trees surrounding burials compare remarkably in some instances with those pecked on the stones of some Irish passage graves. The danger of drawing parallels between the artefacts of communities far removed in time, space and culture needs no emphasis. It is still legitimate to point out that the construction of monuments connected with burial

Figure 1. Rock alignments and sacred rock-piles figure as important archaeological monuments in Australia. This serpentine alignment occurs on Lake Moore, Western Australia.

Figure 2. Burial mound and associated earthworks recorded by John Oxley (1820) on the Lachlan River, New South Wales.

and other ceremonial activity, like the practice of symbolic art, is no monopoly of communities founded on farming. Nearer home, indeed, it has recently been argued that at least two groups of Mesolithic tombs in Europe – the *dysse* and passage-graves of Bohuslan, western Sweden, and the entrance graves of the Celtic Sea – were constructed by people whose economy rested on fishing rather than farming (Clark 1977). This is perhaps something to remember when radiocarbon dating confronts us with the likelihood that megalithic monuments, whether funerary or ceremonial, are indigenous to western Europe. To generalise, the recognition that parts of Europe were inhabited during early Neothermal times by adaptable indigenous Mesolithic communities makes it easier to accommodate ourselves to the findings of radiocarbon dating. As Colin Renfrew has recently been emphasising, a number of key innovations of later Neothermal times need not and in some cases (even without the aid of recalibration) cannot any longer be explained, as Childe would once have had us believe, as mere emanations from the orient.

References

Brown, J.A. 1893. On the continuity of the Palaeolithic and Neolithic periods. *Journal of the Royal Anthropological Institute*, 22: 66-98.
Byers, D.S. (ed.) 1967. *The Prehistory of the Tehuacan Valley*. Austin and London, University of Texas Press.
Childe, V.G. 1927. *The Dawn of European Civilization*. London, Kegan Paul. (2nd. ed.)
Childe, V.G. 1935a. Changing methods and aims in prehistory. *Proceedings of the Prehistoric Society*, 1: 1-16.
Childe, V.G. 1935b. *The Prehistory of Scotland*. London, Kegan Paul.
Clark, G. 1977. The economic context of Dolmens and Passage-graves in Sweden. In V. Markotic (ed.) *Ancient Europe and the Mediterranean*. Warminster, Aris and Phillips: 35-49.
Darwin, C. 1859. *On the Origin of Species by the Means of Natural Selection*. London, Murray.
Dawkins, W.B. 1894. On the relation of the Palaeolithic to the Neolithic Period. *Journal of the Royal Anthropological Institute*, 23: 242-57.
Engels, F. 1884. *The Origins of the Family, Private Property and the State*. English translation by E. Untermann, 1902. Chicago, Kerr and Co.
Gould, R.A. 1969. *Yiwara: Foragers of the Australian Desert*. London, Collins.
Gurina, N.N. (ed.) 1966. *U Istokov Drevnikh Kul'tur. Epokha Mezolita*. Materialy i Issledovaniya po Arkheologii S.S.S.R., No. 126. Moscow and Leningrad, Academy of Sciences.
Higgs, E.S. (ed.) 1972. *Papers in Economic Prehistory*. London, Cambridge University Press.
Higgs, E.S. (ed.) 1975. *Palaeoeconomy*. London, Cambridge University Press.
Howitt, A.W. 1904. *The Native Tribes of South-east Australia*. London, Macmillan.
Lubbock, Sir. J. 1865. *Prehistoric Times*. London, Williams and Norgate.
Marshack, A. 1972. *The Roots of Civilization*. New York, McGraw-Hill.
Mongait, A.L. 1959. *Archaeology in the U.S.S.R.* English translation by M.W. Thompson (1961). London, Penguin Books.
Morgan, L.H. 1877. *Ancient Society*. New York,
Mortillet, G. de. 1872. Classification des diverses périodes de l'âge de la pierre. *Comptes Rendus du Congrès International d'Anthropologie et Archéologie Préhistorique*, 6: 432-44.
Mortillet, G. de, and Mortillet, A. de. 1881. *Musée Préhistorique*. Paris.
Obermaier, H. 1924. *Fossil Man in Spain*. New Haven, Hispanic Society of America.
Oxley, J. 1820. *Journal of Two Expeditions into the Interior of South-East Australia*. London.
Read, H. 1951. *Art and the Evolution of Man*, London, Freedom Press.
Stalin, J. 1950. *Concerning Marxism in Linguistics*. London, Soviet News.
Westropp, H.M. 1872. *Prehistoric Phases*. London, Bell and Daldy.

2

The concept of 'ecology' in Mesolithic research

Stig Welinder

A full description of a Mesolithic culture must include a reconstruction of its settlement pattern – that is, its yearly cycle of movements and changes in its resource exploitation (Fig. 1). The settlement pattern of a hunting/fishing/gathering group and its setting in the natural environment can be regarded as an ecosystem. In such an ecosystem (Fig. 2) the human society is dependent on such basic components as topography, subsoil and climate, while it is both dependent on and itself influencing such components as fauna and vegetation. In the temperate zone at least, the influence upon the environment by a society with a hunting/gathering economy is small, and changes caused by Man are reversible. A farming society, on the other hand, causes irreversible changes in the long run, affecting not only fauna and vegetation but also the much more important factors of topsoil, micro-fauna and micro-flora (Fig. 2).

Ecological research

From an ecological point of view the reconstruction of a Mesolithic settlement pattern is a description, merely a list of components within the prehistoric ecosystem. An ecological analysis deals with the interaction between components of the system, and also with the reaction of the system to outside stress. An ecological analysis of a Mesolithic ecosystem involves:

1. A quantification of the components which make up the system; and

2. A consideration of changes within the ecosystem through time.

In the following paragraphs three examples of this kind of analysis will be demonstrated. They are taken from the Mesolithic of south Scandinavia, and each of them deals with one of the major components of the Mesolithic economy of the area – that is, hunting, fishing and gathering. The aim is not to provide a complete analysis of

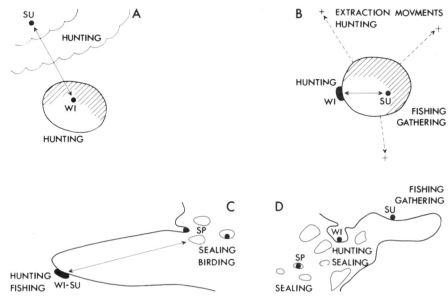

Figure 1. Reconstructed settlement patterns from the north European Mesolithic and Neolithic. The models summarise the yearly movements of hunting/fishing/gathering groups and the seasonal changes in the constraints in the exploitation schemes. A – Maglemosian of England, c. 7,500 bc (from Clark 1972); B – Maglemosian of south Scandinavia, c. 6,500 bc (from Welinder 1971, 1973); C – Komsa culture of arctic Norway, c. 5,000 bc (from Odner 1964); D – Pitted-Ware culture of eastern Sweden, c. 2,500 bc (from Welinder 1976). Diagrams A and B are based on inland lakes, while C and D represent coastal situations. SP = spring; SU = summer; WI = winter.

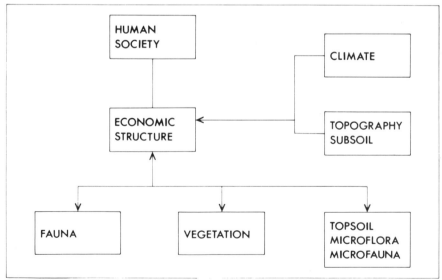

Figure 2. Generalised model of a human ecosystem. The model is valid for both hunting/gathering and farming societies. For societies using large amounts of energy the model must be changed.

Mesolithic settlement patterns in this area but merely to analyse some of the ecological relationships on which these settlement patterns were based.

Example 1: hunting

The relationship between the human society and the fauna of the environment of an area is simply termed hunting. One method of studying Mesolithic hunting patterns is through the examination of fractures on animal bones, both from settlement sites and stray finds. Clearly the occurrence of healed fractures indicates that the same animal has been hunted on at least two occasions, separated by a minimum interval of at least 2-3 months to allow the injury to heal. Changes through time in the ratio of healed to unhealed fractures should therefore demonstrate changes in the relationship between the hunters and their prey, that is, the human society and the fauna of the environment.

In a recent paper Noe-Nygaard (1974) has analysed the evidence for bone fractures in collections of faunal material from both Denmark and north Germany (Table 1). During the late-glacial period, when reindeer was the dominant game animal, healed fractures were found to be absent. This would suggest that the probability of repeated attacks on the same animal was small when hunting the large herds of reindeer on the tundra. The probability was greater in the postglacial forests, where aurochs, elk, red deer, roe deer and wild boar formed much smaller and more sedentary herds. In the material belonging to

Table 1. The occurrence of fractures caused by hunting on animal bones from north-west Germany and Denmark.

Time scale (Nilsson 1964a)	Numbers of fractures recorded Healed	Unhealed	Ratio of healed/ unhealed fractures
Postglacial			
SB 1	2	—	
AT 2	5	1	1.8
AT 1	—	3	
BO 2	1	—	
BO 1	—	1	0.7
PB	1	2	
Late-glacial			
DR 3	—	17	—

The material includes bones from both occupation sites and stray finds. The observations are based on bones of reindeer (in the late-glacial period) and red deer, roe deer, aurochs and wild pig (in the postglacial period). In the case of wild pig, wounds in the forehead region have been excluded, owing to uncertain interpretation. From Noe-Nygaard 1974.

this period healed fractures occur regularly in ribs, shoulder blades and vertebrae.

A further increase in the ratio of healed to unhealed fractures during the later Mesolithic as compared to the early Mesolithic (Table 1) is interpreted as a reflection of the succession from the early postglacial open forests to the more dense broad-leaved forests of the middle postglacial (cf. Fig. 9, C). In the latter type of environment the game was less abundant and the sedentary roe deer and red deer were the major prey species.

Example 2: fishing

The Quaternary biological investigations by Liljegren of the ecological succession in the Litorina lagoon at Spjälkö, Blekinge, south-east Sweden (Fig. 3) represents a useful study of the resources within a well-defined biotope (Liljegren and Welinder 1974). Fishing provided the most obvious way (though not the only possible way) of exploiting this lake/lagoon environment.

It has been possible not only to estimate the total quantity of fish

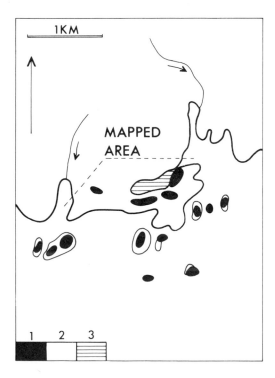

Figure 3. Map of the Spjälkö area in the province of Blekinge, south-east Sweden, during the first Litorina transgression, c. 5,000 bc. 1 – glacial deposits and shore gravel; 2 – primary bedrock; 3 – the Spjälkö lagoon.

SPJÄLKÖ

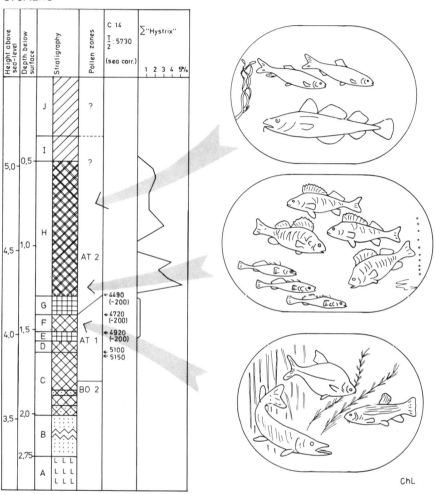

Figure 4. The stratigraphy and fish fauna of the Spjälkö lagoon. The stratigraphic sequence and the fauna are based on the evidence from an excavation in the centre of the lagoon. The main species represented are: pike, bream, tench (layer F); perch, stickleback (layer H, lower part); cod, herring (layer H, upper part). The stratigraphic divisions are as follows: layers A-B, clay and sand; layer C, freshwater mud; layers D-G, slightly brackish-water mud; layer H, brackish-water mud; layer I, carr peat; layer J, mixed layer. From Liljegren and Welinder 1974 and unpublished information from R. Liljegren.

present in the basin, but also to determine the composition of the fish-fauna with the aid of skeletons recovered from an excavation in the *gyttja* sequence of the basin (Fig. 4). We therefore have detailed information not only on the total range of fish species available to Mesolithic communities in the Spjälkö basin, but also on the overall biomass of the fish populations. Both factors changed through time.

Table 2. Quantities of fish in the Spjälkö Lagoon.

	Numbers of skeletons excavated	Weight of fish meat per volume of sediment (in kg./m^3)
Layer H — upper part	12	0.6
Layer H — lower part	66	1.2
Layer F	5	2.8

Archaeological investigations in the Spjälkö area have identified only Neolithic and Bronze Age sites, including both occupation sites and burial mounds. These sites are contemporary with the carr stage of the basin (Fig. 4). No settlement, either seasonal or permanent, has been found that is contemporary with the lake and lagoon stages of the basin. It would appear that during the stage of maximum eutrophy – that is, during the early lagoon stage – human exploitation of the basin was confined entirely to 'extraction' fishing activities. A finely-barbed leister prong from the above-mentioned excavation suggests that the lagoon had been used for spearing pike during this stage. All of the evidence would therefore suggest that throughout the ecological succession of the Spjälkö basin the shallow, slightly brackish-water lagoon stage with a freshwater fish fauna and extensive reeds was most attractive to Mesolithic fishing groups.

Example 3: gathering

A shallow lake passes through three main stages during its ecological succession: open water, the growing-over stage, and carr. The growing-over stage, when the lake is covered by reeds, is usually of short duration. During this stage the biological production of the biotope is at its maximum (Fig. 5). It then offers optimal exploitation possibilities for Mesolithic fishing and gathering groups (Welinder 1973).

The heavily reed-covered environment of the growing-over stage represents the characteristic environment of Mesolithic bog sites (Welinder 1973). Due to the optimal opportunities for economic exploitation, Mesolithic settlement is concentrated in both a time and space perspective on the growing-over stage of shallow lakes. In Figure 6 this is demonstrated for two ancient lakes in Scania, which

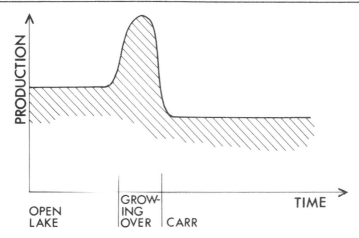

Figure 5. The approximate production of food resources available to man during successive stages in the ecological development of a lake. The production refers to both animal and plant foods. The scale of the diagram is arbitrary. From Westlake 1963 and Welinder 1973.

have since filled up and turned into raised bogs. The extensive bog area which will be referred to here as the 'Ageröds Mosse' changed from an open lake to a carr around the time of the Boreal-Atlantic transition (Fig. 8). The lake which is now represented by the 'Bare Mosse', on the other hand, filled up at the time of the early Boreal-later Boreal transition. At the latter site the Mesolithic occupation ceased when the growing-over phase of the lake was completed.

The general correlation between the occupation of bog sites in Scania and the growing-over stages of lakes is illustrated in Table 3. An initial period favourable to the growing over of lakes occurred during the Preboreal period (Digerfeldt 1972). A second major period of growing-over of lakes in Scania was the late Boreal and early Atlantic. During this second period the occupation of bog sites in Scania reached its maximum.

The archaeological framework

In common with most kinds of archaeological research, any attempt to analyse the ecological relationships of Mesolithic communities must be based on a firmly-established framework of chronology and typology. Most of the basic research in archaeology is concerned with the organisation of this framework. The more detailed this framework is as concerns time and space distributions, the more far-reaching are the interpretations that can be applied to the prehistoric source material. The reconstruction of economic and social structures has to be based upon this archaeological framework, as well as upon models derived from anthropology and ethnography (cf. Gräslund 1974, with

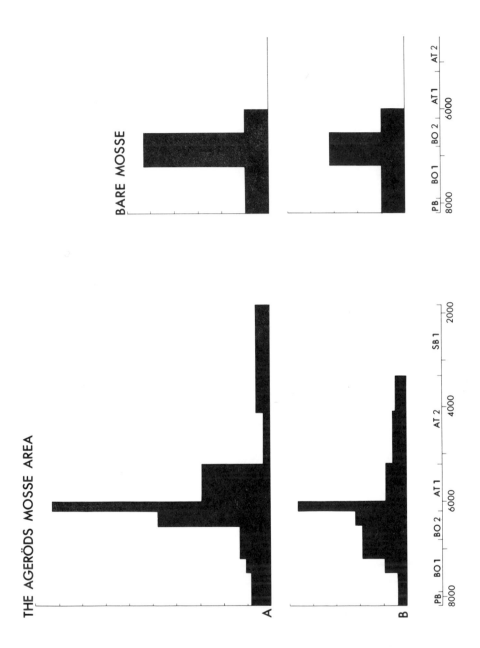

Figure 6. Human activity in the Ageröds Mosse and Bare Mosse areas in the province of Scania, south Sweden. The upper histograms (A) are based on the numbers of arrowheads represented per 100 years, while the lower histograms (B) are based on the numbers of settlement sites (characterized by particular microlith types) per 100 years (cf. Fig. 7). The time scale is based on Nilsson (1964a) modified by Digerfeldt (1975). Derived in part from Welinder 1973.

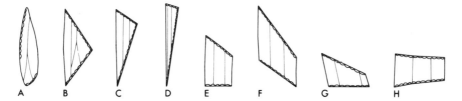

Figure 7. The principal types of microliths and arrowheads in the Mesolithic of south Scandinavia, and their approximate dating according to Althin (1954), Nilsson (1967), Welinder (1971), Larsson (1973) and others. A – lanceolate microliths, c. 8,200 – 6,000 bc; B – isosceles triangles, c. 7,500 – 6,500 bc; C – long, broad triangles, c. 7,200 – 6,500 bc; D – narrow triangles, c. 6,500 – 6,000 bc; E – broad trapezes, c. 6,200 bc; F – oblique arrowheads, c. 6,000 – 5,200 bc; G – transverse arrowheads, c. 5,200 – 1,800 bc. In calculating the numbers of arrowheads used in Figure 6A the types E – G have been calculated as one each, types A – C as half each, and type D as one-sixth each. These adjustments are necessary to compensate for the use of types A – D as parts of composite implements. Derived in part from Welinder 1973.

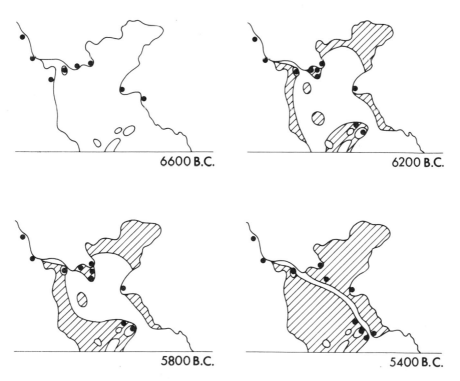

Figure 8. Time and space distribution of Stone Age settlement sites in the Ageröds Mosse area. The reconstructions of the growing-over stages of the ancient lake are compiled from Nilsson 1964a, 1964b, 1967. The sites are mapped according to Althin 1954. From Welinder 1971.

Table 3. Chronological distribution of Mesolithic bog sites and growing-over stages of lakes in Scania, south Sweden.

Time scale	Bog sites (Index)	Lakes growing over (Index)
AT 2	30	20
AT 1	140	70
BO 2	100	100
BO 1	20	0
PB	0	120

From Liljegren and Welinder 1974. The time scale is taken from Nilsson 1964a, modified by Digerfeldt 1975.

further references). Only as a third step in the research process can ecological explanations be looked for. However, it is not necessarily true that this framework must be organised in the same way when one is aiming at ecological explanations as when one is aiming at other kinds of explanations.

Towards an ecological archaeology

A typological/chronological framework that is not concerned with the time and space distributions of artefact types and culture groups, but with resource exploitation methods and settlement patterns, forms the basis of ecological archaeology, or 'human palaeoecology'. Ecological explanations can be arrived at by arranging the elements of this latter framework along time and space gradients, thus correlating the behaviour of Mesolithic hunting/fishing/gathering groups with ecological factors. The two following examples will help to demonstrate this way of thinking. The first example presents a large-scale view of north-west Europe, while the second presents a preliminary attempt to describe the Mesolithic of Scania in ecological terms.

Example 4: north-west European bog sites

As demonstrated in Example 3, the occurrence of Mesolithic bog sites is dependent on the occurrence of a special kind of environment – that is, shallow lakes during the growing-over stage. Thus the time and space distribution of bog sites in north-west Europe summarized in Table 4 is dependent on the main periods of growing-over of lakes during the postglacial period. This in turn is dependent on the humidity of the climate, the chemical composition of the Quaternary deposits and several other ecological factors. Thus it is hardly surprising to observe an approximate time gradient in the occupation

Table 4. Time and space distribution of Mesolithic bog sites along a west-east gradient in north-west Europe.

England	8,200 – 7,000 bc	(PB – BO 1)
Denmark	7,800 – 6,200 bc	(BO 1 – BO 2)
South Sweden	7,000 – 5,200 bc	(BO 2 – AT 1)

The dates indicate only the optimal periods of bog settlements in the different areas. Taken from Liljegren and Welinder 1974, with slight modifications. (For the definition of a 'bog site' see Welinder 1973.) The time scale is based on Nilsson 1964a, modified by Digerfeldt 1975.

of bog sites as one moves from west to east in north-western Europe (Table 4). The earliest bog sites are found in England and the latest in southern Sweden.

Thus the distribution of bog sites is not characteristic of any specific period of time or any particular cultural group, but can be seen simply as a reflection of the distribution of special environmental conditions which rendered these locations especially favourable for human exploitation. This pattern can be seen even more clearly in the time and space distribution of finely-barbed leister prongs, the major function of which appears to have been the spearing of pike in shallow water (cf. Example 2). During the early stages of the postglacial these implements were in use over the whole of north-west Europe (Table 5). In England and Denmark they disappeared towards the end of the Boreal period as the shallow-lake type of environment became rare. In south Sweden, on the other hand, they survived for a much longer period, especially in the area to the north-east of the Scanian fault-lines (dividing the sedimentary rock area from the primary rock area) where the main period of the growing-over of lakes can be dated to the early Atlantic, and where an environment similar to that of the shallow lakes existed in the early Litorina lagoons (cf. Example 2).

Table 5. Time and space distribution of finely-barbed leister prongs along a west-east gradient in north-west Europe.

England	8,200 – 7,000 bc	(PB – BO 1)
Denmark	8,200 – 6,500 bc	(PB – BO 2)
South Sweden	8,200 – 4,500 bc	(PB – AT 2)

The definition of 'leister prongs' is based on Clark 1936, Figure 41, nos. 2-4, 6. Taken from Liljegren and Welinder 1974, with slight modifications.

Example 5: the Mesolithic of Scania, south Sweden

Figure 9 summarises a series of factors that are important to the understanding of the Scanian Mesolithic in ecological terms. It presents three kinds of environment that have successively offered the

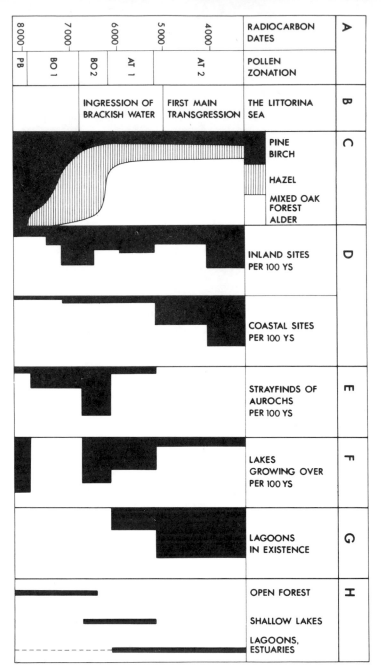

Figure 9. Ecological gradients in the Mesolithic of Scania, south Sweden. A – time-scale by Nilsson 1964a (modified by Digerfeldt 1975); B – the development of the Baltic (from Berglund 1971); C – general changes in vegetational composition from the Boreal to the Atlantic forest periods in south-west Scania (modified from Nilsson 1961); D – human activity calculated as numbers of sites with particular microlith types per 100 years (cf. Fig 7); E – optimal occurrence of big-game populations (from Liljegren and Welinder 1974); F – major periods of growing-over of lakes (from Liljegren and Welinder 1971); G – occurrence of lagoons along the present coastline (compiled from Nilsson 1935); H – succession of landscape-types offering the richest opportunities for economic exploitation within the present topographic limits of Scania.

optimal possibilities for economic exploitations to Mesolithic hunting/fishing/gathering groups – that is: 1. the open forest; 2. shallow lakes during the growing-over stage; and 3. lagoons and estuaries (Fig. 9, C, E-H).

The demographic curve for the inland areas of Scania shows two peaks (Fig. 9, D). The first peak (following a steady rise of the curve from the beginning of the postglacial) coincides with the final phase of the open-forest environment (Fig. 9, C) and the transition to the broad-leaved forest environment. The high density of Mesolithic population at this time can probably be attributed to a number of ecological factors, including a heavy concentration of big game animals (Fig. 9, E), a rich variety of vegetational composition (including an abundance of hazel) (Fig. 9, C), and the beginning of the main period of the growing-over of lakes. Evidently, this combination of ecological conditions offered optimal possibilities for resource exploitation in the inland areas of Scania.

This transition to the broad-leaved forest involved a change in the composition (cf. Example 1) and a temporary increase in the biomass of big-game animals (Fig. 9, E). During this period a general change in the Mesolithic resource exploitation strategy occurred, and settlement patterns based upon the exploitation of shallow lakes (Fig. 1, B) were established (cf. Examples 3-4).

A second peak in the demographic curve for inland Scania (Fig. 9, D) can be identified at the end of the Mesolithic during the later stages of the Atlantic period. This peak also coincides with a peak in the population curve for the coastal part of the province (Fig. 9, D). However, the two curves cannot be combined to provide a population curve for the whole of Scania, since the coastlines dating from before the time of the maximum Litorina transgression (in the second half of the late Atlantic) have been submerged by the rising sea (Fig. 9, B). The relationship between coastal and inland settlements during both the Boreal and Atlantic periods is problematic. However, it is clear that the resource exploitation of the coastal sites during the Atlantic was not based upon sealing or other kinds of sea hunting, but on the exploitation of Litorina lagoons and river estuaries (Fig. 9, G) – that

Table 6. The density of implements on Mesolithic settlement sites in south Sweden.

	Approximate density of implements per square metre
Lagoons and estuaries	2 – 6
Shallow lakes	1 – 2
Open forest	< 1

The figures represent the approximate numbers of implements (axes, scrapers, knives, burins) per square metre. The sites are classified according to the three types of environments defined in Figure 9 (H). Compiled from Althin 1954; Salomonsson 1965, 1969; Welinder 1971; and other sources.

is, on the exploitation of environments that were ecologically similar to the shallow lakes. These biotopes, located at the margins of several ecological zones, formed the basis of the second peak in the demographic curve (Fig. 9, D).

The general trend in the resource exploitation scheme proposed here (Fig. 9, H) runs parallel to a decrease in the mobility of human settlements throughout the Mesolithic period, which appears to be demonstrated by an increase in shooting pressure (cf. Example 1) and an increase in the size of settlement sites (Table 6). A further element in this development was an increase in the part played by fishing and the gathering of plant food, and a corresponding reduction in the importance of hunting.

References

Althin, C.A. 1954. *The Chronology of the Stone Age Settlement of Scania, Sweden: I. The Mesolithic Settlement.* Acta Archaeologica Lundensia, 1, Lund.

Berglund, B.E. 1971. Litorina transgressions in Blekinge, south Sweden. A preliminary survey. *Geologiska Föreningens i Stockholm Förhandlingar*, 93: 625-52.

Clark, J.G.D. 1936. *The Mesolithic Settlement of Northern Europe*, London, Cambridge University Press.

Clark, J.G.D. 1972. *Star Carr: a Case Study in Bioarchaeology.* Addison-Wesley Modular Publications, 10, Reading (Massachussetts).

Digerfeldt, G. 1972. *The Postglacial Development of Lake Trummen. Regional Vegetation History, Water-Level Changes and Palaeolimnology.* Folia Limnologica Scandinavica, 16, Lund.

Digerfeldt, G. 1975. A standard profile for Litorina transgressions in western Skåne, south Sweden. *Boreas*, 4: 125-42.

Gräslund, B. 1974. Befolkning – bosättning – miljö. Några synpunkter på det forntida jägarsamhället i Norden. *Fornvännen* 69: 1-13.

Larsson, L. 1973. Some problems of the Mesolithic based upon finds from the raised bog Ageröds Mosse. In S.K. Kozlowski (ed.), *The Mesolithic in Europe.* Warsaw, University Press: 367-80.

Liljegren, R. and Welinder, S. 1971. Pollen analytical dating of the skeleton of an aurochs. *Geologiska Föreningens i Stockholm Förhandlingar*, 93: 662-72.

Liljegren, R. and Welinder, S. 1974. Time and space distribution and ecological explanation in the north-west European Mesolithic. Paper read at the *Congrès Préhistorique de France* (Martigue). (in press)

Nilsson, T. 1935. Die pollenanalytische zonengliederung der spät- und post-glazialen bildungen schonens. *Geologiska Föreningens i Stockholm Förhandlingar*, 57: 385-562.

Nilsson, T. 1961. *Ein neues Standardpollendiagramm aus Bjärsjöholmssjön in Schonen.* Lunds Universitets Årsskrift, N.F. Avd. 2, Bd. 56, Nr. 18. Lund.

Nilsson, T. 1964a. *Standardpollendiagramm und C14-Datierungen aus dem Ageröds Mosse im Mittleren Schonen.* Lunds Universitets Årsskrift, N.F. Avd. 2, Bd 59, Nr. 7. Lund.

Nilsson, T. 1964b. *Entwicklungsgeschichtliche Studien im Ageröds Mosse, Schonen.* Lunds Universitets Årsskrift, N.F. Avd. 2, Bd. 59, Nr. 8. Lund.

Nilsson, T. 1967. *Pollenanalytische Datierung Mesolithischer Siedlungen im Randgebiet des Ageröds Mosse im Mittleren Schonen.* Acta Universitatis Lundensis, Sectio II (1967), No. 16. Lund.

Noe-Nygaard, N. 1974. Mesolithic hunting in Denmark illustrated by bone injuries caused by human weapons. *Journal of Archaeological Science*, 1: 217-48.

Odner, K. 1964. Erhverv og bosetning i Komsakulturen. *Viking*, 28: 117-28.

Salomonsson, B. 1965. Linnebjär: A Mesolithic site in south-west Scania. *Meddelanden från Lunds Universitets Historiska Museum*, 1964-5: 5-31.

Salomonsson, B. 1969. Mesolithic finds in the early Neolithic settlement at Svenstorp. *Meddelanden från Lunds Universitets Historiska Museum*, 1966-68: 255-68.

Welinder, S. 1971. *Tidigpostglacialt Mesoliticum i Skåne*. Acta Archaeologica Lundensia, Series in 8° minore, No. 1. Lund.

Welinder, S. 1973. Stenålderns mosseboplatser. *Ale. Historisk Tidskrift för Skåneland*, 1973 (1): 1-14.

Welinder, S. 1976. The economy of the Pitted Ware culture in eastern Sweden. *Meddelanden från Lunds Universitets Historiska Museum*, 1974-75: 20-30.

Westlake, D.F. 1963. Comparisons of plant productivity. *Biological Reviews of the Cambridge Philosophical Society*, 38: 385-425.

3

The spatial analysis of Mesolithic occupation floors: a reappraisal

Robert Whallon Jr.

Six concentrations of Mesolithic material near Havelte, Drenthe, Netherlands, were excavated in 1970-2 by the University of Michigan in cooperation with the University of Groningen (Price, Whallon and Chappell 1974). The exact location of every item found in these sites was recorded. The primary reason for such detailed recording of provenance was our intention to use various methods of spatial analysis to study patterns of artefact distribution and thus, hopefully, to provide us with more information about patterns of human activity than had usually been obtained from previous excavations of Mesolithic sites.

A few excellent examples exist of the analysis of spatial patterning of artefacts over occupation surfaces by simple mapping and inspection (Leroi-Gourhan and Brézillon 1966; Lumley 1969). However, at Havelte, as in the majority of sites from which detailed provenance data are available, spatial distributions are not distinctive or clear enough to reveal interpretable patterns when simply mapped. We therefore planned to use statistical methods of spatial analysis to define distributional patterning. Our initial effort in this direction was to establish a methodological basis for the analysis of spatial patterning among artefacts scattered over occupation surfaces (Whallon 1973, 1974).

These methods of spatial analysis, sometimes expanded by the addition of new techniques for statistical manipulation, were extensively applied to the Havelte sites with admittedly rather indifferent results (Price, Whallon and Chappell 1974: 45-53; Price n.d., 1976). Concurrently, a relatively large number of archaeologists in many parts of the world became interested and involved in statistical analysis of patterns of spatial distribution of artefacts within sites. Several symposia on this subject have been held, many papers have been circulated, and new publications are beginning to appear in this field (e.g., Hodder and Orton 1976). All of this activity presently seems to be concentrated on the development of techniques and methods. Few or no substantive and significant results have yet been reported. In this paper I will review our work with the Havelte data, discuss our present plans for continued analysis of this material, and briefly try to review what appear, in the light of our experiences, to be the contributions and major problems of spatial analysis in archaeology at the moment.

Present approaches to spatial analysis usually follow some variant of a 3-step approach as outlined in Whallon (1973). This approach comprises the testing of the 'randomness/non-randomness' of the distribution of artefact types, the delineation of non-random spatial clusters or concentrations on the ground, and the measurement or testing of spatial association or correlation among artefact types. Different approaches may address these steps in different orders and they may emphasise one or more of these steps over, or to the exclusion of, others. Either explicitly or implicitly underlying all such approaches, however, seems to be a common model from which the three steps derive their meaning and analytic importance.

This model predicts that there will be non-random clustering, differential distribution, and spatial associations of different types of artefacts over an occupation area. This follows from the assumptions that human activities were localised in different places within an area of occupation, that different combinations of tools were utilised in these various activities, and that at least some representative sample or characteristic proportions of those tools was left at the scene of the activity in which they were used. From this model, then, come the now-familiar ideas of the 'tool kit' and the 'activity area'. It can also easily be seen how this model leads naturally to 3-part methods of spatial analysis as outlined above for the definition of 'tool kits' and 'activity areas'.

Occasionally this model and the methods of spatial analysis based on it have been found to work well, producing consistent and readily interpretable results. A good example is the cave of Guila Naquitz (Whallon 1973). The materials on the several levels in this site exhibited significant non-random clustering. Moreover, the groups of items defined by spatial correlation made good sense in terms of the subsistence activities and ecology of the group inhabiting the cave, and they were quite consistently definable from level to level. Guila Naquitz is, however, an exception in our experience up to now. Using the same techniques as at Guila Naquitz as well as numerous others, we have made extensive analyses of the scatters of tool types over occupation surfaces at Havelte as already mentioned and at the Abri Pataud (Whallon 1974 and unpublished work). These analyses have produced few interpretable results and virtually no consistency. The results obtained from different kinds of analyses are usually conflicting, and none are more clearly interpretable than others.

A consideration of this recurrent lack of consistency and

interpretability of results eventually leads to the realisation that there are important unsolved problems at all levels of spatial analysis – in the data used, the techniques applied, the accepted method, and in the underlying model itself. A brief review of the most outstanding of these problems will introduce some of our current directions of thought and plans for the continued analysis of the Mesolithic sites at Havelte.

One of the major questions which has presented itself to us time and again in working with the material from Havelte is the degree to which our data are appropriate to our analytical model. Essentially our basic model calls for the analysis of distributions of functional classes of artefacts. After all, the model predicts the existence of spatial clusters, differential distributions, and spatial association on the basis of the assumed use of specific artefacts in specific activities. In practice, we have been assuming that our traditional morphological types or even type-groups (Price, Whallon and Chappell 1974: 27; Price n.d.) represent some sort of functional classes, even if only of a very general sort such as 'cutting', 'scraping', 'piercing', etc. tools. However, evidence has been accumulating rapidly which indicates that this assumption is in large part false. The study of use-wear and breakage patterns, experimental use of tools, edge angle analyses, ethnographic comparisons, etc., all indicate that morphological types are frequently functionally heterogeneous. Nonetheless, virtually all of the spatial analyses with which I am familiar, including our work to date at Havelte, have been based on the use of traditional, morphological types.

We may note here that all but one of the items analysed on the occupation floors of Guila Naquitz were plant and animal remains rather than stone tool types. Perhaps a partial explanation of the success of the spatial analysis of materials at Guila Naquitz and the failure of spatial analysis at other sites lies in the fact that plant and animal remains may be much more direct indicators of areas of activity (in this case related to their procurement, processing or consumption) than are stone tools. Obviously, one of the things we now intend to do in the analysis of the Mesolithic assemblages from Havelte is to redefine the tool types we will use for spatial analysis in an effort to represent more accurately and specifically the functional classes of tools in this material.

However, this is unlikely to change the situation completely or to allow us immediately to produce useful and interpretable results from spatial analysis. There remain a number of significant problems which we have found with the statistical techniques we currently use for spatial analysis. Most of these revolve in one way or another around questions of scale – scale of observation and scale of patterning.

Immediately and directly affected by scale of observation is the detection of non-random clustering of artefacts within a site. The problems are slightly different, though related, for the use of grid-count data or of exact provenance data. At one extreme for both sorts of data we must recognise the influence of the relative size of the area under analysis. If this is significantly different from the area of the site itself, it obviously affects our ability to define non-random clustering within the site.

If only a limited portion of the site is available for analysis we will be limited in the scales of clustering that we can define statistically. Clusters which approach or exceed the size of the area of analysis will obviously be difficult or impossible to detect.

More subtle is the influence of an excavation area larger than the site. Although this at first appears to be the ideal situation, in which artefact clusterings on any scale within the site can be defined, such clusters can in fact be obscured by the effect of the site itself. A site is, by definition, a non-random concentration of archaeological material. Consequently, we have often seen in analysis of the completely excavated Mesolithic concentrations at Havelte that all artefacts are found to be 'non-randomly' distributed simply because the area over which spatial analysis was applied extended clearly beyond the limits of any substantial indication of occupation. Proceeding further with analysis over such an area eventually results in a demonstration that most or all items tend to be associated with each other as a single 'tool kit' simply because they all occur within the site itself. Therefore, an important problem to solve before applying statistical techniques for testing randomness/non-randomness of artefact distributions or for determining correlations or associations among artefact types at Havelte and similar sites will be the definition of site boundaries. We need a clear and objective criterion or method for establishing site boundaries within which it makes sense to search for non-random artefact clusters and associations and outside of which the site itself becomes the dominant cluster.

A more common problem in the analysis of non-random distribution on an occupation floor is how to handle the frequently observed multiple scales of patterning in the clustering of an artefact class. These show up as multiple peaks of variance in dimensional analysis of variance (Whallon 1973: 269) and in analysis with Morisita's index (Price n.d.) and as multi-modal distributions of nearest neighbour distances (Whallon 1974: 33). There is no consistency among these statistical tests as to what scale of patterning is emphasised or tested. Nearest neighbour analysis tests the smallest scale of patterning in exact provenance data. Morisita's index emphasises small-scale groupings of grid count data, while dimensional analysis of variance emphasises larger-scale patterns. In addition, different artefact classes frequently show different scales of clustering and different degrees of unimodal or multimodal clustering. The problem is what to choose out of this often confusing array of choices, on what scale(s) to base further analysis, and particularly how to compare or test the associations among artefacts which exhibit different scales of detectable spatial patterning.

We have faced these problems frequently in the analysis of the Havelte sites. It has become quite clear that the appearance of multiple scales of patterning in our analyses is due to the fact that artefact clusters on the occupation floor, whether of a single artefact type or of a group of artefact types considered together, occur in different sizes, shapes, and densities. In disaccord with this fact, our standard analytical methods of dimensional analysis of variance and nearest neighbour analysis are applied with the implicit assumption that clusters will be relatively uniform in size, shape, and density.

This discrepancy between the nature of the clusters we are trying to define statistically and the assumptions built into the statistical procedures presently in common use has been provisionally solved in one way through the application of a simple, direct clustering method at one of the Havelte sites. The method we have used has been rather 'rough and ready', consisting of a single-link cluster analysis applied to the distances among artefacts of all types. A stopping rule for the clustering procedure has been based on the idea of differential distribution of tool types among activity areas. Clustering stops and the 'activity areas' are defined at the point of maximum average between-cluster variance of the percentage of each artefact type contained in each cluster.

This method is not elegant, and an obvious priority in spatial analysis now is to devise a satisfactory and sound method for the objective definition of artefact clusters of different sizes, shapes, and densities on occupation floors. To do this may require us to abandon the idea of statistically testing the significance of non-random clustering, since all such tests utilise the distribution of densities around a mean, and only unusually high or low density areas will be detected as 'non-random' clusters. However, it may be distributional pattern that is important to our analysis, rather than patches of unusual density. For any test of randomness of distribution, densities may vary within normal limits around the mean, thus giving the appearance of randomness to the results of the statistical test, but the pattern of distribution of those densities over the occupation area may show clear concentrations. Situations like this can be handled, of course, by varying the size of the observation units as in dimensional analysis of variance, but it may also be of value to consider the use of direct cluster-seeking methods that are not based on density-dependent tests of significance.

At Havelte simple, direct clustering outlined a series of artefact concentrations in one site which looked convincing on inspection. We performed the clustering on all artefact types taken together. However, separate analyses of each artefact type with subsequent superpositioning of the individually defined spatial clusters were also made, and they did not essentially change the picture.

The contents of these concentrations were then tabulated to see if tool kits representing specific activities could be identified. The clusters varied considerably in terms of the tools they contained and the proportion of those tools. For some concentrations, possible activities carried out at those spots could be inferred or hypothesised. However, there were no clear, discrete groupings of tool types that consistently tended to occur together in even roughly the same proportions. In other words, there were no 'tool kits' in the sense that we have usually thought of them in spatial analysis. Even allowing for overlap between groups of tools as Price has done (n.d., 1976) is not a realistic representation of the picture of associations and variations in proportions among artefact types in these concentrations. Overlapping of tool groups shows only a degree of gradation in association from one tool type to the next, while the picture presented by the 'activity areas' defined at this one Havelte site is a highly interwoven or reticulate one of changing associations and proportions.

Therefore, if we return to the basic model for spatial analysis with which we began, we must come to the conclusion that, although 'activity areas' may exist and are definable as spatial concentrations of different size, shape, density, and contents, 'tool kits' as we have so far thought of them may not exist, at least at many sites. There is instead an almost continuously variable pattern of artefact association and proportionate representation in such 'activity areas'. One might consider this a more realistic picture of tool use in various activities, but analytically it leads to a bewildering array of numbers with no guide to their interpretation other than sheer speculation and more or less inspired guesses. Although the eventual development of more accurate functional classifications of stone artefacts may bring a partial solution to this confusion, it also seems likely that the integration of tools into the cultural system, their role in human patterns of activity, is much more complex than we have recognised in our models for analysis.

This is obviously an unsatisfactory situation, and on reflection it becomes necessary for us to conclude and admit that our current models and methods for spatial analysis have been at virtually every point over-simplified and leading in the wrong direction to a greater or lesser degree. Recent ethnographic studies (Binford 1973: 241-4) and theoretical statements (Schiffer 1976: 58-78; Ammerman and Feldman 1974) have begun to point this out to us. In short and at its simplest:

Morphological typology is not always able to define 'tools' in the sense of real functional categories of artefacts. This was discussed above, many archaeologists are aware of this, and it seems probable that methods for the functional classification of stone tools will eventually be developed.

Even if we assume that we are able to identify 'tools' as such, we must take into account the facts that most tools will have a multiplicity of uses or functions and that the range of function, that is the degree to which a tool is specialised and tends to serve a single purpose or is generalised and tends to fulfill a wide range of functions, will vary from tool to tool. This, plus the fact that most 'activities' call for different kinds of tool-use in different degrees, leads to the obvious conclusion that different activities will involve the use of different combinations and proportions of tools. Thus, discrete 'tool kits' will not generally be found.

The tools associated with a given activity will be incorporated into the archaeological record as a function of their rate of breakage, loss, and discard. Rates of breakage or loss for any given tool may depend on the activities in which it is used. Such rates need not be a constant for any tool type. Tools will also vary in the degree to which they are 'curated' or 'expediently' used (Binford 1973). Degree of curation is not likely to be a constant over an entire assemblage. Finally, incorporation into the archaeological record will be at the location of the activity or not, depending on the activity itself and on post-activity and post-occupational disturbances such as re-use of the area, cleaning or clearing of the area, and later human or natural disturbances of the ground.

In summary, we can expect to find 'activity areas' on sites and we can expect them to be of different sizes, shapes, and densities and to contain different tools and different proportions of the same tools. But we can also expect them to be generally uninterpretable by inference or by arguing back from the nature of the activity areas to the activities involved, except under certain relatively unusual and restricted circumstances. There are simply too many intervening processes between the activities of a human group and the results of those activities which form the archaeological record to allow regular, accurate inferential reconstructions.

The foregoing does not imply that we must abandon active analysis of artefact scatters on excavated occupation floors and restrict ourselves to 'basic research' – of an ethnoarchaeological or experimental sort for example. It does imply, however, that we can no longer generally accept the basic model which has guided spatial analysis so far and simply continue analysis and the development of statistical techniques along its lines. There are two parallel courses open to us. One is to develop predictive models of artefact distributional patterns (similar to the efforts of Ammerman and Feldman 1974; Schiffer 1976: 58-78). The other is to try to find situations and ways in which the narrow conditions necessary for the applicability of the basic model and method we now use can actually be met.

Building predictive models obviously will be the more powerful approach to spatial analysis. Such models will be complex, as can be seen from the brief survey above of the major elements they must contain. Building and testing these models will also involve, at least at the beginning, a great deal of estimation and perhaps experimentation to establish even the initial values of the various rates, proportions, and ranges necessary to the quantification of the models. Ammerman and Feldman (1974) show how difficult this is for just a skeleton model of this sort, but it seems certain that such models ultimately can be constructed and tested. When they are, we will have made a great step in analytic methods in archaeology.

In the meantime, however, useful and significant results can often be obtained by meeting the necessary conditions as closely as possible and continuing with the methods of analysis presently at our disposal. This is what we propose to do in the next stage of the analysis of the materials from Havelte.

One way in which we can try to meet these conditions at Havelte and similar sites will be by focussing our analysis on the by-products of tool-using activities rather than on the tools themselves. Specifically, this means using the broken remains of tools, particularly the spalls from retouched working edges. We hope in this way to be able to identify actual working areas by spatial analysis. In a sense, such spalls are analogous to the subsistence debris analysed at Guila Naquitz – they form the residue or incidental by-products of activities and are thus perhaps more likely to remain on the spot of an activity than are whole tools which are involved in on-going processes of use, re-use, curation, etc. If such spalls are found in distinct concentrations on the occupation areas, it may be possible to draw some inferences as to the kinds of activities represented from the kinds of spalls – borer tips, spalls from scraping edges, slivers broken from cutting edges, etc., – in each concentration. In this way we may be able, at least partially, to achieve our original aim of developing a picture of the patterns of activity on these sites.

Nevertheless, it must be remembered that, even if we are successful in obtaining useful and significant results from a spatial analysis of spalls and broken tools, these results can provide only a partial picture of the total range of activities on these sites. Obviously, much more information resides in the tools themselves and their distributions, but it now seems clear that it will require the development of more sophisticated and realistic models as discussed above to exploit this potentially rich source of information in the archaeological record.

References

Ammerman, A.J. and Feldman, M.W. 1974. On the 'making' of an assemblage of stone tools. *American Antiquity*, 39: 612-16.

Binford, L.R. 1973. Interassemblage variability – the Mousterian and the 'functional' argument. In A.C. Renfrew (ed.), *The Explanation of Culture Change: Models in Prehistory*. London, Duckworth: 227-54.

Hodder, I. and Orton, C. 1976. *Spatial Analysis in Archaeology*. London, Cambridge University Press.

Leroi-Gourhan, A. and Brézillon, M. 1966. L'habitation Magdalénienne No. 1 de Pincevent près Montereau (Seine-et-Marne). *Gallia Préhistoire*, 9: 263-385.

Lumley, H. de. 1969. *Une Cabane Acheuléenne dans la Grotte du Lazaret (Nice)*. Paris, Société Préhistorique Française, Mémoire 7.

Price, T.D. n.d. *Spatial analysis of grid count data*. Unpublished manuscript.

Price, T.D. 1976. The spatial analysis of lithic artefact distribution and association on prehistoric occupation floors. In D.D. Davis (ed.), *Lithics and Subsistence*. Chicago, University Press. (in press)

Price, T.D., Whallon, R., Jr., and Chappell, S. 1974. Mesolithic sites near Havelte, province of Drenthe (Netherlands). *Palaeohistoria*, 16: 7-61.

Schiffer, M.B. 1976. *Behavioral Archeology*. New York and London, Academic Press.

Whallon, R. Jr. 1973. Spatial analysis of occupation floors I: the application of dimensional analysis of variance. *American Antiquity*, 38: 266-78.

Whallon, R. Jr. 1974. Spatial analysis of occupation floors II: the application of nearest neighbour analysis. *American Antiquity*, 39: 16-34.

4

Shell middens as indicators of postglacial economies: a territorial perspective

G.N. Bailey

Marine molluscs have made some contribution to European subsistence since at least the Middle Pleistocene, when they occur at the 400,000 year-old encampment of Terra Amata on the French Mediterranean (Lumley 1969, 1975). But intensive exploitation of marine resources, whether of molluscs, fish or sea mammals, is scarcely recorded in Europe, or indeed elsewhere, before the postglacial period, when numerous mounds of mollusc shell first begin to form a prominent feature of the archaeological landscape.

The major European midden groupings are shown in Figure 1, the best known being in Denmark, where mounds up to 2000 m³ in size with tens of millions of mollusc shells are found. These coastal middens are of interest both because they show large-scale irregularities of geographical distribution and because they are confined to a relatively restricted period of time, mostly Mesolithic or early Neolithic, whereas shell deposits are apparently smaller, more sporadically distributed or unknown in later as well as earlier periods.

Much attention has focused on the possibility that such evidence might reflect a widespread intensification of economic activity in the late Pleistocene and the early postglacial, triggered by changes in population pressure, changes in the environment, developments in technology, or some combination of these variables, and ultimately culminating in the expansion of agriculture and the transformation of economy and environment over large areas. Alternatively, discontinuities in the distribution of shell middens may reflect nothing more than differential preservation of the data resulting from the eustatic rise of world sea levels or other processes of shoreline displacement.

All of these variables may have impinged to a greater or lesser degree on the archaeological record of coastal economies. But a more precise assessment of their relative influence remains a matter of

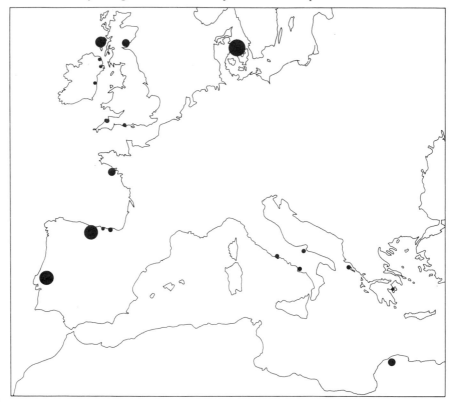

Figure 1. The general distribution of early postglacial shell middens or shell midden groupings in Europe and the Mediterranean.

uncertainty in the absence of a detailed knowledge of the economic factors which affect archaeological site location in general and the occurrence of shell middens in particular.

The brief discussion set out below is not intended as a comprehensive review of these problems, nor does it propose more than an outline of a partial and tentative solution. The intention is rather to concentrate on certain underlying features of potential theoretical importance which offer some insight into the organisational structure of the economies associated with the formation of shell middens. The archaeological examples chosen as illustrations are drawn from Denmark and Spain. For general surveys of the relevant material in these two areas the reader is referred to Brinch Petersen (1973) and Clark (1971) respectively.

Sites, resources and territories: some general considerations

Molluscs as a source of food

It has often been assumed, implicitly more often than by explicit formulation, that shell middens were used by people concerned with the exploitation of molluscs as a primary food resource. However, it is well known that traces of other resources, both marine and terrestrial, are often preserved in middens along with the shells. More recently, there has been a general tendency to downgrade the relative contribution of the molluscs in relation to these other resources (Bailey 1975a, 1975b; Clark, J.G.D., 1975; Parmalee and Klippel 1974).

The ease with which molluscs can be over-rated as a source of food will be swiftly appreciated from the fact that approximately 700 oysters (*Ostrea edulis*) would be needed to supply enough kilocalories for one person for one day, if no other food were eaten, or 1400 cockles (*Cardium edule*), or 400 limpets (*Patella vulgata*), to name the species most commonly found in European middens. I have also estimated that approximately 52,267 oysters would be required to supply the calorific equivalent of a single red deer carcase, 156,800 cockles, or 31,360 limpets, figures which may help to place in their proper nutritional perspective the vast numbers of shells recorded archaeologically. Furthermore, it is arguable, although not proved with certainty, that molluscs tend to be over-represented in archaeological contexts, because their shells are more resistant to disintegration and destruction than is animal bone.

Estimates of the annual production of shellfood, based on ecological and archaeological data, can be compared with the annual production of other resources available for exploitation or with the annual subsistence needs of the local human population, in order to give more precise information on the calorific contribution of molluscs to the annual diet as a whole. In Australia, where the relevant data are most readily available, both archaeological analysis (Bailey 1975b, 1977) and ethnographic studies of modern Aboriginal communities (Meehan 1975) have shown that even in tropical areas with extensive, estuarine shellfish populations and with some of the largest and most densely concentrated prehistoric shell mounds in the world, the relative annual contribution of shellfood ranges between less than 5 percent to not more than 20 percent. In Europe figures towards the lower end of this range have been obtained, on the basis of data which I shall present in more detail below.

In analysing the economic function of shell middens, we are therefore required, at the very least, to consider the possibility that the shell gathering was only one of several diverse exploitation activities integrated into the operation of a single economic unit. Indeed, in many cases it appears that shellfood was a relatively minor resource. Hence, the question arises as to the effect of the non-molluscan resources on the choice of site location and the ways in which the collection of molluscs and the accumulation of their discarded shells might have been influenced by the overall needs of the economy as a whole.

Exploitation territories and the time-distance factor

One approach to the analysis of resource interactions and their effects on site location is the use of territorial concepts such as the site exploitation territory and the economic niche (Higgs 1975; Higgs and Vita-Finzi 1972; Jarman 1972; Vita-Finzi and Higgs 1970). At one level these concepts are simply operational devices, a means of refining and amplifying the analysis of the site and its contents in relation to the physical and biological environment. But they are also theoretical concepts rooted in observations of human behaviour and as such provide a powerful source of explanations for continuities and irregularities of site location and subsistence data.

This theoretical aspect stems from the inherent assumption that distance is a limiting factor on economic behaviour, the increasing distance of a given resource from a given site location resulting in increasing energy costs of exploitation, until certain threshold limits are reached, beyond which the kilocalories expended as human effort exceed those acquired as food. Stated in this way the exploitation territory may be seen as a means of transforming the analysis of energy relationships into a spatial framework which can be directly applied to archaeological data.

The defining parameter of the site exploitation territory, the area potentially within economic reach of a given site, is the time-distance factor, usually defined as the *maximum* radius of *daily* exploitation *on foot* from a given site. It should be stressed that the area so defined refers to the food resources potentially available to the site. It does not necessarily coincide with the area actually used for daily subsistence, which is a matter for further investigation. Nor does it imply exclusive use, ownership or defence by a particular social group, or conscious recognition by the site occupants of the territorial boundary so defined. Exploitation territories are concepts designed for archaeological data and archaeological problems, and they should not be confused with the 'territorial' entities commonly dealt with by other disciplines.

A major variable affecting the time-distance factor for any given resource is the relationship between the kilocalories acquired as food and the effort expended to acquire them. For most hunted and gathered resources the time-distance factor is assumed to be about 10 km. or 2 hours' walking time, significant reduction of that figure occurring only with more labour-intensive activities such as crop cultivation.

Another exception to the 2-hour time-distance factor is found with the exploitation of many molluscan species. For it is often the case that, in order to obtain even a small amount of food in terms of kilocalories, a considerable weight of live shellfood has to be collected. The 700 oysters discussed above, for example, would weigh about 25 kg. Assuming a bag load of 12½ kg., two trips would have to be made simply to supply sufficient kilocalories for the individual shell collector, leaving aside the question of additional mouths to feed. This compares with a single bag load of mongongo nuts, which contains sufficient kilocalories to feed at least five people (Lee 1968). If it is not worth carrying a bag of nuts further than 10 km. (Lee 1968), clearly it is not worth carrying a bag of oysters more than one-tenth that distance.

Measurement of the relationship between live weight and calorific output can be used to assess the time-distance factor for a variety of molluscan species. The results are variable and precise limits are difficult to define, although I have attempted this elsewhere (Bailey 1975a). The essential point is that for many species there is a sharp reduction in the quantities of shellfood that can be transported with increasing distance between source of supply and scene of consumption. For a bivalve species such as the cockle, this limitation will be especially severe, because of the high proportion of the live weight which consists of shell. For the limpet, a gastropod, the shell forms a much smaller percentage of the live weight, and the time-distance limit is correspondingly less severe, approaching the normal maximum of 10 km.

We should therefore expect shellfood to be consumed, or at any rate the shells to be removed, as close as possible to the source of supply. Use of boats, or other improved methods of transportation, may relax the time-distance restraint in some circumstances. At the other extreme, lack of such a modest technological aid as a basket or bag will render foraging the only feasible pattern of exploitation, that is the consumption of the shellfood as it is collected by the individual in the course of the day's activity. In this case shells may be scattered around in small quantities over a wide area in such a way as to leave scarcely any visible archaeological deposit.

Site functions

Given economies where the molluscs play a relatively minor role and where moreover they are unlikely to have been carried very far in large quantities, it is not difficult to perceive that the resulting shell middens may be associated with a diversity of economic functions. At one extreme we might postulate a situation where the supply of molluscs occurs in close proximity to an optimum location for a home-base site integrating a diversity of marine and terrestrial resources, supporting a sizeable community over a considerable part of the year, and repeatedly used from year to year. In this case the resulting shell mound would be a home-base, although the non-molluscan resources would be at least as important determining factors of its location and pattern of use as the shellfood. At the other extreme we might have a situation where the shellfood supply extends beyond the reach of a home-base location, giving rise to shell middens focused exclusively or primarily on shellfood exploitation. In this case, however, the middens would necessarily be transitory sites used only for brief periods of the year and forming only a minor element in the total site distribution.

Specific illustrations of these effects can be found in areas where ethno-archaeological observations of shell middens are available. In the Andaman Islands, for example, Cipriani (1955, 1966) has described shell mounds up to 5 m. high which groups of thirty to forty people used as home-bases every year for two months during the wet season. Molluscs were only collected when other resources were unavailable, more important resources being dugong, turtle and pig, all of which have left archaeological traces in the midden deposits. Localised sources of molluscs, on the other hand, were consumed at temporary camps, which have left no archaeologically visible traces. On the Pacific coast of North America, shell middens used for shellfood consumption, shellfood processing, and fishing are often encountered. In addition one finds home-base sites integrating a range of marine and terrestrial resources and sometimes taking the form of fairly diffuse midden scatters (Drucker 1943; Gould 1966; Kroeber and Barrett 1960).

Table 1 shows a system of classification for the different types of shell middens that may be used in economies where shellfood is a secondary resource with a low time-distance factor. Strictly speaking the classification is a continuum, along which certain key thresholds have been arbitrarily defined, and it may require modification or expansion to suit particular circumstances. But it should help to emphasise the variable nature of shell middens as a focus of occupation and economic activity, and the wide range of factors which may, as a consequence, influence their survival in the archaeological record.

A territorial model

A simplified territorial model incorporating some of the above features is illustrated in Figure 2. The upper site territory is associated with a coastal economy where non-molluscan marine resources – fish or sea-mammals – contribute at least as much to the site economy as do terrestrial resources, a compensation, as it were, for the area of land lost to the site because of its location on the shore. The home-base in this case may be a shell midden, although its primary function will be the integration of terrestrial resources with non-molluscan marine resources.

The lower territory refers to a coastal area where the terrestrial resources are the primary staples, and where, except for molluscs, marine resources are unavailable or inaccessible. The optimum location for a home-base under these conditions is away from the shore, so as to bring the maximum area of land within the site territory. In this case the home-base is less likely to be a shell midden,

Table 1. A palaeoeconomic classification of shell middens.

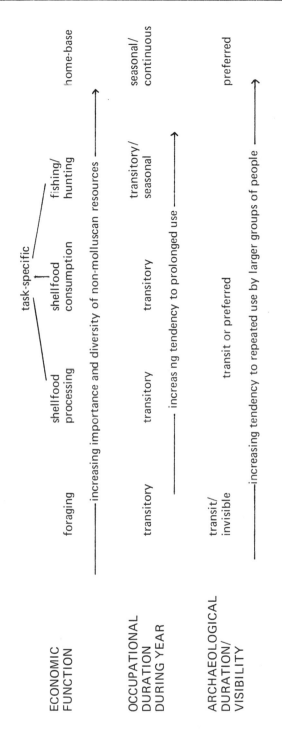

		task-specific		
ECONOMIC FUNCTION	foraging	shellfood processing	shellfood consumption	fishing/ hunting	home-base
	←——— increasing importance and diversity of non-molluscan resources ———→				
OCCUPATIONAL DURATION DURING YEAR	transitory	transitory	transitory	transitory/ seasonal	seasonal/ continuous
	←——— increasing tendency to prolonged use ———→				
ARCHAEOLOGICAL DURATION/ VISIBILITY	transit/ invisible	transit or preferred		preferred	
	←——— increasing tendency to repeated use by larger groups of people ———→				

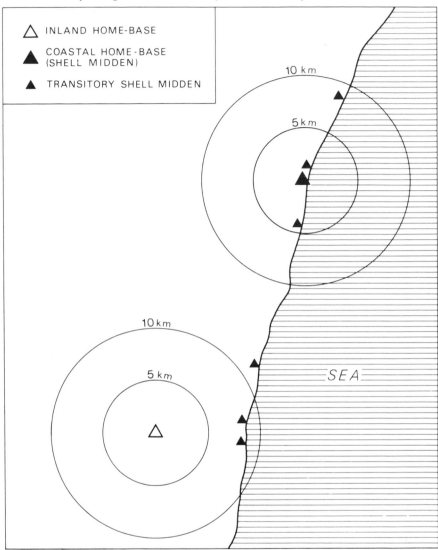

Figure 2. A simplified territorial model for the interpretation of shell middens.

although it may include some mollusc shells. In the following discussion, I shall refer to sites in this position as inland sites, although they may be no further than 10 km. from the shoreline, in order to distinguish them from coastal sites on or near the shore with site territories which incorporate large areas of open sea.

The model is deliberately simplified in ways which should be recognised from the outset: it assumes molluscs to be a minor resource with a low time-distance factor; it assumes a uniform distribution of resources; and it deals with only two extreme types of site among a wider range of alternatives, namely the transitory midden used primarily for shellfood exploitation and the home-base used primarily for non-molluscan resources. Such a model is not, however, intended to prescribe for all possible combinations of variables but to clarify the underlying effects of distance as a limiting factor. It is furthermore intended, by its very simplicity, to highlight discrepancies when confronted with the realities of a given situation, discrepancies which may give direction to further investigation and fuller interpretation of the particular course of events in particular areas.

A Danish example of a coastal home-base

Drawing a territorial boundary round a shell midden located on the sea shore will not of itself tell us whether that site is a transitory midden, a home-base or some intermediate type. For the area so defined is only a measure of what was potentially available to the site occupants for the extraction of their daily subsistence. Whether the site was in fact used as a focus for the exploitation of the resources available within this area remains a hypothesis in need of further corroboration. The size of the deposit alone will also be misleading, since large mounds of shell may accumulate, whatever the function of the site. Both on-site and off-site data are called into play to discriminate between the various possibilities. As an illustration of this point I shall take the case of Meilgaard (Figure 3), one of the classic Ertebølle shell mounds of east Jutland first excavated in the nineteenth century (Madsen 1888).

On-site data

The shell mound originally had a maximum depth of 2 m. and a volume of 2000 m³ (Petersen 1922). The fauna represented in 50 m³ of this deposit, according to the nineteenth-century investigations, is presented in Table 2. The shell data are based on recently excavated samples recovered by the author as part of a long-term programme of excavation under the overall direction of Dr. Søren H. Andersen. The estimated minimum individuals of each resource have been converted to meat weights and kilocalories to allow the closest possible comparison according to a common nutritional standard.

It will be seen that seal are well represented in relation to the terrestrial ungulates, but molluscs are also of primary importance, accounting for 31.9 percent of the diet. Taken at face value these figures suggest either a home-base in which shellfood was a major resource, or a transitory site, both of which are significant deviations from the hypothetical coastal home-base postulated above.

The factors used to convert bone and shell data to nutritional values are subject to some uncertainty. But it is assumed that this has no serious impact on the general order of magnitude of the results. More

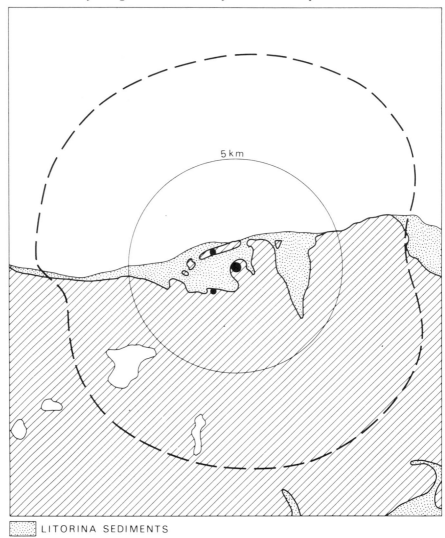

Figure 3. The 2-hour site exploitation territory of Meilgaard. The area of 'Litorina
    sediments' is dry land today but would have been a shallow bay at the time when the
    site was occupied.

serious sources of error stem from the data on fish and shellfish.

Relatively few head bones of fish, such as jaws or otoliths, which
would allow an estimate of minimum individuals, have been recovered
from excavation, although vertebrae, mostly of small size, have been
found in abundance – as many as $3820/m^3$. Too much emphasis,
however, should not be placed on quantity of bone fragments as such,
since large numbers of small fish producing very many vertebrae
would be required to produce a substantial amount of food. For
example, 852 small cod fish, each yielding 1 kg. of flesh, and
representing 44,304 vertebrae in total, would be required to supply

Table 2. The relative representation of resources in 50 cubic metres of deposit at Meilgaard.

Species	Meat weight per animal (kg.)	Kilo-calories per kg.	Minimum number of individuals	Total Kilo-calories	Percentage contribution	Mean Annual Output (1)
Pig	61	3500	11	2,198,000	18.8	1.1
Roe deer	11	1400	7	107,800	0.9	0.7
Red deer	112	1400	9	1,411,200	12.1	0.9
Ringed seal	60	4000	1			
Harp seal	60	4000	1	3,720,000	31.9	0.7
Grey seal	162	4000	5			
Birds	5	3500	27	490,000	4.2	2.7
Fish	1	760	30	22,800	0.2	3.0
Oysters	124(2)	600	100,000	3,720,000	31.9	10,000

[1] Mean annual output for the mound as a whole (expressed in terms of minimum numbers of individuals) assuming a total duration of 400 years.
[2] Meat weight represented by 1 cubic metre of oyster shells.

the same number of kilocalories as a single adult seal carcase. The relative representation of fish is likely to be a minimum estimate, but the degree of correction cannot be established with the available data.

Shellfish, on the other hand, may be over-represented, and it is this which is the major potential source of error. As the Danish marine biologist C.G.J. Petersen (1922) suggested in a pioneering and little known midden analysis of this very site over half a century ago, mollusc shells stand a good chance of being represented in midden deposits in more or less the quantities originally collected, whereas the animal bone is subject to a heavy toll of destruction by human butchery practices and the scavenging activities of domestic dogs or wild animals.

I have therefore recalculated the relative contribution of shellfood by comparing the mean annual increment of shells in the midden with an estimate of the numbers of people occupying the site. Unpublished radiocarbon dates suggest a total duration of at least 400 years for this site (Andersen, personal communication), which is consistent with the radiocarbon chronology for the Ertebølle period as a whole (Tauber 1972). Dividing the total number of shells in the midden by 400 years yields a mean annual increment of 100,000 oysters. Population size can be estimated by applying the Cook and Treganza (1950) logarithmic formula, as corrected by Shenkel (1971), to the base area of the mound. This gives a figure of 39 people. The assumptions of this technique are open to question, but I believe that it offers a sound approximation when applied to isolated mounds, and it does at least provide an independently derived population figure to compare with the dietary data.

At this population level the relative contribution of shellfood to the annual diet is only 1.8 percent, given a dietary requirement of 2000 kcal/person/day. For 25 people the figure would be 2.7 percent, and for 5 people 13.7 percent. All these results are substantially lower than the initial estimate of 31.9 percent.

Off-site data

One possible explanation of this discrepancy is that the archaeologically visible oyster shells are less than the number originally collected by the site occupants. Petersen (1922) estimated that the shallow bay in front of the site could have provided an annual crop of 17,000 oysters by analogy with modern conditions in the Limfjord. The archaeological estimate of mean annual oyster output is, however, 100,000 oysters, higher than the maximum figure predicted from modern ecological data. It is possible that oysters were collected from a wider area than assumed by Petersen, or that the total span of habitation at the site was longer than that indicated by the radiocarbon dates. A more probable explanation is that conditions for the growth of oysters were more favourable in the prehistoric past than at the present day. Whatever the explanation, the data offer no support for the supposition that shells are under-represented archaeologically. Equally, given that the quantity of oysters collected in prehistory approximated the quantities potentially available from the site territory, it follows that the midden was used repeatedly from year to year. Had it been used on a more intermittent basis, say once every 5 years, the mean annual quantities of shell accumulated in the midden would have been only one-fifth of the potential annual output.

With the mammalian resources, on the other hand, the position seems to be reversed. The on-site data suggest a far less intensive exploitation than the off-site data. This can best be examined by determining whether or not the mammalian resources potentially available within the site territory (Fig. 3) could have supported 39 people.

If we assume that the relative percentages of the different mammalian species (Table 2) reflect the relative percentages of animals originally killed, we can estimate the numbers of animals that would have to have been present within the site territory to feed 39 people throughout the year. Given a cropping rate of 10 percent of the live animal populations by human predation, the required standing crop of pig is 400 animals, of roe deer 185, of red deer 345, and of seal 268, assuming a human requirement of 2000 kcal/person/day.

The total area of land within the site territory is 14,580 hectares. Hence the required density of animals is 1: 36.5 hectares for pig, 1: 78.8 hectares for roe deer, and 1: 42.3 hectares for red deer. Modern density figures which might be used to test these predictions are, of course, highly variable, depending on a variety of ecological and behavioural factors which vary over time and from place to place. But a range of figures has been quoted for pig of 1: 40 to 1: 500 hectares, for roe deer 1: 20 to 1: 1000 hectares, and for red deer 1: 14 to 1: 300 hectares (Bay-Petersen 1975; also this volume).

Comparable data are not available for seals, but the offshore islands within easy reach of the site should be noted as a significant feature of the site territory. These could have been seal breeding grounds, although this is uncertain. Clubbing of the seal pups is a favoured method of hunting which is recorded elsewhere in Denmark in the Neolithic period (Møhl 1971), but no immature seal bones have been recorded from the Meilgaard deposits. Alternatively, the adult seals might have been harpooned while using the islands as 'haul-outs' for fishing or basking (Hewer 1974), a practice consistent with the evidence of harpoons from Ertebølle contexts (Andersen 1972). In any case, an annual bag of 27 seals would not seem to lie beyond the capacity of the site territory or the competence of the able-bodied men of a 40-strong community.

These figures do not demonstrate what actually took place in prehistory. The range of values is, afterall, very broad and offers figures which are consistent with an equally broad range of interpretations. But the results do show that sufficient mammalian resources could have been present within the potential site territory to feed 39 people throughout the year. If we take this as the preferred interpretation, it implies that the quantities of bone surviving in the archaeological deposit are a dramatic under-representation of the mammalian resources originally consumed by the site occupants. Indeed the annual cropping rate of mammalian resources suggested by the on-site data, as shown in the final column of Table 2, is only 2.8 percent of the preferred figure derived from the off-site data. Although the scale of under-representation of bone remains implied by these figures is far more drastic than is usually assumed to be the case in conventional midden analyses, it is by no means implausible in the light of ethnographic observations. In Russia, for example, Vereshchagin (1967) observed that only about 1 percent of the cleaned bones were incorporated into the deposits of modern fishing and hunting camps as a result of the depredations of dogs, cats and magpies. Similar results were observed at the modern camp of a group of coastal Aborigines in northern Australia, where mollusc shells were the primary constituent of the midden deposit, although the molluscs had contributed only about 10 percent by weight of the diet (White 1968).

However, the on-site data at Meilgaard cannot be ruled out of consideration simply on the basis of ethnographic analogy. The alternative hypothesis, that the relative representation of bone at this particular site is an acceptable guide to prehistoric diet, requires further consideration, especially in view of the uncertainties inherent in the off-site data.

Seasonal indicators

A means of assessing the reliability of the on-site dietary data is offered by the evidence of seasonality. For if the quantities of archaeologically observed bone are accepted at face value, it follows from the independent estimates of shellfood productivity and size of human population that the site was a transitory one used only for the briefest of visits during the annual round. By contrast, the preferred estimates of ungulate productivity require us to think in terms of sedentary or semi-sedentary habitation.

Deer antler data, the slaughter patterns of juvenile ungulates and the migratory habits of the avifauna represented in the Ertebølle shell mounds have all provided seasonal information and were, in fact, originally held to demonstrate continuous year-round occupation (Madsen *et al.* 1900). More recent analysis incorporating data from inland as well as coastal sites has demonstrated some degree of seasonal movement between coast and hinterland (Andersen 1975, J.G.D. Clark 1975), and renders unlikely the practice of a truly sedentary economy, if by 'sedentary' we mean a self-sufficient

community which occupies a site continuously throughout the year
and draws its total annual subsistence from within the confines of a
single site territory. The data do not, however, exclude the possibility
of a continuous human presence on the middens, and a mobile-cum-
sedentary economy, with a high degree of residential stability on the
coast and occasional movements by some if not all of the coastal
population to other sites, is compatible with the archaeological data.
Whether the coastal economy was a mobile-cum-sedentary one of this
type or a fully mobile economy, seasonal indicators would seem to
exclude the hypothesis of transitory habitation required by a literal
interpretation of the bone remains.

The Litorina shoreline appears then to have been a major focus of
prehistoric settlement where the molluscs, in spite of archaeological
appearances to the contrary, were of scarcely more than incidental
importance. As additional supporting evidence it is worth referring to
the coastal sites of Ølby Lyng (Brinch Petersen 1971), Villingebaek
(Kapel 1969) and Vedbaek Boldbaner (Mathiassen 1946) on the east
coast of Zealand. This area never supported many edible molluscs
because of low salinity, so that shells are relatively rare or absent in the
archaeological deposits. In most other respects these sites are closely
comparable to the large Jutland shell mounds in terms of site location
and site territory, duration of occupation, diversity of faunal remains
and type-range of artifacts. However, they are apparently somewhat
smaller, which might be attributable as much to the lower ungulate
biomass on the island of Zealand in comparison with peninsular
Jutland as to the lack of molluscs. In any case, the absence of a
shellfood supply was clearly no deterrent to the location of major
settlements on the sea shore.

These various lines of evidence consistently corroborate the
hypothesis that the Meilgaard shell mound was used by a community
of approximately 40 people on a prolonged seasonal or mobile-cum-
sedentary basis; that it was repeatedly occupied from year to year;
and that it was dependent on a diversity of resources, among which
molluscs were of minor importance, while the non-molluscan marine
resources contributed at least as much to the site economy as the
terrestrial resources.

Cantabrian Spain

Cantabrian Spain has a mountainous coastline of marked contrasts to
the Danish coastal environment examined above. On the seaward side
the exposed rocky shores and narrow, restricted river estuaries
support a molluscan fauna of limited abundance, consisting
principally of the limpet (*Patella vulgata*), while the narrow, steeply
sloping continental shelf is an unproductive environment for any kind
of inshore marine life. On the landward side the topography is

dominated by the Cantabrian *cordillera*, whose mountain peaks range up to a maximum height of about 2700 m. The watershed runs approximately parallel to the coastline and between 25 and 50 km. distant from it. Level land is inevitably confined to the coastal plain, although numerous broad valleys provide good access to the immediate hinterland and in some cases easy routes across the watershed to the upland plateau of the northern *meseta*. On flatter ground a rich growth of vegetation is encouraged by the humid climate, and the area is capable of maintaining a diverse and abundant ungulate fauna. During the final stages of the Pleistocene and the early postglacial the principal species was red deer (*Cervus elaphus*), with chamois (*Rupicapra rupicapra*) and ibex (*Capra pyrenaica*) on higher and steeper ground (Clark 1971; Freeman 1973).

The many caves and rock shelters of the region show evidence of human occupation extending back at least 50,000 years. Throughout this period the resource base appears to have undergone relatively little change, although there are fluctuations in species representation, especially on land, where animals characteristic of a 'forest biotope' (red deer, roe deer and pig) become increasingly prominent over time at the expense of the open-country biotope represented by horse and bovids (Freeman 1973). From a territorial point of view, the chief effects of the last glaciation would have been an extension of the coastal plain by the lowered sea level and some restriction on the use of the hinterland by localised glaciation in the Cantabrian mountains and a general lowering of the snowlines. Because of the topography, human settlement at all periods would have been centred on the coastal plain. Furthermore the steep submarine topography is such that even with the maximum lowering of the sea level, existing sites would still have remained within fairly close proximity to the Pleistocene shoreline. This area therefore offers unusual opportunities for the examination of a coastal exploitation system in time depth.

It is likely, as I have argued elsewhere (Bailey 1973), that occupation on the coast was associated with an economic niche which included a mobile exploitation of the hinterland. But, in this paper, I shall be mainly concerned with the resources in the immediate vicinity of the sea shore and the problems of their integration at the level of the site territory.

About 30 shell middens are concentrated in the provinces of eastern Asturias and western Santander, and isolated examples are scattered elsewhere along the Cantabrian coastline. Some of the middens are stratified above Palaeolithic deposits in which shells are less abundant or lacking. Recent radiocarbon dating suggests that a major period of shell accumulation took place between 9,000 and 7,000 B.P. in association with an industry called the 'Asturian' and characterised by a pick something like a small, pointed handaxe made on a pebble, although both earlier and later shell middens associated with other industries are known (Clark 1971).

The largest of the shell middens is estimated as about 1000 m³ but analysis of individual middens using the techniques applied in Denmark has not so far proved possible because of the erosion or removal of deposits at most existing sites. A diverse fauna including red deer as the dominant species, with lesser quantities of pig, roe deer, chamois and ibex, has been reported from previous excavations. This variety suggests a wide-ranging exploitation on land (Clark 1971), and it is generally assumed that the middens were closely associated with a home-base focus of exploitation, whether or not they themselves were the actual scene of habitation. Small quantities of fish bone have also been recorded, but the finds are few, the only identified specimen being of flatfish (*Solea sp.*). Given the relatively small size of the shell accumulations and the low economic potential of the marine environment, it is most unlikely that marine resources played as great a role in the economies of this area as in Denmark.

The major shell deposits show a marked clumping in time and space, and any attempt to explain such a pattern by reference to territorial organisation must be qualified at the outset by uncertainties arising from the uneven quality of archaeological investigations, the restriction of the known shell middens to cave locations, the damage or destruction of many of the deposits, and the comparative scarcity of radiocarbon dates. The possibility cannot be excluded that substantial shell middens were formed at other periods of time and at other places along the coast. Recognition of this possibility, however, should not impede the consideration of others. Differential preservation of the data is itself an hypothesis, and one difficult to corroborate except by positive elimination of the alternatives. Even if correct as a means of removing apparent disorder in site-distributional data, such an hypothesis by itself cannot bring us appreciably closer to an understanding of the archaeological record in terms of human behaviour.

Santander

The Asturian shell middens are generally located at varying distances from the present-day shoreline, mostly within 5 km. of it, but in rare cases somewhat further than this. An extreme case is the site of El Pendo in Santander (Fig. 4). This is one of a group of four sites with multiple occupation sequences which, in aggregate, extend from at least as early as the Mousterian to the Neolithic period, the best known being Cueva Morín (González Echegaray and Freeman 1971). The other sites illustrated have fewer periods of occupation or less substantial cultural remains. Almost all the deposits include mollusc shells in some quantity, including many of the Palaeolithic levels. In addition an 'enormous' Asturian shell midden composed mostly of limpet shells was recorded in the uppermost part of the Pendo sequence (Carballo and González Echegaray 1952; González

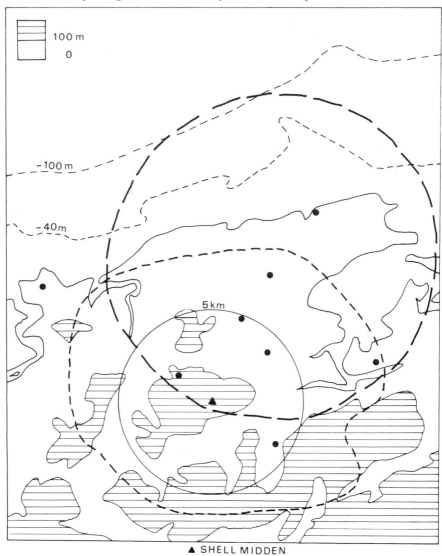

▲ SHELL MIDDEN

Figure 4. The 2-hour site exploitation territories of El Pendo (*lower*) and Peña Castillo (*upper*). Sites within the 5 km. circle are, from left to right: Cobalejos, El Pendo, Juyo, Camargo and Morín. Other sites are, from left to right: Cuchía, Peña Castillo, Liencres and Los Moros. Sources: Carballo and González Echegaray (1952); G.A. Clark (1975); González Echegaray and Freeman (1971); González Echegaray *et al.* (1963); Janssens and González Echegaray (1958); Obermaier (1925).

Echegaray, personal communication). Since this deposit was destroyed soon after its discovery, nothing further is known about it except that by virtue of its stratigraphic position and its association with an Asturian industry it is presumably of postglacial date.

A significant factor in determining changes over time in the representation of marine resources within the occupational sequence of a given site is the eustatic fluctuations of sea level and the consequent variation in distance between the site and the sea shore.

Radiocarbon dating of freshwater sediments on the Atlantic coastal shelf has allowed the reconstruction of a generalised curve of sea level change over the past 36,000 years (Emery and Milliman 1970). Between 36,000 and 30,000 B.P. sea level appears to have been similar to the present level. After that it dropped, slowly at first, and after about 19,000 B.P. more dramatically, to reach a maximum lowering of −130 m. at about 16,000 B.P. From about 14,000 B.P. it rose rapidly again to reach −20 m. by 7,000 B.P. and thence more slowly to its present level. Dates before 16,000 B.P. are scattered and the interpretation less certain than those for the succeeding period, but the maximum extension of the coastal plain would appear to have been a relatively short-lived episode which would have had its greatest effect on the human economy between about 16,000 and 14,000 B.P.

Use of modern submarine contours as a guide to the extension of the Cantabrian coastal plain at the maximum of the last glacial is subject to potential errors arising from two processes which may have taken place in the intervening period: tectonic disturbance and accumulation of sediment on the sea bed. The former can be disregarded for present purposes, since the area has remained fairly stable over the period in question, exhibiting, if anything, only minor residual effects of the tectonic upthrust which mostly took place in earlier epochs (Mary *et al.* 1975). However, there is no information on sediment accumulation. Where the continental shelf is steeply sloping, as here, lateral variations in the position of the shoreline are likely to be insensitive to all but the grossest of errors in assessing the vertical displacement between land and sea. But as a conservative guide to the extension of the coastal plain the −100 m. contour has been used. Also shown is the −40 m. contour, which represents the approximate position of the shoreline at about 9,000 B.P.

Few radiocarbon dates are available for the Cantabrian archaeological sequence, but there are good reasons for supposing that the low sea level stand corresponded rather closely with the Lower Magdalenian phase (Magdalenian III). This is dated at Altamira to 13,550 ± 700 bc (M-829) and at Juyo to 13,350 ± 700 bc (M-830), that is 15,500 and 15,300 B.P. respectively. Radiocarbon dates for industries of the preceding Solutrean and succeeding Upper Magdalenian throughout the Franco-Cantabrian province further indicate that the Lower Magdalenian as a whole can be bracketed with some confidence between about 18,000 and 15,000 B.P., and it would thus seem to be the period most likely to have been affected by the maximum extension of the coastal plain.

It is therefore of considerable interest that, among the sites shown in Figure 4, the major occupations of this period are found at Juyo and Peña Castillo, while the four sites of Cobalejos, El Pendo, Camargo and Morín, which were the central focus of occupation at other periods, all show an occupational hiatus at this point in the sequence.

The Juyo deposit contains large numbers of shells, but improved access to marine resources can hardly have been a primary motivation in the choice of site location, since the sea shore would have remained peripheral to the site territory of this period. A similar comment applies to Peña Castillo. Furthermore Freeman (1973) has emphasised the exceptional quantities of deer bones recovered from Juyo, a clear indication of a continued emphasis on terrestrial resources. It makes better sense to suppose that these sites were occupied in order to gain access to productive, low-lying ground exposed by the maximum retreat of sea level. As further support for this hypothesis is the evidence that these two sites ceased to be occupied in subsequent periods, as if the loss of substantial areas of land from their site territories with the rise in sea level were detrimental to their continued use.

Both Freeman (1973) and González Echegaray (1973) have interpreted the data of site location and subsistence in the Lower Magdalenian period, in particular the data from Juyo, as evidence of increased regional specialisation and the adoption of new and more effective exploitation strategies. However, the explanation proposed above offers at least as likely an alternative hypothesis, that the data reflect a shift of site territory in response to lowered sea level, an adjustment of the pre-existing exploitation system to a changed environment rather than a fundamental shift towards the more intensive utilisation of an unchanged resource base.

From 9,000 B.P. onwards, the rise of sea level would have brought the shoreline close to its present position. Although at least three of the existing sites shown in Figure 4 would have become optimally placed for the intensive exploitation of marine resources by this time, there is no evidence to show that this occurred. Indeed the best studied site is the open-air site of Liencres, which was used during the Asturian period primarily as a workshop site related to a nearby source of flint (Clark, G.A. 1975). Rather the major occupation at this time appears to have been centred on El Pendo. Even if allowances are made for the destruction of evidence elsewhere, the existence of a large shell midden at this site at least 5 km. from the nearest shoreline is a measure of the dominating influence of terrestrial resources on the use of the site and the distance over which people were prepared to carry their limpets to accommodate the overriding needs of the economy.

The evidence from Santander, then, suggests that the preferred focus of occupation throughout the prehistoric period was adjusted in such a way as to maintain an essentially inland site territory, the degree to which molluscs were incorporated in the resulting archaeological deposits depending largely on the extent to which the sea shore encroached on the peripheries of the site territory with changes in sea level.

Asturias

In eastern Asturias, where the majority of shell middens occur, sites tend to form clusters with multiple occupations extending throughout the prehistoric sequence, as in Santander, indicating a fairly stable, generalised focus of occupation. A typical example is shown in Figure 5, centred on the cave of Lloseta. This site is best known for its substantial Lower Magdalenian deposits (Jordá 1958), and, like its

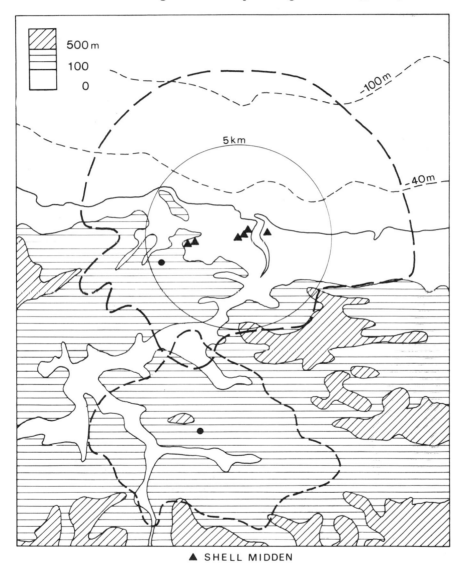

▲ SHELL MIDDEN

Figure 5. The 2-hour site exploitation territories of Lloseta (*upper*) and Buxu (*lower*). Sites within the 5 km. circle are, from left to right, Cova Rosa, Pedroses, Cierro, Lloseta, Rio, Cuevona and San Antonio. Sources: Clark (1971); Jordá Cerdá (1958); Obermaier and Vega del Sella (1918); Vega del Sella (1923).

Lower Magdalenian counterparts in Santander, would have been associated with an essentially inland site territory, given the lowered sea level. Mollusc shells are present in the deposit of this period, although not in quantities that would justify its description as a shell midden, which is hardly surprising, given that the sea shore would have been at the very edge of the site territory, if not beyond it.

Concentrated accumulations of shell make an early appearance, the earliest being at Lloseta itself (Clark 1971) with a radiocarbon date of 13,250 ± 412 bc (GAK-2549). This is considerably earlier than the earliest shell midden at Pendo, but may reflect no more than the inadequacies of the data and the uneven quality of investigations in this area. Equally it is consistent with the fact that Lloseta is closer to the shoreline than Pendo and would have been brought within economic reach of the sea shore at an earlier stage of the eustatic sea-level rise.

A later shell midden dated to 8,450 ± 515 bc (GAK-2548) occurs at Cierro (Clark 1971), and postglacial shell middens, whether of the Asturian period or later, at Lloseta, Rio, Pedroses and San Antonio (Fig. 5). Although the data are fragmentary, there is a well-marked tendency for the number and size of shell accumulations to increase in the later periods, which is consistent with the progressive transgression of the sea and the increasing proximity of the molluscan supply.

However, in contrast to the pattern in Santander, there is little indication here that the major centres of settlement retreated inland in response to the rising sea level in spite of the loss of large areas of land from the territories of the coastal sites. Although habitable rock shelters and caves were available for use in the immediate hinterland behind the coastal plain, evidence of occupation in them is sparse at all periods of the prehistoric sequence. Whereas in Santander the postglacial sites adjacent to the shore appear to have supported only transitory occupation and the home-base sites were associated with inland site territories, in Asturias the reverse applies: the inland sites are the minor ones, while the home-bases are in locations apparently disadvantageous for the pursuit of economies based primarily on terrestrial resources.

One resolution of this discrepancy would be to invoke an intensive exploitation of the sea in postglacial Asturias. But such an explanation is intrinsically unlikely in an area where the economic potential of marine resources is generally low. There is, in any case, no independent archaeological support for it, nor is there any justification for supposing that marine resources were available in greater abundance in Asturias than in Santander.

An alternative hypothesis is suggested by the nature of the topographical restraints on the terrestrial economy, for eastern Asturias is one of the most mountainous sectors in the whole of Cantabria. The coastal plain is at its narrowest here, and the hinterland rises steeply from the sea shore to a maximum height of 2677 m. within 30 km. of the sea. Even at quite small distances inland from the coast, the ever-steepening landscape distorts the 2-hour territorial boundary severely enough to reduce substantially the area of land within the potential site territory. The site of Buxu (Fig. 5), an art site with traces of Palaeolithic occupation, has a site territory whose area is actually slightly less than the area of land within the truncated portion of the postglacial site territory of Lloseta. Not all hinterland locations are quite so severely limited as this. But it is generally the case in this area that any increase in the proportion of land brought within a potential site territory at increasing distances from the shore margin is rapidly offset by a progressive decline in the total area of land available for exploitation. From the point of view of terrestrial exploitation there would be little advantage in moving the home-base very far inland.

Furthermore the location of home-base sites close to the postglacial sea shore in Asturias would have offered two small advantages: easy access to marine resources and the benefits of the mild, oceanic climate which prevails on the immediate coastal plain. Neither of these features can be regarded as primary factors in site location. Indeed, the minor role of marine resources and their marginal effects on territorial organisation have been stressed throughout. However, it is important to recognise that, where the major food resources are uniformly distributed, and several alternative sites offer equally favourable access to them, the presence at one site of some additional factor, however small an addition to the total resource base, whether it is a minor food supply or some small amelioration of microclimate, may be sufficient to tip the balance in favour of that site and to reinforce its continued selection over time as the centre of occupation. In this way we may account for the differences in patterns of postglacial site location between Santander and Asturias, and the concentration of settlement along the shoreline in the latter area in preference to sites situated further inland, without recourse to unsupported assumptions about differential preservation of the data, differential distribution of marine resources, or differences in the perception of their environment by the respective communities of the two areas.

Recognition of these additional influences on site location brings into focus another aspect of the site distribution which has already been noted in passing both in Asturias and Santander, and that is the tendency of sites with similar or largely overlapping site territories to proliferate within clustered groupings, rather than for exploitation to be centred on a single home-base. Two possible explanations may be mentioned here: either the site territory was capable of supporting a larger population than could be accommodated within the confines of a single cave or rock shelter, in which case all the sites within each cluster would have been occupied simultaneously by several groups of people; or the sites were used in alternate seasons, alternate years or on some other rotational basis to form what Sturdy (1972) has defined as the 'annually mobile home-base', where several sites offer a similar economic position with respect to the site territory but different positions with respect to other needs, for example shelter, firewood, freshwater, or avoidance of insect pests. Precisely what these factors were in the Cantabrian case lies beyond the resolution of the existing data, and we can do no more than observe that they may have discernible effects on site location.

Taking the territorial analysis as a whole, the results indicate that the concept of the annually mobile home-base can be generalised to include sites which offer a similar economic position with respect to the major staple resources but different positions with respect to other needs including localised supplies of other resources such as molluscs. The results further indicate that these other needs, although they may sometimes influence changes of site location over considerable distances, should be regarded as small-scale factors which operate within more or less narrow limits constrained by the large-scale directives of economic exploitation.

Conclusion

In the foregoing examples I have attempted to outline something of the diversity of factors which affect archaeological site distributions, and the analytical methods by which the complexity of their interaction might be disentangled, as well as to emphasise some of the common denominators of economic organisation in different environmental contexts. The results are of a preliminary nature, but with that qualification in mind it is appropriate to conclude by considering their impact on the problem raised at the beginning of this paper, that of long-term economic trends extending back into the Pleistocene. Since northern Spain is one of the few coastal areas in Europe with a sufficient time span to focus on this question, discussion is inevitably dominated by the reconstruction of events in this region.

The hypothesis advanced above in connection with Cantabria, although derived from the initial model, goes considerably beyond it, in order to cope with a complexity of data not originally envisaged. It is of particular interest in offering a unified explanation of both chronological and geographical variations in the distribution of shell middens. In this case the unifying directive on the exploitation system would appear to have been the essentially stable relationship with the ungulate basis of the food supply, while the discontinuities arose from the differential spatial relationship between changes of sea level and a varied and generally restrictive landscape. Where living by the sea shore was unavoidable or even marginally advantageous for the exploitation of terrestrial resources because of topographical restraints, molluscs could be incorporated in large quantities into the site economy. Where the topography was less limiting, and the home base could be located further inland, the mollusc supply, because of its greater distance from the settlement, was exploited either less intensively or at transitory sites now destroyed.

If this hypothesis applies throughout the prehistoric sequence, we should expect shell middens to have accumulated during earlier periods of high sea level also, although the data in this area are at present inadequate to pursue this point. However, evidence may ultimately be forthcoming to reject this hypothesis in favour of the alternative, that exploitation became progressively more intensive over time under the impetus of cumulative pressures, whether stemming from external factors in the biotope or 'internal' changes of human behaviour. That possibility cannot be excluded. But the essential point would remain, that the time-distance factor imposes a structural unity on the relationship between resource integration and site location, one which can account for at least some of the observed variation in archaeological data, and which will require more detailed consideration than hitherto if processual models are to fulfil their declared aim of explaining change in prehistory.

Acknowledgements

I am grateful to Dr Søren H. Andersen, Institut for Forhistorisk Arkaeologi, Aarhus University, for the opportunity to examine the Danish material at first hand and for discussion of the Danish evidence. I would also like to thank Prof. M. Almagro Basch, Prof. F. Jordá Cerdá and Prof. J.M. Gomez Tabanera in Spain, and H.N. Jarman and N.J. Shackleton for discussion of the text.

References

Andersen, S.H. 1972 Ertebøllekulturens harpuner. *Kuml*, 1971: 73-125.
Andersen, S.H. 1975. Ringkloster: en jysk inlandsboplads med Ertebøllekultur. *Kuml*, 1973-4: 10-108.
Bailey, G.N. 1973. Concheros del norte de España: una hipótesis preliminar. *XII Congreso Arqueológico Nacional de Arqueología*, 12: 73-83.
Bailey, G.N. 1975a. *The Role of Shell Middens in Prehistoric Economies*. Unpublished Ph.D. thesis, University of Cambridge.
Bailey, G.N. 1975b. The role of molluscs in coastal economies: the results of midden analysis in Australia. *Journal of Archaeological Science*, 2: 45-62.
Bailey, G.N. 1977. Shell mounds, shell middens, and raised beaches in the Cape York Peninsula. *Mankind* 11: 132-43.
Bay-Petersen, J.L. 1975. *Pre-Neolithic Faunal Exploitation in Southern France and Denmark*. Unpublished Ph.D. thesis, University of Cambridge.

D

Brinch Petersen, E. 1971. Ølby Lyng: en østsjaellands kystboplads med Ertebøllekultur. *Aarbøger for Nordisk Oldkyndighed og Historie*, 1970: 5-42.

Brinch Petersen, E. 1973. A survey of the late Palaeolithic and Mesolithic of Denmark. In S.K. Kozlowski (ed.), *The Mesolithic in Europe*. Warsaw, University Press: 77-127.

Carballo, J. and González Echegaray, J. 1952. Algunos objetos inéditos de la cueva de El Pendo. *Ampurias*, 14: 37-48.

Cipriani, L. 1955. Excavations in Andamanese Kitchen-middens. *Actes du IV Congrès International Scientifique, Anthropologique et Ethnologique*, 2: 250-3.

Cipriani, L. 1966. *The Andaman Islanders*. London, Weidenfeld and Nicolson. (Edited and translated by D.T. Cox, assisted by L. Cole.)

Clark, G.A. 1971. The Asturian of Cantabria: subsistence base and the evidence for post-Pleistocene climatic shifts. *American Anthropologist*, 73: 1244-57.

Clark, G.A. 1975. Liencres: una estación al aire libre de estilo Asturiense cerca de Santander. *Cuadernos de Arqueología de Deusto, Seminario de Arqueología, Bilbao*.

Clark, J.G.D. 1975. *The Earlier Stone Age Settlement of Scandinavia*. London, Cambridge University Press.

Cook, S.F. and Treganza, A.E. 1950. The quantitative investigation of Indian mounds. *University of California Publications in American Archaeology and Ethnology*, 40(5): 223-62.

Drucker, P. 1943. Archaeological survey on the northern Northwest coast. *Smithsonian Institution, Bureau of American Ethnology*, 133: 17-132.

Emery, K.O. and Milliman, J.D. 1970. Quaternary sediments of the Atlantic continental shelf of the United States. *Quaternaria*, 12: 3-18.

Freeman, L.G. 1973. The significance of mammalian faunas from Paleolithic occupations in Cantabrian Spain. *American Antiquity*, 38(1): 3-44.

González Echegaray, J. 1973. Consideraciónes climáticas y ecológicas sobre el Magdaleniense III en el norte de España. *Zephyrus*, 23: 167-87.

González Echegaray, J. and Freeman, L.G. 1971. Cueva Morín: Excavaciónes 1966-1968. *Patronato de las Cuevas Prehistóricas de la Provincia de Santander*, 6.

González Echegaray, J., García Guinea, M.A., Begines Ramírez, A. and Madariaga de la Campa, B. 1963. Cueva de la Chora. *Excavaciónes Arqueológicas en España*, 26.

Gould, R.A. 1966. Archaeology of the Point St. George site, and Tolowa Prehistory. *University of California Publications in Anthropology*, 4.

Hewer, H.R. 1974. *British Seals*. London, Collins.

Higgs, E.S. (ed.). 1975. *Palaeoeconomy*. London, Cambridge University Press.

Higgs, E.S. and Vita-Finzi, C. 1972. Prehistoric economies: a territorial approach. In E.S. Higgs (ed.), *Papers in Economic Prehistory*. London, Cambridge University Press: 27-36.

Janssens, P. and González Echegaray, J. 1958. Memoria de las Excavaciónes de la Cueva del Juyo (1955-6). *Patronato de las Cuevas Prehistóricas de la Provincia de Santander (España)*.

Jarman, M.R. 1972. A territorial model for archaeology: a behavioural and geographical approach. In D.L. Clarke (ed.), *Models in Archaeology*. London, Methuen: 705-33.

Jordá Cerdá, F. 1958. Avance al estudio de la cueva de la Lloseta (Ardines, Ribadesella, Asturias). *Memorias del Servicio de Investigaciónes Arqueologicas*, 3.

Kapel, H. 1969. En boplads fra tidlig-Atlantisk tid ved Villingebaek. *Nationalmuseets Arbejdsmark*: 85-94.

Kroeber, A.L. and Barrett, S.A. 1960. Fishing among the Indians of northwestern California. *Anthropological Records of the University of California*, 21.

Lee, R.B. 1968. What hunters do for a living, or how to make out on scarce resources. In R.B. Lee and I. DeVore (eds.), *Man the Hunter*. Chicago, Aldine: 30-48.

Lee, R.B. and DeVore, I. (eds.). 1968. *Man the Hunter*. Chicago, Aldine.

Lumley, H. de. 1969. A Paleolithic camp at Nice. *Scientific American*, 220(5): 42-50.

Lumley, H. de. 1975. Cultural evolution in France in its paleoecological setting during the Middle Pleistocene. In G. Ll. Isaac and K.W. Butzer (eds.), *After the Australopithecines: Stratigraphy, Ecology and Culture in the Middle Pleistocene.* The Hague and Paris, Mouton: 745-808.

Madsen, A.P. 1888. Undersøgelse af Kjøkkenmøddingen ved Meilgaard i 1888. *Aarbøger for Nordisk Oldkyndighed og Historie*, 3: 299-309.

Madsen, A.P., Muller, S., Neergaard, C., Petersen, C.G.J., Rostrup, E., Steenstrup, K.J.V. and Wingc, H. 1900. *Affaldsdynger fra Stenalderen i Danmark.* Copenhagen, C.A. Reitzel.

Mathiassen, T. 1946. En boplads fra aeldre stenalder ved Vedbaek Boldbaner. *Søllerødbogen*: 19-35.

Mary, G., Medus, J. and Delibrias, G. 1975. Le Quarternaire de la côte Asturienne (Espagne). *Bulletin de l'Association Française pour l'Etude du Quarternaire*, 42: 13-23.

Meehan, B. 1975. *Shell Bed to Shell Midden.* Unpublished Ph.D. thesis, Australian National University, Canberra.

Møhl, U. 1971. Fangstdyrene ved de Danske strande: den zoologiske baggrund for harpunerne. *Kuml*, 1970: 297-329.

Obermaier, H. 1925. El hombre fósil. *Comisión de Investigaciónes Paleontológicas y Prehistóricas*, 9.

Obermaier, H. and Vega del Sella, Conde de la, 1918. La cueva del Buxu. *Comisión de Investigaciónes Paleontológicas y Prehistóricas*, 13.

Parmalee, P.W. and Klippel, W.E. 1974. Freshwater mussels as a prehistoric food resource. *American Antiquity*, 28(1): 421-34.

Petersen, C.G.J. 1922. Om tidsbestemmelse og ernaeringsforhold i den aeldre Stenalder i Danmark. *Det Kongelige Danske Videnskabernes Selskab, Biologiske Meddelelser*, 3: 3-20.

Shenkel, J.R. 1971. *Cultural Adaptation to the Mollusc: a Methodological Survey of Shellmound Archaeology and a Consideration of the Shellmounds of the Marismas Nacionales, West Mexico.* Unpublished Ph.D. thesis, State University of New York at Buffalo.

Sturdy, D.A. 1972. *Reindeer Economies in Late Ice Age Europe.* Unpublished Ph.D. thesis, University of Cambridge.

Tauber, H. 1972. Radiocarbon chronology of the Danish Mesolithic and Neolithic. *Antiquity*, 46: 106-10.

Vega del Sella, Conde de la, 1923. El Asturiense: nueva industria Pre-Neolitíca. *Comisión de Investigaciónes Paleontológicas y Pre-históricas*, 32.

Vereshchagin, N.K. 1967. Primitive hunters and Pleistocene extinctions in the Soviet Union. In P.S. Martin and H.E. Wright, Jr. (eds.), *Pleistocene Extinctions: the Search for a Cause.* New Haven and London, Yale University Press: 365-98.

Vita-Finzi, C. and Higgs, E.S. 1970. Prehistoric economy in the Mount Carmel area of Palestine: site catchment analysis. *Proceedings of the Prehistoric Society*, 36: 1-37.

White, C. 1968. *Report on Field Survey, June-August 1968.* Canberra, Australian Institute of Aboriginal Studies, Document 68/738 (mimeographed).

5

Ecological aspects of population size and growth in late-glacial and early postglacial north-western Europe

Christopher Meiklejohn

Local group size, total regional population and population growth are concepts central to understanding the dynamics of any region. They are factors in social organisation, itself a measure of the complexity of a group, a concept that cannot be divorced from its absolute size (Carneiro 1967). They are also major factors in the control of the genetic systems. In this paper I will expand upon these concepts as they relate to the shift from late-glacial to early postglacial conditions. An elegant balance appears between these factors and observable ecological shifts in northern and western Europe.

The period under consideration saw the last extensive occupation of Europe by hunting and gathering communities. There is clear evidence that these groups fell within the general framework of 'band' societies as used by such workers as Lee and DeVore (1968) and Damas (1969). The band concept serves to define the activity patterns of people at this economic level for the purposes discussed below. Attempts to view European populations of this time horizon as more complex do not appear to have a reliable archaeological basis. They also clash with what we know of the ecology of this period and therefore, if proposed, require far more evidence than has currently been provided.

The economic basis

The populations considered here were subject to certain economic constraints that show both continuity and extensive change. They display continuity in that there is little change in the *nature* of the economic base. Changes do occur, however, both in the components that make it up and in its variability. These are fundamental to understanding the differing statuses of late-glacial and postglacial human groups.

A considerable body of evidence now exists for the diet of Upper Palaeolithic populations during the late-glacial period. During actual glacial episodes very high dependency upon large herd mammals is apparent (see Meiklejohn 1974). In the majority of cases *one* large herd mammal is predominant, and in the overwhelming number of cases it is reindeer. This was clearly documented by Bouchud (1966) and is supported by a wealth of further publication over the last ten years. Only in Mediterranean Europe is this pattern not seen, as recently documented by Freeman (1973). The nature of the economic base in the latter area may provide a closer parallel to populations of postglacial Europe than to those of the contemporary Palaeolithic to the north. The degree of specialisation seen in these Upper Palaeolithic groups has few living analogues outside modern arctic and subarctic populations (Lee 1968). In addition there is little evidence for exploitation of subsidiary food resources – especially plant foods. There may even be a *prima facie* case for suggesting that plant-food exploitation was considerably below that seen in most modern 'hunting' populations (Meiklejohn 1974).

It has been argued that the shift to postglacial conditions resulted in fundamental changes in the *nature* of the economy (Binford 1968). The published evidence, however, suggests that the changes are of degree rather than kind. That some changes have occurred would appear self evident. There is no doubt that the degree of climatic change occurring between c. 12,000 and 5,000 bc was accompanied by substantial shifts in flora and fauna. This was first documented in the classic pollen sequences published in the last century by pioneers such as Blytt. That these represent natural phenomena related to climatic change is underlined by the fact that insect faunas in northern Europe show the effect of climatic amelioration somewhat earlier than those seen in the flora (Osborne 1974). This adds weight to the evidence that pollen-zone boundaries are not continentally synchronous, but instead show clear wave progression (Hafsten 1971; Hibbert, Switsur and West 1971; Smith and Pilcher 1973). The modifying effect of local ecological factors can also be measured (see Walker 1975).

Under such climatic and resulting ecological change the economic basis of human communities could not have resisted modification. What is marked, however, is that while the actual species of exploited animals did change, the *type* of species under exploitation remained strikingly unaltered. A society oriented towards the exploitation of large herd mammals remained.

Major changes appear to have begun in the Bölling oscillation, accelerating during the Allerød and continuing into the postglacial. The Older and Younger Dryas periods saw short-term halts to this change but no meaningful reversal occurred. The reindeer was the only major element of the Upper Palaeolithic dietary which survived into the Younger Dryas. The major period of effective extinctions appears to have been the Allerød interstadial. During the early Preboreal the last reindeer were displaced to the north (see Hansen 1961). The earlier herd-oriented fauna was replaced by more solitary species adapted to the developing forest vegetation. Red and roe deer, wild cattle and pig predominated, providing the major subsistence basis until the development of the Neolithic after 4,500 bc.

An examination by the author (Meiklejohn 1974) suggests that the pattern of Mesolithic dietary preferences described by Clark (1952) for Northern Europe is still largely valid. In seven recently published sites from the United Kingdom and France a total of eleven large mammal species were reported. The sites are: Star Carr, Thatcham, Westward Ho!, Roc d'Abeilles, Chambre des Fées, La Borie del Rey and Gramari (Clark 1972; King *in* Wymer 1962; Churchill and Wymer 1965; Bouchud 1970; Poulain *in* Hinout 1964; Coulonges 1963; Poulain *in* Paccard *et al.* 1971). From 2 to 7 were reported for individual sites and levels, with an average of 4.1. This is in sharp contrast to the late Palaeolithic dependency upon a single species. In addition there may be an increase of up to one-third in the number of species present between early and late Mesolithic sites. The central complex noted above was apparent and had been reported several years ago by Schwabedissen (1962) and Waterbolk (1962) and more recently by Jarman (1972). In addition, a higher number of small mammals were reported from these sites and levels. It is also possible to document the seasonal exploitation of aquatic mammals, waterfowl, fish and shellfish. An economic base of considerable breadth is thus apparent to a degree totally absent in late-glacial contexts (see also Bay-Petersen, this volume).

There are, in addition, some indications that plant food exploitation during the postglacial era may be more of the form documented in recent hunter-gatherer populations (see Lee 1968). Edible plant foods have been obtained in some numbers from certain sites with good preservation. Examples would be the presence of *Phragmites* and *Menyanthes* at Star Carr (Clark 1972) and the large numbers of hazel nut shells reported from many sites in northern Europe. Recent work on Mongongo nut exploitation by the !Kung Bushmen shows that a very high percentage of the total diet can come from a single plant food resource (Lee 1973).[1]

In conclusion, there is overwhelming evidence for marked change in the economic base at the Pleistocene-Holocene transition, which is clearly the result of gradual postglacial forest development. Large mammals remain the central focus of the subsistence strategies, supplemented by secondary resources, often of a seasonal nature, and increased gathering. The trend to small game hunting suggested by Binford (1968) is not a true conveyor of the dynamic pattern seen. The above pattern is involved in the controls of both local group size and regional population, and thus of population growth.

Local group size and regional population

Of the variables that control the social system of any group, population size is one of the most important. As alluded to above, sociopolitical complexity is almost certainly best viewed structurally as the means by which a population controls its members. The larger the group, the more complex must be the control mechanisms required to keep that group intact. This has been clearly shown by Lee for Bushmen undergoing acculturation (1972b, 1972c). Social complexity and the cultural material which is associated with this complexity leaves an archaeologically clear record. At present it seems obvious that the kinds of complexity which are related to increased group size, political control and long term static communities are essentially Neolithic phenomena. Complexity as seen in pre-Neolithic societies occurs in areas not concerned with the above-mentioned features, but rather in those such as the artistic which are not size related. The richness that is seen, for example, in the Magdalenian is analogous to that of small group cultures such as the Canadian Eskimo and not to large scale settled communities such as those of the Northwest Coast.

The archaeological evidence relating to late Palaeolithic and Mesolithic communities suggests a society that is artistically rich (extending to the decoration of utilitarian items) but with little extended material culture and showing little evidence for permanence in their site occupation. Groups within the general size range reported for modern hunter-gatherers can explain all the known archaeological evidence. They also fit well with what we know of the ecology. Differences between the groups seen in Pleistocene and early postglacial times appear to be ecologically based.

Sites of late Palaeolithic populations tend in general to be relatively conspicuous phenomena. In contrast there has always been a dearth of large Mesolithic sites. This led, in the last century, first to the concept of the 'Ancient Hiatus' thought to separate Palaeolithic and Neolithic populations and, later, to concepts of cultural degeneration that still rear their heads in the literature (cf. Clark, this volume). It seems profitable to examine whether group size differences are to be expected in the changing ecology of the Pleistocene-Holocene transition.

Hunter-gatherer societies are cyclic in nature. As both seasonally-based resources and group-needs vary, so does the internal composition of the groups. This has been well documented by workers such as Campbell (1968), Leacock (1969) and Slobodin (1969). In most of these societies a clear dichotomy between periods of aggregation and dispersion is apparent. The applicability of such patterning to Upper Palaeolithic society has been clearly demonstrated by David's (1973) analysis of the Perigordian Vc (Noaillian) occupation in western France. The 'visibility' of any culture in archaeological terms is related to the degree of agglomeration and its duration. Both Campbell and David note that most sites within the dispersal phase will be effectively unrecognisable in the archaeological record. An obvious corollary is that groups that spend much of their annual round within the 'dispersed' phase will leave a weak archaeological record.

The dynamics of late Palaeolithic hunting communities have not been sufficiently closely studied. Only recently have we gained some insight into the factors that control such a society, especially those related to the behaviour of the exploited game species. In an important example Burch (1972) has documented that reindeer exploitation provides a far less stable economic base than has generally been assumed. Though reindeer may well provide almost the total range of food and other economic requirements to an exploiting group in certain circumstances, they are not nearly so eager to oblige as some authors have envisaged. They are difficult to capture during certain periods of the year, and are subject to fluctuations, both in terms of total numbers and regional distribution. They can only be followed throughout their annual cycle at extreme energy cost that leads to excessively low population densities (Burch 1976). They are not simply an ever available walking larder. This places several constraints on exploiting groups. I will discuss those concerned with population control and growth below. Others affect local group size and aggregation patterns.

Wilmsen (1973) has argued that when a primary resource is both scattered and mobile a central site location for groups is adaptive, reducing the area that must be covered in attempting to locate game. It is thus a conserver of energy expended, an important factor in such small groups (Lee 1972a). Group aggregation can therefore be expected in Palaeolithic populations exploiting a mobile resource such as reindeer. In the spring and fall migrations this will lead to aggregations employing what Burch (1972) refers to as the 'head-'em-off-at-the-pass' hunting technique. Thus aggregation would have been highly adaptive for late Palaeolithic groups both in searching for the primary food resource and after locating it. The aggregation thus performs a major economic function as well as having certain social concomitants. A major portion of the yearly round thus will have a correspondingly high degree of archaeological 'visibility'.

A pattern such as that described above may lead to an exaggerated impression of population stability at any one site and, by extrapolation, for any given region. If exploiting mobile resources such a group would need to move from one central site to others during the course of the year. A group might therefore occupy several sites, each with considerable evidence of continuity. Distinguishing between continuous occupation of a site for several years and annual but seasonal occupation of a site is not easy. One of the primary reasons for assuming year round occupation of such sites in south-western France has been the evidence of reindeer remains so extensively documented by Bouchud (1966). Binford (1973) has, however, shown that certain assumptions of the method may lead to overestimation of the seasonal range of reindeer presence for any given site. Occupation of such sites for short seasonal periods fits far better with modern hunter-gatherer analogues. The classic abri site of south-western France is, moreover, especially prone to such misinterpretation due to the limitation of occupiable area. Consecutive occupations must *perforce* overlie each other and the opportunities for sterile layers to develop between successive occupations are considerably reduced.

Problems such as those described above have led to considerable variation in population estimates for late Palaeolithic Europe. Extremes in the recent literature are indicated by the figures suggested for Upper Palaeolithic France by Bordes (1968) and David (1973). The discrepancy seen is between five and ten-fold, Bordes' figures being the higher. Converting the figure-estimates to densities yields outer limits of 0.008 to 0.090 persons per square kilometre. Both are well within the range of densities known from modern hunter-gatherer populations. However, only the lower figures stem directly from a site and territory analysis for a specific area and period. They are thus the only ones that can be compared directly to modern group studies. Furthermore, modern populations exploiting reindeer fall at the lower end of the above density range (Burch 1976).

Other estimations can be derived from the above. In simulation studies Wobst (1976) has shown that self-sufficient mating networks cannot normally operate with population numbers much below 475. The minimal figure is possible only under idealised conditions of social structure and an operative figure closer to 1000 is suggested by studies such as those of the Central Eskimo (Damas 1975). Using David's density estimates (calculated from his estimates of total population numbers) this implies a minimum territory for such a group of 24-60,000 square kilometres. The higher figure implies a territory of 50-125,000 square kilometres. If equal density of habitation over habitable western Europe north of the Mediterranean basin is assumed (a dubious proposition), from eight to twelve genetically autonomous groups could operate under ideal circumstances of stability. Each of these groups would contain a number of locally defined 'bands', groups of closely interrelated extended families. The total group might well come together in larger seasonal aggregations for hunting and for social purposes such as mate exchange. Such aggregations could account for suggestions that a number of adjacent abris might be occupied at the same time. These aggregations would, however, be of short duration. Such a major aggregation would probably account for almost the total population of a regional zone such as the Perigord, southern England, etc.

Such full aggregations are, however, not easy to document

archaeologically. Even major sites such as Dolni Vestonice must involve much smaller groups. Klima's estimate of the population at the latter site is 100-125, and involves the assumption that all the habitations were contemporary (in Butzer 1971). Such a site, can, however, provide much lower population estimates if viewed as a series of accumulating temporary camps as seen at Muller-Beck's Umingmak site. Smaller aggregations would be interactive with others over a large geographical area. In times of stress such groups would require access to a considerably larger geographical area (Lee 1972a). The number of major groups extant in western Europe over any considerable duration of time would thus, in all probability, be less than the eight to twelve units noted above. Bordes' figures would probably only allow twenty groups over any extended period, David's about four to six at most. This probably can be taken as defining the possible range of variability for this parameter. An area such as the Perigord would support, at most, one or two such macro-units. The area required in a less densely populated area such as the Ile-de-France would be considerably greater (see Schmider 1971). The extent to which such groupings would have formed discrete units is a separate issue which has been discussed elsewhere (Meiklejohn 1976, 1978).

The shift to postglacial conditions would affect many of the variables noted above. The change from herd to solitary mammals would result in an immediate decrease in the potentially available biomass. This was probably at least partially offset by the increased exploitation of secondary, less mobile, food resources. Some of these secondary resources may also have proven more reliable over any extended period of time. A shift to more locally-oriented forms would lead to patterns of incipient sedentism. Whether any stresses would be placed upon the population by the apparently competing factors of lowered potential biomass and increased regionalism needs further exploration. I will return to this below.

An offsetting factor to regionalism is the observation by Wilmsen (1973: 6) that more stable resources are more effectively garnered where 'each user position controls an equal but limited and nearby set of resource locations'. In practical terms this translates into a population of smaller, more evenly distributed groups (Meiklejohn 1974: 179). Such a model of smaller units could result in denser spatial packing. Group competition for space in times of resource scarcity would be expected to be considerably dampened by any broadening of the economy.

The above model of changing patterns of aggregation and density would result in a lowering of the number of large sites of Upper Palaeolithic type, such as Dolni Vestonice mentioned above. Aggregations which did take place would most probably be for social rather than economic reasons, and of shorter duration. Such a pattern would result in a considerably less 'visible' set of sites for early postglacial northern and western Europe. Other factors involved in reduced visibility include postglacial alluviation, absence of loess deposition and a general abandonment of cave occupation. Sites have also been lost in coastal areas as a result of the postglacial rise in sea level – as chance opportunities for examination have revealed (Waals and Waterbolk 1976).

Evidence for mobility centred around specific economic foci is evident from many sites. At Star Carr an annual pattern based on variations in seasonal abundance and ecological zonation is apparent (Clark 1972). In the sites of the Dutch Havelte region there is evidence for group return to an area on a regularised basis (Price, Whallon and Chappell 1974). Cultural means of increasing the local availability of resources may also be evident, as seen in the high percentages of ivy pollen reported in some Mesolithic sites (Simmons and Dimbleby 1974).

If seasonal distributions of 'band' groupings in the Mesolithic became localised there is a more than reasonable presumption that total regional populations would have never actually decreased in the early Holocene. The decrease in individual group size would have been countered by the number of groups per unit area. No meaningful break would therefore have occurred in population growth, though the variables may have altered.

Population growth

I have argued above that the parameters of local group size altered in response to the changing ecology of the Pleistocene-Holocene interface. At the same time the total regional population showed continuity in size, though with a differing spatial configuration. Within this framework I would like to consider a factor of primary importance in demographic terms, namely population growth. Does a simple continuity of pattern emerge from the above or does this parameter also exhibit change?

It has often been assumed that the Upper Palaeolithic economy of northern and western Europe provided an unlimited base for population development, a 'larder on the hoof' as mentioned above. However, as Burch (1972) has pointed out, our understanding of large herd-mammal dynamics, especially reindeer, has contained many misleading or false assumptions. Reindeer cannot normally be followed during their annual round. Over any appreciable period of time they show both cyclic variations and regional displacements. For any particular regional population such resource fluctuation would provide a strong mechanism of population control, following Liebig's Law. Fitzhugh (1972: 171-86) has documented periodic starvation and group fragmentation in the Naskapi-Montagnais population of Labrador and Quebec. It is pointed out that the factors leading to the collapse of a primary resource may also affect secondary resources. This is also documented by Waisberg (1975). Such conditions are not confined exclusively to arctic environments. Ecological stress may well be worse in subarctic and Boreal forest conditions, where fire and winter icing are major factors (op. cit.). These conditions are likely to occur during mild winters and during periods of reforestation. David (1973) has documented two apparent population crises during Perigordian Vc times in south-western France. The second of these crashes probably dates to the 'Tursac' oscillation. It cannot therefore be argued that population control by economic means applies only to periglacial regions. It is in fact probable that the severity of population crises would be greater in more southerly regions where higher population densities may have prevented alternate exploitation of other areas.

The above comments suggest that population growth in the Upper Palaeolithic would have been anything but smooth and gradual. A cyclic pattern is far more likely, though overall growth through time as measured in millennia most probably occurred. Using site density data Butzer (1971) estimated a ten-fold increase in population for Europe for the duration of the Weichsel glaciation. Translated into annual rate of growth, a figure of less than 0.01 percent per annum emerges and if evenly spread over the total 60,000 years, only 0.004 percent per annum. When viewed over the time scale of a single generation or even a century, these figures imply almost no net increase in local group size (Meiklejohn 1974: 368): a group of 100 would require over 250 years to show a net increase of one person using the lower figures cited above!

The preceding comments on group size and density suggest that the effect of resource cyclicity would increase as population density increased. Thus, the populations of the Mousterian and early Upper Palaeolithic may have been less likely to show the effects of resource-based stress in reduced numbers. Lower population density would have permitted a larger margin of local group displacement to meet regional resource crashes. Bordes' density estimates are for terminal Upper Palaeolithic times. The total number of effective populations in the early Mousterian would have been less than half a dozen using Bordes' figures. If David's figures are correct, the whole Neanderthal population of western Europe can only have had two or three subgroups at most, and may have been encompassed within a single breeding unit!

As population size increased during the last glacial the effect of resource cyclicity would have become more apparent. By the late Perigordian, David records marked effects on group distribution and site numbers. If a fifty percent drop in population occurred in such a crash it would take 500 years for the population to regain its former size, using the upper level of population increase rates calculated for the Neolithic (0.14 percent) (Carneiro and Hilse 1966). To double in

100 years would require a rate of 0.7 percent – a level hard to visualise for a hunter-gatherer population, especially in the light of recent work suggesting that low growth-levels in hunter-gatherers may be related to the interaction of fertility with female body-fat levels (Howell 1976) and not simply to culturally-derived phenomena such as work effort (Lee 1972*a*). Very rapid rates of growth which have been postulated for populations faced with an open territory may make sense in cultural terms (Mossiman and Martin 1975) but they run foul of biological mechanisms.

The comments above suggest that a pattern of population decline and rebound may have characterised the late Upper Palaeolithic period. The frequency of such resource-mediated declines would be such that overall growth as measured in millennia would not exceed the figures proposed by Butzer. Indications that both population density and climatic amelioration would exacerbate the situation suggest that this model would extend through the late-glacial oscillations and into the Preboreal period. Only slight relief might come from a slightly more stable resource base during late-glacial oscillations.

The postglacial shift in the economic base has implications for population growth. There is a suggestion of a lowered potentially available biomass. However, a more important question concerns the availability of that biomass to the exploiting population. A considerable portion of the high biomass of late Pleistocene herd mammals was unavailable to human populations as I have indicated above. In response to fluctuating resources, population numbers would have been controlled by the periods of least availability of those resources (see Smith 1972; Casteel 1972). Viewed within this light the decrease in actual available biomass during the postglacial is likely to have been more apparent than real. The shift to a broad-based economy would have increased the dependability of the food base and may even have increased the long-term available yield, especially if the shift included an increased use of plant food resources as I have suggested above.

If dependable biomass increased during the Mesolithic a quite different relationship between the ecological system and population growth can be expected. A dependable biomass would militate against some of the controls on population growth controlled by physiological factors (Howell 1976). If reduction below critical body-fat levels occurs effective sterility results, and in critical cases menstrual function may cease (amenorrhea). Under a regime where the food base is reliable, mothers would be more likely to retain their body-fat levels above critical thresholds, thus reducing birth-spacing intervals. This would be even more marked if a simultaneous tendency to sedentism was occurring, thus reducing the total caloric requirements of women as measured over the course of the year. Under such conditions a tendency toward increased population growth would be a reasonable prediction.

To what degree a change in population growth was a sudden postglacial development remains to be answered. It is probable that the shift in the dietary took little more than a millennium, being largely completed by the end of the Preboreal, some shifts in emphasis occurring later. Thus it is probably fair to say that Holocene diets *in toto* were broader-based and more reliable than those of the late Pleistocene. The counter-effect of other variables may, however, have slowed down the overall process. Forest succession is a major point. As alluded to above, Waisberg (1975) has documented the kinds of instability inherent in a situation of forest succession. This appears to be especially true if the forest is of the Boreal type. Regular cycles of burning are only one of the problems encountered. This area has hardly been discussed in a European context. It may be fair to propose that successional problems were a major factor in the early Holocene, becoming increasingly less severe as the deciduous maximum of the Atlantic period was approached. The result would be for population growth to be considerably dampened in the Preboreal and early Boreal periods as compared to the later Boreal and Atlantic.[2]

What kinds of growth rate can be postulated for the Mesolithic? As noted above I have previously estimated that steady-state Upper Pleistocene growth rates lay in the range of 0.004-0.010 percent per annum. If these figures are used to calculate population growth during the period 10,000-4,000 bc an increase of between 27 and 82 percent results. If the upper growth rate figure is doubled to 0.020 percent per annum (as might be expected from the comments above) the increase would be 332 percent. The increase at 0.040 percent (i.e. *half* the minimal figure calculated for the Neolithic by Carneiro and Hilse (1966)) would be over eleven-fold! These figures show that only a minor change in growth rate would produce a startling increase in population size during the Mesolithic as compared to the late Palaeolithic.

Two sets of recently published data provide results that supply at least some confirmation for the above model. Brinch Petersen (1973) has shown that population growth in Denmark proceeded slowly throughout the Preboreal and Boreal, was somewhat stagnant in the early Atlantic, but showed marked expansion during the late Atlantic 'Ertebølle' phase. Population growth, especially in the late Mesolithic, has also been demonstrated by Newell (1973).

The question of site visibility in the Mesolithic is closely related to the above suggestions. The initial response of Mesolithic populations to early postglacial ecological conditions would be a dispersion of local groups into smaller units, albeit probably more closely distributed in space. This, together with a reduced tendency to supragroup or 'band' aggregation, would result in a considerable lessening of archaeological visibility. The shift in ecological position of the community would, however, lead to an increased population growth. At first this would be dampened by factors in the local environmental succession that would result in population disruption. By the Atlantic period, however, the development of a climax forest would offset these constraints, leading to more rapid population growth, continuous with that so better documented in the succeeding Neolithic.

Acknowledgements

The current paper is derived from two that were written for the IX International Congress of Prehistoric and Protohistoric Sciences, held in Nice in September 1976. Support for attendance at that meeting was provided by the Canada Council General Grant to the University of Winnipeg. I would like to thank Dr Paul Mellars for suggesting that the discussed topic would be appropriate to this volume.

Notes

[1] The probable importance of plant food resources in the economy of Mesolithic communities in Europe has been emphasised even more strongly in a recent paper by D.L. Clarke (1976). Such a shift in the food base may have been sufficient to overcome apparent drops in the available biomass suggested for large mammals.

[2] The effects of forest fires on the ecology of early postglacial communities has been discussed in detail in a recent article by Mellars (1976). As Mellars points out, burning of forests on a *limited* scale can be highly beneficial to hunter-gatherer communities by increasing the yields of both animal and plant food resources. However, the kind of large-scale, high-intensity fires frequently encountered in the coniferous forests of the sub-arctic zone must be seen in a different light. Such fires can effectively eliminate the forage resources available to both moose and caribou populations over areas of several hundred square miles for periods of several years (cf. Mellars 1976: 26-7, 29-30). Burning on this scale would inevitably create a major economic crisis for human groups who relied heavily on the exploitation of these animal resources.

References

Binford, L.R. 1968. Post-Pleistocene adaptations. In S. Binford and L.R. Binford (eds.), *New Perspectives in Archeology*. Chicago, Aldine: 313-41.

Binford, L.R. 1973. Interassemblage variability – the Mousterian and the 'functional' argument. In C. Renfrew (ed.), *The Explanation of Culture Change; Models in Prehistory*. London, Duckworth: 227-54.

Bordes, F. 1968. *The Old Stone Age*. New York, McGraw Hill.

Bouchud, J. 1966. *Essai sur le Renne et la Climatologie du Paléolithique moyen et supérieur*. Périgueux, Imprimerie Magne.

Bouchud, J. 1970. Determination de la faune du Roc d'Abeilles (Dordogne). *Gallia Préhistoire*, 13: 23.

Brinch Petersen, E. 1973. A survey of the late Palaeolithic and Mesolithic of Denmark. In S.K. Kozlowski (ed.), *The Mesolithic in Europe*. Warsaw, University Press: 77-128.

Burch, E.S. Jr. 1972. The Caribou/Wild Reindeer as a human resource. *American Antiquity*, 37: 339-68.

Burch, E.S. Jr. 1976. The Caribou-Eater Chipewayen and their prey, 1600-1800. Paper read to the *Conference on the Prehistory of the North American Sub-Arctic: The Athapaskan Question.* Calgary.

Butzer, K. 1971. *Environment and Archaeology.* Chicago, Aldine.

Campbell, J.M. 1968. Territory among ancient hunters: interpretations from ethnography and nature. In B.J. Meggers (ed.), *Anthropological Archaeology in the Americas.* Washington, The Anthropological Society of Washington: 1-21.

Carneiro, R.L. 1967. On the relationship between size of population and the complexity of social organization. *Southwestern Journal of Anthropology,* 23: 234-43.

Carneiro, R.L. and Hilse, D.F. 1966. On determining the probable rate of population growth during the Neolithic. *American Anthropologist,* 68: 177-81.

Casteel, R.W. 1972. Two static maximum population-density models for hunter-gatherers: a first approximation, *World Archaeology,* 4: 19-40.

Churchill, D.M. and Wymer, J.J. 1965. The kitchen midden site at Westward Ho!, Devon, England: ecology, age and relation to changes in land and sea level. *Proceedings of the Prehistoric Society,* 31: 74-84.

Clark, J.G.D. 1952. *Prehistoric Europe, The Economic Basis.* London, Methuen.

Clark, J.G.D. 1972. *Star Carr: a Case Study in Bioarchaeology.* Addison Wesley Modular Publications, 10. Reading, Massachussets.

Clarke, D.L. 1976. Mesolithic Europe: the economic basis. In G. de G. Sieveking, I.H. Longworth and K.E. Wilson (eds.), *Problems in Economic and Social Archaeology.* London, Duckworth: 449-81.

Coulonges, L. 1963. Magdalénien et Périgordien postglaciaires, La Grotte de la Borie del Rey (Lot-et-Garonne). *Gallia Préhistoire,* 6: 1-29.

Damas, D. (ed.) 1969. *Contributions to Anthropology: Band Societies.* National Museums of Canada Bulletin, 230.

Damas, D. 1975. Demographic aspects of central Eskimo marriage practices. *American Ethnologist,* 2: 409-18.

David, N.C. 1973. On Upper Palaeolithic society, ecology and technological change: the Noaillian case. In C. Renfrew (ed.), *The Explanation of Culture Change; Models in Prehistory.* London, Duckworth: 277-303.

Fitzhugh, W.W. 1972. *Environmental Archaeology and Cultural Systems in Hamilton Inlet, Labrador. A survey of the central Labrador coast from 3000 bc to the present.* Smithsonian Contributions to Anthropology, 16.

Freeman, L.G. 1973. The significance of mammalian faunas from palaeolithic occupations in Cantabrian Spain. *American Antiquity,* 38: 3-44.

Hafsten, U. 1970. A sub-division of the late Pleistocene period on a synchronous basis, intended for global and universal usage. *Palaeogeography, Palaeoclimatology, Palaeoecology,* 7: 279-96.

Hansen, S. 1961. The Quaternary of Denmark. In K. Rankama (ed.), *The Geologic Systems: The Quaternary.* New York, Interscience, 1: 1-90.

Hibbert, F.A., Switsur, V.R. and West, R.G. 1971. Radiocarbon dating of Flandrian pollen zones at Red Moss, Lancashire. *Proceedings of the Royal Society of London,* Series B. 177: 161-76.

Hinout, J. 1964. Gisements Tardénoisiens de l'Aisne. *Gallia Préhistoire,* 7: 65-106.

Howell, N. 1976. Toward a uniformitarian theory of human palaeodemography. *Journal of Human Evolution,* 5: 25-40.

Jarman, M.R. 1972. European deer economies and the advent of the Neolithic. In E.S. Higgs (ed.), *Papers in Economic Prehistory.* London, Cambridge University Press: 125-47.

Leacock, E. 1969. The Montagnais-Naskapi band. *National Museums of Canada Bulletin,* 228: 1-17.

Lee, R.B. 1968. What hunters do for a living; or, how to make out on scarce resources. In R.B. Lee and I. DeVore (eds.), *Man the Hunter.* Chicago, Aldine: 30-48.

Lee, R.B. 1972a. Work effort, group structure and land-use in contemporary hunter-gatherers. In P.J. Ucko, R. Tringham and G.W. Dimbleby (eds.), *Man, Settlement and Urbanism*. London, Duckworth: 177-85.

Lee, R.B. 1972b. Population growth and the beginning of sedentary life among the !Kung Bushmen. In B. Spooner (ed.), *Population Growth: Anthropological Implications*. Cambridge, MIT Press: 329-42.

Lee, R.B. 1972c. The intensification of social life among the !Kung Bushmen. In B. Spooner (ed.), *Population Growth: Anthropological Implications*. Cambridge, MIT Press: 343-50.

Lee, R.B. 1972d. !Kung spatial organization: an ecological and historical perspective. *Human Ecology*, 1: 125-47.

Lee, R.B. 1973. Mongongo: the ethnography of a major wild food resource. *Ecology of Food and Nutrition*, 2: 307-21.

Lee, R.B. and DeVore, I. 1968. *Man the Hunter*. Chicago, Aldine.

Meiklejohn, C. 1974. *The Bio-social Basis of Upper Palaeolithic and Mesolithic Man in Western Europe*. Unpublished Ph. D. thesis, University of Toronto.

Meiklejohn, C. 1976. Population structure models and the interpretation of the European Upper Palaeolithic-Neolithic transition. *American Journal of Physical Anthropology*, 44: 194.

Meiklejohn, C. 1978. Genetic differentiation and deme structure: considerations for an understanding of the Athapaskan/Algonkian continuum. *Conference on the Prehistory of the North American Sub-Arctic: The Athapaskan Question*, Calgary.

Mellars, P.A. 1976. Fire ecology, animal populations and Man; a study of some ecological relationships in prehistory. *Proceedings of the Prehistoric Society*, 42: 15-45.

Mosiman, J. and Martin, P. 1975. Simulating overkill by Palaeoindians. *American Scientist*, 63: 304-13.

Newell, R.R. 1973. The postglacial adaptations of the indigenous populations of the Northwest European Plain. In S.K. Kozlowski, (ed.), *The Mesolithic in Europe*. Warsaw, University Press: 399-440.

Osborne, P.J. 1974. An insect assemblage of early Flandrian age from Lea Marston, Warwickshire, and its bearing on the contemporary climate and ecology. *Quaternary Research*, 4: 471-86.

Paccard, M., Livache, M., Dumas, C., Poulain, T. and Miskovsky, J.-C. 1971. Le camp Mésolithique de Garmari à Méthamis (Vaucluse). *Gallia Préhistoire*, 14: 47-137.

Price, T.D., Whallon, R. Jr. and Chappell, S. 1974. Mesolithic sites near Havelte, Province of Drenthe (Netherlands). *Palaeohistoria*, 16: 7-61.

Schmider, B. 1971. *Les Industries Lithiques du Paléolithique Supérieur en Ile-de-France*. Gallia Préhistoire, Supplement 6.

Schwabedissen H. 1962. Northern Continental Europe. In R.J. Braidwood and G.R. Willey (eds.), *Courses toward Urban Life*. Chicago, Aldine: 254-66.

Simmons, I.G. and Dimbleby, G.W. 1974. The possible role of Ivy (*Hedera helix* L.) in the Mesolithic economy of Western Europe. *Journal of Archaeological Science*, 1: 291-96.

Slobodin, R. 1969. Leadership and participation in a Kutchin trapping party. *National Museums of Canada Bulletin*, 228: 56-89.

Smith, A.G. and Pilcher, J.R. 1973. Radiocarbon dates and vegetational history of the British Isles. *New Phytologist*, 72: 903-14.

Smith, P.E.L. 1972. Changes in population pressure in archaeological explanation. *World Archaeology*, 4: 5-18.

Waals, J.D. van der, and Waterbolk, H.T. 1976. Excavations at Swifterbant – discovery, progress, aims and methods. *Helinium*, 16: 3-14.

Waisberg, L.G. 1975. Boreal forest subsistence and the Windigo: fluctuation of animal populations. *Anthropologica*, n.s. 17: 169-85.

Walker, M.J.C. 1975. Late-glacial and early postglacial environmental history of the central Grampian Highlands, Scotland. *Journal of Biogeography*, 2: 265-84.

Waterbolk, H.T. 1962. The Lower Rhine Basin. In R.J. Braidwood and G.R. Willey (eds.), *Courses toward Urban Life*, Chicago, Aldine: 227-53.

Wilmsen, E.N. 1973. Interaction, spacing behaviour, and the organization of hunting bands. *Journal of Anthropological Research*, 29: 1-31.

Wobst, M. 1976. Locational relationships in Palaeolithic society. *Journal of Human Evolution*, 5: 49-58.

Wymer, J.J. 1962. Excavations at the Maglemosian sites at Thatcham, Berkshire, England. *Proceedings of the Prehistoric Society*, 28: 329-61.

6

Mesolithic settlement systems in the Netherlands

T. Douglas Price

Until very recently much of our knowledge of the Mesolithic period in north-west Europe has consisted primarily of typologies of lithic artefacts. The geographic distribution of these artefact types and limited data on the economic activities of various Mesolithic cultures has supplemented a focus on the classification of artefacts. Suggested, but generally unverified, characteristics for these Mesolithic cultures have been low population density, small group size, ephemeral settlement, and a dependence upon a wide range of subsistence resources. Most of our impressions of the Mesolithic are derived from a very small number of sites that belong primarily to the 'Maglemose' component[1] of the Mesolithic in the coastal areas of north-west Europe.

More recent studies of the Mesolithic, again primarily in the areas of 'Maglemose' occupation, have emphasised the study of human settlements in addition to lithic typology. Several of these studies (e.g. Clark 1954, 1972; Brinch Petersen 1973) have resulted in preliminary descriptions of settlement patterns for the 'Maglemose'. The excellent preservation of organic remains at certain settlements in Denmark and Great Britain provides a rather complete record of the season and duration of occupation and permits direct faunal and floral evidence to be used in the investigation of variation in settlements.

Very little is known however of the inland western European Mesolithic. This absence of information can be attributed in part to extremely poor conditions for the preservation of organic material in this area. The vast majority of inland Mesolithic sites in north-west Europe occur in sandy, acidic soils where carbonised remains provide the only evidence for organic materials. In most cases, only wood charcoal and occasional burned nut shells are recovered. For this reason, direct information on the season or duration of settlement is generally not available at these sites and variations in the settlements have not been considered.

There is, however, information at the sites of the western European Mesolithic that can be used in the investigation of settlements. Data on the type and distribution of artefacts in the concentrations that define the sites and on the size of the sites in this area are available from a number of excavated sites. The present study then is focused on this inland western European Mesolithic of the North European Plain and is an attempt to define settlement systems in this poorly understood region. Both archaeological data from the sites and a predictive model involving resource utilisation will be employed in this investigation.

Settlement systems

The concept of settlement system, as defined by Winters (1969) or Streuver (1968), provides a useful perspective for viewing the operation of prehistoric cultures, particularly for hunter-gatherers. The concept refers to the functional interrelationships among different kinds of settlements within a region and their articulation with the natural environment. More specifically, the concept provides a framework in which to place the variety of sites that may appear in the record of an archaeological culture. These seemingly diverse remains may thus be understood as the 'seasonal' poses or postures (Gearing 1958) that human groups may take during the course of a yearly cycle of activity. In this sense, the concept of settlement system simply formalises a general pattern of behaviour that has been described for many ethnographically-known groups of hunter-gatherers.

Clearly, for most groups of hunter-gatherers, group size and subsistence activity are important aspects of settlement and are closely related to environmental conditions (Price 1973). Strategies for the optimal utilization of resources include a seasonal cycle of activity as a necessary adaptive response to varying resources, that is reflected in shifts in group size and activity. A more detailed examination of the relationships between these components emphasises their importance as useful handles for understanding the behaviour of hunter-gatherers. While the following paragraphs are focused on the nature of hunting-gathering adaptations in temperate forest areas, much of the discussion applies to pre-agriculture adaptations in general.

The relationship of human demography to environmental conditions for groups of hunter-gatherers has been discussed in a number of publications (Hallowell, 1949; Birdsell 1953; Yengoyan 1968; Rogers 1969). Population size is maintained within a certain range by biological and cultural controls such as miscarriage, infanticide, abstinence, taboos, etc. (cf. Hayden 1972; Janzen 1973; Divale 1972). A population, maintained within a specific size range, is also distributed over an area of space by factors related to available resources. Wilmsen (1973) has argued that population spacing, in areas of stable resources, operates so that each unit of population is evenly distributed, controlling an 'equal but limited and nearby set of resource locations'. According to this argument, members of the population are distributed over all the available area. Distribution in small groups is fostered by processes related to the distribution and behaviour of subsistence resources. Animals in a temperate forest ecosystem, for example, are generally solitary and well dispersed throughout an area, with limited home ranges. In order to exploit such resources optimally, the distribution of the human population must approximate to that of its resources. Thus, in a forested environment, hunter-gatherers are dispersed into small subsistence units over a large area. This 'primary subsistence unit' is the minimum group of individuals that cooperate in subsistence activities for the major portion of the year (Steward 1969: 290).

The size of the primary subsistence unit is determined by a variety of factors which impose maximum and minimum constraints in order to maintain this unit within a certain size range. Biological requirements dictate that the primary subsistence unit must be of sufficient size to form a reproductive unit. Culturally this is translated into the nuclear family. A single nuclear family, however, is not a long-term viable unit (Wobst 1974). Such a small unit is unstable because of unpredictable fluctuations in the numbers of producing and reproducing individuals. The unit would be unlikely to survive in the event that a primary producer were eliminated. By increasing the size of the primary subsistence unit to a group larger than an individual nuclear family, a number of advantages are gained. If one of the primary producers is incapacitated (a rather frequent occurrence) other productive members of the unit can sustain the family through mechanisms such as food-sharing and child care, fostered by obligations of kinship. Moreover, with a unit of increased size, age groups vary so that maximum information and experience are constantly available and may be transmitted to younger generations. Certain tasks may also require performance by more than one individual in order to maximise efficiency, as in the case of resources that are most effectively procured through a strategy that requires several people to hunt a certain species of animal or to gather a resource that is abundantly available for a very limited period of time.

Group size must be regulated below a certain maximum size as well. The size of the subsistence unit must be maintained at a relatively low level in order to prevent conflicts in procurement activities with other units, and so that the resources of a particular area will not be exhausted. A large group very quickly uses up the resources of a given locale. Units of smaller size make less demands on resources. Two consequences of too large a subsistence unit would be (1) the stripping of resources from an area and (2) the necessity of more frequent moves as supplies are more quickly consumed.

Mobility may be hampered during certain periods of the year and large groups thus immobilised would face rapid starvation. This, however, is not the case among most groups of hunter-gatherers (cf. Dunn 1968: 223). Indeed, an abundance of resources per capita seems to distinguish most hunter-gatherers (Lee and DeVore 1968). Malnutrition and starvation are rare occurrences. Hunters and gatherers utilise strategies that extract only the natural 'interest' of the home range, leaving the natural resource 'capital' untouched (Janzen 1973). Subsistence units are clearly maintained within a specific size range by systemic mechanisms of population control, dispersal and mobility.

A subsistence unit cannot exist alone however. It must function as part of a larger breeding population in order to secure an adequate number of mates. In a subsistence unit composed of only a few nuclear families, the probability of the occurrence of a suitable mate for an individual is quite low (Wobst 1974). The aggregation process allows for the collection of subsistence units into a larger group for the exchange of mates, information, and materials. Short-term aggregation is predicated on the presence of sufficient resources to support a large group for a certain period of time. The size of this collected group, the time of the year it collects, and the duration of the collection are primarily functions of available resources. During aggregation, changes in unit membership take place, information is exchanged regarding observations and expectations of resource availability for the coming year, and hunting areas are realigned with respect to anticipated potentials. In short, the collection provides an opportunity for the reconstitution of the subsistence unit and the reaffirmation of its ties with other such units.

Mobility characterises both unit membership and procurement activities. Fluidity of membership in the primary subsistence unit has certain advantages: (1) it allows for the readjustment of group size in response to severe changes in resource availability within the hunting area of the unit, (2) it permits the general exchange of information along with individuals (access to accurate information is critical for the successful continuation of the group), (3) it provides for strong relationships among a number of subsistence groups, reducing inter-unit conflicts, and (4) it allows for the resolution of intra-unit conflicts by fission.

Mobility with regard to subsistence activities accommodates seasonal variation in resources and provides buffers against situations of stress. The seasonal regulation of subsistence activities has been recognised for some time (cf. Thompson 1939). Scheduling of activities to correspond to those periods and areas when and where certain resources are optimally available allows subsistence units to maximise their utilisation of resources within a limited area. Areas of exploitation are delimited by the presence of adjacent subsistence units regularly distributed throughout a region. A 'seasonal cycle' also prevents the exhaustion of stable and limited resources within the unit's area. Rapid depletion of stable resources will occur unless regular movement provides for the recovery of resource areas. Yearly cycles, determined by the availability of resources ('seasonality') and regulated by the 'scheduling' of subsistence activities (Flannery 1968), are thus highly adaptive features of a hunting-gathering existence in that they (1) maximise the subsistence consumption of the group, (2) promote the maintenance of the ecosystem by allowing short-term seasonal service areas to rebound, (3) minimise the size of the area needed for support, and (4) eliminate sources of conflict.

In summary, a tentative model can be suggested for the operation of settlement systems of prehistoric hunter-gatherers in temperate forest ecosystems with stable and limited resources. The density and dispersal of population is closely linked to food resources and maintained within a certain range. The primary subsistence group is the basic unit of population and the size of this unit is maintained by cultural and biological mechanisms that operate primarily in response to environmental cues. Organisation of subsistence activities is based upon the availability of resources and regulated by decisions taken to avoid situations of stress and conflict. Mobility and aggregation are two mechanisms which interrelate the components of the adaptive system for the maximisation of the exchange of information and materials and for minimising conflicts. The normal pattern seems to be one in which subsistence units of small size move regularly in a seasonal cycle that most effectively organises food quest activities and maintains the viability of the population.

Two major classes of sites that characterise the settlement systems of many groups of hunter-gatherers may be distinguished by the types of activity taking place at a site (Binford and Binford 1969). Extractive activities involve the acquisition of specific foods, fuels, or materials from the environment. Maintenance activities include those fundamental, general-purpose, routine activities of daily life: food processing and preparation, manufacture and repair of tools, construction for shelter and protection. Among hunter-gatherers, maintenance activities frequently take place at *base camps* – the settlement of a co-resident unit of population involved in such general-purpose activities. *Extraction camps* are more special-purpose localities such as hunting camps, kill sites, quarries, gathering stations, etc. that reflect the acquisition of specific environmental resources. Extraction camps may correspond to the activities of only a segment of the co-resident unit of population (a 'task group') and are generally ancillary to base camps. Other general classes of sites that may appear are transient camps – temporary, perhaps overnight, settlements intermediate in location to base camps or base camps and extraction camps – and symbolic sites – special locales for ritual or ceremonial activities, not directly articulated to the physical environment.

Base camps are expected to be the most visible settlements

represented in the archaeological record and variations in the character of base camps should reflect the differential utilisation of various resources. Significant characteristics of base camp settlements from the perspective of settlement systems would be the size of the co-resident human group, the season and duration of settlement, and the nature of the subsistence activities undertaken. Differences in these characteristics should help to define the relevant postures of a human group during the course of a year.

Frame of reference

The frame of reference for the investigation of these settlement characteristics is the Mesolithic of the Netherlands during the Boreal period, from roughly 7,000 to 5,500 bc. The Boreal period in the Netherlands represents a time of continental climate with summer temperatures some 2-4° centigrade higher than today (Waterbolk 1965-66). The vegetation of this region was dominated by rather open pine forests with interspersed hazel and a few remnant birch. During the course of the Boreal period, oak, elm, and lime appeared in small numbers in the higher areas, with more alder and ash in the lower, wetter zones. Certainly a wide variety of shrubs and herbs would have been present in the undergrowth of the forest and in clearings. The presence of boulder-clay at varying depths in the subsoil and concomitant differences in the ground water level would have produced a mosaic of vegetation types over the region. As a result of the general postglacial rise in sea level and the higher water table, the landscape may well have been somewhat marshy with numerous streams and shallow lakes in the low-lying areas (Waterbolk 1965/66).

The many small lakes and brook valleys should have been rich in fish and waterfowl. Moreover, the higher, half-open pine woods and the lower, marshy areas would have provided excellent conditions for populations of aurochs, elk, red deer, roe deer, and wild boar. Numerous small mammals are also known to have been present at this time including beaver, pine marten, otter, badger, wild cat, wolf, squirrel, and hare. From the perspective of a hunter-gatherer this must have represented an extremely favourable environment.

For the analysis of settlement characteristics, then, Mesolithic sites dating from the pre-Atlantic period in the Netherlands are used. This frame includes sites from the Early to the Late Mesolithic as defined by Newell (1973), but does not include the De Leien-Wartena complex, an Atlantic period Mesolithic manifestation in the Netherlands.[2] It must be reiterated that the perspective employed here is oriented towards the definition of a static or equilibrium model of human settlement systems in the Mesolithic. Optimally, of course, we should tightly control the chronological and chorological variation in the settlements under analysis and attempt to deal only with a short span of time in a restricted area. This is not possible at the present time, however, because of the nature of archaeological data in general and the nature of the specific data used in this study. Settlements covering a period of roughly 1,500 years or more and distributed throughout the Netherlands are considered to represent aspects of the same general pattern of behaviour; that is, prior to the Atlantic period, settlement systems in the Mesolithic of the Netherlands are assumed to have remained relatively stable. The homogeneous nature of the Dutch landscape and the absence of any conspicuous changes in archaeological remains during this period would seem to justify such a general assumption. Nevertheless, one of the goals of a long-term investigation of settlement systems in the Mesolithic of north-west Europe must be the refinement of the time and space parameters of the materials under investigation.

The archaeological data

Although the general absence of organic remains at inland Mesolithic sites on the North European Plain has generally discouraged the investigation of settlement systems, there are several types of data that are particularly useful and abundant in the area. Over the last thirty years, the Biologisch-Archaeologisch Instituut of the University of Groningen has undertaken or sponsored the excavation of many Mesolithic occupations.[3] In addition, the Museum of Anthropology of the University of Michigan, in collaboration with Biologisch-Archaeologisch Instituut, completed the excavation of six more Mesolithic sites in the northern Netherlands in 1972 (Price, Whallon, and Chappell 1974).[4] A total of more than twenty-five excavated sites are now available for study.

These sites are generally characterised by open-air concentrations of lithic artefacts and cultural features. Because of the procedures employed in the excavation of these sites, ground plans (distribution maps) are available for a majority of the sites that provide exact provenience data on the distribution of various types of artefacts, features, and the approximate size of the settlements. Most of these sites appear to represent brief, single occupations so that the general confusion often encountered with multiple occupation surfaces is not a significant problem in this area. Reliable information on several settlement attributes is thus available from relatively complete single-occupation sites and this information is readily amenable to the analysis of settlement types.

Twenty-five sites were considered in the original analysis and the following attributes were recorded for each site where possible:

    (1) *Artefact density*. This value was defined as the mean number of artefacts per square metre, not including the zero-count

squares. This value may be expected to vary in part as a function of the recovery accuracy at a particular excavation.

(2) *Site size*. Settlement area was measured using a method which eliminated differences due to the accuracy of artefact recovery in the original excavations. The number of metre squares with more than the mean artefact density was multiplied by 1.8 to obtain a value reflecting 90 percent of the area covered by the concentration of artefacts. This measure was corrected for sites which were only partially excavated by interpolating the number of missing squares. (The reason for using the 90 percent area will become clear in the following discussion. 100 percent of the area could have been estimated by multiplying the number of metre squares with more than the average density of artefacts by 2.0.)

(3) *Number of features*. In most cases, the features at a site were indicated on a ground plan and could simply be counted. A few ground plans, however, showed no features and for these sites, this attribute must be considered as unknown.

(4) *Counts for the artefact type-groups*. In order to have functionally discrete categories for the analysis of the sites and to have samples of adequate size for comparison, the traditional types of retouched artefacts from these sites were grouped into ten major categories: points, backed blades, scrapers, borers, burins, knives, retouched flakes, retouched blades, notched pieces, and cores.

(5) *Total amount of waste material*. This value provides a reasonably good measure of the size of the artefact assemblage at a site; it will, however, vary with the accuracy of excavation techniques.

(6) *Two measures of the spatial patterning of artefacts*. Nearest neighbour distances (Clark and Evans 1954; Whallon 1974; Price 1978) and a measure of artefact clustering between type-groups, the index of segregation (Pielou 1961; Price 1978), were computed. Nearest neighbour distance is a simple measure of the average distance between all members of a single type-group on an occupation floor. Nearest neighbour distances for large, easily identified artefacts such as cores or scrapers should be comparable between sites since they are difficult to miss during excavation and readily recognised. In these cases, nearest neighbour distance may provide a better measure of artefact density for certain categories of artefacts. The index of segregation is a measure of association based on distances between members of different type-groups. These two measures, nearest neighbour distance and the index of segregation, were calculated only for the four most common type-groups: points, backed blades, scrapers, and cores. The remaining type-groups were absent or rare at some sites and measures of spatial patterning could not be calculated.

Measures of spatial patterning of artefacts were originally considered in an attempt to define spatially associated clusters of artefacts or tool kits on the ground plans of the individual Mesolithic sites (Price 1975, 1976). However, no consistent patterns of artefact association could be found among the sites considered in the analysis; 'tool kits' *per se* do not regularly appear in these Mesolithic assemblages. Measures of spatial patterning were useful however for the definition of settlement types. In addition to providing (1) a better measure of density for some categories of artefacts, and (2) more measures for comparison between sites, these statistics aided in removing from further consideration a few of the sites where problems of multiple occupation or recording errors made the site unsuitable for analysis.

Seventeen sites were used in the final classification of Mesolithic sites.[5] These sites were considered to be the most reliable, well-excavated, single-occupation settlements. Values for several of the site attributes for these seventeen sites are presented in Table 1.

Two points should be considered prior to the description of the site types in the Mesolithic of the Netherlands. First, the classification is based heavily on the similarities and differences among the Havelte sites. These sites are clearly the most reliable and useful for the measurement of the site attributes. Secondly, the classification of sites is necessarily polythetic; that is, members of the same type may share various characteristics but they are not required to share a specific common trait. This form of classification is more reasonable for data such as the attributes of archaeological sites where the vagaries of excavation technique and recording may produce a wide range of values for any given attribute.

Although there are a number of potential sources of error, analysis of the site attributes did reveal five relatively discrete clusters or types of sites:

Small sites – circular or oval concentrations of 2-5 metres in diameter with less than 1,000 total artefacts and generally less than 25 retouched tools. Two types were distinguished:

1. Small sites with a predominance of a particular type-group, e.g., scrapers or cores or points. This type was characterised by small, dense, circular concentrations of artefacts.
2. Small sites with low counts for the major type-groups of points, backed blades, scrapers, and cores; minor type-groups of borers, knives, retouched flakes, retouched blades, and notched pieces are generally rare or absent.

Medium sites – characterised by elongated oval concentrations of artefacts, generally 5-10 metres in length and 4-8 metres in width. Ninety percent size varies from 30 to 100m² with an average of

Table 1. Classification of Mesolithic Settlements in the Netherlands

	Artefact Density/ m²	90% Size Estimate (m²)	Number of Features	Points	Number of: Backed Blades	Scrapers	Cores	Total Waste	Estimated Site Population
SMALL SITES									
Extraction Camps									
18 Moerkuilen I	–	–	1	10	2	0	20	–	–
19 Moerkuilen II	–	–	1	10	0	4	21	–	–
20 Nijnsel 1–5	8.5	27.0	1	3	0	22	5	256	–
24 Waubach	–	–	1	1	0	5	44	–	–
Base Camps									
10 Havelte 1:III	17.5	16.2	3	2	5	4	9	703	–
15 Hazeputten II	16.6	10.8	1	2	5	6	14	245	–
23 Siegerswoude	16.5	50.4	9	3	9	6	7	1186	9
MEDIUM BASE CAMPS									
Short-Term									
1 Acht	34.0	49.5	–	16	13	36	5	2247	9
8 Havelte 1:I	14.7	72.0	2	13	18	10	31	1956	11
9 Havelte 1:II	13.7	81.0	2	2	9	12	38	1691	12
13 Havelte 3	12.4	59.4	6	8	16	10	33	1820	10
14 Hazeputten I	22.2	31.5	2	7	13	14	3	647	–
21 Nijnsel II	16.7	99.0	3	27	16	19	51	1944	14
Long-Term									
4 Duurswoude III	17.5	100.8	23	36	62	12	106	3430	14
11 Havelte 2:I	43.0	82.8	4	19	44	71	151	9618	12
12 Havelte 2:II	28.7	88.2	0	43	33	26	112	6218	13
LARGE AGGREGATION CAMP									
22 Rotsterhaule	26.9	288.4	9	47	53	19	104	7887	28

approximately 75m². The medium sites are generally similar in size and shape and in the proportion of artefact types represented. All of the type-groups are generally present. Two types of medium sites are distinguished on the basis of the number and density of artefacts (cf. Table 2):

3. Medium sites with 1,500-2,500 artefacts.
4. Medium sites with 2,500-10,000 artefacts, i.e., a much higher density of material. Scrapers are less common than expected at this type of site.

Large sites

5. A single large site (Rotsterhaule) covering an area of almost 300m² was also distinguished and contained several observable concentrations within the larger area.

Examples of the site types are shown in Figure 1. In this illustration all of the sites are shown at the same scale and with the same contours of artefact density. The artefact density contours indicate 10, 20, 40, 80, 160, and 320 artefacts per square metre. The numbers adjacent to each ground plan correspond to the site type numbers given above. All of the ground plans appear to represent single occupations with the exception of Waubach. At this site there are three distinct, small concentrations, each representing a special-purpose (Type 1) camp.

In the classification of sites no significant differences are observed that can be related to geographical factors. Sites from throughout the Netherlands occur in all three major categories of small, medium and large. Moreover, there are no distinctions made in the classification between sites belonging to different chronological periods of the Mesolithic. The fact that this classification cross-cuts both regional and chronological variations among the sites suggests that indeed the same general settlement systems were in operation and remained relatively stable throughout the Late Mesolithic and prior to the Atlantic period.

In the earlier discussion of settlement systems, certain characteristics were emphasised. Site population, subsistence activities, and the season and duration of occupation were suggested to be critical aspects of settlements from this perspective. Two of these characteristics, site population and duration of occupation, may be investigated in the light of the recorded site attributes of size and artefact density. However because of the lamented absence of organic remains at these sites, we have no direct information to use in the investigation of season of occupation or subsistence activities. Discussion of these latter two characteristics will be deferred until the next section of this paper.

Relatively few attempts have been made to estimate the number of

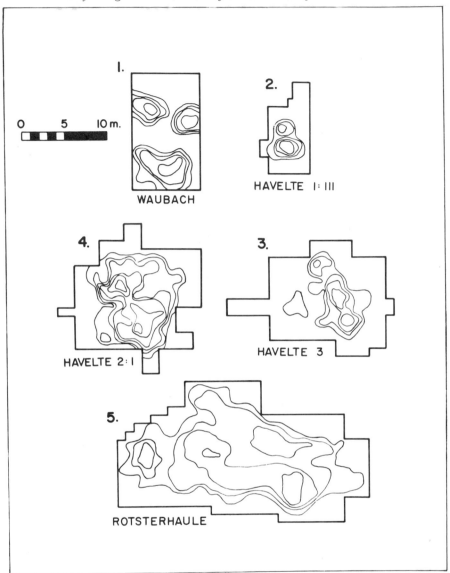

Figure 1. Settlement types in the Mesolithic of the Netherlands. The artefact concentrations are represented by contours of the artefact density, using contour intervals of 10, 20, 40, 80, 160 and 320 artefacts per square metre. All of the concentrations are drawn to the same scale. The numbers adjacent to each concentration correspond to the five site types discussed in the text.

individuals occupying a site. Methods have been suggested for predicting the number of inhabitants of sedentary villages using the area of covered floor space (cf. Naroll 1962), or using the quantity of food remains left at a site for hunter-gatherers (cf. Clark 1972). None of these methods are practical for occupations of the Dutch Mesolithic

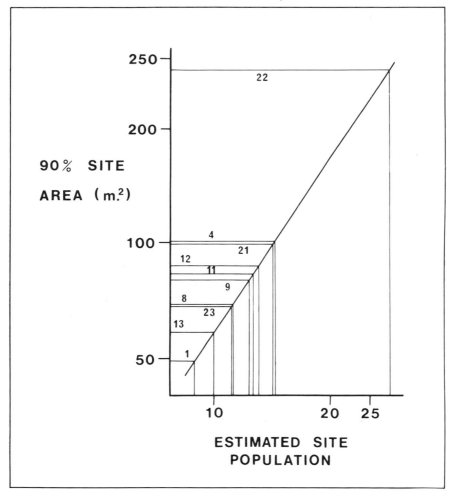

Figure 2. A logarithmic curve for predicting site population from site size (modified from Wiessner 1974). The site numbers on the graph correspond to the site numbers in Table 1.

however, because of the absence of both structures and organic remains.

One recent attempt has been made to estimate site population for hunter-gatherers on the basis of the area of the living floor. Using data from ground plans of contemporary Bushman encampments, Wiessner (1974) suggests a formula for predicting group size using approximately 90 percent of the living area as defined by the distribution of discarded materials. Although the formulation has not been adequately tested for groups other than the Bushman, it can be used to make a preliminary estimate for co-resident group size at the Mesolithic settlements in the Netherlands. The logarithmic curve predicted by Wiessner's formula is given in Figure 2. The 90 percent

E

areas of the Mesolithic settlements, given in Table 1, are used to predict site population with this curve. The formula is applicable to areas of 50-250 square metres in area and predicts a site population ranging from 10 to 25 individuals. This formula generally cannot be used for the group of small sites since they are less than 50 square metres in area, but estimates for a site population of 10-15 individuals for the medium sites appear reasonable. The single large site is predicted to have a population of greater than 25 individuals, or roughly twice as many people as the medium sites.

Estimates of the length of occupation for a few Mesolithic sites have been derived from the specific seasonality of floral and faunal remains (Clark 1954; Andersen 1975) but again this is not possible for inland Mesolithic sites because of the absence of organic materials. There is information, however, from the excavated Mesolithic sites in the Netherlands that can be used to examine the relative differences between sites in terms of the length of occupation. Differences in artefact density should be a good indicator of the relative duration of occupation, particularly in the case of the medium sites. The single assumption is made that the longer a site is occupied, the more artefacts will be deposited. The Havelte sites again provide the major focus for this comparison since these six sites were excavated in exactly the same manner and excavation technique is not expected to contribute to the variation in artefact density. Comparison of the Havelte sites for both types of medium sites suggests that the higher density medium sites are occupied two to three times longer than the medium sites with fewer artefacts. Artefact density at several of the small sites is comparable to the short-term medium sites. For the large site, density is roughly comparable to the density of artefacts at the long-term medium sites but direct comparison of the length of occupation is not feasible since there is only one example of the large site. Thus, the major difference seen in the comparison of artefact density is between the two types of medium sites which appear to reflect short-term and long-term occupations respectively. More specific periods of occupation cannot be attached to these sites until much more is known about discard rates for various categories of artefacts.

In the light of these estimates for group size and duration of occupation, a preliminary interpretation of the five site types in a general inland Mesolithic settlement system can be suggested:

Type 1. *Small extraction camps* – specific-activity locations, exhibiting only a limited range of artefacts and occupied for a brief span of time, probably by a task group.

Type 2. *Small base camps* – general purpose maintenance camps with a low number of several artefact types, probably occupied by a nuclear family.

Type 3. *Medium, short-term base camps* – settlements of the primary subsistence unit (cf. Steward 1968), a group of two to four nuclear families co-operating in subsistence activities for the major portion of the year. These sites contain a full range of artefact types and were occupied for a short term, roughly one-half the period of occupation for the long-term medium base camps.

Type 4. *Medium, long-term base camps* – similar settlements of the primary subsistence unit, occupied for a longer period of time.

Type 5. *Large aggregation camps* – aggregation settlements of several primary subsistence units, a total of perhaps 30 individuals. This type of site is represented by only one example in the present analysis.

Thus, four basic demographic arrangements for the base camps, ranging from a single nuclear family to an aggregation of perhaps as many as ten families, are suggested in an annual cycle for inland Mesolithic groups in the Netherlands. Extraction camps should represent task locations ancillary to these base camps. There is, however, no direct information that can be used to articulate these specific demographic arrangements with a particular season of the year or with certain kinds of subsistence activities. Several other factors contribute as well to the more general problem of interpreting site activities. It is virtually impossible, for example, to define meaningful tool kits or areas of specific activity on the ground plans of these Mesolithic sites. Moreover, many of the artefacts found at the sites appear to be 'secondary' tools – that is, tools to make other tools. Many of these implements appear to have been used as wood or bone working tools (Price, Whallon, and Chappell 1974: 41) and it is impossible to determine at present if these tools were used to fashion a bow, to make a trap, to shape a digging stick, or to construct a fishing device, among numerous possibilities. With the possible exception of points, then, none of the various artefact types are diagnostic of specific subsistence activities and even projectile points are indicative only of 'hunting' activities and may have been used to procure a wide variety of species. In addition, there is very little differentiation among the sites in terms of the types and proportions of stone tools present. The small sites show some differences but the proportions of the various type-groups present at the medium and large sites are almost identical.

Some general activities can be suggested for certain of the 'small' sites. Locations such as Waubach, with a predominance of cores in the artefact assemblage, suggest 'chipping stations', that is, sites where cores are being worked for the manufacture of stone tools. The finished tools do not appear on the site and are assumed to have been transported elsewhere. This type of site has also been noted in surface collections from the province of Drenthe in the northern Netherlands

Table 2. Average counts and percentages of major implement types in three Mesolithic Site Types in the Netherlands.

TYPE-GROUP	MEDIUM SHORT-TERM SITES		MEDIUM LONG-TERM SITES		LARGE SITE	
	Counts	Percentages	Counts	Percentages	Counts	Percentages
Points	11.6	11.9	38.5	11.4	47	18.8
Backed blades	15.4	15.7	48.3	14.3	53	21.2
Scrapers	16.4	16.8	38.5	11.4	19	7.6
Cores	29.4	30.1	123.0	36.6	104	41.6
Burins	1.9	2.0	4.5	1.3	12	4.8
Borers	1.9	2.0	8.0	2.4	2	0.1
Knives	5.0	5.0	16.0	4.8	0	0
Retouched pieces	13.7	14.0	48.7	14.5	11	4.4
Notched pieces	2.5	2.6	11.0	3.3	2	0.1
Total	97.8	100.1	336.5	100.0	250	98.6

(Price 1975) where a number of collections were represented only by a few cores and a quantity of debitage. Small sites with a high proportion of points and/or scrapers may be the remains of hunting stations or 'butchering sites' where one or several individuals, probably male, made or repaired equipment for the hunt, perhaps camping for several days. These sites may also be simply the remains of a location where an animal was killed and butchered – indicated by the presence of the projectile points and scrapers. Other small sites, with relatively equal proportions of the various type-groups, may represent the remains of a base camp occupied by a single nuclear family, as suggested earlier.

The medium and large sites are the most common type of settlement among the excavated Mesolithic sites and contain all or most of the defined artefact type-groups. These artefacts are suggested to represent the general group of tools associated with maintenance activities. Although there is some variation in the proportions of the type-groups between individual sites, comparison of the average percentages of the type-groups for the two medium sites and the large site is useful. These values are given in Table 2 and are based on eight medium short-term sites, four medium long-term sites, and the single large site.[6]

The majority of the values are remarkably similar. The percentages of points, backed blades, knives, and retouched pieces are almost identical. The differences between burins, borers and notched pieces may be significant but the samples are so small that these categories must be regarded as similar for the present time. Scrapers and cores do show divergent values between the two types of medium sites. In the assemblages of artefacts from the medium short-term occupations, scrapers average 16.8 percent of the tools, while at the medium long-term sites these tools average 11.4 percent. Cores are relatively more abundant at the long-term sites, 36.6 percent compared to 30.1 percent at the short-term sites. It appears that scrapers are used more commonly at the short-term sites and that cores are relatively more abundant at the long-term sites. This difference suggests a basic contrast between the two types of sites in terms of activities: the manufacture of stone tools is emphasised at the long-term medium sites while the manufacture of wood/bone/antler tools is of greater importance at the short-term medium sites. The significance of this contrast in terms of season or subsistence activities is not clear. It should be noted as well that very small differences in the proportions of other type-groups may reflect important variations in subsistence activities but we are not yet in a position to interpret these slight differences.

Some general differences between the large site and the medium sites are also to be noted in Table 2 but these must be viewed with caution since there is only one example of the large site. Microlithic tools are much more common at the large site – a total of 40 percent for the points and backed blades compared to 26.6 percent and 25.7 percent for the two categories of medium sites. Scrapers are much less common and the proportion of cores is slightly higher at the large site. The proportions of the remaining type-groups are low with the exception of burins which represent 4.8 percent of the type-group assemblage at the large site of Rotsterhaule. Again, however, the significance of these differences (if they are valid in the light of a single example) cannot be assessed. Resolution of this impasse of attempting to articulate settlement types with subsistence activity and seasonality requires another approach to these questions.

Predicting resource utilisation

Jochim (1976) has recently shown that certain characteristics of subsistence resources can be used to predict resource utilisation patterns and significant economic seasons for hunter-gatherers, independent of direct archaeological data. Jochim's model deals specifically with the subsistence resource categories available to the prehistoric inhabitants of an area. Estimates of resource weight, mobility, density, aggregation size, and non-food yields may be used to predict the proportional monthly utilisation of various resources and thereby suggest significant seasonal changes in the types of resources being procured. The model has been employed successfully for both prehistoric and ethnographically-known groups.

Two primary goals are assumed to dictate the relative utilisation of the various categories of available resources: (1) the provision of sustenance, a basic biological requirement, along with non-food products such as hide, antler, and bone for manufacturing needs; and (2) the minimisation of energy expenditure, a common goal for almost any human society and well documented for hunter-gatherers. Basic patterns of resource utilisation should be determined by how well the various resource categories serve to meet these goals. Secondary goals such as the maximisation of the procurement of good-tasting foods, of variety in the diet, of prestige resources, or the maintenance of the differentiation of sex roles in procurement activities are not directly considered in the formulation. Clearly these secondary goals may have a significant bearing on subsistence patterns when an abundance of resources permits greater choice and flexibility in procurement, but the basic pattern of resource utilisation should be determined by the two primary goals.

The performance of a resource category in meeting the two primary goals is measured by indices composed of various attributes of each resource category. Fulfilment of goal one, secure income of food and non-food items, is measured by resource weight multiplied by non-food yields, multiplied by density, divided by mobility. Thus, a resource category is of greater significance in terms of secure income the greater its weight and non-food yields, the higher its density, and the lower its mobility. Goal two, minimum expenditure of effort, is measured by weight multiplied by non-food yields multiplied by aggregation size divided by mobility; that is, a resource requires less expenditure of energy the greater its weight and non-food yields, the larger its aggregation size, and the less its mobility.

The percentage of utilisation of each resource in the yearly diet is determined by the proportional average score for each resource category in terms of fulfilling these two primary goals. This stage in the model assumes that the two goals are of equal importance. In other words, scores for the indices of the performance of each resource category in accomplishing each goal may be calculated, the average of the two scores determined, and the proportion of that average score to the sum of the average scores for all resource categories will indicate the relative utilisation of a particular resource category during the year. This figure for the proportional utilisation of a resource category should reflect the relative contribution of the category to the diet in terms of the weight consumed.

Monthly changes in the resource attributes of weight, non-food yields, aggregation size, and mobility permit the same proportional scores to be calculated for each of the twelve months of the year. Similar months may then be grouped to reflect potential seasons of economic importance.

Application of this model to the inland Mesolithic of the Netherlands may help to illustrate its operation. Specifically for the Boreal period I have employed the following resource categories: aurochs, elk, red deer, roe deer, wild boar, small game, fish, fowl, and plants. Materials from archaeological sites in areas adjacent to the Netherlands clearly indicate the presence and utilisation of these categories by prehistoric groups: for example, in Great Britain (Clark 1954; Mellars 1976), in Belgium (Bouchud 1974), north Germany (Bokelmann 1971), and Denmark (Brinch Petersen 1973). Recent evidence from the bed of the North Sea also confirms the availability of many of these resources (Louwe Kooijmans 1970-71). These resources are thus assumed to have been readily accessible to the inland inhabitants of the Netherlands during the Boreal period.

The values for the attributes used in the model are given for these resource categories in Table 3. Clearly these values are only rough approximations and may vary widely. However, since we are interested primarily in summary percentage figures, it is not the precise values that will affect the outcome of the model but rather the relative differences in the attributes between the resource categories. For the large game categories of elk (*Alces alces*), red deer (*Cervus elephas*), roe deer (*Capreolus capreolus*), and wild boar (*Sus scrofa*), the average values for the attributes of weight, aggregation size, and density have been taken from studies of modern populations[7] with some modifications appropriate for the Boreal period. For example,

Table 3. Estimated values for resource attributes and the percentage contribution to the yearly diet for different resource categories in the Dutch Mesolithic.

Resource	Weight (kg.)	Relative non-food yields	Aggreg-ation size	Density per km^2	Relative mobility	Percentage of yearly diet
Aurochs	600	1.05	6.0	.56	1.4	15.8
European elk	380	1.10	2.0	.70	1.15	5.5
Red deer	220	1.10	13.0	5.0	1.5	16.6
Roe deer	34	1.05	2.5	8.0	1.2	2.1
Wild boar	135	1.05	13.5	8.0	1.4	15.7
Small game	3.6	1.05	2.0	103.0	.2	14.2
Fish	1.0	1.00	2.0	70.0	.05	10.0
Fowl	—	—	—	—	—	5.0
Plants	—	—	—	—	—	15.0

most of the large game categories were somewhat larger in size in the Boreal period than their modern descendants (Degerbøl 1964) and the attribute of weight has been adjusted accordingly. In another case, the density for aurochs (*Bos primigenius*), an extinct species, was unknown. In this instance I have used an archaeological occurrence of aurochs to estimate its density. I have assumed that aurochs was hunted opportunistically along with red deer at the site of Star Carr. The density of aurochs can then be adjusted relative to that of red deer. At Star Carr there is one aurochs for every nine red deer (Clark 1972: 27); thus if red deer have an estimated density of five animals per square kilometre, aurochs are assumed to occur in the same relative proportion and thus at a density of .56 animals per square kilometre.

Aggregation size is a measure of the average number of animals that may be found together in a group; for example, red deer and wild boar are generally found in small herds while roe deer and elk are more solitary and dispersed. These differences are indicated in the values for the attribute of aggregation size.

Relative non-food yields are rough estimates of the useful inedible portion of the various resources based on remains found at various Mesolithic sites. Red deer and elk, for example, provide antler, hide, and bone materials and are weighted higher than the other categories. Aurochs, roe deer, and wild boar provide bone and/or dentition that are known to have been used in Mesolithic contexts and are rated slightly below red deer and elk for relative non-food yields.

Relative mobility is a rating of the movement of a resource category and thus of the relative ease of capture. For example, red deer are reported to make seasonal migrations and thus receive a high rating for relative mobility. Roe deer are relatively stationary and receive a low rating.

For the remaining resources, a number of individual species have been grouped into single categories. A variety of small mammals make up the category of small game: badger (*Meles meles*), beaver (*Castor fiber*), fox (*Vulpes vulpes*), hare (*Lepus europaeus*), hedgehog (*Erinaceus europaeus*), pine marten (*Martes martes*), otter (*Lutra lutra*), polecat (*Mustela putoris*), squirrel (*Sciurus vulgaris*), wolf (*Canis lupus*), and wild cat (*Felis silvestris*), among others. Values for the attributes for the category of small game (Table 3) represent an average for all these species.

A variety of species of fish are known to havé been taken by Boreal Mesolithic groups (Clark 1948, 1975; Brinch Petersen 1973): pike (*Esox lucius*), tench (*Tinca tinca*), roach (*Rutilus rutilus*), bream (*Abramis brama*), wels (*Siluris glanis*), eel (*Anguilla anguilla*), and perch (*Perca fluviatilis*). Certainly there was a well developed technology for fishing in the Mesolithic (Clark 1975: 142-4, 223-4) including the use of nets, hooks and weirs. Again, all species are grouped into a single category for fish and the resource attribute ratings for this category represent an average value (Table 3). The value for density is estimated from similar environments in North America (Rostlund 1952).

For the two remaining categories, fowl and plants, estimates of the various attributes are more difficult. Although a wide range of avifauna are known from Mesolithic contexts (including some thirty species in Denmark alone: Brinch Petersen 1973), the availability of fowl in specific areas of north-west Europe is unknown and estimates of density are not possible. For this reason fowl are not used in the calculation of the proportional yearly use of resources but are simply assumed to represent five percent of the total yearly diet. Similarly, plants may have played an important role in Mesolithic subsistence (cf. Mellars 1976) but there is no information at present on their relative importance in the diet. I have simply used a value of 15 percent for plants in the total yearly diet. Clearly either category of plants or fowl could contribute much more heavily to the diet and more information is needed on this question.

The performance of the remaining resource categories (not including fowl and plants) in providing secure income and minimising the expenditure of energy can be calculated using the measures described above. The mean of the two indices gives the average score for a particular resource category. The proportional utilisation of each category is determined by dividing its average score by the sum of the average scores for all resources, including 5 percent for fowl and 15 percent for plants. These values are given for each resource category in Table 3.

Interestingly, several categories make approximately the same contribution to the yearly diet. Aurochs, red deer, wild boar, and small game each provide about 15 percent of the yearly diet; fish contribute 10 percent and elk and roe deer provide 5 percent or less. For several reasons it is difficult to verify these figures from archaeological data. There are, of course, no known year-round settlements for the Boreal

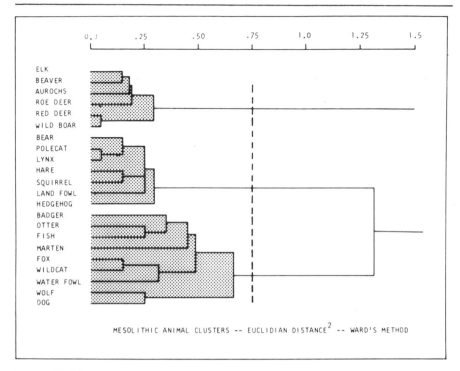

Figure 3. Cluster analysis of 22 animal species recorded from Mesolithic sites in
north-west Europe. The analysis is based on material from 20 sites, for which the
names and bibliographic references are given in note 8 at the end of the text. The
dashed line indicates the level at which the three shaded clusters were
distinguished.

Mesolithic in north-west Europe. Moreover, there are only a few sites
where faunal remains are adequately reported and from these the
analyses usually provide only a count of identifiable bones rather than
the minimum number of individuals or caloric values for the various
species that have been utilised.

The limited data that do exist generally confirm the pattern
predicted by the model. A cluster analysis of some twenty Mesolithic
sites[8] from north-west Europe with identified faunal remains provides
an indication of the species which are commonly found together. The
initial data for this analysis are simply the presence or absence of the
various species at the sites. Squared Euclidian distance was used as a
measure of similarity between the species and Ward's error sum of
squares method was the linkage procedure used in the cluster
analysis. The analysis was performed using the suite of computer
programs 'CLUSTAN IA' (Wishart 1970) on the computer system of
the Academic Computer Centre at the University of Wisconsin-
Madison. The results of this analysis are presented in the form of a
dendrogram in Figure 3. Three major clusters are indicated below a
level of similarity of .75 as shown by the dashed line in Figure 3. These

three clusters are shaded in the dendrogram. The upper cluster of elk, beaver, aurochs, roe deer, red deer, and wild boar represents the species of animals found most commonly at the twenty sites. These six species would appear to be major staples in the diet and to be hunted concurrently from most Mesolithic settlements. The second major cluster, composed of bear, polecat, lynx, hare, squirrel, terrestrial fowl, and hedgehog, represents a group of animals that appear only rarely in Mesolithic sites. These species were most likely not systematically exploited. The third major cluster of animals indicates those small game species that occur commonly on Mesolithic sites. Of these, fox and wildcat occur together most frequently and are probably the result of trapping activities. Otter and fish are the second most common pairing of species and must represent the remains of procurement activities in lakes and streams. Waterfowl, badger, and marten join these two pairs at a lower level of similarity and again would appear to be the results of specialised trapping or hunting activity. Finally, wolf and dog occur commonly together and are linked to the third cluster at a relatively low level of similarity. In sum, the diversity of the subsistence base in the Mesolithic is clearly indicated by the remains at the sites used in this analysis and the results of the analysis suggest that several species were indeed hunted concurrently at individual settlements. This diversity is also indicated in the predictions of the model where a number of species contribute relatively equal amounts to the yearly diet.

Of even greater interest in the predictive model are the specific monthly contributions of the resource categories that result in the prediction of potential economic seasons for the Boreal Mesolithic in the Netherlands. In the calculation of the proportional monthly utilisation of each category, the resource attributes (with the exception of density) are varied according to reported changes in biological and behavioural characteristics during the course of a year. As an example, the monthly variations in the critical attributes of red deer are given in Table 4. Non-food yields of red deer are greater in the months when the deer carry antler. Food yields, indicated by animal weight, are greatest for red deer just before the rut. Aggregation size also increases during the rut and mobility is limited. Similar adjustments can be made for the remaining species of large game.

Plants are assumed to be available primarily during the warmer months of the year with somewhat greater utilisation of bulbs and roots in the spring and of nuts and berries in the fall. Fish are most readily available in the spring during spawning and should be still numerous in the summer months. Fowl are weighted slightly higher in the spring and fall when migratory waterfowl may have been more numerous in the area. Finally, in the projection of the monthly contributions of the resource categories, small game are considered to have been used to make up the deficiencies in those months when total

Table 4. Monthly variation in resource attributes for red deer.

	J	F	M	A	M	J	J	A	S	O	N	D
Weight	205	197	209	220	207	203	225	230	245	220	225	222
Aggregation	21.7	21.7	21.5	11.4	4.9	5.7	12.3	14.1	10.0	10.0	11.6	11.4
Non-food yield	1.15	1.15	1.15	1.05	1.05	1.05	1.05	1.05	1.15	1.15	1.15	1.15
Mobility	1	1	1	1.5	1.7	2	2	2	1.3	1.3	1.7	1.7
Density	5	5	5	5	5	5	5	5	5	5	5	5

Table 5. Hypothetical utilisation of different economic resources throughout the annual cycle in the Dutch Mesolithic (percentages).

	J	F	M	A	M	J	J	A	S	O	N	D
Aurochs	13.2	13.2	12.2	13.9	14.3	13.9	14.2	18.2	19.3	16.9	19.4	14.9
European elk	6.6	5.8	5.5	5.0	5.2	4.6	4.8	4.6	6.1	6.0	4.8	4.7
Red deer	29.2	28.0	29.6	13.7	8.5	7.2	10.7	11.6	14.6	13.5	13.7	14.9
Roe deer	3.1	2.9	3.2	2.3	1.5	1.3	1.5	1.7	1.6	1.6	1.8	2.3
Wild boar	23.2	19.3	19.8	7.4	7.4	10.4	11.4	12.2	10.6	12.0	26.3	25.5
Fish	1.6	2.1	3.3	9.7	30.2	17.0	15.8	15.8	13.8	3.2	2.7	2.4
Fowl	1.8	3.6	5.5	7.2	7.2	3.6	3.6	3.6	4.4	6.1	7.2	3.6
Plants	0	0	0	12.1	24.2	24.2	24.2	12.1	29.6	40.7	0	0
Small game	21.2	25.1	21.1	16.5	1.3	17.5	13.7	20.0	0	0	24.1	31.5

resource utilisation does not reach one-twelfth of the yearly diet. In this sense, small game are treated as a contingency resource, available when needed.

The proportional monthly contribution of each category, as determined by its performance in fulfilling the two primary goals, is

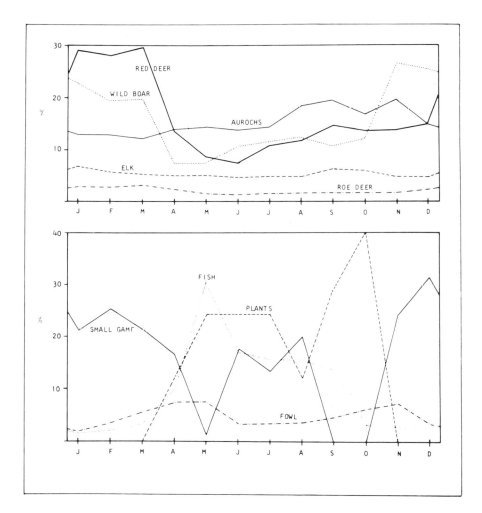

Figure 4. Percentage monthly utilisation of different resource categories in the Boreal Mesolithic of the Netherlands. The upper graph shows large game species; the lower graph portrays the remaining categories.

given in Table 5. These values, graphed in Figure 4, show several clear peaks that can be used to differentiate seasonal changes in the patterns of resource use. Five major seasons can be defined by inspection of the graphs:

1. Winter (January, February, March): dominated by the utilisation of red deer, small game, and wild boar which together provide 72 percent of the diet.
2. Spring transition (April, May): characterised by the use of fish, plants, aurochs, and red deer.
3. Summer (June, July, August): plants, small game, fish, and aurochs.
4. Fall Transition (September, October): marked by the utilisation of plants, aurochs, red deer, and wild boar.
5. Late Fall (November, December): small game, wild boar, aurochs, and red deer.

The average percentage utilisation for each resource category for these five seasons is given in Table 6.

This then is the pattern of seasonal resource utilisation predicted by the application of Jochim's model to the Boreal Mesolithic of the Netherlands. Distinct differences in seasonality and subsistence activities are suggested that should be reflected in Mesolithic settlements. Clearly the borders of these seasons would be flexible and yearly variations in climate may, for example, permit longer summer subsistence patterns or force longer winter occupations. Nevertheless, the five seasons predicted by the model should appear in a long-term, stable pattern of resource utilisation.

Several additional observations can be made regarding the predicted patterns. Aurochs, red deer, and wild boar are the primary large game species and are heavily exploited throughout much of the year. Roe deer and elk are of less importance because of their low density and dispersed distribution. Small game are also very important, particularly during the late fall and winter, as a contingency

Table 6. Average percentages of resource utilisation during suggested economic seasons.

	Winter (Jan-Mar)	Spring transition (Apr-May)	Summer (Jun-Aug)	Fall transition (Sept-Oct)	Late fall (Nov-Dec)
Aurochs	12.9	14.1	15.4	18.1	17.1
European elk	6.0	5.1	4.9	6.0	4.7
Red deer	28.9	11.1	8.8	14.1	14.3
Roe deer	3.1	1.9	1.5	1.6	2.0
Wild boar	20.8	7.4	11.3	11.3	25.9
Fish	2.3	20.0	16.2	8.5	2.6
Fowl	3.6	7.2	3.6	5.3	5.4
Plants	0	18.1	20.3	35.2	0
Small game	22.5	8.9	17.1	0	27.8

resource. Beaver may be the small game species of greatest significance during these months. Although plants are estimated to comprise only 15 percent of the total yearly diet, they are clearly indicated to play a major role in subsistence during the warmer months from the spring to the fall. At the fall transition, hazel nuts must have been particularly important and groves of hazel would have provided a strong attraction for human groups as well as for numbers of large herbivores such as aurochs, red deer, and wild boar. Hazel nuts may also have been stored to provide sustenance during the late fall and winter (cf. Mellars 1976). There is no definitive evidence for such a practice but caches of hazel nuts have been reported from several sites in north-west Europe (Newell 1973: 416). The possible storage and subsequent use of nuts during the late fall and winter may have provided an alternative food source for Mesolithic groups during the colder, harsher months of the year. This possibility has not been incorporated into the predictive model. More information is clearly needed regarding not only plants but fish and fowl as well. These three categories of resources remain the least understood in Mesolithic economies.

Summary and conclusions

Two distinct approaches to the investigation of settlement systems in the Mesolithic of the Netherlands have been employed in an attempt to define the critical aspects of group size, subsistence activities, and the duration and season of occupation. The initial approach, utilising archaeological data from this area, indicated four basic demographic arrangements defined by variations in group size and the duration of occupation. A second approach employed a predictive model to generate seasonal patterns of resource use, based on the biological and behavioural characteristics of available resources. This procedure indicated five major seasons of economic importance and their associated subsistence activities.

Ideally, it should be possible to articulate these two approaches. Shifts in economic seasons should correspond to changes in group size and the length of occupation. Among most groups of hunter-gatherers, changes in group size and settlement location show a strong correlation with the distribution and abundance of resources (Price 1973). We should anticipate a relationship between the archaeologically-defined characteristics of group size and duration and the predicted characteristics of season and resource utilisation. No direct correspondence can be demonstrated at the present time, however, between the results of the two approaches. Some suggestions can be made but refinement and further investigation of both approaches will be necessary before the results of the two methods can be articulated.

On the basis of the archaeological data alone we might have expected a different alignment of seasons to have been predicted by the model of resource utilisation. Specifically a pattern of four seasons might have been anticipated: three seasons of approximately the same length and one season two to three times longer than the others, corresponding to the three types of short-term base camps and the one long-term type. This pattern did not appear in the economic seasons predicted by the model; three seasons of approximately two months and two seasons of approximately three months duration are indicated. Nevertheless, some correspondence between the two approaches may be suggested in spite of the discrepancies.

Initially, human group size should be proportional to the abundance and concentration of resources, as discussed earlier. Aggregation camps should be expected in those seasons when resources are most concentrated and abundant. Two of the predicted seasons would appear to meet this requirement. The spring transition should witness abundant fish resources capable of supporting a large group. The fall transition as well is a period of resource concentration, in this case in the groves of hazel where an abundant mast yield should attract man, aurochs, red deer, and wild boar. Either or both of these transitional periods could provide for the larger aggregation of several primary subsistence units.

Late fall activities in November and December occur during a period of relative instability in terms of access to resources. Red deer, aurochs, and elk are dispersing following the early fall rut and the abundance of plants and fish during the warmer months has greatly diminished or disappeared. This period may well witness the smallest co-resident human groups, fragmenting in a pattern of dispersion, in response to the scattering of resources at this time. Perhaps the settlements of small nuclear families would occur during this season.

Although the summer and winter seasons are of approximately the same length in the predicted pattern, the types of resources present and the nature of seasonal catchment areas may imply quite different behaviour on the part of human groups. Because of the limiting conditions in the winter, imposed by cold and snow, site catchments may well be smaller and movement more restricted during this season. In contrast, improved mobility in the summer and the potential exhaustion of stationary plant resources within a site catchment may cause several locations to be settled during this single season. If such is the case, the archaeologically-defined long-term medium camps may represent winter settlements and the short-term medium sites may reflect summer occupations focused on plants, small game, and fish.

Clearly, this discussion is highly speculative and no direct correspondence between the two models can be demonstrated at the present time. A number of potential problems must be considered. Certain types of sites may simply not appear in the archaeological record. For example, sites at the margins of streams and small lakes may have completely disappeared through process of erosion or more serious human disturbances of the landscape such as peat-cutting and the reclamation of bogs for agricultural land. Certainly the enigmatic relationship between stone tools and human activity may also play an important role. Stone tools may not occur at some types of settlements – for example, fishing stations or locations of plant gathering activities – and these sites, without lithic artefacts, would no longer remain in the acidic soils of the sand areas of the Netherlands. Settlements from certain seasons may now lie beneath the waters of the North Sea, transgressed during Atlantic times, and no longer visible. The absence of such sites can clearly distort any interpretation of settlement systems.

In addition, the characteristics of settlements discussed here cannot be directly articulated with variations in the postglacial landscape. In many ways the Netherlands appears to have been a homogeneous area during the Boreal period but certain contrasts in the landscape, such as the brook valleys versus the higher and drier sandy areas, may have had important consequences for Mesolithic subsistence strategies. Unfortunately the location for many of the excavated sites is not adequately reported so that potential differences in site setting cannot be adequately evaluated. Even in the situation of the Havelte sites, where site location and setting is well known, there is no distinction between the types of sites present. The Havelte sites occur along a minor sand ridge in the upland area of the Drenthe plateau in the northern Netherlands (Price, Whallon, and Chappell 1974). All six of the Havelte sites occur within 100 metres of one another along this ridge. Of these six sites, one is a small occupation, two are medium long-term occupations, and three are medium short-term occupations. Such patterning does not suggest that geographic location plays a major role in the distribution of settlement types, but rather reinforces the impression that the landscape was remarkably homogeneous. Again, further investigation of the significance of settlement location is necessitated.

In several areas of north-west Europe, tentative formulations have been presented dealing with the nature and appearance of settlement systems in various areas. Mellars (1976) in Great Britain, Brinch Petersen (1973) in Denmark, Indrelid (this volume) in Norway and Newell (1973)[9] and the present discussion for the Netherlands, have attempted to elucidate the varieties of settlement present in their respective areas. In spite of a wealth of problems and a dearth of data, it is through the continued investigation, alteration, expansion, and refinement of formulations such as these that we may effectively discuss the operation of specific settlement systems in the Mesolithic , demonstrating the functional interrelationships among human activity, settlement, and population in the context of specific environmental regimes. Hopefully, such projections, continuously realigned in response to new data, can be elaborated to accommodate the variety of materials and information that define the Mesolithic period in north-west Europe.

Notes

[1] Newell (1973: 429) has suggested a useful distinction which avoids some of the confusion inherent in the term 'Tardenoisian'. 'Maglemose' is used to denote all the northern Mesolithic cultures with core axes. These sites generally are found along the Baltic and North Sea coasts. The term Western European Mesolithic is used to denote the various Mesolithic cultures characterised by microlithic points and backed blades but lacking core axes. The term Tardenois*ien* is to be used exclusively for the specific Mesolithic culture of the Fer-en-Tardenois region of France.

[2] The De Leien-Wartena Complex (Newell 1970) and the Oldesloe Stufe (Schwabedissen 1962) represent the final phase of the Mesolithic occupation of the north-west European Plain. The De Leien-Wartena Complex is characterised by the first appearance of core axes in this area along with several new point types. The size of human settlement appears to be much larger than in previous phases (Newell 1973) and, in many respects, the De Leien-Wartena Complex represents a major transition in human adaptation in this area.

[3] Ground plans of excavated Mesolithic sites in the Netherlands were made available through the courtesy of Prof. H.T. Waterbolk and Dr R.R. Newell of the Biologisch-Archaeologisch Instituut of the State University of Groningen, Netherlands. The majority of the original excavations were conducted by A. Bohmers or amateur groups in collaboration with the Instituut (e.g., Heesters 1967, 1968). Many of these ground plans will appear in a forthcoming publication by Dr Newell (in press).

[4] The investigation of Mesolithic settlement systems in the Netherlands was made possible by a grant for the support of doctoral dissertation research from the National Science Foundation (GS-29688). The excavations at Havelte were funded by an NSF grant to Dr Robert Whallon, Jr., of the Museum of Anthropology of the University of Michigan. The assistance of the National Science Foundation is gratefully acknowledged.

[5] A more detailed discussion of the individual sites and the analysis of the site types appears in Price, 1975. The data and ground plans from several of the sites (Waubach, Siegerswoude, Acht, Duurswoude, and Rotsterhaule) will be published by Dr R.R. Newell (in press).

[6] Three additional sites were used in the compilation of this Table – Een, Borger, and Ede (Newell, in press). These sites are not listed in Table 1 because adequate information is not available from the ground plans.

[7] The following are good general sources on European mammals and provide access to additional references for particular species: van den Brink 1967; Degerbøl 1964; Grzimek 1971; Southern 1964; Walker, *et al.* 1964. Syntheses by archaeologists of some of the relevant literature on species present in the Boreal period appear in G.A. Clark (1971), Mellars (1975, 1976), and Jochim (1976).

[8] The following sites were used for the analysis of animal clusters at Mesolithic settlements in north-west Europe; references which report the faunal remains are also given: in Denmark, Vinde Helsinge (Brinch Petersen 1966), Melsted (Brinch Petersen 1966), Holmegaard (Clark 1936), Mullerup (Clark 1936), Svaerdborg II (Brinch Petersen 1971), Hallebjgaard (Murray 1970), Hesselbjergaard (Murray 1970), Øgaarde (Murray 1970), Tingbjergaard (Murray 1970), and Ringkloster (Andersen 1975); in Sweden, Agerød (Althin 1954), and Dalkarstroop (Welinder 1975); in East Germany, Hohen Viecheln (Schuldt 1961), Rüde (Nobis 1962), Förster Moor (Nobis 1962), and Bonde Bruck (Nobis 1962); and in England, Thatcham (Wymer 1962), Star Carr (Clark 1954), Creswell (Clark 1936), and Westward Ho! (Churchill 1965).

[9] Newell (1973) has formulated a tentative classification of settlement types in the Dutch Mesolithic on the basis of similarities and differences in the size and shape of sites. Three settlement types belong to the pre-De Leien Wartena periods. Settlement type 1 of Newell is roughly 'trapezoidal' in shape and averages 500m² area. The average number of tools at sites of this type is 240. Settlement type 2 is oval, roughly 25m² in area, and contains an average of 37 retouched tools. Settlement type 3 is represented by small, round concentrations of flint, approximately 7m² in area with an average of 18 retouched tools. This settlement type closely resembles the small concentrations in the Pennines of Great Britain, described by Clark (1972). Newell suggests that settlements of type 1 represent maintenance camps. Settlement types 2 and

3 are considered to be extractive camps associated with type 1 settlements.

Newell's type 1 sites correspond directly to the one large site type (type 5) defined in this analysis, the site of Rotsterhaule. There is no correspondence between Newell's type 2 and the medium settlements (types 3 and 4) described in this discussion. Much more differentiation between the sites is recorded in the present study: a distinction is made between long- and short-term medium settlements and these sites are considered to be base camps of the primary subsistence unit. Newell's type 3 settlements correspond in part to the extraction camps (type 1) defined in the present study but small base camps (type 2) have also been distinguished.

The discrepancies between the classification of sites by Newell and the present study are due, in part, to the use of information from the Havelte excavations and to the consideration of a larger number of variables in this study. Future excavations and analysis will undoubtedly elaborate on the present classification and will serve to determine if it will remain as a useful framework for the study of the Mesolithic in the Netherlands.

References

Althin, C.A. 1954. *The Chronology of the Stone Age Settlement of Scania, Sweden.* Acta Archaeologica Ludensia, 4. Lund.

Andersen, S. 1975. Ringloster: en jysk indlandsboplads med Ertebøllekultur. *Kuml,* 1973-74: 10-108.

Binford, L.R. and Binford, S.R. 1969. Stone tools and human behaviour. *Scientific American,* 220: 78-84.

Birdsell, J.B. 1953. Some environmental and cultural factors influencing the structuring of Australian Aboriginal populations. *American Naturalist,* 87: 169-207.

Bokelmann, K. 1971. *Duvensee, ein Wohnplatz des Mesolithikums in Schleswig-Holstein, und die Duvenseegruppe.* Inaugural-Dissertation zur Erlangung des Doktorgrades der Mathematisch-Naturwissenschaftlichen Fakultät der Universität zu Köln.

Bouchud, J. 1974. Etude de la faune Ahrensbourgienne de Remouchamps. In Michel C. Dewez (ed.), Nouvelles récherches à la Grotte de Remouchamps. *Bulletin de la Sociétié Royale Belge d' Anthropologie et Préhistoire,* 85: 119-27.

Brink, F.H. van den. 1967. *A Field Guide to the Mammals of Britain and Europe.* London, Collins.

Brinch Petersen, E. 1966. Klosterlund-Sønder Hadsund-Bøllund. Les trois sites principaux du Maglemose ancien en Jutland. Essai de typologie et de chronologie. *Acta Archaeologica,* 37: 77-185.

Brinch Petersen, E. 1971. Svaerdborg II. A Maglemose hut from Svaerdborg Bog, Zealand, Denmark. *Acta Archaeologica,* 42: 43-77.

Brinch Petersen, E. 1973. A survey of the Late Paleolithic and the Mesolithic of Denmark. In S.K. Kozlowski (ed.), *The Mesolithic in Europe.* Warsaw, University Press: 71-127.

Churchill, D.M. and Wymer, J.J. 1965. The kitchen midden site at Westward Ho!, Devon, England: ecology, age and relation to changes in land and sea level. *Proceedings of the Prehistoric Society,* 31: 74-84.

Clark, G.A. 1971. The Asturian of Cantabria: subsistence base and the evidence for Post-Pleistocene climate shifts. *American Anthropologist,* 73: 1245-57.

Clark, J.G.D. 1936. *The Mesolithic Settlement of Northern Europe.* London, Cambridge University Press.

Clark, J.G.D. 1948. The development of fishing in prehistoric Europe. *The Antiquaries Journal,* 28: 45-85.

Clark, J.G.D. 1954. *Excavations at Star Carr.* London, Cambridge University Press.

Clark, J.G.D. 1972. *Star Carr: a Case Study in Bioarchaeology.* Addison-Wesley Modules in Anthropology, 10. Reading, Massachussetts.

Clark, J.G.D. 1975. *The Earlier Stone Age Settlement of Scandinavia.* London, Cambridge University Press.

Clark, P.J. and Evans, F.C. 1954. Distance to nearest neighbour as a measure of spatial relationships in populations. *Ecology*, 35: 445-53.

Degerbøl, M. 1964. Some remarks on Late- and Post-glacial vertebrate fauna and its ecological relations in northern Europe. *Journal of Animal Ecology*, 33: 71-85.

Divale, W.T. 1972. Systematic population control in the Middle and Upper Paleolithic: inferences based on contemporary hunters and gatherers. *World Archaeology*, 4: 222-43.

Dunn, L. 1968. Epidemiological factors: health and disease in hunter-gatherers. In R.B. Lee and I. DeVore (eds.), *Man the Hunter*. Chicago, Aldine: 221-28.

Flannery, K.V. 1968. Archaeological systems theory and early Mesoamerica. In B.J. Meggers (ed.), *Anthropological Archeology in the Americas*. Washington, Anthropological Society of Washington: 67-87.

Gearing, F. 1958. The structural poses of 18th century Cherokee villages. *American Anthropologist*, 60: 1148-57.

Grzimek, B. (ed.) 1971. *Grzimek's Animal Life Encyclopedia*. New York, Van Nostrand Reinhold Company.

Hallowell, I. 1949. The size of Algonkian hunting territories: a function of ecological adjustment. *American Anthropologist*, 51: 33-45.

Hayden, B. 1972. Population control among hunter/gatherers. *World Archaeology*, 4: 205-21.

Heesters, P.W. 1967. Mesolithicum te Nijnsel. *Brabants Heem*, 19: 167-78.

Heesters, P.W. 1968. Een Vroeg-Mesolithische Kultuur te Nijnsel. *Brabants Heem*, 20: 98-118.

Janzen, D.H. 1973. Review of *Amazonian Cosmos* by G. Reichel-Dolmatoff. *Natural History*, 82: 86-90.

Jochim, M. 1976. *Hunter-Gatherer Subsistence and Settlement: a Predictive Model*. New York and London, Academic Press.

Lee, R.B. and DeVore, I. 1968. Problems in the study of hunters and gatherers. In R.B. Lee and I. DeVore (eds.), *Man the Hunter*. Chicago, Aldine: 3-12.

Louwe Kooijmans, L.P. 1970-71. Mesolithic bone and antler implements from the North Sea and the Netherlands. *Berichten van de Rijksdienst voor het Oudheidkundig Bodemonderzoek*, 20-21: 27-73.

Mellars, P.A. 1975. Ungulate populations, economic patterns, and the Mesolithic landscape. In J.G. Evans, S. Limbrey, and H. Cleere (eds.), *The Effect of Man on the Landscape: the Highland Zone*. Council for British Archaeology, Research Report No. 11: 49-56.

Mellars, P.A. 1976. Settlement patterns and industrial variability in the British Mesolithic. In G. de G. Sieveking, I.H. Longworth and K.E. Wilson (eds.), *Problems in Economic and Social Archaeology*. London, Duckworth: 375-99.

Murray, J. 1970. *The First European Agriculture*. Edinburgh, University Press.

Naroll, R. 1962. Floor area and settlement population. *American Antiquity*, 27: 587-88.

Newell, R.R. 1970. *The Mesolithic Affinities and Typological Relations of the Dutch Bandkeramik Flint Industry*. Unpublished Ph.D. thesis, Institute of Archaeology, University of London.

Newell, R.R. 1973. The post-glacial adaptations of the indigenous populations of the Northwest European Plain. In S.K. Kozlowski (ed.), *The Mesolithic in Europe*. Warsaw, University Press: 399-40.

Newell, R.R. In press. *The Mesolithic Settlement of the Northwest European Plain*.

Nobis, G. 1962. Die Tierreste prähistorischer Siedlungen aus den Satrupholmer Moor. *Festschrift für Tierzuchtung und Zuchtungsbiologie*, 77.

Pielou, E.C. 1961. Segregation and symmetry in two-species populations as studied by nearest neighbor relations. *Journal of Ecology*, 49: 255-69.

Price, T.D. 1973. A proposed model for procurement systems in the Mesolithic of northwestern Europe. In S.K. Kozlowski (ed.), *The Mesolithic in Europe*. Warsaw, University Press: 455-76.

Price, T.D. 1975. *Mesolithic settlement systems in the Netherlands*. Unpublished Ph.D.

thesis, Department of Anthropology, University of Michigan.

Price, T.D. 1978. The spatial analysis of lithic artifact distribution and association on prehistoric occupation floors. In D.D. Davis (ed.), *Lithics and Subsistence*. Nashville, Vanderbilt University Publications in Anthropology, 20.

Price, T.D., Whallon, R., and Chappell, S. 1974. Mesolithic sites near Havelte, province of Drenthe (Netherlands). *Palaeohistoria*, 16: 7-61.

Rogers, E.S. 1969. Band organization among the Indians of eastern subarctic Canada. In D. Damas (ed.), *Contributions to Anthropology: Band Societies*. National Museum of Canada, Bulletin 228: 21-50.

Rostlund, E. 1952. *Freshwater Fish and Fishing in Native North America*. University of California Publications in Geography, 9.

Schuldt, E. 1961. *Hohen Viecheln: Ein Mittelsteinzeitlicher Wohnplatz in Mecklenburg*. Schriften der Section für Vor- und Frühgeschichte, 10. Berlin, Deutsche Akademie der Wissenschaft.

Schwabedissen, H. 1962. Northern continental Europe. In R.J. Braidwood and G.R. Willey (eds.), *Courses Towards Urban Life*. Chicago, Aldine: 254-66.

Southern, H.N. 1964. *The Handbook of British Mammals*. Oxford, Blackwell.

Steward, J.H. 1969. Postscript to bands: on taxonomy, processes, and causes. In D. Damas (ed.), *Contributions to Anthropology: Band Societies*. National Museum of Canada, Bulletin 228: 288-95.

Streuver, S. 1968. Woodland subsistence-settlement systems in the Lower Illinois Valley. In L.R. Binford and S.R. Binford (eds.), *New Perspectives in Archeology*. Chicago, Aldine: 285-312.

Thompson, D.H. 1939. The seasonal factor in human culture. *Proceedings of the Prehistoric Society*, 5: 209-21.

Walker, E.P. *et al.* (eds.) 1964. *Mammals of the World*. Baltimore, Johns Hopkins Press.

Waterbolk, H.T. 1965-66. The occupation of Friesland in the prehistoric period. *Berichten van de Rijksdienst voor het Oudheidkundig Bodemonderzoek*, 15-16: 13-35.

Welinder, S. 1975. Agriculture, inland hunting, and sea hunting in the western and northern region of the Baltic, 6000-2000 B.C. In W. Fitzhugh (ed.), *Prehistoric Maritime Adaptations of the Circumpolar Zone*. The Hague, Mouton: 21-39.

Whallon, R. 1974. Spatial analysis of occupation floors II: application of nearest neighbor analysis. *American Antiquity*, 39: 16-34.

Wiessner, P. 1974. A functional estimator of population from floor area. *American Antiquity*, 39: 343-50.

Wilmsen, E.N. 1973. Interaction, spacing behaviour, and the organization of hunting bands. *Journal of Anthropological Research*, 29: 1-31.

Winters, H.D. 1969. *The Riverton Culture*. Illinois State Museum Reports of Investigations, 73.

Wishart, D. 1970. *Clustan IA.* St. Andrews, Computing Laboratory, St. Andrews University.

Wobst, H.M. 1974. Boundary conditions for Paleolithic social systems: a simulation approach. *American Antiquity*, 39: 147-78.

Wymer, J.J. 1962. Excavations at the Maglemosian sites at Thatcham, Berkshire, England. *Proceedings of the Prehistoric Society*, 28: 329-61.

Yengoyan, A.A. 1968. Demographic and ecological influences on Aboriginal Australian marriage sections. In R.B. Lee and I. DeVore (eds.), *Man the Hunter*. Chicago, Aldine: 185-99.

7

Animal exploitation in Mesolithic Denmark

J.L. Bay-Petersen

The concept of hunting economies in prehistory has traditionally implied a random unstructured exploitation, based on chance encounter between the individual hunter and his prey (e.g. Ducos 1968: xiv). Since the methods by which pre-Neolithic man exploited animal populations are still largely unknown, the validity of such an assumption is doubtful. As Higgs and Jarman (1972) have pointed out, pre-Neolithic faunal exploitation is likely to have comprised a diversity of economic systems, some of which may have resembled the Neolithic in intensity of exploitation and/or extractive capacity. It may be that many of the features associated with animal domestication are the results of constraints imposed by an agricultural economy rather than any intrinsic increase in animal productivity. Certainly it seems that animal products, and meat in particular, play a much less important role in the diet of the peasant farmer than in that of the meat-dependent hunter (see Bay-Petersen 1975).

Present-day hunting societies wholly or primarily dependent on meat all occupy areas within or near the Arctic Circle in an environment where edible plant species are much sparser than those which are likely to have been available in Mesolithic Denmark. Outside this area, the most intensively studied surviving hunter-gatherer groups are those from tropical forest and desert regions, who seem to have depended more on vegetable than animal food resources. It has been suggested in a comparative study of such societies that the hunting of mammals is inherently less productive and less reliable as a resource base than the gathering of vegetable foods (Lee 1968: 41). We must remember however that faunal densities in both tropical forest and desert regions are very low. Sparse ungulate populations mean not only a low animal biomass, but also that the chances of effective man-animal contact are relatively small: in order to maximise the chances of encountering prey, animals are generally exploited on an individual basis (Lee 1968; Woodburn 1968; Driver 1961; Lawrence 1971). On the other hand there seems to have been a widespread use of communal hunting methods amongst peoples dependent on free-ranging social ungulate species as a primary food resource. Anell's comprehensive survey of hunting techniques in North America shows that a heavy utilisation of social ungulate species is characteristically associated with the use of communal hunting methods (Anell 1969). Forest cover does not seem to have been a limiting factor in communal hunting: there are several records of mass drives of wild reindeer by forest Lapps using wooden corrals (e.g. Vorren and Manker 1962), and Forde (1934: 80) mentions large deer drives in the woodlands of British Columbia. Such techniques of course imply a much greater animal population density, but also seem to result in a much higher economic return per unit of effort than individual hunting (Bay-Petersen 1975; Van Etten *et al.* 1965). The relative productivity of animal as opposed to vegetable foods is likely to be determined primarily by the economic potential of the particular environment.

In the collection of vegetable foods, the leafy part of the plant seems to be of little value: it is the storage systems and seeds of plants with their concentrated nutritional resources that are important. These parts of plants are well developed in a desert environment, where species are adapted to survive in conditions of very low and intermittent rainfall. In the heavily wooded environment of Mesolithic Denmark the main edible plant species seem to have been hazel nuts and the fruit and tubers of aquatic plants. As a dispersed food resource these would have required a comparatively high expenditure of time and labour for collection: they are also available for only a short period of the year. Outside desert areas it is competition between species rather than environment that acts as the major limiting factor in germination and growth, and the short-lived fruits of a non-desert environment are not the equivalent, as a food resource, to the resistant desert fruits which can provide an annual, not merely short-term seasonal, food supply.

The presence of potential food species in a territory exploited by man does not necessarily imply their maximum utilisation. Lawton's (1973) study of the energy costs of food-gathering found the ratio of energy gained to energy expended to be very similar in a large number of species, including birds and insects, in spite of great variation in absolute rates of energy expenditure. Lawton (1973: 66) writes: '... energetically expensive food-gathering techniques in animals can only be applied to food sources which guarantee a high rate of energy return.'

It is impossible to define in detail the role of vegetable foods in the economy of the Danish Mesolithic, but it seems likely that their contribution to the annual subsistence of human groups was intermittent, and relatively small. Birds and fresh-water fish also seem to have been of minor importance in the Mesolithic economy, probably for similar reasons. Fishing was practised from inland sites throughout the Mesolithic, as is evidenced by skeletal remains of pike and sheat-fish, but such fishing probably gave a rather low return on time and energy expended compared to the exploitation of terrestrial mammals, especially if, as Clark suggests, line and spear fishing were practised rather than netting (Clark 1975: 143). For example, at Svaerdborg 64 pike are represented by the left mandible: assuming an average weight of one kilogram each, the nutritional contribution they provide is 76.8 x 10³ calories (Muus and Dahlstrom 1967), compared to the 165 x 10³ calories represented by a single adult male red deer (Table 2). The numbers of fish and bird bones in inland sites is generally low. At the lacustrine site of Ringkloster there were 38 bones of large ungulates for every fish and bird bone, and this difference in economic importance is of course increased considerably when comparative body size is taken into account (Andersen 1973-4). Both birds and fresh-water fish can probably be viewed as a subsidiary rather than as a primary food resource.

The economy of the Danish Mesolithic seems to have been based predominantly on the exploitation of terrestrial mammals, and particularly of large ungulates. This appears to have been true of coastal as well as inland sites, although complementary resources on the coast seem to have played a much more important role: the most productive of such resources seem to have been marine mammals rather than shell-fish (see Bailey 1975 and this volume; Bay-Petersen 1975).

Ungulate exploitation in the Danish Mesolithic was based on five species – elk, red deer, roe deer, pig, and aurochs – the first four of which still survive in northern Europe. Carnivores and rodents comprise an appreciable percentage of the site fauna, generally over 10 percent and sometimes as high as 40 percent, but most of these species were probably of minor value as a food resource (Fig. 1). Most carnivore species were probably killed, as they are today, for their furs rather than their meat. Gubser (1965), for example, states that the Nunamiut did not consider wolf, fox, lynx or wolverine to be suitable food species, and killed them only for their fur. Bears were highly valued by the Nunamiut as a food resource because of their high fat content (Gubser 1965). Although the European brown bear is a large animal, weighing 200-250 kg. (Burton 1962), approximately the weight of a male adult red deer, it does not seem to have been of major economic importance. Bear are absent from the majority of Danish Mesolithic sites, and where present are in very small quantities of 1-3 individuals. Beaver are common in a number of both coastal and inland sites in Zealand, though not in Jutland. The largest concentrations are in the Atlantic and Boreal sites of the Aamose area, and at Svaerdborg and Holmegaard, where they contribute between 6 and 15 percent of the total fauna. As well as providing high-quality

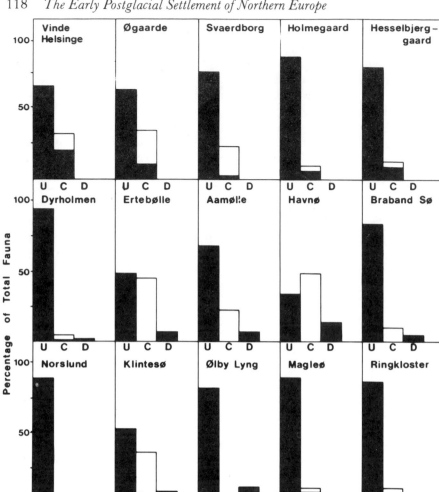

Figure 1. Percentage of edible and non-edible animal species in faunal assemblages from Danish Mesolithic sites. For references to the site faunas see Table 1.

furs, beaver were probably also a valuable food resource: they were highly esteemed by the North American Indian both for their furs and their meat. C.H.C. Clarke (1942) states that in many areas beaver lodges were regarded as individual property, and could be exploited only by their owners: the animals were killed mainly over the winter. However, beaver are much less common in sites of the Danish

Table 1. Relative frequencies of different ungulate species in Danish Mesolithic sites, calculated as percentages of the total ungulate fauna.

	Red Deer	Roe Deer	Pig	Aurochs	Elk	Sample size
BOREAL						
Vinde Helsinge ⎰	37.5	12.5	25.0	12.5	12.5	8 (A)
⎱	45.1	13.7	19.6	2.0	27.5	51 (B)
Øgaarde	44.6	21.7	16.9	12.0	4.8	83 (A)
Svaerdborg ⎰	12.0	31.0	38.0	7.0	12.0	100 (A)
⎱	12.6	23.1	34.1	8.6	21.6	880 (B)
Holmegaard	30.8	24.6	33.8	4.6	6.2	65 (A)
Hesselbjgaard ⎰	16.7	16.7	16.7	33.3	16.7	6 (A)
⎱	30.4	13.0	13.0	34.8	8.7	23 (B)
ATLANTIC						
Dyrholmen ⎰	34.3	25.4	32.8	6.0	1.5	67 (A)
⎱	35.2	14.8	38.8	8.5	2.7	1442 (B)
Ertebølle	17.1	43.4	35.5	1.3	2.6	76 (A)
Aamølle	35.3	41.2	17.6	5.9	–	17 (A)
Havnø	28.6	28.6	28.6	14.3	–	7 (A)
Braband Sø	51.0	10.2	20.4	15.8	2.6	196 (B)
Norslund	25.9	13.1	32.6	27.6	0.8	659 (B)
Ringkloster	15.8	2.2	74.0	7.3	0.6	1445 (B)
Klintesø	23.1	53.8	23.1	–	–	26 (A)
Ølby Lyng	58.0	29.6	12.3	–	–	1114 (B)
Magleø	56.0	24.0	12.0	4.0	4.0	25 (A)
Hallebygaard	90.0	5.0	5.0	–	–	20 (A)
Kildegaard ⎰	62.5	12.5	25.0			8 (A)
⎱	77.0	6.6	16.4	–	–	61 (B)
Tingbjerggaard ⎰	61.5	7.7	15.4	7.7	7.7	13 (A)
⎱	58.3	13.0	19.4	2.8	5.6	36 (B)
Faareville	10.0	50.0	40.0	–	–	20 (A)

The figures are based on either the minimum numbers of individuals (A) or total numbers of specimens (B) identified. Owing to certain ambiguities in the literature, all of the figures quoted should be regarded as approximate. Data from Broholm 1926-31; Degerbøl in Mathiassen *et al.* 1942; Degerbøl in Matthiassen 1943; Friis-Johansen 1919; Møhl in Andersen and Malmros 1965; Møhl in Brinch Petersen 1970; Thomsen and Jessen 1906; Winge in Madsen *et al.* 1900; Petersen *et al.* 1888 and other sources.

Mesolithic than ungulate species, and also much smaller than all ungulate species except roe deer (adult beaver weigh 15-20 kg. (Burton 1962), cf. Table 2).

Figure 1 shows the relative percentages of the main groups of food species in Danish sites – ungulates, *Carnivora* and *Rodentia*, and *Delphinidae* and *Phocidae* – based on the numbers of identified remains. It shows that ungulates provided by far the most important source of animal protein. The importance of the edible species of carnivores and rodents (bear and beaver), though always small, does not seem to be related to the *overall* abundance of carnivores and rodents in the site fauna, implying perhaps some spatial or seasonal differentiation in their exploitation for fur and their exploitation for meat. This is

Table 2. Body weights and calorific value of various ungulate species.

Species	MALE Weight (Kg.)	Calories	FEMALE Weight (Kg.)	Calories	JUVENILE Weight (Kg.)	Calories
Red Deer	220	165.0×10^3	170	127.5×10^3	50	37.5×10^3
Roe Deer	19	14.3×10^3	18	13.5×10^3	12	9.0×10^3
Pig	166	155.6×10^3	68	63.8×10^3	20	18.8×10^3
Woods Bison	800	600.0×10^3	600	450.0×10^3	150	112.5×10^3
Elk	500	375.0×10^3	346	259.5×10^3	100	75.0×10^3

Body weights of red deer, pig and elk are taken from Heptner *et al.* 1966; those of roe deer and Woods Bison from Prior 1968 and Krysiak 1963 respectively. The proportions of edible meat are calculated as 60 percent of body weight for cervids and bovids, and 75 percent of body weight for pig (Bay-Petersen 1975:88-9). The calculations assume that 100 gm. of edible meat = 125 calories.

particularly marked at Havnø and Ertebølle, where there are unusually large numbers of *Rodentia* and *Carnivora*, none of which are edible species. The variation between sites in this respect seems likely to be related to site location rather than season of occupation, in that it seems likely that beaver, the fur-bearing species, and probably bear, were all exploited most heavily in the cold months of the year, when such species are in their best condition, and, particularly in the case of beaver, most vulnerable to exploitation. The *Carnivora* and *Rodentia* are present in appreciable, though varying, proportions in all sites, which may support other evidence that there does not seem to have been a simple one-season exploitation of either coastal or inland resources in Mesolithic Denmark (Bay-Petersen 1975).

Table 1 and Figure 2 show the relative frequencies in different sites of the ungulate species which seem to have provided the primary food resource in the Danish Mesolithic. Table 1 shows species representation in terms of both the number of specimens and the minimum number of individuals (where this is available). In Figure 2 the minimum number of individuals of each species is translated into terms of meat weight (see Table 2): this shows that the resource contribution of both elk and bovid is fairly high, although their remains are generally relatively sparse; conversely roe deer, although one of the most common species, is usually the least productive as a meat resource.

The faunal evidence from these sites, whether expressed in terms of the number of specimens (reflecting the number of kills made) or as meat weights (reflecting the relative contribution of each species to the site economy), seems to indicate a broad-based ungulate exploitation. By broad-based exploitation we mean one based on a number of complementary species in the site territory, no one of which is markedly dominant in the site fauna. Naturally one species must always be dominant in a site assemblage, but the role played by the

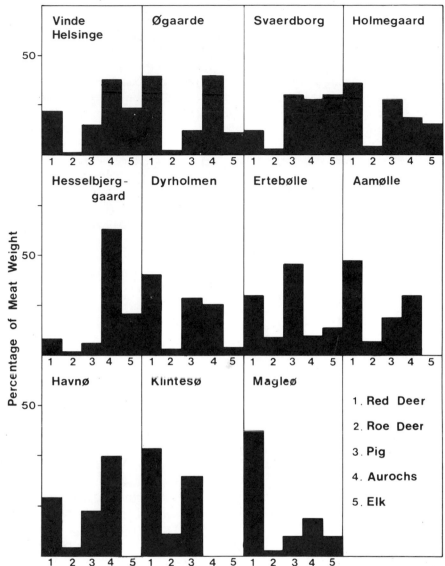

Figure 2. Ungulate meat weights in sites of the Danish Mesolithic. For data on the meat weights of different species see Table 2, and for references to site faunas see Table 1.

dominant species cannot be sharply differentiated from that played by subsidiary species.

There are some exceptions: red deer seem to play a comparatively major role at Braband Sø, Ølby lyng and Magleø compared to other species, although they still represent less than 60 percent of the site fauna. The relative meat contribution of cattle at Hesselbjerggaard is fairly high (64 percent), but in view of the very small size of the faunal sample (in which the cattle remains represent only two individuals) it would clearly be dangerous to accept this as evidence of a specialised economy. The sole example of what may have been a specialised site economy is at Ringkloster, where pig represent 74 percent of the ungulate fauna (Andersen 1973-4). This is all the more remarkable in that it is unusual for pig to be the dominant species in a faunal assemblage; generally red deer is the most common species.

In general, however, site economies in Mesolithic Denmark seem to have depended upon the exploitation of multiple ungulate species. This does not of course imply that no specialised faunal exploitation orientated towards a particular species took place – indeed, since there is considerable variation in the distribution and behaviour of the species exploited it seems likely that each hunting activity, possibly resulting in a multiple kill, was designed with a particular species in mind – but such activity seems to have co-existed with the major exploitation of complementary species from the same habitation base. It seems likely therefore that sites were located with a view to maximising the potential exploitation of multiple ungulate species.

The environment

In considering the environment of Mesolithic man in Denmark, two main aspects are of particular economic importance. The first is the physical environment itself, in terms of topography and vegetation: the second is the nature of the faunal community available for human exploitation. Man as a predator must obey environmental imperatives, and the limitations imposed by the behaviour of the species he hunted were a basic factor in his environment.

Although the site faunal assemblages of the Danish Mesolithic indicate that the economy was based on complementary ungulate species, not all of these species were necessarily of equal abundance within the site territory, or equally accessible to human predation. Wilkinson (1972a, 1975) has suggested that variable patterns of animal behaviour may largely determine animal exploitation systems, and has convincingly demonstrated this in an analysis of musk-ox exploitation. Musk-oxen may be atypical in this respect, in that their behaviour seems to delimit much more rigidly potential exploitation systems than most other species – as a meat supply they can be exploited in the long term only periodically as a critical resource (see Wilkinson *ibid.*). However, even if animal behaviour did not determine exploitation patterns – in that most species can be exploited by a number of alternative systems – it is likely to have been an important limiting factor.

One measure of the economic potential of a species is its population density, and Table 3 shows the observed population densities of pig, red deer, roe deer and elk in a number of habitats. It can be seen that densities vary enormously among different populations of the same

Table 3. Recorded population densities of various ungulate species in different habitats.

Region	Hectares per Animal
Red Deer	
N.W. Scotland	16
Crimean Reserve, U.S.S.R.	14
Belovezhsk Reserve, U.S.S.R.	21
Dune Plantations, Denmark	20—25
Voronezh Reserve, U.S.S.R.	36
Caucasus Reserve, U.S.S.R.	100
Bohemia, Czechoslavakia	40
Sikhote-Alin Reserve, U.S.S.R.	140
Tokko Valley, Yakutia, U.S.S.R.	300
Roe Deer	
Yakutia, U.S.S.R.	220
Baikal Area, U.S.S.R.	35—40
Crimea Nature Reserve, U.S.S.R.	25
Belovezhsk Nature Reserve, U.S.S.R.	55—1000
Ilmenisch Nature Reserve, U.S.S.R.	33—40
Tuwinisch Nature Reserve, U.S.S.R.	20—40
Pig	
Kazakhstan (Maximum), U.S.S.R.	16—20
Mongolia (Maximum), U.S.S.R.	25—33
Astrakhan Reserve, U.S.S.R.	40
Belovezhsk Reserve, U.S.S.R.	
end 19th Century	77
Caucasus Reserve, U.S.S.R.	125—250
Black Forest, Germany:	
end 19th Century	500
1936—39	200
Elk	
Isle Royale (1945), U.S.A.	120
Ontario — early regrowth of woodland	62
— plus 16—30 years	125
— plus 30—45 years	250
Oka Nature Reserve, U.S.S.R.	40—50
Prioksko-Terrasny Reserve, U.S.S.R.	40—50
Pechoro-Ilych Reserve, U.S.S.R.	240
Yakutia, U.S.S.R.	260
European Russia — mixed forest	1000—1200
— coniferous forest	1400
Siberian taiga	1500—1600

Data from Heptner *et al.* 1966; Darling 1969; Jensen 1968; Egorov 1967; Oloff 1951; Peterson 1955.

species, to the extent that it is difficult to distinguish any significant inter-specific variations. However it appears that elk have generally a much lower population density than the other ungulate species: on the other hand they are also much larger in size, and if the body weights of the four species with surviving wild populations are combined with their population densities in preferred and marginal habitats (with respectively the highest and lowest recorded animal populations per unit area) elk would appear to have a species biomass greater than either roe deer or pig (see Table 4). Red deer seem to have by far the highest biomass in both preferred and marginal habitats, while roe deer have very much the lowest.

This may be related in part to social behaviour, in that pig, roe deer and elk are generally solitary animals, and roe deer maintain an individual defended territory (Tegner 1951). Social behaviour is likely to have been an important determinant of exploitation efficiency, in that an animal which moves in large aggregates provides a more concentrated and easily available food resource than a species whose members live solitarily or in very small groups. Red deer characteristically move in larger groups than the single family unit, and have been observed in aggregations of several hundred animals, but these are uncommon and are probably temporary (Heptner *et al.* 1966; Darling 1969). The aurochs is now extinct, but seems to have been very similar in size and behaviour to the North American woodland bison, which also forms social groupings. Apart from a few marginal areas which support only the mother-young group at all times of the year except the rut, 4-5 animals appear to represent the minimum social unit of both red deer and Woods bison. Under favourable conditions both species move in larger social groups, and are probably capable of supporting, at least seasonally, large-scale communal exploitation.

Pig behaviour would seem to impose a different · pattern of exploitation. Although pig exist in fairly high population densities they are widely scattered, and apart from the rut do not form social units larger than mother and young (Heptner *et al.* 1966). Since free-ranging pigs have a dispersed distribution, we might expect efficient human exploitation to follow the same pattern, with a maximisation of hunting units, possibly to the level of single hunters, in order to increase the chances of man-animal contact. Roe deer exploitation, for similar reasons, would probably follow the same pattern. Elk are also a non-social species, but since they show a tendency to cluster at localised feeding grounds – lake edges in summer and small feeding yards in winter – they may provide better opportunities for intensive forms of exploitation (Peterson 1955).

Another factor determining the productivity of a species is its reproductive potential, since this factor determines the level of the viable long-term cull which can be compensated by herd increase. The rate of increase in pig is particularly high. Females begin

Table 4. Estimated biomass of different ungulate species in a hypothetical site territory of 10 km radius (= 31,428 hectares).

| Species | Number of hectares per animal | | Number of Animals in Site Territory | | | | | | | | Biomass in Kg | |
	Preferred	Marginal	Tot.	Preferred Male	Female	Juv.	Tot.	Marginal Male	Female	Juv.	Preferred	Marginal
Roe Deer	20	1000	1571	628.4	628.4	314.2	31	12.4	12.4	6.2	27.0×10^3	0.5×10^3
Pig	25	500	1257	377.0	628.5	251.4	62	18.6	31.0	12.4	110.3×10^3	5.4×10^3
Elk	40	1600	786	314.4	314.4	157.2	20	8.0	8.0	4.0	281.7×10^3	7.2×10^3
Red Deer	14	300	2245	673.5	1122.5	449.0	105	31.5	52.5	21.0	361.4×10^3	16.9×10^3

The calculations assume a population structure comprising 30 percent males, 50 percent females and 20 percent juveniles for polygamous species; and 40 percent males, 40 percent females and 20 percent juveniles for monogamous species. Densities of animals in preferred and marginal habitats are taken from Table 2; animal body weights are from Table 1.

F

breeding in the second year, and on average in Europe, 5.5 young are born in each litter; in poor years the average figure is only 3.0 young, rising to 8.9 under favourable conditions (Oloff 1951). The highest recorded rate of increase in wild pig, based on the number of yearlings one year after parturition, is 64 percent in the Belovezhsk Reserve; the Ili River has a comparable rate of 60 percent (Heptner *et al.* 1966).

The reproductive rates of cervids and bovids are much lower. Cervids begin breeding in the second or third year, but multiple births are very rare in red deer. Twins are fairly common among both elk and roe deer, but since both species are monogamous the ratio of adult males to females is approximately equal, which reduces the potential rate of population increase. The incidence of twins varies in different populations, but usually represents 30-40 percent of births in both species (Tegner 1951; Egorov. 1967; Peterson 1955; Heptner *et al.* 1966). Roe, red deer and elk populations generally have an annual recruitment level of 12-20 percent (Bay-Petersen 1975).

Since pig have a very high rate of increase, correspondingly high predation levels are possible without altering the overall population balance. Dasmann and Mossman (1961) record a 50 percent annual exploitation rate for African wart-hog and bush pig with a similar reproductive pattern to the European wild pig. This high productivity must have compensated considerably for the two disadvantages of wild pig as a food species – their dispersed distribution and relatively small body size. We could expect the maximum viable long-term cull of the cervid species and aurochs to be appreciably lower.

Since animal densities, and the social behaviour of red deer and bovid, seem to vary considerably among different local populations of the same species, it is also relevant in assessing species productivity to consider Mesolithic Denmark as an ungulate habitat. The landscape of Denmark represents a fairly uniform environment, with flat to undulating sandy and glacial clay uplands, and in the glacial depressions closed drainage basins with consequent lake and swamp formation, in some cases of considerable extent. No point is higher than 150 metres. Within this environment Mesolithic inland sites in Denmark show a marked tendency to cluster around restricted resource zones, in particular the marshy water catchment areas of the glacial basins. The sites either lay on the marsh edge (like Holmegaard V) or else are found on small islets and peninsulas of higher ground surrounded by swamp and open water. Sites in the latter type of location include the largest Maglemosian habitation bases such as Svaerdborg 1, Holmegaard, Øgaarde, Maglelyng and Kongsted. Such clustering of settlement, despite the relative uniformity of soils, climate and topography, implies a repeated intensive exploitation of spatially limited areas and of the associated ungulate populations, presumably in response to a marked disparity in resource distribution within the context of the Mesolithic economy.

The most common tree species in Boreal pollen samples is pine, although during this period deciduous species were advancing from the south, with hazel a particularly common pioneer species. The Atlantic period is represented by a replacement of mixed pine by a climax deciduous forest, the most important species of which were lime, elm, and oak. The available radiocarbon dates seem to support the general assumption that pollen transition zones were approximately synchronous in Jutland and the present Danish islands, although there seem to be some differences between the postglacial vegetation of Mid-Jutland and the rest of the country. Pollen analyses from the former area seem to show a mixed oak-birch forest with a high grass and heather component reflecting a very open forest. Elsewhere the Atlantic forest seems to be fairly homogeneous on a broad regional basis, though with local variations depending on soil type and drainage. In particular, lime is likely to have been found on higher ground, with elm on rich soils and oak on poorer soils (Iversen 1960). Outside Mid-Jutland the pollen diagrams seem to indicate a heavy forest cover. Iversen (1941: 43) writes: 'The surprisingly low percentages of grass and herb pollen in Atlantic times ... show that before the Neolithic forest clearances the country was covered by a continuous primeval forest, with no openings other than swamps and moors.' As the same author has remarked, such an environment is unlikely to have provided a favourable habitat for ungulate populations. The five ungulate species exploited by man in the Danish Mesolithic all characteristically favour an open woodland in a state of succession or regeneration, with open glades and plentiful ground cover, rather than a dense climax forest with a closed leaf canopy. This is true even of those species such as elk which depend very little on grasses and forbs. It is notable that in western Siberia the elk attains its greatest population density in the southern belt of the taiga, where the tree cover is broken by a mosaic of clearings. Similarly in Canada it has been found that populations of elk reach their highest densities in the early stages of forest regeneration and decrease progressively as the forest becomes more mature (Peterson 1955). Since water plants are a favourite food in summer, elk also prefer areas near open water, and in particular lake shores with a rich aquatic flora. Studies of the feeding habits of red deer in Europe and North America show a decided preference for grasses as opposed to browse foods whenever these are available (Darling 1969; Jensen 1968; Stoddart and Smith 1943), and a corresponding preference for open ground or light forest cover. A study of the rumen content of 119 red deer in Jutland showed that shoots and leaves of deciduous trees were almost untouched throughout the year: grasses and forbs provided the most important food source, while conifer browse was only eaten extensively during the later part of the winter, when grasses and forbs were in short supply (Jensen 1968). Typically, leaves and shrubs are dominant in the diet of roe deer, but all authorities seem to agree that roe deer dislike dense forest, preferring open woodlands with frequent clearings and dense ground cover (Heptner *et al.* 1966; Egorov 1967; Tegner 1951; Prior 1968). Similarly wild pig appear to show a preference for forest fringes, while bovids are characteristically grazers rather than browsers.

It would seem that the narrow lacustrine zone between the forest edge and open water would have represented the optimum ungulate resource zone during the Danish Mesolithic . At least two of the important food species (red deer and aurochs) seem to prefer grasses and sedges to browse foods, and exploit the latter mainly at times of winter food shortage. The open lake-margin swamp vegetation would have provided the major grazing resource in the environment of that time. Not only red deer and aurochs would have been attracted to this zone. Water plants in the shallow lake edges were probably exploited intensively by elk, who show a decided preference for such foods, while pig and roe deer would find a favourable habitat, as they do today, on the woodland fringe.

Although the present extensive peat bogs in Denmark are the result of a long and continuous process of lake infill, pollen samples show that marsh vegetation was well developed even before the Boreal period. Layer 2 of the Vinkel Mose pollen diagram shows a thick Preboreal bull-rush (*Typha*) swamp on the lake margin, overlain by a reed swamp vegetation community in Layer 3, dated to the early Boreal: on top of this reed swamp was found an early Maglemosian arrow shaft, overlain by sphagnum bog (Troels-Smith 1961). Pollen samples from the Maglemosian site of Lundby and its vicinity indicate that the eastern shore of the lake was covered by a layer of reeds, and cultural layers at both Holmegaard and Svaerdborg were enclosed by a *Cladium-Phragmites* swamp vegetation.

The pollen analysis of Svaerdborg also showed, amidst the swamp-plant communities that in places maintained a meadow-like vegetation, small patches of alder (Jessen 1935). Danish pollen samples seem to indicate that sedges rather than woodland were the predominant swamp vegetation cover: this is supported by Jasnowski's (1972) study of fossil and sub-fossil peats in northern Poland, an area at the same latitude as Denmark, and geologically and environmentally very similar. 'Woodland bog associations ... occurred very seldom in the past ... the main trend in vegetation consists in the development of woods ... while in more extensively drained and eutrophized habitats – the development of meadow plant communities' (Jasnowski 1972: 152). In the environmental context of the Danish Mesolithic, open swamplands would have represented a highly favourable feeding zone for ungulate populations. Two of the most common species in Mesolithic swamp vegetation – *Cladium* and *Phragmites* – are used today in unimproved swamp grazing in both northern Europe (e.g. the coastal areas of Poland) and southern Europe (e.g. the Camargue), and constitute a highly productive grazing resource. Once the growing season has commenced, the vegetation in such swamplands is dense and lush: an experimental cropping of *Cladium* in a peat-bog in north-west Poland yielded on average 34.45 kg. per m^2 of above-ground growth (Rieley and Jasnowski 1972).

Peat marshes seem to have been highly regarded as a grazing resource in northern Europe during historic times, even at a stage when most arable (and potential pasture) land had been cleared of its original forest cover. In Great Britain there seems to have been a close link between the presence of marshland pastures and the existence of intensive animal husbandry. The Romney marshes and the fenland areas of Cambridgeshire, north-west Suffolk and Lincolnshire, were all major livestock centres, and although drainage has since allowed the conversion of much of the peatland areas to intensive arable farming, they still maintain high animal populations at the present day (Thirsk 1957; Young 1969; Thirsk and Imray 1958). The economic value of such marshlands is reflected in their high land prices. In 1334 the tax assessments per acre in the peat fens of Lincolnshire were the third highest in the kingdom, and such land was regarded as considerably more valuable than the fertile arable clays (Thirsk 1957). Similarly Darby (1940) records that in medieval times an acre of fen meadow was worth more than two acres of the best arable land, and that rents for meadowland were proportionally high.

The quality of such natural pastures is generally much inferior to that of sown and improved pasture, but the establishment of the artificial pastures which support most intensive animal husbandry today has developed only during the last 250 years. Before the eighteenth century natural grasses on wet pastures, either naturally flooded or artificially so by the construction of water meadows, seem to have been regarded as optimum grazing zones, noted both for their high carrying capacity and their fast rate of regeneration (cf. Fortrey 1685; Lamond 1890; Darby 1968).

If marshland pastures were of considerable economic value in an environment where a long-established agricultural economy had largely cleared the original woodland, they must surely have been even more important in the colonisation in historic times of dense virgin forest similar to that encountered by Mesolithic man in northern Europe. We must remember that before forest clearance such marshland zones were the only extensive natural pastures in northern Europe, and they seem to have played a major role in the agricultural colonisation of northern Scandinavia in the eighteenth century. Historical accounts of such colonisation in Scandinavia and Finland indicate that arable farming was not an important food resource in the early stages of settlement, but was dependent on the prior establishment of a successful economy based principally on fishing and animal husbandry, particularly of cattle (Campbell 1948). Although the species exploited in Mesolithic Denmark differ to some extent from those exploited by the early farmers to the north (particularly in the greater utilisation of cervids) the two economies do bear a basic resemblance, in that both were heavily dependent on ungulate resources within a northern European virgin forest habitat.

Campbell (1948) records that natural marshlands in northern Scandinavia were the primary cattle pastures, and were also used as hay meadows to provide winter feed. The presence of suitable natural pasture, and in particular marshland pasture, seems to have been a major requirement in the location of early settlements, and farmsteads were characteristically attracted to this zone.

That these marshlands served as a favoured grazing area for wild as well as domesticated ungulates in this area is reflected in the heavy utilisation by present day elk populations of abandoned *seter* pasture. Thus Ahlen writes (1975: 62-4) of the Lima-Alveden region of central Sweden: 'The most utilised natural vegetation was mire and other peat land on low levels ... The more productive the areas were as meadows or pastures, the more productive they are today as [elk] browsing habitats.' Since it appears that the northern European peat marshes were generally regarded as favoured grazing zones, the comparative productivity of which was particularly marked in a dense forest habitat with few alternative grazing resources, it would seem likely that they fulfilled a similar role in the animal-based economy of the Danish Mesolithic. As we have discussed earlier, exploitation of lacustrine resources such as water birds, fish and water plants can probably be viewed as a subsidiary economic activity, contributing little to the human economy and relatively much less productive than ungulate exploitation both in terms of their calorific contribution to the subsistence basis and of yield per unit area and per man-hour of effort.

In addition to the intrinsic productivity of the lacustrine marshes as an ungulate resource zone, the location of sites by lakes also offered the considerable economic advantage that boats could be used to gain access to farther lake shores, and facilitate the transport of game home to the site. The use of boats must have greatly increased both resource potential and exploitation efficiency. It is difficult to evaluate the economic importance of water transport compared to access to the optimum available ungulate resource zone as a factor in determining lacustrine site location: it seems likely that both were of prime importance in maintaining a successful exploitation system.

The use of boats would have extended the viable site territory considerably, but in a predominantly linear manner in that the narrow lacustrine zone would probably have been the main focus of animal exploitation. This is not to suggest that movement of either ungulates or humans was confined to lake edges, but whatever the exploitation system practised by Mesolithic man, it seems likely that it was within this area of the site territory that man-animal contact was most predictable and most frequent. Even in chance-encounter hunting, animal exploitation does not consist of random forays, but a systematic coverage of the most likely encounter points where animals could be expected to cluster periodically – especially in favoured feeding grounds (Bay-Petersen 1975). It seems likely therefore that a disproportionately large number of the kills were made within the spatially limited lacustrine zone. It is interesting that a recent study of site distribution in northern Sweden shows a marked clustering of elk pits in close proximity to water edges, indicating that a large proportion of elk kills took place on lacustrine and riverine shores (Anderson 1976).

If we accept that the lacustrine swamp zone was a major focus of animal exploitation and consequently of human settlement, then it would appear that a relatively limited area supported a recurrent intensive culling of local ungulate populations. Such exploitation may have been only seasonal, but the abundance of faunal and cultural remains in numerous lacustrine sites indicates that it was highly productive and frequently repeated: on ethnographic analogy it is likely that it represented a regular consecutive exploitation within a stable annual economic system. Under such circumstances it is likely that the incentive to conserve and yet make maximum effective long-term use of animal resources would be particularly marked. Such conservation, if it took place, would presumably be reflected in both prey selection and methods of exploitation; the actual level of the cull is impossible to determine from archaeological data, since we are unable to define either the original population density, or how many of the site faunal remains represent a separate annual kill.

Animal exploitation

It is generally assumed that a maximisation of herd productivity by use of a predetermined and controlled policy of prey selection is reflected in a particular type of cull, in which females are maintained as breeding units and young males are selected for slaughter. Since it is generally impossible to distinguish skeletal remains of male from female juveniles, in effect such a system is believed to be demonstrated by a high percentage of juveniles in the site fauna. On the other hand a heavy juvenile cull may reflect the differential vulnerability of young animals rather than conscious selection. In all ungulate species it is the first few months of life which carry the greatest risk of death from predation. Healthy adults, particularly of large ungulate species, are almost immune from the attacks of non-human predators. A study by Mech (1970) of wolf predation showed that in the winter study period 94 percent of the Isle Royale moose killed by wolves were either calves less than one year old or animals over 8 years old. (This must be related to the fact that approximately 80 percent of the same herd were aged from 1-7 years). Similar results have been found in the population structure of caribou, big-horn sheep and musk-oxen killed by wolf predation (Banfield 1954; Cowan 1947; Tener 1954). The same pattern of differential exploitation of more vulnerable individuals has also been observed in African carnivores (e.g. Schaller 1972).

While a high proportion of juveniles in a site may indicate selective killing of non-productive herd members, it may also indicate a primitive non-selective pattern where existing economic techniques were inadequate to exploit any but high-risk prey. Certainly an incidence of juveniles equivalent to, or lower than, their expected occurrence in a natural population implies a fairly sophisticated and efficient exploitation pattern encompassing those individuals with the strongest escape and defence mechanisms.

Prey selection does not necessarily imply the close long-term man-animal contact of the domesticate system. All predation is selective, in that it presses unequally on different segments of an animal population, but whereas non-human prey selection is largely governed by the differential vulnerability of prey, human technology and organisation allow a highly efficient form of predation potentially encompassing any age class of any ungulate species, and which may operate on different selective criteria. From ethnographic data it would appear that the pre-determined selection of individual ungulate prey is compatible with the exploitation of free-ranging animals. There is no ethnographic evidence of such hunting exploitation oriented towards juvenile males, but selection of individual animals was practised in the game drives of the American Indian. In the autumn hunt, fat individual buffalo (usually females) were preferentially killed. Bulls at this season were lean with poor quality meat as a result of the rut. Autumn was also the season when hides for winter clothing were essential, and the buffalo pelage was in good condition. Since bull hides were almost unworkable it was necessary to kill a sufficient quantity of cows (Roe 1970: 117-8, 860). The fact that the largest communal hunts took place in the autumn, when calves were no longer weak and dependent on their mothers, would tend to conserve animal populations, not necessarily consciously since the purpose of autumn hunts was to procure winter food. Conscious conservation is apparent in the practice of taking only a defined and limited number of necessary animals from the potential kill (Hassrick 1964). Also, although the calf foetus was regarded as a great delicacy by the Indian, not only was there no selective exploitation of pregnant females, but herds were guarded during parturition from human and animal predators (Roe 1970: 116-18). The caribou hunting of the Tungus shows a similar conservation of pregnant females and fawns (Jarman and Wilkinson 1972: 95).

Since selective killing of individuals is known to have been practised within the exploitation of free-ranging species, there is no technical reason why selective killing of this kind should not be orientated towards young males, although ethnographic evidence seems to show rather a general conservation of pregnant females and young. A possible explanation may be that the selective killing of males in free-ranging animal populations is not necessary, since the natural population structure of present-day wild polygamous ungulate species shows a high ratio of females to males as a result of high male mortality (see e.g. Darling 1969; Heptner *et al.* 1966; Bannikov 1967). (The heavier male mortality seems to be compensated in monogamous species such as elk by a preponderance of male calves at birth: e.g. Heptner *et al.* 1966.) It could perhaps be argued that the selective slaughter typical of 'domesticated' animal economies is simply an artificial replica of the natural death toll, made necessary by the partial or complete insulation of domesticates from natural mortality factors.

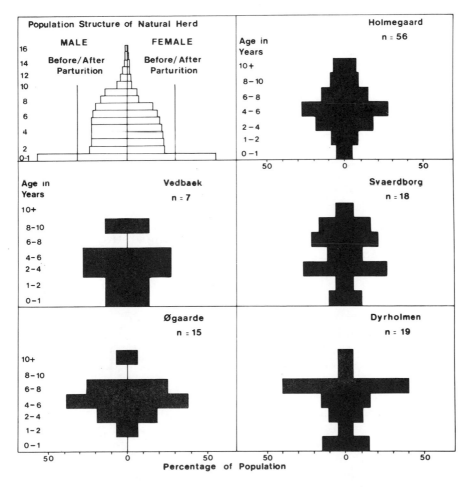

Figure 3. Age distribution of red deer mandibles in Danish Mesolithic sites. Data on the population structure of a modern red deer herd are taken from Lowe 1969.

In order to determine the pattern of prey selection in the Danish Mesolithic, the population structure of the most common food species – red deer – was established on the basis of dental age classes of faunal assemblages in a number of Boreal and Atlantic sites (cf. Fig. 3). The dental age classes of red deer are based on data in Lowe (1967). All classes in Lowe's sample later than the first year are from animals killed during the autumn and early winter. Since the animals were not of known age, it is difficult to estimate the extent to which progressive dental age classes represent annual age classes. Tooth wear rates seem to differ considerably among animals of the same species: sexual variation seems to be marked in at least some cervids, and there is also a pronounced variation among different local populations, depending on environment and diet. Flook's work on the wapiti (*Cervus canadensis*) of the Jasper and Banff National Parks (less than 200 km. apart) showed not only a marked difference in tooth wear between animals of the same age in the two areas, related to dietary differences, but also a marked sexual variation. On average male wapiti reached the 8-year wear pattern two to three years earlier than females. This is related to larger-than-average body size in males and a correspondingly higher food intake (Flook 1970). It is possible therefore that the animals in a particular dental age class at one site could be several years older or younger than the same dental age class at another site. This possibility becomes increasingly stronger with progressively older age classes.

When establishing age classes for the purpose of evaluating prehistoric faunal exploitation, however, these difficulties are of minor significance. It is *relative* rather than *absolute* age that is the main point of interest – in other words, whether animal exploitation was spread evenly over the whole population or whether it depended heavily on particular age sections while others were comparatively free from human predation.

In all ungulate populations individuals with extreme tooth wear are near the end of their lives, whatever their absolute age, and such tooth wear can be considered the terminal condition of a dental aging sequence. Although correlation with absolute age is only approximate, tooth wear classes offer a useful series of stages between birth and the terminal wear condition that can be accepted as descriptive of the actual kill population represented, especially if presented in terms of fairly broad age classes.

If the patterns of faunal exploitation in Mesolithic Denmark had taken a cull from each age class proportional to its representation in a natural population, one would expect to find a high proportion of young animals in the site fauna. A natural population structure is pyramidal, with a broad base of juvenile animals narrowing rapidly through successive age classes. The smallest age classes are composed of animals showing pronounced tooth wear and other indications of old age. Figure 3a presents diagrammatically a natural red deer population on the island of Rhum (from Lowe 1969), and it can be seen that male and female individuals in the 10-17 age classes account for a very small proportion when compared to the number born into the herd every year. Natural mortality is particularly high during the first year of life.

The Danish material shows that the population structure of red deer exploited by man during the Mesolithic differs considerably from that of a natural herd (Fig. 3). In particular, juveniles and young animals are markedly under-represented. At Dyrholmen, which shows the highest proportion of juvenile animals, only 16 percent of the red deer mandibles are from animals less than a year old, and in other sites juvenile representation is considerably lower than this. Holmegaard has the largest sample of 56 mandibles, only 5 percent of which are juvenile, while at Øgaarde no juveniles are present at all. The bulk of the animals exploited in all of the sites seem to be between 4 and 8 years of age, while animals over 8 years old (i.e. in late middle and old age) are considerably more common than in a natural herd. In all of the sites examined mandibles from red deer over 2 years of age comprise between 74 and 93 percent of the population: as Jarman (1972: 134) remarked with reference to Vlaardingen (where 65 percent of the red deer killed were over 3 years of age) 'this means that an unusually large percentage of the crop came from a relatively small percentage of the herd'.

The same type of population imbalance, in which juveniles are markedly under-represented, has been recorded in pre-Neolithic killing patterns elsewhere. In a comprehensive study of the population structure of reindeer from over 20 Palaeolithic sites in southern France, all with appreciable quantities of reindeer remains and showing a heavy economic dependence on this species, Bouchud (1966) found the percentage of juveniles to be between 2 percent and 13 percent in 32 out of the 34 individual assemblages analysed. In 28 of the occupation layers, juveniles in the first year of life were found to contribute less than 10 percent and in 9 layers less than 5 percent of the total reindeer population. The proportion of juveniles in a natural herd is much larger than this: Bouchud quotes an average figure of 19 percent based on varying percentages of juveniles in modern herds as recorded by several different authorities. Since rates of annual increase are directly related to the annual total of surviving juveniles, and since reindeer herd increase is usually between 10 percent and 30 percent per annum (on average approximately 20 percent, c.f. Parker 1972), Bouchud's figure presumably represents the percentage of juveniles immediately before parturition, when the annual juvenile mortality has already taken its toll. Immediately *after* parturition the percentage of juveniles must always be very much higher than this, since there is a high mortality in the first year of life, especially in the few weeks after parturition and during the following winter. Parker (1972) records an overall annual juvenile mortality among the

Kaminuriak reindeer herds of 78 percent: comparable figures from other areas seem somewhat lower, but are still substantial. Even if all reindeer exploitation in southern France had taken place immediately before parturition, the percentage of juveniles would still be surprisingly low. The inherent unlikelihood of such a pattern is supported by the seasonal evidence from reindeer antlers, which indicates that reindeer exploitation from different sites in fact covered all months of the year (Bouchud 1966; Bay-Petersen 1975).

Sturdy's analysis of reindeer remains from Stellmoor in northern Germany also showed a very low percentage of juveniles, with only 7 percent of a large faunal sample in the first year of life. Since the antler study also showed that the majority of kills were made in the autumn before the heavy winter juvenile death toll, it would seem that juveniles are markedly under-represented in this site compared to their probable frequency in the natural herd. It is also interesting that 69 percent of the antlers were from mature adults, predominantly of males in the fifth year and older (Sturdy 1972; 1975).

The great abundance of reindeer compared to other species at both Stellmoor and the French sites indicates that an intensive, highly specialised pattern of faunal exploitation was carried out from these sites. A similar pattern of intensive animal exploitation and a predominantly adult cull is recorded from the famous horse-bone horizon at Solutré, containing the remains of several thousand individual horses (Combier 1956; Arcelin and Ferry 1867). The published analyses of Solutré are based mainly on material excavated in the last century, and our interpretation of the site economy may be revised considerably in the light of the material from Combier's current excavations, but a strong indication of pre-determined prey selection which excluded juveniles is implied by Toussaint's statement that nearly all the teeth from this horizon belonged to horses between 5 and 7 years of age (Toussaint and Ducrost 1873).

It is not suggested that there is an invariable correlation between intensive hunting and an absence of juvenile prey. Remains of juveniles were common in the upper Mousterian layers of the Hortus cave in southern France, for example, in an abundant fauna consisting mainly of ibex (Pillard 1970). The very low occurrence of juvenile red deer in sites of the Danish Mesolithic, and the similar under-representation of juveniles at Solutré and the reindeer-intensive sites of south-west France is an interesting feature, however, since it is difficult to account for except by a selective avoidance of juveniles in faunal exploitation. Juveniles are invariably high-risk prey, and must inevitably have been vulnerable to any exploitation system that encompassed the low-risk adult. All present-day non-human predators, although they also press heavily on aged or diseased individuals, take a juvenile cull at least proportional to their occurrence in the natural herd; generally the proportion of juvenile prey is much higher than this (see pp. 131-2 above).

A similar exploitation emphasis on adult deer has been reported by Elder (1965) from five Indian sites in Missouri, three with prehistoric occupation and two dating from the historic period. In all five sites fawns were uncommon and accounted for 8 percent or less of the total sample. These figures are not directly comparable to the European evidence presented above, since in this case fawns were regarded as animals up to 6 months in age, whereas juveniles in Europe are usually presented as animals in the first year of life, but they provide an interesting contrast to the modern sporting cull in the same area in which nearly a third of the kill are fawns (Elder 1965). A further difference is that a large percentage (20-26 percent) of the deer in the prehistoric sample were $6\frac{1}{2}$ years old or more, whereas the percentage of deer of comparable age in the modern sporting kill is only 2 percent. The evidence would seem to suggest a strong negative correlation between the presence of fawns in the kill and the importance of deer as a staple food resource.

Since guns are always used in the modern cull, there is also an interesting correlation between technological efficiency in killing prey and the exploitation of high-risk individuals. Elder (1965: 369) remarks that '... most modern hunters shoot the first deer they see and hence get the numerous and vulnerable fawns in greatest proportion.' In an experimental cropping of the same deer species (*Odocoileus virginianus*) in a square mile enclosure over a period of seven years, Van Etten records that 'fawns appeared most vulnerable to hunting and adult bucks least vulnerable' (Van Etten *et al.* 1965).

It would seem therefore that in sites with a low incidence of juveniles some factor other than prey vulnerability determined which animals were taken as prey. This factor may have been related to the economic return per unit of energy expended. In a recent study of the hunting of buffalo, warthog, zebra and other species in the Central Luangwa Valley, Marks (1973) records that 88 percent of all kills were adults. The majority of these (60 percent) were males, and Marks states that adult males were consciously selected because they were larger in body size and provided a higher return for hunting efforts. On the other hand these animals were all killed by guns: they were also of secondary importance in a predominantly agricultural economy.

Certainly adult ungulates represent a much greater food resource per animal unit than that provided by juveniles (cf. Table 2). Adult red deer, elk, bovid and pig represent a meat weight some three or four times greater than that of a six-month-old juvenile. The meat yield of a herd is likely to be determined, therefore, not by the number of animals, but by the number of adults killed while maintaining a stable population.

A further factor is the need in a long-term exploitation system to ensure the adequate recruitment of juveniles into older age classes. All free-ranging ungulates have a high rate of juvenile mortality which is probably largely irreducible. Lowe (1967) has suggested that juvenile teeth are inherently less efficient at processing winter feed. For this reason severe winters are likely to take a high toll of juveniles, regardless of overall animal population densities.

The depth of winter snow cover and minimum winter temperatures were probably to some extent unpredictable factors in the Danish Mesolithic, as in southern France during the Würm glaciation and in Missouri. Under these circumstances it may have been of decided long-term advantage to take a very low juvenile cull, in order to maximise the survival of the year's calf crop. Otherwise a heavy summer cropping followed by a harsh winter might almost exterminate the whole age group. If bad winters were repeated for two or three years, this, combined with a heavy rate of juvenile predation, could almost eliminate the whole breeding stock from the area.

In areas where there is consistently and predictably no winter snow cover, selective killing of juveniles would probably represent an efficient economic mechanism, since the winter death toll would not be sufficiently severe to prevent the survival of an adequate number of juveniles. Similarly, an exploitation system where animals are provided with winter fodder, and possibly artificial shelter, would constitute a similar, though artificially produced, context where juvenile survival was sufficiently predictable and assured to permit an annual juvenile cull. Such factors probably account for the high proportion of juvenile red deer at the Italian (snow-free) site of Molino Casarotto, and the similarly high percentages of juveniles of various domesticated ungulates recorded from the majority of Neolithic and later sites (Jarman 1972). There is no evidence of any increase in winter food resources in the Danish Mesolithic by the use of artificial fodder, such as that suggested by the extremely high percentages of ivy pollen (from 40 percent to over 100 percent of the tree pollen) recorded in a number of Mesolithic sites in northern Europe (Simmons and Dimbleby 1974). Ivy percentages in the Mesolithic of Denmark are all fairly low, and can be accepted as representative of natural deposits from adjacent woodlands.

A further interesting feature of red deer exploitation in Mesolithic Denmark is that older animals appear to be more common than in a natural herd; this feature is also found in the prehistoric Missouri sites, while most of the adults killed at Stellmoor and Solutré appear to be several years past sexual maturity. This exploitation of older animals represents a further increase in efficiency, since by pressing down the demographic structure it would maintain the herd in a state of maximum productivity.

The selective avoidance of juvenile prey which seems to have characterised the red deer exploitation of Mesolithic Denmark does not apply to all species: juvenile pig for example are fairly common in Danish Mesolithic sites. They are the most common age class at Ertebølle, and are present in appreciable quantities at Vedbaek and

Svaerdborg (Bay-Petersen 1975). Similarly Andersen (1973-4) records that the majority of pig remains at Ringkloster derive from animals between 8-12 months and 17-24 months of age. This may be related simply to the much higher reproductive rate of pig, which results in a high proportion of juveniles to adults in a natural population, and also means that the killing of juveniles is unlikely to endanger recruitment levels. On the other hand it may also be related to differences in exploitation patterns. As we remarked earlier, since wild pig have a dispersed distribution, they are likely to be most efficiently exploited by small human groups equally dispersed to maximise the chances of man-animal contact. Red deer on the other hand are a social species, and when encountered are likely to be accompanied by a fairly large social group.

In a recent paper Geist (1971) has suggested that the fear of human beings generally displayed by present-day wild populations is a learned, not an innate, behavioural characteristic. The causative factor is behaviour interpreted by the animal as dangerous (particularly stalking and approach by stealth) which terminates in the animal's flight rather than its death. Since in social animals the disturbance influences all members of the social group, hunting by stealth has a particularly marked effect on gregarious species. Geist produces an impressive number of examples to illustrate that the rapid flight reaction displayed by hunted wild animals is a result of earlier human contact, which can be modified to produce a very different behavioural response. He writes: '... wild but unhunted populations of ungulates can be habituated to humans; tamed in their native habitats; ... and can be cropped without hunting ... They will be free to roam and continue their normal life, but will live with man as a constant part of their environment' (Geist 1971: 416). A large number of exploitation systems are practised at the present day in which wild species are killed without hunting, including some of the species exploited in the Danish Mesolithic. Red deer ranches have been established in Scotland, and elk – which are usually considered to be extremely wary of human beings – are subject to controlled slaughter in the Pechoro-Ilych Reserve in the U.S.S.R. The elk are free-ranging, with unrestricted grazing in the taiga, and are not attended by herdsmen. They are periodically rounded up and held in temporary corrals for calving and selective slaughtering (Yazan and Knorre 1964).

Outside Europe a considerable number of 'wild' species have been incorporated into a 'domesticated' economy. Free-ranging musk-oxen can be handled and tamed a few days after birth, and remain tolerant of human beings with only an occasional contact at calving and for wool collection (Wilkinson 1972a, 1972b). In Africa, species such as eland, kob and oryx are successfully exploited on ranches, and are in fact estimated to give a much higher meat yield per unit area than domesticated cattle (Kyle 1972).

This is not to suggest that all ungulates before the Neolithic were exploited in a ranching system, but it does seem significant that there appears to be no innate behavioural difference in wild as opposed to domesticated ungulates which determines the pattern of animal response to human contact. We must remember that in any ranching system, man-animal contact is usually minimal (sometimes as little as once a year). Animals are free-ranging within very large spatial units, and seldom encounter man (e.g. Grigg 1974). Within this system animals can be rounded up and driven, selectively culled and branded. That the ranching system is possible at all is dependent on the fact that this type of contact does not evoke the flight reaction in the exploited species.

Conclusion

The exploitation system of Mesolithic man in Denmark is not comparable with modern hunting, since encounter hunting with guns inevitably disturbs animal populations considerably. Nor is it likely to resemble the animal exploitation of hunter-gatherer groups in marginal areas where ungulate distribution is sparse and unpredictable and the economy is dependent on vegetable foods. The closest parallels are likely to be found in the historic records of meat-dependent hunters such as the American Indian, and in such economies there seems to have been frequent use of the game drive, often utilising the artificial corral, implying a potentially high level of control over the movement of free-ranging ungulates. There are in fact marked similarities between the buffalo exploitation of the North American Indian and the subsequent extensive cattle ranching in the same area (Bay-Petersen 1975). The location of Mesolithic sites in Denmark would appear to indicate that animal exploitation was concentrated mainly within a relatively limited area, involving the repeated, intensive exploitation of the some local ungulate populations. Since the economy seems to have been heavily dependent on ungulates as a primary food resource, it could operate successfully only insofar as the ungulate species tolerated coexistence with man as a predator within the site territory. Under such circumstances there would be a strong selective pressure towards adopting exploitation methods which minimised animal disturbance. This would be particularly important with regard to social species, since hunting by stealth or by any other method which evokes the flight reaction reduces considerably the chance of successfully exploiting surviving members of the social group.

The population structure of red deer in sites of the Danish Mesolithic seems to indicate that there was a marked tendency to avoid the juvenile prey inherently most vulnerable to predation. This feature is found in a number of other prehistoric hunting economies, all based on the exploitation of social ungulate species, and can probably be related to the much higher meat yield of adult animals, and the desirability of maximising annual recruitment levels by conserving juvenile ungulates.

All predation is selective, but a predation system which exploited predominantly adult prey is likely to reflect a highly effective exploitation pattern in that it focuses on that segment of the population with the strongest escape and defence mechanisms, and is sufficiently productive to conserve the most vulnerable and accessible prey. Since in the context of a primitive hunting technology the selected animals were probably killed at close range, it also implies that animals may have tolerated human contact to a much greater degree than present-day hunted populations of 'wild' animals.

This is not to suggest that exploitation was continuous throughout the year. On present evidence it would seem that coastal and inland areas were exploited as complementary resource zones (Bay-Petersen 1975, Bailey 1975). In view of the uniform environment of Denmark there is no reason to suspect a parallel movement of animal populations; animal and human annual territories were probably not coincidental. An imposed transference of herds would not only have been difficult, it would probably have reduced the meat yield per unit area in that the same animal populations would have occupied successive site territories. If domestication involves continuous contact between a proprietary human group and a separate identifiable animal population, there seems no reason to suggest any hypothetical domestication of red deer in Mesolithic Denmark.

On the other hand animal exploitation during this period may have resulted in some modification of ungulate behaviour, of a kind not typical of present-day hunted populations. Hunters dependent on free-ranging ungulates, and therefore necessarily in close association with them, could be expected to have a very wide knowledge of animal response to human exploitation, and it seems likely that their system of hunting took advantage of the flexibility of ungulate behaviour. In short, the response of wild ungulates to human contact is determined largely by the manner, rather than the fact, of their exploitation.

References

Ahlen, I. 1975. Winter habitats of moose and deer in relation to land use in Scandinavia. *Viltrevy Swedish Wildlife*, 9, No. 3: 45-192.

Andersen, S.H. 1973-4. Ringkloster: en jysk inlandsboplads med Ertebøllekultur. *Kuml*: 10-108.

Andersen, S.H. and Malmros, C. 1965. Norslund: en Kystboplads fra aeldre Stenalder. *Kuml*: 35-114.

Anderson, A. 1976. *Prehistoric Competition and Economic Change in Northern Sweden*. Unpublished Ph.D. thesis, University of Cambridge.

Anell, B. 1969. Running down and driving of game in North America. *Studia Ethnographica Upsaliensia* XXX: 1-129.

Arcelin, A. and Ferry, H. 1867. L'Age du renne en Mâconnais; Mémoire sur la station du Clot du Charnier à Solutré. *Annales de l'Académie de Mâcon.*

Bailey, G. 1975. *The Role of Shell Middens in Prehistoric Economies.* Unpublished Ph.D. thesis, University of Cambrige.

Banfield, A.W. 1954. Preliminary investigation of the barrenground caribou, Parts 1 and 2. *Wildlife Management Bulletin.* Series 1, No. 10 (A and B). Dept. Nat. Resources and Northern Development, Ottawa.

Bannikov, A.G. (ed.) 1967. *Biology of the Saiga.* Israel Program for Scientific Translations, Jerusalem.

Bay-Petersen, J. 1975. *Pre-Neolithic Faunal Exploitation in Southern France and Denmark.* Unpublished Ph.D. thesis, University of Cambridge.

Bouchud, J. 1966. *Essai sur le Renne et la Climatologie du Paléolithique Moyen et Supérieur.* Périgueux, Imprimerie Magne.

Brinch Petersen, E. 1970. Ølby Lyng: en ostsjaellandsk Kystboplads med Ertebøllekultur. *Aarbøger for Nordisk Oldkyndighed og Historie*: 5-42.

Broholm, H.C. 1926-31. Nouvelles trouvailles du plus ancien âge de la pierre: les trouvailles de Holmegaard et de Svaerdborg. *Mémoires de la Société des Antiquitaires du Nord*: 1-128. Copenhagen.

Burton, M. 1962. *Systematic Dictionary of Mammals of the World*, London, Museum Press.

Campbell, A. 1948. *Fra Vildmark till Bygd: en Etnologisk Undersokning av Nybyggari Kulturen i Lappland.* Copenhagen.

Clark, J.G.D. 1975. *The Earlier Stone Age Settlement of Scandinavia.* London, Cambridge University Press.

Clarke, C.H.D. 1942. The Indian as conservationist. *The Canadian Field-Naturalist*, 56: 127-8.

Combier, J. 1956. *Solutré: Les fouilles de 1907 à 1925.* Mâcon.

Cowan, I.M. 1947. The Timber Wolf in the Rocky mountains national parks of Canada. *Canadian Journal of Research*, 25: 139-74.

Darby, H.C. 1940. *The Mediaeval Fenland.* London, Cambridge University Press.

Darby, H.C. 1968. *The Draining of the Fens.* (2nd ed.). London, Cambridge University Press.

Darling, F.F. 1969. *A Herd of Red Deer: A Study in Animal Behaviour.* London, Oxford University Press.

Dasmann, R.F. and Mossman, A.S. 1961. *Commercial Use of Game Animals on a Rhodesian Ranch.* (Mimeographed circular)

Degerbøl, M. 1943. Dyreliveti Aamosen i Stenalderen. In Mathiassen, T. *Stenalderbopladser i Aamosen*, Nordiske Fortidsminder III, 3.

Driver, H.E. 1961. *Indians of North America.* Toronto, University Press.

Ducos, P. 1968. *L'Origine des Animaux Domestiques en Palestine.* Publications de l'Institut de Préhistoire de l'Université de Bordeaux.

Egorov, O.V. 1967. *Wild Ungulates of Yakutia.* Israel Program for Scientific Translations, Jerusalem.

Elder, W.H. 1965. Primeval deer hunting revealed by remains from American Indian middens. *Journal of Wildlife Management*, 29: 366-9.

Flook, D.R. 1970. A study of sex differential in the survival of wapiti. *Canadian Wildlife Service Report.* Series No. 11.

Forde, C.D. 1934. *Habitat, Economy and Society.* London, Methuen.

Fortrey, S. 1685. *Bedford Level. The History or Narrative of the Great Level of the Fenns, called Bedford Level.* London, Moses Pitt.

Friis-Johansen, K. 1919. Une station du plus ancien Âge de la Pierre dans la Tourbière de Svaerdborg. *Mémoires de la Société des Antiquaires du Nord*: 241-359.

Geist, V. 1971. Management of wild ungulates. In E. Duffey and A.S. Watts (eds.) *The Scientific Management of Animal and Plant Communities for Conservation.* Oxford, Blackwell Scientific Publications.

Grigg, D.B. 1974. *The Agricultural Systems of the World: An Evolutionary Approach.*

London, Cambridge University Press.

Gubser, N.J. 1965. *The Nunamiut Eskimos: Hunters of Caribou.* New Haven, Yale University Press.

Hassrick, R.B. 1964. *The Sioux: Life and Customs of a Warrior Society.* Norman, University of Oklahoma Press.

Heptner, V.G., Nasimovic, A.A. and Bannikov, A.G. 1966. *Die Säugetiere der Sowjetunien.* Jena.

Higgs, E.S. and Jarman, M.R. 1972. The origins of plant and animal husbandry. In E.S. Higgs (ed.), *Papers in Economic Prehistory.* London, Cambridge University Press: 3-14.

Iversen, J. 1941. Landnam i Danmarks stenalder. *Danmarks Geologiske Undersøgelse*, II Rk., No.66: 7-68.

Iversen, J. 1960. Problems of the early postglacial forest development in Denmark. *Danmarks Geologiske Undersøgelse*, IV Rk., No.3: 1-32.

Jarman, M.R. 1972. European deer economies and the advent of the Neolithic. In E.S. Higgs (ed.) *Papers in Economic Prehistory.* London, Cambridge University Press: 125-48.

Jarman, M.R. and Wilkinson, P.F. 1972. Criteria of animal domestication. In E.S. Higgs (ed.) *Papers in Economic Prehistory.* London, Cambridge University Press: 83-96.

Jasnowski, M. 1972. Threat to peatlands and their protection in Poland. *Proceedings of the 4th International Peat Congress.* Otaniemi, Finland: 149-58.

Jensen, P. 1968. Food selection of the Danish Red Deer (*Cervus elephas* L.) as determined by examination of the rumen content. *Danish Review of Game Biology*, 5, No.3: 3-44.

Jessen, K. 1935. The composition of the forests in northern Europe in epipaleolithic times. *Det Kongelige Danske Videnskabesnes Selskab. Biologiske Meddelelser* XII: 1.

Kyle, R. 1972. Will the antelope recapture Africa? *New Scientist* 53, (23 March): 640-3.

Lamond, E. (ed.) 1890. *Walter de Henley, fl 1250. Husbandry: together with an anonymous husbandry, seneschaucie and Robert Grosseteste's rules.* London, Longman's, Green and Co.

Lawrence, R. 1971. Habitat and economy: a historical perspective. In D.J. Mulvaney and J. Golson (eds.), *Aboriginal Man and Environment in Australia.* Canberra, Australian National University: 249-61.

Lawton, J.H. 1973. The energy cost of food-gathering. In B.B. Cox and J. Peel, (ed.) *Resources and Population.* Proceedings of the Ninth Annual Symposium of the Eugenics Society, London.

Lee, R.B. 1968. What hunters do for a living, or how to make out on scarce resources. In R.B. Lee and I. De Vore (eds.), *Man the Hunter.* Chicago, Aldine: 30-48.

Lee, R.B. and De Vore, I. (eds.) 1968. *Man the Hunter.* Chicago, Aldine.

Lowe, V.P.W. 1967. Teeth as indicators of age with special reference to red deer (*Cervus elaphus*) of known age from Rhum. *Journal of Zoology*, 152: 137-53.

Lowe, V.P.W. 1969. Population dynamics of the red deer (*Cervus elaphus* L.) on Rhum. *Journal of Animal Ecology*, 38: 425-56.

Madsen, A.P., Muller, S., Neergaard, C., Petersen, C., Rostrup, E., Steenstrup, K.J.V., and Winge, H. 1900. *Affaldsdynger fra Stenalderen i Danmark.* Copenhagen.

Marks, S.A. 1973. Prey selection and annual harvest of game in a rural Zambian community. *East African Wildlife Journal*, 11: 113-28.

Mathiassen, T. 1943. Stenalderbopladser i Aamosen. *Nordiske Fortidsminder* III, 3.

Mathiassen, T., Degerbøl, M., and Troels-Smith, J. 1942. *Dryholmen: en stenalderboplads paa Djursland.* Det Kongelige Danske Videnskabesnes Selskab, Copenhagen.

Mech, L.D. 1970. *The Wolf. The Ecology and Behaviour of an Endangered Species.* New York, Natural History Press.

Møhl, U. 1970. Oversigt over dyreknoglerne fra Ølby Lyng: en Østjaellansk kystboplads med Erteb∮llekultur. *Aarb∮ger for Nordisk Oldkyndighed og Historie*: 43-77.

Muus, B.J. and Dahlstrom, P. 1967. *Freshwater Fishes of Britain and Europe*. London, Collins.

Oloff, H.B. 1951. *Zur Biologie und Ökologie des Wildschweines. Beiträge zur Tierkunde und Tierzucht*, 2. Frankfurt-am-Main.

Parker, G.R. 1972. *Biology of the Kaminuriak Population of Barrenground Caribou*. Canadian Wildlife Science Report. Series no.20. Part 1.

Petersen, C.G.J., Winge, H., and Winge, J. 1888. Dyrelevninger fra aeldre og yngre Stenalders Bopladser. *Aarb∮ger for Nordisk Oldkyndighed og Historie*: 310-22.

Peterson, R.L. 1955. *North American Moose*. Toronto.

Pillard, B. 1970. *La Faune de Grands Mammifères de la Grotte Moustérienne de l'Hortus (Valflaunès, Hérault): Interpretations paléontologiques et palethnographiques*. Thesis presented to Faculty of Sciences, University of Paris. Marseille, Imprimerie Leconte.

Prior, R. 1968. *The Roe Deer of Cranbourne Chase*. London, Oxford University Press.

Rieley, J.O. and Jasnowski, M. 1972. Productivity and nutrient turnover in mire ecosystems: 1. Comparison of two methods of estimating the biomass and nutrient content of *Cladium mariscus (L) Pohl. Oecologia Plantarum*, 7, No.4: 403-8.

Roe, F.G. 1970. *The North American Buffalo: A Critical Study of the Species in its Wild State* (2nd ed.). Toronto, University Press.

Sarauw, G.F.L. 1903. En stenalderboplads i Maglemose ved Mullerup: Sammenholdt med beslaegtede Fund. *Aarb∮ger for Nordisk Oldkyndighed og Historie*: 148-315.

Schaller, G.B. 1972. *The Serengeti Lion*. Chicago, University Press.

Simons, I.G. and Dimbleby, G.W. 1974. The possible role of Ivy (*Hedera helix* L) in the Mesolithic economy of Western Europe. *Journal of Archaeological Science*, 1, No.3: 291-6.

Stoddart, I.A. and Smith, A.D. 1943. *Range Management*. New York, McGraw-Hill.

Sturdy, D.A. 1972. *Reindeer Economies in Late Ice Age Europe*. Ph.D. thesis, University of Cambridge.

Sturdy, D.A. 1975. Some reindeer economies in prehistoric Europe. In E.S. Higgs (ed.), *Palaeoeconomy*, London, Cambridge University Press: 55-96.

Tegner, H.S. 1951. *The Roe Deer, Their History, Habits and Pursuit*. London, Batchworth Press.

Tener, J.S. 1954. A preliminary study of the musk-oxen of Fosheim Peninsula, Ellesmere Island. *Northwest Territories Canadian Wildlife Service, Wildlife Management Bulletin*, Series 1, No.9: 1-34.

Thirsk, J. 1957. *English Peasant Farming: The Agrarian History of Lincolnshire from Tudor to Recent times*. London, Routledge and Kegan Paul.

Thirsk, J. and Imray, J. 1958. Suffolk farming in the nineteenth century. *Suffolk Records Society*, Vol. 1.

Thomsen, T. and Jessen, A. 1906. Braband-fyndet fra den aeldre Stenalder. *Aarb∮ger for Nordisk Oldkyndighed og Historie*: 1-75.

Toussaint, H. and Ducrost, Abbé. 1873. Le cheval dans la station préhistorique de Solutré. *Compte Rendu de l'Association Française pour l'Avancement des Sciences* (Lyon): 586-600.

Troels-Smith, J. 1961. Et Pileskaft fra Tidlig Maglemosetid. *Aarb∮ger*: 122-46.

Van Etten, C., Switzenberg, D.F. and Eberhardt, L. 1965. Controlled deer hunting in a square-mile enclosure. *Journal of Wildlife Management*, 29, No.1: 59-73.

Vorren, O. and Manker, E. 1962. *Lapp Life and Customs: A Survey*. London, Oxford University Press.

Westerby, E. 1927. *Stenalderbopladser ved Klampenborg: Nogle Bidrag til studiet af den Mesolitiske Periode*. Copenhagen, H.H. Thieles Bogtrykken.

Wilkinson, P.F. 1972a. *The Relevance of Musk Ox Exploitation to the Study of Prehistoric Animal Economies*. Unpublished Ph.D. thesis, University of Cambridge.

Wilkinson, P.F. 1972b. Current experimental domestication and its relevance to prehistory. In E.S. Higgs (ed.), *Papers in Economic Prehistory*, London, Cambridge University Press: 107-18.

Wilkinson, P.F. 1975. The relevance of musk ox exploitation to the study of prehistoric animal economies. In E.S. Higgs (ed.), *Palaeoeconomy*, London, Cambridge University Press: 9-53.

Woodburn, J. 1968. An introduction to Hadza ecology. In R.B. Lee and I. De Vore (eds.), *Man the Hunter*. Chicago, Aldine: 49-55.

Yazan, Y. and Knorre, Y. 1964. Domesticating elk in a Russian national park. *Oryx*, 7: 301-4.

Young, A. 1969. *A General View of the Agriculture of the County of Norfolk*. Newton Abbot (Devon), David and Charles.

8

Mesolithic economy and settlement patterns in Norway

Svein Indrelid

Introductory remarks on the Mesolithic

Traditionally, the Mesolithic of Norway has been divided into three broad cultural units, of which the Fosna and Nøstvet cultures represent a chronological sequence in the southern parts of Norway, while the Komsa culture encompasses the entire Mesolithic period in the northernmost parts of the country.

The distribution of Komsa sites is concentrated along a 400-km. stretch of the coastline in the extreme northerly areas of Norway in the Finnmark province (Fig. 1). The Komsa culture was originally described as a pre-slate lithic industry of macrolithic character, in which discoidal cores, various types of core tools, flake axes, burins and tanged points were the most frequent artefact types. There is also a strong element of smaller artefacts, particularly projectile points, although true microliths are absent (Nummedal 1927, 1929b; Bøe and Nummedal 1936). A variety of local rocks, especially quartz, quartzites, dolomite flint and chert, were employed as raw materials (Fig. 2). The age of the Komsa culture has generally been estimated to cover the range from around 7,000/8,000 to 2,500 bc, but at present no reliable radiocarbon determinations are available to test this dating. Similarly, attempts to identify chronological subdivisions within the Komsa industries (Bjørn 1928, 1929; Odner 1966: 105-7) have been disputed (Bøe and Nummedal 1936: 197-211; Gjessing 1945: 62; E. Helskog 1974: 263-4).

Komsa sites are located either on the coast or along the margins of fjords, and are usually situated between present-day sea level and the maximum of the *Tapes* marine transgression. Owing to this strongly coastal distribution it has generally been assumed that the economy of the Komsa people was oriented predominantly towards the exploitation of the arctic marine fauna. Despite the lack of faunal evidence from Komsa sites, an economy based largely on fishing and whale and seal hunting has therefore been suggested, although the possibility of additional reindeer and moose hunting has also been

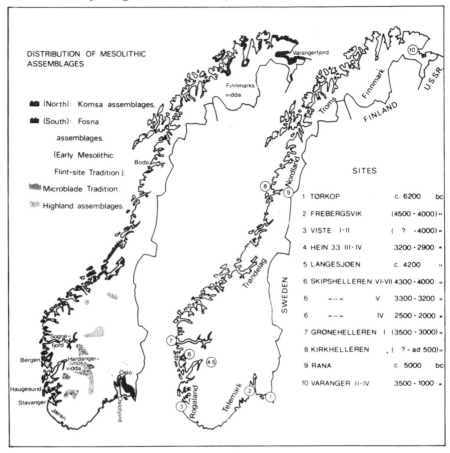

Figure 1. Map to show the distribution of Mesolithic assemblages in Norway (*left*) and the location of sites discussed in the text (*right*).

discussed (Bøe and Nummedal 1936: 251-5; Gjessing 1945: 72-5; Odner 1964: 121-6). Recent surveys in the interior areas of Finnmark, however, have revealed that Mesolithic sites are by no means confined to the coast, and it may well be that further investigations in these areas will change considerably our understanding of both the spatial distribution and the subsistence-settlement systems of the Komsa culture (E. Helskog 1974: 262-3).

Sites belonging to the Fosna culture are found in two main areas in the more southerly parts of Norway: firstly along a 1,000-km. stretch of the western coastline from the Bodø district to the vicinity of Haugesund; and secondly in a relatively localised area to the east of the Oslofjord in south-eastern Norway (Fig. 1). The lack of sites in the intervening 500 km. has been attributed to a submergence of the coastline due to the eustatic rise in sea level, but for obvious reasons this explanation is difficult to test (Nummedal 1933: 239-44).

Unlike those of the Komsa culture, assemblages belonging to the

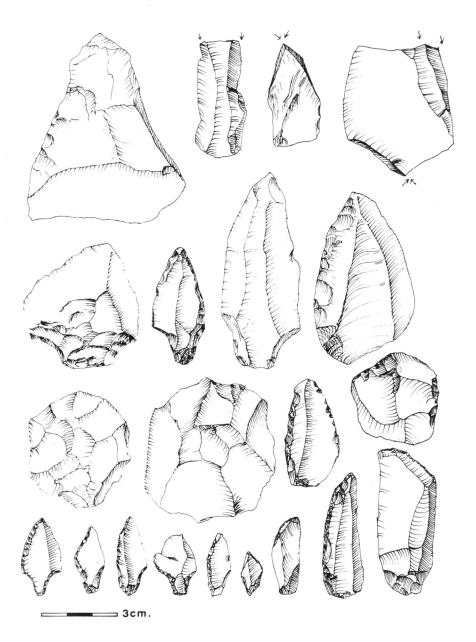

Figure 2. Quartz and quartzite artefacts from Komsa assemblages.

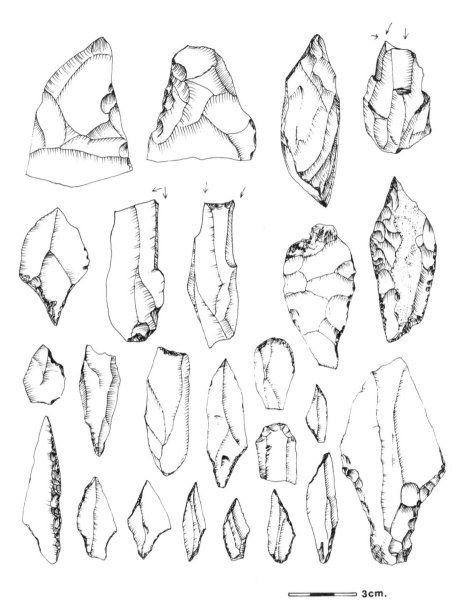

Figure 3. Flint artefacts from Fosna assemblages (= 'Early Mesolithic Macro-Tradition').

Fosna culture are characterised by the extensive use of flint (Rygh 1911, 1912; Shetelig 1922; Nummedal 1924, 1929a; Bjørn 1929; Gjessing 1945). Once again the industry comprises mostly macrolithic forms, with an abundance of core tools, coarse blades, burins and scrapers. Flake axes are more frequent than core axes. Projectile points are characteristic, especially small tanged points and single barbed forms (Fig. 3). Lanceolate microliths occur on some sites, but a true microlithic technique is effectively confined to the Fosna sites in eastern Norway and is virtually absent from sites along the western coast (Gjessing 1945: 46; Indrelid 1975: 8-9; Mikkelsen 1975b: 27).

No faunal remains have so far been recovered from Fosna sites, but the general distribution of the sites would appear to indicate a strongly maritime adaptation. Most authors have regarded the Fosna culture as descending from the late-glacial reindeer-hunting cultures of north Germany and the adjacent areas of the north European plain (Gjessing 1945: 48-52; Hagen 1963: 139-42; Indrelid 1975: 9-15). This supposition is based partly on the 'archaic' typological character of the assemblages (especially on the distinctive forms of the projectile points) and partly on the fact that reindeer is known to have inhabited the west coast of Norway during both the late-glacial period and the earlier stages of the postglacial. No radiocarbon dates have so far been published from Fosna sites, but there are grounds for thinking that the whole of this culture must be assigned to the period prior to 6,000 bc (Indrelid 1975: 8).

The Nøstvet culture (Hansen 1904; Brøgger 1905; Shetelig 1922; Gjessing 1945; Mikkelsen 1975b) is essentially a microlithic industry characterised by micro-blades and small, cone-shaped cores. Although true microliths occur on Nøstvet sites they are by no means common. Most of the assemblages include small blade borers and scrapers, while projectile points, burins, flake axes and core axes of flint are less common.

Originally the 'Nøstvet axe', a roughly chipped core axe or hoe made of greenstone, diabase, or other finely grained volcanic or contact-metamorphic rocks, was regarded as the sole diagnostic artefact of the Nøstvet culture (Fig. 4) (Hansen 1904: 127; Brøgger 1905: 64). At some sites, however, pecked and edge-ground round-butted axes made of the same rock types are also found. Indeed, in western Norway the chipped and polished greenstone axe is far more common than the Nøstvet axe.

Sites with Nøstvet elements have been reported as far north as Nordland province (Gjessing 1943: 135; 1945: 92-5) and occur along the whole coast of southern Norway, and to some extent also along the lower reaches of the east Norwegian rivers. The most characteristic sites are located along the course of former shore lines from Telemark province to the Swedish border, where similar archaeological assemblages are generally attributed to the 'Lihult culture'. Most of the Nøstvet sites are surface sites, in which faunal remains are usually

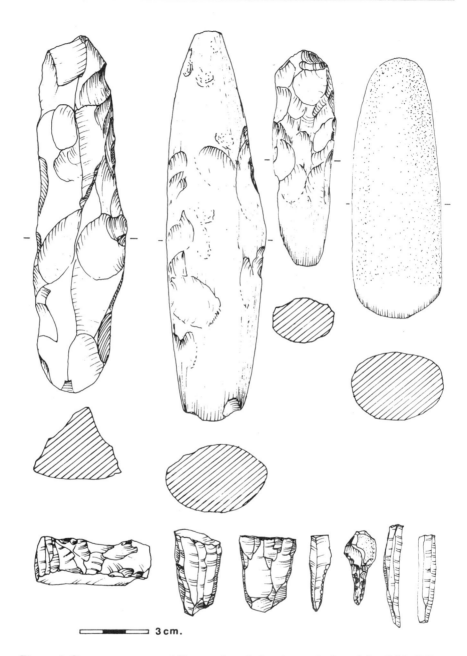

3 cm.

Figure 4. Greenstone axes and flint artefacts belonging to the later Mesolithic 'Micro-
blade Tradition'.

totally lacking. Substantial assemblages of faunal remains have however been found in association with Nøstvet artefacts in the lower levels of a number of rock-shelter sites along the west coast (Bøe 1934; Degerbøl 1951; Lund 1951) and these remains provide valuable information on the economy of the coastal-living groups in these areas during the later stages of the Mesolithic.

The lack of clear definitions and the strong emphasis placed on one single artefact type (the Nøstvet axe) has led to considerable confusion regarding the character and the dating of the Nøstvet culture. Recently a dating of 5,400-4,300 bc has been proposed for the most characteristic assemblages from the south-eastern sites. However, if we take into account all of the later Mesolithic industries in this area (i.e. all of those which cannot be attributed to the Fosna grouping) it is clear that this time range should be extended to the region of 6,300-3,000 bc (Mikkelsen 1975b: 31).

If we turn now to the Mesolithic sites in the highland areas of Norway, recent investigations have shown that the cultural sequences established on the basis of lowland material have little meaning when applied to these upland regions. Diagnostic artefact types such as axes, burins and microliths are almost totally absent from the highland sites, and the most frequent types in the latter areas are less distinctive forms such as points and scrapers. There are nevertheless certain general points of similarity between the material from the upland and lowland sites. On typological grounds it has been possible to distinguish between a 'northern' and 'southern' Mesolithic tradition in the south Norwegian highlands, and to show that the affinities of these groupings lie respectively with the Fosna and the Nøstvet cultures of the coastal zone (Indrelid 1975: 4-6).

When viewed as a whole, however, the material from the highland areas of Norway demonstrates clearly the inadequacy of the traditional cultural concepts within the Norwegian Mesolithic. On the one hand the existing cultural groupings are too vaguely defined. On the other hand it is becoming clear that many of the diagnostic implement types of these cultures are associated with specialised economic activities and therefore have little bearing on the definition of discrete 'cultural' groupings in the conventional archaeological sense. Moreover, the spatial distribution of these forms is so limited that a large proportion of the recorded Mesolithic material cannot be accommodated within any of the existing cultural divisions.

In response to these problems there has been a tendency in recent Norwegian archaeological research to replace the traditional Mesolithic cultures by more operational concepts which place more emphasis on the *technological* aspects of the lithic assemblages than on the presence or absence of specific artefact types. In this way it is hoped to recognise certain basic divisions within the archaeological material which are much less sensitive to the effects of 'activity specialisation' on the composition of the artefact assemblages

(Indrelid, in press). Some suggestions as to how these divisions might be organised will be presented in the final section of this paper.

Data on Mesolithic economy

The major problem in attempting to reconstruct economic patterns in the Norwegian Mesolithic is posed by the scarcity of faunal material from sites of this period. Owing to generally unfavourable geological conditions for the preservation of bone, only a small number of Mesolithic sites in Norway have yielded substantial samples of faunal remains, and of these only the finds from the Viste Cave near Stavanger have been fully published (Degerbøl 1951). It is anticipated that the rich faunal remains from the rock shelter of Skipshelleren, east of Bergen (Bøe 1943), will be published in the fairly near future.

Very few of the numerous Mesolithic open-air sites in Norway have produced any traces of animal bones. Small collections of faunal material have been recovered from a number of sites in the Oslofjord district (Sørensen 1974: 16; Mikkelsen 1975a: 129-31) and on the Hardangervidda highland plateau (Indrelid 1973b: 84-6), but most of these remains are inadequate for any detailed quantitative analysis.

Another potential source of information on Mesolithic economy is provided by rock carvings and paintings of the 'Arctic' type (Fig. 5). These representations have a fairly wide geographical distribution in Norway, although none have so far been located in either the eastern part of the Finnmark province or in the highland areas of the interior. Unfortunately, the potential information which can be derived from these sources is limited by two factors. First, the age of the carvings is very difficult to establish. However, most if not all of the carvings are generally assumed to belong to the Stone Age, and recent discoveries have suggested that at least some of these representations can be attributed to the Mesolithic period (Bakka 1975: 17-18, 39-40). Secondly, although animal motifs form the dominant element in the art, it is clear that these motifs reflect only a selection of the animals actually exploited – and in some cases perhaps not even the most important. As examples of this it may be noted that although bones of seal are particularly common (and sometimes dominant) in the faunal assemblages from Stone Age sites, representations of these animals are so far known from only a small number of localities. Similarly, remains of wild boar (*Sus scrofa ferus*) are well represented in faunal collections from Mesolithic settlements but this species has not so far been recorded among any of the carvings from Norwegian sites.

A third possible source of information is provided by accidental discoveries of sub-fossil animal bones. The main problem posed by these discoveries stems in many cases from the inaccuracies and uncertainties surrounding the dating of the remains. Discoveries of this kind can however be of considerable value in helping to establish

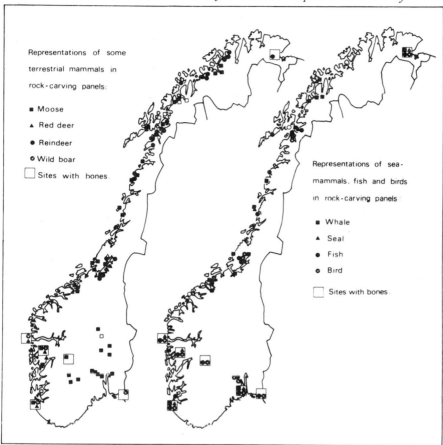

Figure 5. Representations of terrestrial mammals (*left*) and sea mammals, fish and
birds (*right*) in rock carvings of the 'Arctic' type. Open symbols indicate dubious
identifications. Large squares (enclosing symbols) indicate sites with bones
belonging to species represented in the rock carvings. Distribution of rock carvings
after Hagen 1976.

how far the earlier geographical distributions of particular species
may have differed from that of the present-day populations of the
same animals.

If we combine the three lines of evidence discussed above the main
point which emerges is that, with the notable exception of the wild
boar, the general distribution of the major species of land mammals
during the Mesolithic period appears to have been broadly similar to
that of the modern populations – or at least up to the nineteenth
century. This means that we can to some extent base models of
Mesolithic subsistence patterns on the distributions of species as
documented in historical times. On the other hand, however,
significant fluctuations in the relative numbers and geographical
distribution of certain species are known to have occurred during the

past 400 years, and this provides a warning of the numerous potential sources of error in this direction which are at present impossible to control. The observations of Mesolithic subsistence patterns in the sections which follow should therefore be read with these reservations in mind.

On the basis of the existing faunal assemblages, the species of land mammals which would appear to have been of greatest importance to Mesolithic communities in Norway were the reindeer (*Rangifer tarandus*) moose (*Alces alces*) and red deer (*Cervus elaphus*). At the present day the geographical distributions of these three species are rather sharply differentiated and show very little overlap. The reindeer, of course, is adapted to living in 'barren ground' conditions and at the present time is found in the wild state only in the southern parts of Norway in areas above the altitudinal tree limit. In the seventeenth century, however, this species had a much wider distribution incorporating most of the highland areas of Norway and extending onto the plains of the Finnmark region. The moose is most commonly found in the coniferous forests in the eastern and south-eastern parts of the country, but also occurs in the Trøndelag provinces and in the southern part of Nordland. The red deer is the dominant big-game animal of the deciduous forested regions of western Norway, and is at present distributed along the coastal and fjord areas from northern Rogaland to Nord-Trøndelag province. As we have already observed, the major contrast between prehistoric and modern animal distributions is shown by the wild boar, which was clearly an important component of the Norwegian fauna during Atlantic times. Rather surprisingly, there would appear to be no records whatever of the presence of this animal in Norway during historic times.

The exploitation of sea mammals, fish and wildfowl can be demonstrated both from the content of faunal assemblages and the general distribution of Mesolithic sites in the coastal areas of Norway. Evidence for the exploitation of shell-fish is more limited, and can at present be documented only from a few sites on the south-west coast.

Subsistence patterns in northern fjord and coastal areas

In 1964 K. Odner put forward a model for the resource exploitation and settlement patterns of Komsa settlements in the area around the Varanger Fjord in Finnmark province (Odner 1964). In the absence of faunal remains, Odner's model was based on the geographical location of the sites and on the relative sizes of the settlements as reflected by the distribution of the artefacts. According to Odner, the sites located at the head of the fjord are considerably larger than those located on the coast. Working from this basis – and assuming that the quantities of implements and flaking debris provide an approximate indication of the length of occupation of the respective sites – Odner went on to suggest that the Mesolithic communities in this area had practised a 'mobile' economy based on the occupation of two seasonally-contrasting types of settlement.

The coastal sites in this area are usually situated either on small islands or on narrow spits of land, where the nesting places of sea birds and breeding colonies of seals would provide attractive and easily accessible sources of food during the summer months. During the winter season, however, these locations would be far less attractive to the human communities, not only because of changes in the availability of food resources but also because of severe weather conditions along the coasts. Odner therefore suggested that the coastal settlements were occupied primarily during the summer months, and that human groups spent the remainder of the year in the more sheltered settlements at the head of the fjord.

Unfortunately, the general absence of faunal remains from sites belonging to the Komsa period has made it impossible to test Odner's model in any systematic way. Extremely rich samples of faunal material have however been recovered from a series of younger Stone Age settlements at the head of the Varanger Fjord (totalling approximately 120,000 faunal specimens), and the composition of these faunal assemblages goes a considerable way towards validating the general patterns of seasonal exploitation postulated by Odner for the earlier Komsa-period sites (Olsen 1967, 1975). The dating of these younger Stone Age settlements (represented by periods II to IV of the Varanger succession) has generally been estimated in the region of 2,200 B.C. to 100 A.D. (Simonsen 1962: 7-8) but more recent radiocarbon determinations from northern Norway and Finland indicate that this dating is almost certainly too young. K. Helskog has recently suggested (1974: 100-2) that the occupation represented by periods II-IV of the Varanger sequence spans the period from approximately 3,500-1,000 bc.

Analysis of the faunal assemblages from these younger Stone Age settlements by Olsen (1967, 1975) has revealed a total of 65 different species, of which bones belonging to 10 different species of fish account for slightly more than half (55.6 percent) of the total number of identified remains. Mammals are represented by no less than 27 different species and account for 36.75 percent of the remains, whilst birds (represented by 28 species) make up the remaining 7.6 percent (Olsen 1967: 14-17) (Table 1).

The bone material clearly demonstrates the heavy reliance on maritime economic resources at these sites. From the nine sites where the total samples of mammalian bones were identified, 63.5 percent were found to belong to seals, while a further 28 percent belonged to whales. Only 8.5 percent of the mammalian bones belonged to terrestrial species, of which reindeer (5.7 percent) and domestic dog (1.3 percent) accounted for the bulk of the identified bones (Olsen

G

1975: 3, 7, 12). A similar reliance on marine species is apparent in the bird bones, among which remains of various species belonging to the auk family comprised 66 percent of the bones. The only species of land bird of any importance was the arctic willow grouse (*Lagopus lagopus*), which accounted for 15 percent of the bird-bone sample (Olsen 1967: 176-7). Among the fish bones 77 percent belonged to cod (*Gadus callarias*), 10 percent to coalfish (*Pollachius virens*) and a further 10 percent to haddock (*Melanogrammus aeglefinus*). No remains whatever of fresh-water species were identified among the fish-bone remains (Olsen 1967: 20).

From the composition of these faunal remains there can be little doubt that the occupation of the sites was confined largely if not entirely to the winter and spring months of the year. Winter occupation is suggested particularly clearly by the bird remains, among which are four species of arctic breeders which are typical winter visitors in Finnmark. For example, the little auk (*Plotus alle*), which is represented by 2.9 percent of the identified bird bones, remains in the Varanger area from October to January or February and is absent from the area for the rest of the year (Olsen 1967: 81, 87-9, 165). Essentially the same pattern of occupation is suggested by the fish-bone remains. Thus the high percentage of cod recorded amongst the fish bones is strongly indicative of fishing during the late winter and early spring months (i.e. April and May), while the complete absence of salmon bones would suggest that the sites were abandoned during the summer months. A further argument in favour of the abandonment of the site during the summer season is provided by the complete absence of remains of fledglings among the bird-bone remains (Olsen 1967: 31-6, 54, 60-2, 79).

The interpretation of the reindeer bones from the sites is more problematic. During historical times reindeer do not appear to have been present in coastal areas during the winter months. However, palaeoclimatic evidence suggests that at the time of the Younger Stone Age occupations the area around the Varanger Fjord would have supported a more luxuriant vegetational cover than during historic times, and under these rather different ecological conditions it may well be that concentrations of reindeer would have been accessible to the occupants of the Varanger sites during the winter months (Olsen 1975: 11). An interesting feature which emerged from the faunal analyses was that although reindeer accounted for only 3 percent of the total bone material, approximately 90 percent of the bone *implements* from the sites were manufactured from either the bones or antler of reindeer. This therefore raises the possibility that a further component in the economic exploitation patterns of the Varanger communities may have included sites devoted primarily to the hunting of reindeer herds in some other areas, and presumably at a different time of the year (Simonsen 1973: 177).

Taking into account these different lines of evidence, Simonsen

(1973: 177-8) has recently proposed a more complex model for the subsistence-settlement strategies of Stone Age communities in the Varanger area, which incorporates four major components:

1. Settlements located at the head of the Varanger Fjord and devoted primarily to marine fishing and the hunting of sea mammals during the months of October or November to May.
2. The possibility of spring-season settlements on the coast, oriented towards the exploitation of breeding colonies of sea birds during June and early July. A number of sites which have yielded large numbers of bird bones (including remains of fledglings) might belong to this category.
3. Fishing camps located along the course of inland rivers and occupied during the months of July and August. The existence of such settlements is suggested by the location of certain sites, but cannot at present be verified on the basis of faunal material.
4. Possible autumn settlements devoted to the hunting of reindeer. No sites which can certainly be attributed to this category have so far been identified.

This is clearly an interesting, if necessarily hypothetical, model, which will need to be systematically tested in the course of future research.

A western fjord settlement

The rock shelter of Skipshelleren is situated 40 km. to the north-east of Bergen near the mouth of the Voss river. In the late Mesolithic period the river valley would have formed a fjord, stretching several kilometres further inland. At this time the Skipshelleren shelter would have been located close to the shore at a shallow part of the fjord.

The excavations revealed seven cultural levels of which the lowermost four horizons (layers 4-7) belonged to the Stone Age (Bøe 1934). Recently, a series of bone samples from the site have been dated by radiocarbon, yielding the following results for the Stone Age levels:

Layer 6   : (T-2127) : $4,280 \pm 140$ bc
Layer 6   : (T-1959) : $4,170 \pm 90$ bc
Layer 6   : (T-1958) : $4,050 \pm 100$ bc
Layer 5/6 : (T-2196) : $3,310 \pm 80$ bc
Layer 5   : (T-2128) : $3,210 \pm 90$ bc
Layer 4   : (T-1961) : $2,450 \pm 80$ bc
Layer 4   : (T-1960) : $2,050 \pm 90$ bc

The site produced a total of 175,900 faunal remains, of which the majority were recovered from the Stone Age levels (Bøe 1934: 13-19). No full report on the fauna has so far been published but according to Olsen (1967: 65) approximately 85 percent of the bones belonged to mammals, 14 percent to fish and approximately 1 percent to birds. Further details are provided by Fasteland (1969) who reports that a total of 18 different mammalian species are represented in the different levels. Among these remains bones of red deer account for approximately 50 percent of the identified specimens, while wild boar and seals are represented by approximately 12 percent each. In addition there are bones belonging to 17 species of fish and an unspecified number of birds. According to Olsen, the composition of the faunas suggests that the settlement was occupied during the summer months (Olsen 1967-61).

Large numbers of shell fish were found in layers 4 and 6, but were far less abundant in layer 5 and almost absent in layer 7. The majority of the shells in the midden levels belonged to mussels (*Mytilus edulis*) but remains of the common periwinkle (*Littorina littorea*) and other gastropods were also abundant (Bøe 1934: 13-19).

The overall composition of the food refuse reveals a strong emphasis on the exploitation of terrestrial mammals, although it is clear that both fish and shell fish made a significant contribution to the food supply. Clearly, the diversity of this subsistence basis indicates that the Stone Age occupants of the Skipshelleren rock shelter must have been acquainted with a wide range of technologies for exploiting both the terrestrial and aquatic aspects of the local environment. It is therefore particularly interesting to observe that the range of artefacts recovered from levels 4-7 of the site provides little indication of this technological diversity, and instead reflects what would appear to be pronounced bias towards the exploitation of fish and sea mammals. Thus the most common bone artefacts recovered from the site were fish hooks, of which the majority of the 120 specimens were found in levels 6 and 7. The excavations also yielded 18 specimens of harpoon heads and leister prongs, together with at least 12 fragments of slotted bone points and 25 smaller forms of bone points (Bøe 1934: 23-38, 60-2, Plates I-VI). By contrast, artefacts which are usually associated with the hunting of land mammals were remarkably scarce in all of the Stone Age levels on the site. Arrowheads were completely lacking in the two lowermost levels, and only a single slate point is reported from layer 5. A larger number of slate points and stemmed points of flint and quartzite were recovered from layer 4, but even in this level these artefacts are far rarer than one might have anticipated from the large quantities of animal bones recovered. One possible explanation for this anomaly may be that most of the land mammals were hunted by means of techniques which would leave no trace in the archaeological record – for example, by means of cliff-fall hunting in the case of the larger land mammals, or by the use of traps or nets in the case of the smaller game. The alternative would seem to be that these animals were hunted with the use of such artefacts as the slotted bone points or barbed harpoon heads recovered from the site.

Nevertheless the impression remains that the bulk of the artefacts represented on the site were associated with the exploitation of specifically maritime resources. The harpoon-heads are similar to those used by recent Eskimo groups for seal hunting. Line fishing is documented by the numerous fish hooks, and also by the presence of line sinkers. The presence of deep water species such as ling (*Molva molva*) indicate that at least some of the fishing was carried out from boats, and with the aid of relatively long fishing lines. Whether or not net fishing was also practised from the site is clearly more difficult to ascertain, but it may be recalled that four artefacts recovered from layers 6 and 7 were interpreted by Bøe as netting needles (Bøe 1934: 38-9, 62-3, Plate VI).

A midden on the south-west coast

The Viste Cave lies 5 km. to the north-west of Stavanger in the northernmost part of Jaeren. The site has been excavated on a number of occasions and has yielded a rich collection of both faunal remains and artefacts (Brøgger 1908, 1910; Degerbøl 1951; Lund 1951). Of the three archaeological levels identified, the lowermost two horizons (layers I and II) belong to the Mesolithic period. Layer II is typologically and technologically closely related to levels 6 and 7 in the Skipshelleren rock shelter (dated to the 5th millenium bc), while the lowermost horizon (layer I) appears to be significantly older (Mikkelsen 1971: 29, 35).[1]

Layer II may be regarded as a typical shell-midden accumulation, in which the dominant species were the common periwinkle (*Littorina littorea*) and limpet (*Patella vulgata*). By contrast, remains of shell fish were almost absent in layers I and III. Most of the animal bones were found in the Mesolithic levels (Lund 1951: 11-12, 50-1).

A total of 70 species have been identified among the faunal remains, including 22 species of mammals, 37 species of birds and 11 species of fish. Unfortunately, most of the bone material has been published in a way that makes it impossible to calculate the relative contributions of these different resources to the food supply. From the excavations carried out in 1939 and 1941, however, at least 1,029 bones of mammals and 235 bones of birds were identified; the number of fish bones is not specified (Degerbøl 1951: 56-82).

Relatively detailed information is available on the composition of the mammalian bones and indicate that the major reliance was placed on terrestrial species. Only 10 percent of the mammalian bones belonged to sea mammals, and all of these were seals. From the heavy predominance of typically forest-living species in the fauna (wild boar, moose, red deer and brown bear, comprising 69 percent of the mammalian bones) it may be inferred that the area of Jaeren – which is at present treeless – was extensively forested during later Mesolithic times.

Bones of wild boar accounted for 56.8 percent of the identified mammalian bones and show that this species provided the major focus of the hunting activities during the Mesolithic occupation. Next in order of importance among the land mammals were remains of moose which made up 7.8 percent of the mammalian bones. Moose is at present found in western Norway only in a few small and scattered populations, and it may be inferred from the remains found at both this site and in the Skipshelleren shelter (Fasteland 1969) that this species had a wider distribution during the Atlantic period than it has today. Remains of red deer are much rarer than those of moose and account for only 1.7 percent of the mammalian remains (Degerbøl 1951: 53, 72-3).

The overall composition of the faunal remains from the Viste Cave points strongly to occupation during the summer months, although a small number of bones of typically winter-season visitors has been identified amongst the bird-bone remains (Degerbøl 1951: 77, 81). Bones representing new-born pups of the grey seal (*Halichoerus grypus*) would similarly point to occupation during the late autumn or winter months (Olsen 1967: 90). Needless to say, there is no reason to see these different seasonal indications as necessarily contradictory, and the positive indications of summer settlement do not exclude the possibility of occupation at other seasons of the year as well.

The bone implements from the Mesolithic levels include 29 fish hooks, 12 slotted bone points, 3 harpoon heads, 8 chisels, and some 70 bone points of unknown function (possibly representing bodkins or needles). All of these types are similar to those found at the Skipshelleren site (Mikkelsen 1971: 22). With the exception of blades (213) and micro-blades (20), stone implements are few. There are 12 axes of various types manufactured from greenstone, and only a single example of a flake-axe manufactured from flint. The other implements manufactured from either flint or quartzite include 16 scrapers, 5 knives, 2 borers and 1 microlith (Mikkelsen 1971: 22-3). In view of the extensive range of bone implements it is interesting to note that only two burins were found at the site; in the material from the Skipshelleren site, burins were completely absent.

When viewed in functional terms, the artefacts which can be related to hunting and fishing show the same bias towards the exploitation of maritime resources (i.e. fishing and sea mammal hunting) as that encountered in the material from the Skipshelleren shelter. Here again we can see the same contrast between the functional orientation of the artefact assemblage and the clear emphasis on the exploitation of terrestrial food resources reflected in the composition of the faunal remains.

Smaller bone assemblages

Grønehelleren

The rock shelter of Grønehelleren is located near the mouth of the Sognefjord in western Norway. The diagnostic artefacts from the basal layer ('stage I') include a slotted bone point, a harpoon head, 4 fish hooks, greenstone axes of typical late Mesolithic types, and a strong element of micro-blades (Jansen 1972: 43-9). The evidence available from other sites points strongly to a date for this assemblage in the latter part of the 4th millennium bc (Indrelid, in press), and the two radiocarbon dates of 2,230 $\pm$ 70 bc (T-759) and 2,330 $\pm$ 60 bc (T-761) which are claimed to relate to this level are difficult to accept; in all probability these determinations relate to the overlying level which contains a slate industry.

The faunal remains recovered from the stage I level show a predominance of fish bones (58 percent of the 263 identified bones) among which remains of coalfish, cod and pollack are the most frequent species. Bones of mammals account for 34 percent of the faunal assemblage and bird bones the remaining 8 percent (Jansen 1972: 52-4).

In view of the location of this site on the outer part of the west Norwegian coast one might have expected that the hunting of sea mammals would be more profitable than the exploitation of terrestrial species. Nevertheless seals (the only sea mammal represented) account for only 35 percent of the mammal bones, while remains of red deer (32.6 percent), wild boar (20 percent) and otter (12.4 percent) make up the remaining 65 percent (Jansen 1972: 52). However, in view of the relatively small size of this assemblage (only 89 bones) it might be unwise to draw too far-reaching conclusions from these results.

The presence of wild boar at this site is of interest in providing a further indication that the west coast of Norway – which is at present essentially treeless – must have been at least partially forested during later Mesolithic times.

Frebergsvik

Small assemblages of faunal material have been recovered from two late Mesolithic sites located on the western shore of the Oslofjord in south-eastern Norway. On the basis of the evidence of shore-line displacement curves and typological comparisons the dating of these two sites at Frebergsvik has been estimated in the region of 4,000-4,500 bc (Mikkelsen 1975a).

In the combined faunal assemblage from these two sites mammals are represented by 725 bones (94.3 percent), birds by 41 bones (5.3

percent) and fish by 3 bones (0.4 percent). Only 127 of the bones are identifiable as to species and of these 85 belong to whales, 6 to seals, 2 to otter, 1 to fox, 1 to dog and 32 to birds of the auk family (Mikkelsen 1975a: 130).

Despite the limited size of the bone assemblage, the remains would seem to indicate that whaling was a major economic activity at these sites. Among the whale bones, two species have been identified: the porpoise (*Phocaena phocaena*) and the white-nosed dolphin (*Lagenorhynchus albirostris*).

At the time of occupation two narrow inlets extended inland at Frebergsvik, presenting an excellent situation for whale hunting (Mikkelsen 1975a: 137-8). The main point of uncertainty is whether or not these remains can be assumed to indicate the active hunting of whales, or whether they could represent simply the exploitation of animals which were accidentally stranded in the area.

Hardangervidda

Only two sites in the highland areas of southern Norway have so far yielded identifiable traces of faunal remains. From the site known as 'Hein 33' on the Hardangervidda highland plateau a few bones of moose were recovered. These bones have been dated by radiocarbon to around the time of the transition from the Mesolithic to the Younger Stone Age (2,970 ± 90 bc : T-1076; Indrelid 1973b: 58). In addition, both this site and a rather earlier site at Langesjøen (locality 1039) in the same region have yielded a number of fish bones identified as belonging to trout (*Salmo trutta*). The dating of the latter site to 4,200 ± 100 bc (T-1616) provides the earliest evidence for the presence of fish in the Norwegian highlands.

The occurrence of moose at the first-mentioned sites suggests that this animal may well have been present in parts of the highland areas of Norway during the period of the postglacial climatic optimum. If so, then the implications would be that the territories occupied by reindeer at that time were less extensive than they are at the present day, since moose and reindeer have rather different ecological requirements and do not normally occupy the same ranges. Accordingly it may be suggested that the economic exploitation of these highland areas by Mesolithic hunters may not have been associated exclusively with the exploitation of reindeer, but may have included the hunting of other species at certain periods.

The early occurrence of fish bones at an altitude of 1,200 metres above sea level points strongly to the conclusion that Mesolithic Man was in some way responsible for the spread of these resources into the rivers of the interior. Almost certainly the existence of waterfalls would have provided an insurmountable obstacle to the migration of fish into these areas by natural means.

Table 1. Numbers of species and relative proportions of mammals, birds and fish represented at some Mesolithic sites in Norway.

Region	Site	Settlement Location	MAMMALS		BIRDS		FISH	
			Number of species	Percent of bones	Number of species	Percent of bones	Number of species	Percent of bones
North Norway	Varanger	Fjord	27	36.75	28	7.6	10	55.65
West Norway	Skipshelleren	Fjord	18	85	?	1	17	14
West Norway	Grønehelleren (Stage I)	Coast	4	34	10	8	8	58
South-west Norway	Viste	Coast	22	?	37	?	11	?
South-east Norway	Frebergsvik	Fjord	6	94.3	3	5.3	?	0.4

The data are derived from the following sources: Varanger – Olsen 1967, 1975;
Skipshelleren – Olsen 1967, Fasteland 1969; Grønehelleren – Jansen 1972; Viste –
Degerbøl 1951; Frebergsvik – Mikkelsen 1975a.

Comparison of economies

From the data presented in the preceding sections it will be apparent that the existing faunal assemblages from Norwegian Mesolithic sites must inevitably present a rather biassed picture of the range of economic strategies practised during this period. All of the sites of major importance date from either the late Atlantic or early Sub-boreal periods, they are all located either on the coast or along fjords, and their geographical distribution is not very representative. Even allowing for these factors, however, a number of conclusions of general importance can be drawn.

Table 1 shows that regardless of the location of the sites, a wide variety of faunal species was exploited. Perhaps the most striking feature in this regard is that in spite of the large numbers of bird species represented at all of the sites in question, the overall representation of bird-bone material in the faunal assemblages is invariably very low. Clearly, birds were only exploited on a sporadic basis, and formed only a minor portion of the diet. Nevertheless the varying behavioural patterns of the different bird species indicate that the Mesolithic communities must have been familiar with a variety of techniques for the exploitation of this aspect of the food supply.

If we turn now to Table 2 it is interesting to observe the very strong representation of terrestrial mammals in the faunal assemblages from the two coastal sites of Viste and Grønehelleren. As already noted, the coastal areas of western Norway are virtually treeless at the present day, but during later Atlantic and early Sub-boreal times these areas would have been extensively forested and would have provided very favourable conditions for such species as wild boar, red deer and moose. All of these animals form relatively stable portions and could most probably have been exploited from the coastal sites without the need to organise specialised seasonal hunts.

Both the composition of the faunal assemblages and the character of the contemporary vegetation would therefore support the view that the late Mesolithic coastal adaptation in southern Norway included the systematic exploitation of both maritime and terrestrial economic resources. If the material from the Skipshelleren rock shelter can be regarded as representative it would appear that this pattern of exploitation was equally characteristic of the fjord settlements. The major difference in this regard would appear to be a somewhat greater reliance on maritime resources at the settlements located on the outermost parts of the west coast. When seen in the context of the other sites the extreme predominance of whales in the fauna from the Frebergsvik site must surely represent the contents of a 'specialised activity' camp.

To judge by the faunas from the Younger Stone Age settlements in the neighbourhood of the Varanger fjord, the character of the fjord

Table 2. Relative proportions of land and sea mammals, land and sea birds, and fresh-water and salt-water fish, represented at some Mesolithic sites in Norway.

Sites	PERCENTAGES						PREDOMINANT SPECIES					
	1. Land mammals	2. Land birds	3. Fresh-water fish	1. Sea mammals	2. Sea birds	3. Salt-water fish	1. Land mammals	2. Land birds	3. Fresh-water fish	1. Sea mammals	2. Sea birds	3. Salt-water fish
Varanger	8.5	15	0	91.5	85	100	Reindeer, dog	Willow grouse		Greenland seal, White-nosed dolphin	Auks, eiders	Cod, coalfish, haddock
Skipshelleren	89	?	2.8	11	?	97.2	Red deer, wild boar	?	Salmon/trout	Harbour seal	?	Cod, coalfish, pollack
Grønehelleren Stage 1	65	5	0	35	95	100	Red deer, wild boar	Swan	–	Seals	Cormorants, Great auk	Coalfish, cod, pollack
Viste	90	12	0	10	88	100	Wild boar, moose	Capercailzie, thrush	–	Grey seal	Common guillemot, Great auk	Cod
Frebergsvik	3	0	?	97	100	?	Otter	–	?	Porpoise, White-nosed dolphin	Auks	?

The data are taken from the following sources: Varanger – Olsen 1967, 1975; Skipshelleren – Olsen 1967, Fasteland 1969; Grønehelleren – Jansen 1972; Viste – Degerbøl 1951; Frebergsvik–Mikkelsen 1975a.

adaptation in the most northerly parts of Norway would appear to differ from that of southern Norway in a more pronounced emphasis on maritime food resources. The same tendency can be seen in the unpublished faunal material from the coastal site of Kirkhelleren in Nordland province. At the same time, however, the content of the rock art in these areas would appear to indicate that the subsistence patterns represented in the bone material from the Varanger and Kirkhelleren sites may not be representative of all parts of northern Norway.

A wide range of animals is represented in the rock art of north Norway and Trøndelag (Fig. 5). Although representations of whales, seals, fish and birds are by no means uncommon in this art, the frequent occurrence of representations of both moose and reindeer would appear to suggest a more diversified subsistence basis than that represented in the faunal assemblages from the Varanger sites. Perhaps the most likely explanation of this dichotomy is that the selection of animal motifs represented in the rock art reflects the activities carried out in the course of specialised seasonal hunts. One feature which remains somewhat anomolous in this regard is that representations of both moose and reindeer have frequently been found together on the same rock panel (Hagen 1976: 12-15, 120-2, 207-12). From our knowledge of the ecology of these two animals it seems unlikely that both species would occur together in precisely the same areas, and indeed the moose usually shows a tendency to avoid the reindeer (Collett 1912: 498, 530). If we assume that the rock carvings do provide a reliable indication of the animals actually exploited, we must probably accept that the hunting of these two animals would have been carried out in separate ecological zones.

Settlement patterns during the late Boreal, Atlantic and Sub-boreal periods

Northern Norway

The possible subsistence and settlement patterns of Mesolithic communities in the northernmost parts of Norway have been discussed in describing the evidence from sites in the region of the Varanger fjord in the north-east part of Finnmark province. It will be recalled that an original model by Odner (1964) postulating the existence of two major seasonally-regulated settlements (summer settlements along the coast and winter settlements at the head of the fjord) was elaborated by Simonsen (1973) into a more complex model involving the occupation of four economically and seasonally specialised settlement types. It may well be that Simonsen's model is equally applicable to other parts of the north Norwegian coast (for example, in the provinces of Troms and Nordland) but in the absence of faunal remains from sites in these areas there is at present no way of evaluating this possibility.

Indications of a rather different pattern of seasonal exploitation have been reported recently by Gaustad (1973) from a study of the distribution and typological affinities of a series of sites dated to around 5,000 bc in the Rana district of Nordland. In the highland areas a large number of lake-shore sites have been excavated which are interpreted as the summer-season camps of reindeer hunting groups. A systematic survey of the neighbouring coastal and fjord areas has revealed sites with assemblages which could well represent economically and seasonally complementary settlements to those in the highlands (Gaustad 1973: 186-9). Once again, the absence of faunal remains from both the upland and lowland sites makes it very difficult to test this model.

Moving further to the south, no radiocarbon-dated Mesolithic sites have so far been published from either the Trøndelag provinces or the northern parts of Møre. Indeed, very little is at present known of the middle and later stages of the Mesolithic in this region.

Western Norway

The greater part of the Mesolithic sites in the more southerly parts of western Norway (i.e. from the province of Møre southwards) are located along the coast, and in many cases on islands. Occasional sites are known from the outer parts of the fjords, but no clear traces of Mesolithic sites have so far been discovered at the heads of the major western fjords. Sites appear to be similarly lacking in the western highland regions and in the mountainous areas between the fjords, despite a number of systematic archaeological surveys in these areas.

It would therefore appear that the economic strategies of Mesolithic groups in the western areas of Norway did not include the exploitation of resources in the interior. The faunal assemblages from Skipshelleren and Grønehelleren have demonstrated the existence of stable populations of several species of terrestrial mammals within the vicinity of these sites, and it may well be that these resources provided an adequate economic basis for the Mesolithic communities without the need to exploit the upland areas of the interior. In particular it may be recalled that both the available faunal assemblages and the selection of motifs in the rock art suggest that the principal terrestrial animal exploited in this region was the red deer (cf. Fig. 5). Both the natural vegetation and the terrain in this area are well suited to this animal, and the extent of the seasonal migrations of present-day populations of red deer along the western coast are relatively short. It follows that the year-round exploitation of this animal by Mesolithic communities could have been achieved by equally short movements on the part of the human groups themselves. It is entirely possible therefore that rock shelter settlements of the kind represented at

Skipshelleren, Viste and Grønehelleren could have been occupied as base camps throughout the greater part of the year, and that the numerous smaller sites in this area represent either sites occupied for a relatively brief period or the sites of some specialised economic activities.

South-eastern Norway

Several lines of evidence suggest that the exploitation of moose is likely to have played an important part in the economic activities of Mesolithic communities in the south-eastern parts of Norway. Moose is the characteristic big game species of this region at the present day, and the content of the rock carvings suggests that this was true during at least the later part of the Stone Age. The finds from the Hardangervidda highland plateau referred to earlier show that moose was being hunted up to an elevation of at least 1,130 metres above sea level around 3,000 bc, and isolated discoveries of animal bones show that moose populations were present in the interior areas of south-eastern Norway during the Boreal period (Henningsmoen 1975).

Sites of presumed Atlantic age have been found along the rivers and lake sides of the interior areas of south-eastern Norway, as well as along the coast. Some of the coastal settlements – like the two sites at Frebergsvik – show a strong orientation towards the exploitation of maritime resources, but from the great majority of the sites no form of direct evidence bearing on the economy is available. The Boreal site of Tørkop near the Swedish border, dated to 6,230 ± 170 bc (T-1872: Mikkelsen 1975c: 19), has yielded a few bones of wild boar, but no identifiable remains of moose (Sørensen 1974: 16).

Sites dated to the late Boreal and early Atlantic periods in the interior highland areas of Hardangervidda would appear on the basis of both typological affinities and the sources of the flint resources exploited to be more closely related to the Mesolithic sites of south-eastern Norway than to those of the west. These highland sites are usually interpreted as seasonal settlements devoted primarily to the hunting of reindeer during the late summer and autumn months (Hagen 1963: 131-3, 141; Indrelid 1973c: 5-7, 14). The implications of this interpretation are that the winter and spring settlements would be located elsewhere, presumably at lower elevations. The easiest access routes to several of these highland areas – including Hardangervidda – is by means of the valleys leading towards the south-east coast.

Unfortunately, no systematic surveys have so far been carried out in the interior river valleys in this region. As already noted, a number of sites of Atlantic and Sub-boreal age are however known to exist in these areas, and the hunting groups represented at the highland sites would certainly have had to pass through these valleys to gain access to their flint supplies. In the absence of faunal evidence the types of economic exploitation practised in these interior valley habitats must inevitably remain a matter for speculation, but it may be significant that a number of rock carvings showing representations of moose are known from several localities adjacent to rivers at altitudes below 700 metres above sea level (Hagen 1976: 127-8, 132-4, 194). Though most of these rock carvings in south-eastern Norway appear to date from the Sub-boreal period, they might well perpetuate older subsistence-settlement traditions extending back into the Mesolithic period.

The more variable economic resources and the relatively easy access to contrasting ecological zones are likely to have fostered a greater degree of economic and cultural variability in the south-eastern part of the country than in the west. As we have seen, the archaeological finds show that all of the major ecological zones were exploited – the coast, the interior river valleys and the highlands. In these circumstances it is reasonable to postulate the existence of economic cycles with a more pronounced degree of seasonal differentiation than those apparent in the coastal and fjord areas of the west. Indeed, the possibility that several different patterns of economic adaptation may have existed in this area (for example, pure coastal, coastal/interior, pure interior, and interior/highland) should not be overlooked.

Some archaeological indications of this kind of specialised adaptation can perhaps be detected in the distribution of certain artefact types within the south-eastern region. Thus it may be significant that while projectile points of the single-barbed and transverse-edged types are relatively common on the southern highland sites of the late Boreal and Atlantic periods, they are rarely found on contemporary sites in the lower parts of the interior and along the coast. On the whole it seems difficult to envisage any functional reason why arrowheads which proved effective in the hunting of reindeer in the highlands and moose on the outer areas of the highland plateau should not have proved equally effective in the hunting of moose and wild boar in the more low-lying areas of the interior and on the coast. This systematic difference in the character of the artefact assemblages from the two areas may therefore reflect the existence of two separate forms of economic adaptation, associated with rather different traditions in the patterns of tool manufacture.

Environmental history and cultural change

From what has been said in the preceding section it will be apparent that the regional variations in economy and settlement patterns which can be observed in the later stages of the Norwegian Mesolithic can be attributed very largely to the great variety of environments and ecological zones in different parts of the country.

When compared with the marked *geographical* variations in environmental conditions, the extent of the *chronological* changes in climatic and vegetational conditions during the course of the Boreal and Atlantic periods appear relatively insignificant. While progressive changes in climatic conditions and the vegetational cover during these periods must inevitably have resulted in some fluctuations in the distribution and relative abundance of certain animal species, it is unlikely that these changes were of sufficient significance to require any dramatic modifications in the character of the human economic and cultural adaptations. Throughout these periods we would therefore expect to observe an essentially stable pattern of cultural development, with only gradual modifications during the course of time.

This pattern of environmental stability appears to have been established during the first half of the Boreal period (c. 7,000-6,500 bc) when the southern parts of Norway became forested. The transition from an essentially open, tundra-like environment to relatively dense forest which took place at this time must be seen as the critical development in the history of postglacial environmental conditions in southern Norway, and it is at this point that the major adaptations among the human populations of the area would be expected to occur.

Indications of a fundamental change in at least the technological aspects of human culture can in fact be observed in the southern areas of Norway shortly before 6,000 bc. This change is marked in the coastal sites by a replacement of the older, coarse flake and blade tradition of the 'Fosna Culture' by a technology based on the production of smaller 'micro-blade' forms. Owing to the overall abundance of micro-blades in sites belonging to the general time range between 6,000/6,300 bc and 3,200/3,300 bc, I have recently proposed that the term 'Micro-blade Tradition' should be introduced as a general term to cover assemblages belonging to this period (Indrelid, in press). Geographically, this concept of a Micro-blade Tradition can be applied to all parts of southern Norway, including parts of Nordland province (Fig. 1). The main impression conveyed by sites belonging to this 3,000-year period is one of an essential stability in settlement patterns and only relatively minor changes in the character of the artefact assemblages. The only variations of any significance which can be detected within these assemblages are certain tendencies towards regional differentiation (which are particularly apparent in the form of the axes) and a gradual modification in the form of certain implement types through the course of time. In the more northerly parts of Norway there are at present no radiocarbon dates relating to this time range (6,300-3,200 bc) so that the patterns of cultural development in this area are impossible to establish.

The question of the dating and the character of the earliest postglacial occupation of Norway poses a number of problems. It is known that parts of southernmost Norway and the west coast became free of ice at the end of the Oldest Dryas period, and that the same areas were probably similarly exposed on a number of occasions during the last glaciation. Bones of reindeer recovered from a Bølling-age deposit to the north-east of Bergen have been dated by radiocarbon to 10,250 ± 350 bc and 10,750 ± 350 bc (T-138 and T-139; Mangerud 1970: 132-7) and show conclusively that reindeer were present on the west coast during at least certain stages of the late-glacial period. During the 8th millennium bc it would appear that reindeer withdrew from the lowland areas of southern Norway and retreated to the newly-deglaciated areas of the highlands (Indrelid 1975: 15-16).

Problems associated with the dating of the earliest human occupation of southern Norway have been discussed at some length in a recent paper by the writer (Indrelid 1975). The hypothesis was advanced in this paper that the earliest colonisation of this region may have been achieved by late-glacial reindeer hunting groups who were able to make the crossing between the former 'North-Sea Continent' and the south-west coast of Norway by means of ice connections during the winter months (Indrelid 1975: 14-15). This hypothesis remains to be tested, but it would help to explain the apparently early dating of some west-Norwegian finds. In the eastern parts of Norway, the earliest sites would appear to date from the Preboreal period, although the possibility remains that some of these finds could be of Younger Dryas age (Johansen 1964: 177-8).

The composition of the artefact assemblages from Fosna sites along both the west coast and in the areas to the east of the Oslofjord is extremely variable. The only feature which appears to be common to all of the sites is an abundance of coarse flakes and blades, all manufactured from flint. Distinctive artefact types such as points, axes, burins and microliths occur on some of the sites, but in many cases these forms are totally lacking. In such cases it is impossible to assign the assemblage to the 'Fosna Culture' in any meaningful taxonomic sense. The most likely explanation is that these assemblages characterised by a very restricted range of artefact types represent the sites of some specialised economic activity.

In contrast to the variation in the composition of the tool inventories, however, the basic technological patterns underlying the production of these industries are essentially homogeneous. For this reason I would propose that the term 'Fosna Culture' should be abandoned as a general descriptive label for these early industries, and be replaced by the term 'Early Mesolithic Macro-Tradition', as an equivalent to the original 'Flintpladse' term applied to these finds by Rygh in 1911. As we have already noted, current dating evidence suggests that the whole of this tradition in southern Norway is earlier than c. 6,300 bc.

The assumption that this initial colonisation of Norway was associated with the specialised hunting of reindeer is of course impossible to demonstrate on the basis of faunal remains and rests essentially on the typological similarities between the early Norwegian artefact assemblages and those of the Ahrensburg culture in the areas further to the south. Perhaps the strongest argument in favour of this hypothesis has been provided by the recent discovery of evidence for human exploitation in the highland areas of southern Norway as early as 6,500 bc. This occupation of the highland areas must have taken place only a few hundred years after these areas were deglaciated, and it is frankly difficult to envisage what other economic resources, other than reindeer, could have drawn the hunters into the highlands at this early date. There can be little doubt that a combination of climatic and vegetational changes during the earlier part of the Boreal period would have exerted strong ecological pressures on the reindeer populations in the lowland areas of southern Norway, and a shifting of the annual ranges of the reindeer herds into the highland habitats would have been a natural reaction to these environmental changes. Although certain typological similarities can be detected between the highland assemblages dated prior to 6,000 bc and those of the Early Mesolithic Macro-Tradition in the coastal area, it would be premature on the basis of the existing information to interpret them as seasonal occupations by the same groups of people.

As we have already seen, a fundamental change in this economic and technological pattern appears to have been brought about by a rapid succession of environmental changes in southern Norway during the later part of the Preboreal and the earlier part of the Boreal period. Economically, one aspect of this change appears to have been a greater reliance on the exploitation of maritime food resources. Technologically, the change seems to have been marked by a replacement of the Early Mesolithic Macro-Tradition by the very different industries of the Micro-blade Tradition. In my opinion these two traditions represent more operational concepts (in a pragmatic sense) than the two 'cultures' which they partly replace. These two broad technological traditions, as they are now defined, are applicable to wider geographical areas and are able to incorporate the assemblages from specialised activity sites which may lack diagnostic artefact types and which are accordingly difficult to accommodate within the more narrowly defined cultural divisions.

Regional differences within these broad traditions, characterised by specific artefact types, may be regarded as 'sub-traditions', of which the 'Nøstvet Culture', for example, may prove to be one. Within these sub-traditions, regional chronological sequences will need to be worked out. Similarly, studies of the varying composition of the artefact assemblages from different sites may throw light on the varying economic activities carried out at different locations. Based on activity analysis and studies of bone assemblages it may be possible to construct regional models of subsistence-settlement patterns, and to study their changes over time. Needless to say, a correct understanding of these developments will only be possible when the observed changes in human behaviour are placed clearly within the context of contemporary changes in animal populations, vegetation and climate.

Notes

[1] Four radiocarbon dates obtained whilst the present article was in press (April 1978) provide confirmation of the expected ages of the two lower levels in the Viste Cave:

Layer II : 4,320 ± 170 bc (T-2665)
            2,580 ±   90 bc (T-2667)
Layer I: 5,900 ± 120 bc (T-2664)
            5,830 ± 130 bc (T-2668)

References

Bakka, E. 1975. Geologically dated arctic rock carvings at Hammer near Steinkjer in Nord-Trøndelag. *Arkeologiske Skrifter fra Historisk Museum, Universitetet i Bergen*, 2: 7-48.

Bjørn, A. 1928. Noen norske stenaldersproblemer. *Norsk Geologisk Tidsskrift*, 10: 53-75.

Bjørn, A. 1929. *Studier over Fosnakulturen*. Bergens Museums Årbog, Historisk-Antikvarisk Rekke, no. 2.

Brøgger, A.W. 1905. *Øxer af Nostvettypen Bidrag til kundskaben om aeldre norsk stenalder*. Norges Geologiske Undersøgelse, 42.

Brøgger, A.W. 1908. *Vistefundet, en aeldre stenalders kjøkkenmødding fra Jaederen*. Stavanger Museums Aarshefte (1902), 2.

Brøgger,'A.W. 1910. Vistefundet. Ny utgravning sommeren 1910. *Naturen*: 332-47.

Bøe, J. 1934. *Boplassen i Skipshelleren på Straume i Nordhordland*. Bergens Museums Skrifter, no. 17.

Bøe, J. and Nummedal, A. 1936. *Le Finnmarkien: les origines de la civilisation dans l'extrême-nord de l'Europe*. Institutt for Sammenlignende Kulturforskning, Ser. B, 32. Oslo, Aschehoug.

Collett, R. 1912. *Norges Pattedyr*. Kristiania, H. Aschehoug & Co.

Degerbøl, M. 1951. Det osteologiske materiale. In H.E. Lund, *Fangst-boplassen i Vistehulen*. Stavanger, Stavanger Museum: 52-84.

Fasteland, A. 1969. *Skipshelleren – Bustad i 3000 år*. Historisk Museum, Universitetet i Bergen.

Gaustad, F. 1973. Kyst og innland i Nordland. *Tromsø Museums Skrifter*, 14: 183-9.

Gjessing, G. 1943. *Traen-funnene*. Institutt for Sammenlignende Kulturforskning, Ser. B, 41. Oslo, Aschehoug.

Gjessing, G. 1945. *Norges steinalder*. Oslo, Norsk Arkeologisk Selskap.

Hagen, A. 1963. Mesolittiske jegergrupper i norske høyfjell. *Universitets Oldsaks Samling Årbok*, 1960-61: 109-42.

Hagen, A. 1975. *Bergkunst. Jegerfolkets Helleristninger og Malninger i Norsk Steinalder*. Oslo, Cappelen.

Hansen, A.M. 1904. *Landnåm i Norge: en Vdsigt over Bosaetningens Historie*. Kristiania, Fabritius.

Helskog, E. 1974. The Komsa culture: past and present. *Arctic Anthropology*, 11: 261-5.

Helskog, K. 1974. Two tests of the prehistoric cultural chronology of Varanger, North Norway. *Norwegian Archaeological Review*, 7, no. 2: 97-103.

Henningsmoen, K. 1975. Elghornet fra Hov i Løten. *Norsk Skogbruks Museums Årbøk*, 7 (1972-75): 62-73.

Indrelid, S. 1973a. En mesolitisk boplass i Dysvikja på Fjørtoft. *Arkeo*: 7-11.

Indrelid, S. 1973b. *Hein 33 – En Steinalderboplass på Hardangervidda: forsøk på Kronologisk og Kulturell Analyse*. Universitetet i Bergen Årbok, Humanistisk Serie, 1972, no. 1.

Indrelid, S. 1973c. Mesolitiske tilpasningsformer i høyfjellet. *Stavanger Museums Årbok*, 1972: 5-27.

Indrelid, S. 1975. Problems relating to the Early Mesolithic settlement of Southern Norway. *Norwegian Archaeological Review*, 1: 1-18.

Indrelid, S. (in press). Das Spätmesolithikum und die Anfänge des Neolithikums im westlichen Norwegen. In H. Schwabedissen (ed.), *Die Anfänge des Neolithikums vom Orient bis Nordeuropa*. Fundamenta. Monographien zur Urgeschichte. Köln, Böhlau.

Jansen, K. 1972. *Grønehelleren, en Kystboplass*. Unpublished M.A. thesis. University of Bergen.

Johansen, E. 1964. Høgnipen-funnene. Et nytt blad av Norges eldste innvandringshistorie. *Viking*, 27: 177-9.

Lund, H.E. 1951. *Fangst-boplassen i Vistehulen*. Stavanger Museum, Stavanger.

Mangerud, J. 1970. Late Weichselian vegetation and ice-front oscillations in the Bergen district, Western Norway. *Norsk Geologisk Tidsskrift*, 24: 121-48.

Mikkelsen, E. 1971. Vistefunnets kronologiske stilling. Trekk av Rogalands eldre steinalder. *Stavanger Museums Årbok*, 1970: 5-38.

Mikkelsen, E. 1975a. *Frebergsvik. Et Mesolitisk Boplassområde ved Oslo-fjorden*. Universitetets Oldsaksamlings Skrifter. Ny rekke, No. 1. Oslo.

Mikkelsen, E. 1975b. Mesolithic in south-eastern Norway. *Norwegian Archaeological Review*, 1: 19-35.

Mikkelsen, E. 1975c. Noen betraktinger omkring C-14-datering av Tørkopboplassen i Idd. *Nicolay*, 19: 19-21.

Nummedal, A. 1924. Om flintplassene. *Norsk Geologisk Tidsskrift*, 7: 89-141.

Nummedal, A. 1927. Stenaldersfunnene i Alta. *Norsk Geologisk Tidsskrift*, 9: 43-7.

Nummedal, A. 1929a. Et steinaldersfund i Ski. *Norsk Geologisk Tidsskrift*, 10: 474-81.

Nummedal, A. 1929b. *Stone Age Finds in Finnmark*. Institutt for Sammenlignende Kulturforskning, Ser. B, 13. Oslo, Aschehoug.

Nummedal, A. 1933. Kan det finnes flintplasser på Kyststrekningen mellem Kristiansand og Ålesund? *Naturen*: 227-44.

Odner, K. 1964. Erhverv og bosetning i Komsakulturen. *Viking*, 28: 117-28.

Odner, K. 1966. *Komsakulturen i Nesseby og Sør-Varanger*. Tromsø Museums Skrifter, 12. Tromsø, Universitetsforlaget.

Olsen, H. 1967. *Varanger-funnene: IV: Osteologisk materiale: Innledning – fisk – fugl*. Tromsø, Universitetsforlaget.

Olsen, H. 1975. *Varanger-funnene*. Zoologisk Museum, Universitetet i Bergen. (Stencil)

Rygh, K. 1911. Oversigt over Videnskabsselskabets Oldsagsamlings tilvaekst i 1910 af Sager aeldre end Reformationen. *Det Kongelige Norske Videnskabers Selkabs Skrifter*, (1910), no. 10, Trondhjem.

Rygh, K. 1912. Flintpladsene paa Trøndelagens kyst. *Oldtiden* II, Stavanger.

Shetelig, H. 1922. *Primitive Tider i Norge: en oversigt over Stenalderen*. Bergen, Greig.

Simonsen, P. 1962. Nord-Norges bosetningshistorie i Oldtiden. *Ottar*, no. 32-33. Tromsø.

Simonsen, P. 1973. Jaeger og nomade i Finnmark. *Tromsø Museums Skrifter*, 14: 174-83.

Sørensen, S.A. 1974. Villsvinjegere og nøttesankere i Idd. *Nicolay*, 18: 10-21.

9

Prehistoric settlement in northern Sweden: a brief survey and a case study

Noel D. Broadbent

In the earliest archaeological literature a distinction was made between a southern Scandinavian and a northern Scandinavian cultural area. Hans Hildebrand (1866) and J.J.A. Worsaae (1872) distinguished between the hunting economy of the north and the agricultural economy of the south, and the border was drawn through northern Uppland, Västmanland and Värmland, corresponding roughly with the Dal river, or c. 60°N. This *Limes norrlandicus* is still considered as being the boundary zone (Stenberger 1964: 145). In both a botanical and geographical sense the boundary has a certain validity, although, as in the case of the archaeological finds, it is not a sharp one.

Phytogeographically, the Swedish transition zone is confined to a narrow belt of land – unlike, for example, the situation in Finland. North of this zone the topography becomes more hilly with uplands of 300-400 metre elevations separated by broad river valleys. There is a general increase in precipitation and the soil is more podsolic. The border zone corresponds to certain climatic gradients brought on largely by the differences in topography. The *Limes* corresponds with the 4-5°C. yearly average temperature isotherm and the 120-day snow cover, 200 frost-free day zone (Fransson 1966; Angstrom 1968).

The vegetation of northern Sweden (Swedish *Norrland*) is predominantly coniferous taiga, with a subalpine birch region in the mountainous west starting at c. 500-metre elevation. While the *Limes* represents a rough limit for the mixed oak forest, elm (*Ulmus glabra*), lime (*Tilia cordata*) and hazel (*Corylus avellana*) penetrate far above the 60° parallel along the coast, due to the maritime influence of the Gulf of Bothnia. Some scattered stands of elm can even be found in Lappland, due to especially suitable conditions on high, sunny, southern slopes (Lundquist 1965: 216). Hazel grows as far north as the Angermanland coast at c. 63°N.

The warming effect of the Atlantic Gulf Steam and the Gulf of Bothnia make it possible to carry out limited agriculture on coastal marine and river valley sediments as far north as the Arctic Circle. During the Atlantic climatic maximum thermophylous plants extended even further north and the tree level was some 200 metres higher than today.

Despite the possibilities for agriculture and livestock raising in Norrland, however (the first traces of which are dated to around 2,500 bc), the economic emphasis in this region throughout almost the whole of the prehistoric period was on hunting and fishing (cf. Figure 4).

The geology of Norrland

The Fennoscandian Shield consists of very ancient Pre-Cambrian bedrock broken on the Scandinavian peninsula by the Caledonian mountain chain. Pleistocene glaciation has shaped the topography, and the subsoil consists mainly of glacial till. In Norrland very characteristic north-west to south-east running eskers extend roughly parallel to the river and lake systems which extend from the mountains in the west to the Bothnian coast in the east. The three geographical zones (coastal, interior forest and bog, and mountain *fjäll*) are traversed partially or wholly by 18 river systems (Fig. 1). The eskers and waterways form natural east-west lines of communication and it is along these systems that most prehistoric settlements have thus far been found (Janson and Hvarfner 1960).

The use of raw materials by Stone Age man was determined by the local availability of different bedrock types and morainic deposits, as well as the distance from south Scandinavian and eastern flint sources. True flint was not locally available in Norrland. On the coast, and to some extent in the interior forest and *fjäll* regions, the main silica raw material in use was quartz. The quartz is found in pegmatites within the largely granite and gneiss bedrock. Its use extends into middle Sweden as far south as Ostergötland (Welinder 1973) and Södermanland (Florin 1959). It also predominates in the whole of Finland. In the mountains, the eastern foothills and the interior, there is a greater availability of cryptocrystalline silicas including quartzites, breccia quartzes, fine-grained porphyrys etc. Slates and schists are also found in the interior (especially red and green slates), although similar stones of tool-making quality can also be found in some coastal areas. However, moraine deposits can provide sources of transported stone, so that contact with special source areas was not always necessary.

Culturally, the use of quartz, quartzite and slate has been viewed as a surrogate for flint (Santesson 1941) and bone (Brögger 1909; Almgren 1914) respectively, and the northern cultures have been

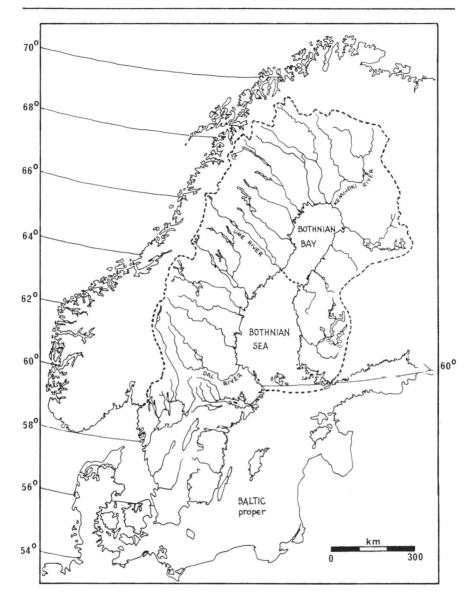

Figure 1. Lake and river systems in northern Sweden and Finland with drainage into the Gulf of Bothnia.

considered either as extensions of the south Scandinavian cultures (Hallström 1942) or eastern circumpolar influences (Gjessing 1944). With the time depth as we know it today, influences can be traced both south and east during different time periods.

Quartz and slate are an early technological manifestation in northern Sweden and show a specialised and independent development. The choice of different raw materials corresponds largely to what is locally accessible, but a certain degree of cultural preference can be seen. During the oldest Boreal settlement, flint-like porphyritic stone was preferred, no doubt as a substitute for flint. During Atlantic times quartz dominates, even in the interior, perhaps reflecting the quartz-using traditions coming from the east in Finland. Flint was imported from southern Scandinavia as far north as the Västerbotten coast at c. 2,000 bc, although quartz and slate were still extensively used. At c. 1,300 bc flat-hewn projectiles are introduced from the east and quartzite becomes the preferred raw material.

Research in northern Sweden

The earliest archaeological work in Norrland was largely in the hands of amateurs: Knut Tinnberg in Jämtland, O.B. Santesson in Angermanland and Knut Dahlberg in Kalix, to mention but the best known among numerous individuals. The first large-scale, systematic investigations were the results of the building of hydro-electric power plants, which necessitated extensive surveys along the river valleys. In Sweden this started in 1942 and is still being carried out. In 1968, a special project was organised for the cross-disciplinary analysis of this material. The project is called '*Early Norrland*', or 'NTB', and is in the process of publishing its results (Baudou 1970: 10; Biörnstad 1966: 65-72).

Another project with which the author has been associated has concentrated on the Västerbotten coastal region. Shoreline displacement has been used as the chronological framework. This project is called '*Nordarkeologi*' (Christiansson 1971, 1974).

In Norway a number of similar salvage and research projects have been organised in association with river and lake regulation: in south-west Norway (Martens and Hagen 1961; Indrelid 1969, 1975), Rana (Gaustad 1969) and Laerdal (Johanssen 1969). In Finland, salvage has been carried out in the Kemi river drainage area (Erä-Esko 1957, 1975).

All of these investigations have made available an extensive new archaeological source material, and greatly stimulated interest in the archaeology of the north. New attempts at artefact and culture analysis have been made, and this is certainly one of the most exciting new areas of Scandinavian research.

Settlement in northern Sweden: a survey

The question of when man entered northern Sweden can be answered in part by looking at the withdrawal of the continental ice-sheet which covered the land. According to *Atlas över Sverige* (1971), the ice was limited to the innermost parts of northern Sweden by 6,500-7,000 bc.

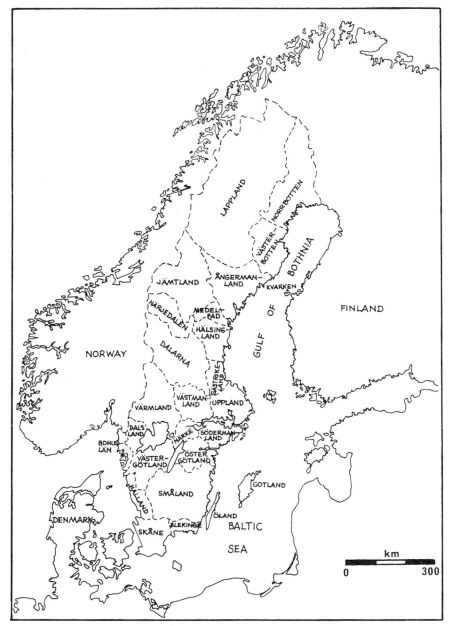

Figure 2. The provinces of Sweden.

Thus practically the whole area was free to be occupied by this time. The withdrawal was extremely fast, moving some 500 metres per year during its last stages (Bergström 1968). Because of the warm Boreal conditions, the landscape was quickly colonised by the birch-pine forest, with possibly a very short-lived tundra phase preceding it. These conditions, and the absence of reindeer remains in Norrland on

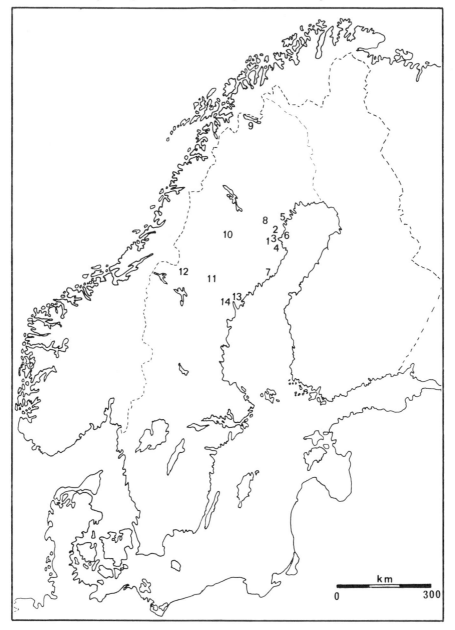

Figure 3. Map showing sites mentioned in the text: 1 – Lundfors; 2 – Bjurselet; 3 –
   Heden; 4 – Falmark; 5 – Jävre; 6 – Stor Kåge; 7 – Obbola (Umeå); 8 – Garaselet; 9 –
   Torne Träsk; 10 – Tjikkiträsk; 11 – Bellsås; 12 – Föllinge; 13 – Överveda; 14 –
   Norböle.

Stone Age sites and in the rock art, indicate that reindeer hunting and herding came late in the prehistory of the area.

Due to a lack of excavation until a few years ago the prehistoric record could not be pushed back further than c. 3,000 bc. Despite some rather primitive-looking material from the Torne Träsk area which was compared with the Komsa finds of Finnmark (Bagge 1937: 89), there has been very little evidence for a Boreal settlement in the north. Surface collections from Dalarna (Lannerbro 1975: 54), Härjedalen (Gräslund 1970: 143), Jämtland, Norrland and south-west Svealand have brought to light keeled core-scrapers and handle cores, but none of this material is datable and it could represent artefact survivals of much later date than in southern Scandinavia. Similar material has nevertheless recently been excavated by *Nordarkeologi* in northern Västerbotten's interior at the Garaselet site on the Byske river at 65°19'N., 20°18'E. The finds consist of several keeled scrapers, at least one handle core, and microblades, all of porphyritic stone. Three radiocarbon dates associated with this material gave dates of 6,220 $\pm$ 110 bc. (ST-5190), 5,935 $\pm$ 300 bc. (ST-5191) and 6,090 $\pm$ 100 bc. (ST-5193).

The animal bone thus far identified at Garaselet consists of brown bear, and one can count on the presence of a normal Boreal forest fauna in the area at the time.

The concentration of similar finds in south-west Norrland suggests that the origin of these people is to be sought on the Swedish west coast or in Norway, although the handle core dates correspond better to those of Scania (introduced c. 6,500 bc). The west coast datings (c. 5,000 bc), which are based on shoreline displacements, are debatable (Cullberg 1972; Welinder 1974: 146-53).

The quartz-slate technocomplex

The next archaeological period which can be distinguished is characterized by quartz and slate implements. These sites have been found in interior Jämtland, Angermanland, Norrbotten and Västerbotten, and also on the coast in Angermanland and Västerbotten. The following radiocarbon dates have been obtained for sites of this kind in different parts of Norrland (Fig. 3):

Lundfors (Västerbotten coast): 3,430 $\pm$ 70; 3,355 $\pm$ 245; 3,205 $\pm$ 250 bc (Broadbent, in press).
Bellsås (Angermanland interior): 3,795 $\pm$ 110; 3,475 $\pm$ 140; 3,150 $\pm$ 100 bc. (Baudou 1973: 168).
Föllinge (Jämtland): 4,765 $\pm$ 125 bc (Robertson-Akerlund 1976: 101-10).
Tjikkiträsk (Lappland): 5,135 $\pm$ 90; 4,445 $\pm$ 90; 3,350 $\pm$ 80; 2,495 $\pm$ 110 bc (Meschke 1967: 51).

The full development of the quartz and slate technology can be demonstrated as early as 4,000 bc and perhaps as early as 5,000 bc. From the lower levels at Bellsås there are small tanged and barbed projectiles of slate. At Lundfors, single and double-edged knives, including small curved (*ulo*) forms, pendants and projectiles are represented (Fig. 7). One of the best known slate sites, Överveda on the Angermanland coast, which can be dated through shoreline displacement to c. 3,000 bc, has yielded a wealth of fine slate implements: projectiles, knives and the peculiar T-shaped implements (Fig. 8) (Santesson 1941). This site was a manufacturing centre, and, as in the case of Lundfors which is discussed in more detail below, probably played an important part in the trading relations along the Bothnian coast.

The use of quartz is also typical of these sites, and large amounts of core and flake material, as well as tools, litter the sites. Another distinctive feature is the presence of enormous quantities of fire-cracked stones. In the interior in Jämtland, Angermanland and

Table 1. Faunal assemblages from coastal (Lundfors and Heden) and inland (Tjikkitrask) sites in northern Sweden.

		Identified pieces	Percent
LUNDFORS SITE A (Västerbotten coast, c. 3,400 bc)			
Ringed seal	*(Phoca hispida)*	237	99
Elk	*(Alces alces)*	1	0.5
Bream	*(Abramis brama)*	1	0.5
LUNDFORS SITE B (Västerbotten coast, c. 3,400 bc)			
Ringed seal		97	96
Beaver	*(Castor fiber)*	2	2
Hare	*(Lepus timidus)*	1	1
Pike	*(Esox lucius)*	1	1
HEDEN (Västerbotten coast, c. 2,700 bc)			
Ringed seal		200	88
Elk		19	8
Beaver		6	3
Pike		2	1
TJIKKITRASK (Meschke 1967:62) (Southern Lappland, from 5,000 bc)			
Elk		175	91
Beaver		14	7
Bream		2	1
Harbour seal	*(Phoca vitulina)*	2 (phalanges)	1

Västerbotten, huge mounds and ring-walls of these stones are encountered. Sites with quartz, slate and fire-cracked stones are long-lived in Norrland and predominate until 2,500-2,000 bc.

The economic bases of the settlements are quite distinctive and show what appears to be an extreme seasonal specialisation. The coastal sites are dominated by finds of ringed seal (*Phoca hispida*) and the interior sites by elk (*Alces alces*). The faunal samples listed in Table 1 will serve to illustrate this pattern. In addition to the samples listed in the table it may be noted that two further sites for which radiocarbon dates have been given were shown to contain 100 percent elk bones. They are Bellsås (S-65) in Angermanland and Föllinge (158) in Jämtland, both interior locations (Baudou 1973: 161; Iregren 1976: 16-20).

This material would appear to imply a migratory coastal-inland way of life. The Harbor seal bone (*Phoca vitulina*) from Tjikkiträsk is an unusual find and, as suggested by Gräslund (1967: 247), could have been transported to the site attached to a seal skin.

Neolithic settlement and contact

The next point of departure is seen in the growth of south Scandinavian Neolithic trading contact and settlement. This is strongest on the Bothnian coast, but is also seen in the interior along fertile river valleys and lake systems. A special inland region during these times was Jämtland, which was the meeting place for trade with middle Sweden, Norway, and the Medelpad and Angermanland coasts. The contact starts in the early Neolithic of southern Scandinavia, as seen by the presence of polygonal battle axes in southern Norrland and extending as far north as Angermanland. Contact continues throughout the Neolithic, and double-edged battle axes, boat axes, simple shaft-hole axes and flint daggers etc. are found, some finds coming from as far north as Norrbotten. The greatest contact, to judge from the imported articles, took place during the middle Neolithic (Nilsson 1969: 84).

Flint adzes of the thick-butted type were also imported from the south (South Baltic) and are found along the Norrland coast with special concentrations in Västerbotten where both agriculture (barley) and livestock raising (cattle and sheep) have been demonstrated (Christiansson 1974; Königsson 1970; Lepiksaar 1975). Further research has shown the presence of similar colonisation in Angermanland, at Norrböle (Huttunen and Tolonen 1972: 9-31).

The analysis of the Bjurselet fauna has thrown considerable light on the question of why the colonists settled on the Upper Bothnian coast. Eighteen different species of animals were identified from 4,041 bones: 9 mammals (88 percent), 5 birds (0.22 percent) and 4 fish (11.78 percent). Cattle (5 bones), sheep (64 bones) and pig (3 bones of recent date) comprised only 2 percent of the total mammal bone. Seal bones, however, constitute 97 percent of the total (3,463 bones), of which the majority of the identifiable specimens belong to ringed seal. Harp seal (*Pagophilus groenlandicus*) was identified from 4 bones.

The birds (golden eagle, goshawk, black grouse, capercailzie and a small sea duck) were identified from a total of 6 bones. The fish (pike, atlantic salmon, whitefish and dab) were represented by 476 bones, of which whitefish totalled 460 bones (96.6 percent).

On the basis of this material it would appear that seal hunting was the main activity at Bjurselet, together with fishing. The absence of elk is notable and sets the site apart from the normal Norrland type. Unlike other sealing sites in Västerbotten, Bjurselet did not produce any net weights, so one must assume that ice hunting and harpooning were the techniques used. The agriculture and livestock could not have provided more than a subsidiary to the economy this far north, but formed a link in the economy perhaps otherwise taken by elk hunting. Some 200 flint adze blanks were found at the site and it is possible that they were meant for trade – in which case the venture was apparently a failure as no adzes have been found in the interior.

It has been proposed that these people came from the Southern Baltic where they also lived as seal hunters. Greatly reduced ice conditions in the south would have caused a northern concentration of ringed seals, which could have been catastrophic for an economy dependent on them. The move to the north was necessitated by their dependence on this game (Christiansson and Broadbent 1976).

Along with the imported axes there was an indigenous production of finely ground and polished slate and schist adzes and chisels. While also found in the interior, these are found most frequently along the coast, and located at elevations indicative of Neolithic and Bronze Age associations. Ground slate implements reach a high level of development. Typical of this period are large tanged and barbed projectiles, knives (daggers) and animal-headed knives (Fig. 8b).

Parallel with the coastal settlements, the interior hunting, fishing and gathering peoples continued to live as before with a technology based on quartz, quartzite and slate. Trade was active between the coast and interior as well as with Norway, Finland, middle Sweden and the Baltic islands, Aland and Gotland. The slate trade was extensive and organised.

The Bronze Age

The coastal zone assumes special prominence during the Bronze Age in Norrland. This horizon is marked by the appearance of coastal cairns, some three thousand in number, which follow the ancient coastline from southern Norrland (Gästrikland) up to the Kalix area in Norrbotten. In form and construction they correspond to south

Scandinavian types and are round, oval and sometimes rectangular in shape. The oldest, highest lying, have body-length cists (Baudou 1968). Similar cairns are also found on the Aland islands and the Finnish Bothnian coast. The number of Bronze Age cairn finds is small in northern Sweden, but indicates a dating to the older Bronze Age, which is in accordance with the shoreline displacement datings. During the Bronze Age (and certainly before and afterwards) petroglyphs and rock paintings were made. The elk was the main motif, but at the largest site at Nämforsen in Angermanland a variety of animals, boats and men are found together with traditional south Scandinavian Bronze Age symbols: footprints, sun discs etc. (Hallström 1960).

While this settlement may be said to have its roots in the south Scandinavian Bronze Age, there are also strong eastern influences. The occurrence of asbestos-tempered and textile-impressed pottery and flat-hewn, transverse-based projectiles witnesses contact, if not a migration of peoples from the Ural-Siberian areas. The pottery can be linked with the Russian Andronovo culture. Asbestos pottery is found in Sweden as far south as Uppland, but is otherwise concentrated in northern Scandinavia, northern Finland and the Kola Peninsula, but only sparsely in interior and southern Finland where textile pottery predominates (Stenberger 1964: 307-18; Kivikoski 1964: 104-9). Radiocarbon datings of organic substances found on asbestos pottery sherds from northern Sweden have given a dating range from as early as c. 1,250 bc to as late as c. 100 A.D. (Linder 1966). Asbestos pottery has been found on the coast in northern Hälsingland, together with flat-hewn quartz and quartzite projectiles and is datable through the shoreline level to c. 1,300 bc (Sundlin 1974: 68). A similar find of projectiles on the Västerbotten coast at Falmark has been dated by the same means to c. 1,300-1,200 bc (Broadbent in press).

In Finland, the points, made of both eastern flints and quartzite, have been dated to 1,300-600 bc (Carpelan 1962). Eastern bronzes, both moulds and socketed celts, are also found and can be linked with the Ananjino culture (600-200 bc) in the Volga-Kama area. This extended eastern contact is believed by some to mark the entrance of the Lapps into northern Fennoscandia (Tallgren 1949; Toivonen 1948: 161; Westerlund 1969).

Recent pollen analysis in upper Norrland has given some new perspectives on the Bronze and Iron Age settlement. The area of investigation is located near the city of Umea in Västerbotten (Engelmark 1976, in press). Numerous cairns are found within the raised coastal area. At c. 1,000 bc, the colonisation of spruce (*Picea albies*), an aggressive eastern hybrid, took place on the Bothnian coast. This coincides roughly with the growth of eastern cultural influence, and there is some suggestion that the spread is due to a common climatic background.

The *Picea* forest is subject to clearance, however, during the period

700-400 bc, presumably in an effort to revitalise the deciduous vegetation for leaf fodder and to open the landscape for grazing and agriculture. Pollen evidence for the cultivation of barley, wheat and oats has been established for the area at this time.

This evidence for human impact on the environment ends abruptly around 400 bc; after this date the spruce forest dominates totally and it looks as though the agricultural way of life ceased altogether. The period between 400 bc and 500 A.D. lacks any trace of human influence on the environment in the Umea region.

In Angermanland (Norrböle) there is not such an extreme break, although during the period 1,000-500 bc and some time after the birth of Christ, there is a decrease in human influence which otherwise was more or less continuous (Huttunen and Tolonen 1972: 29).

The beginning of the economic breakdown in Umea corresponds to the Sub-atlantic climate deterioration (the *Fimbul winter* of the sagas) which, of uncertain influence in the south, was strongly felt in the peripheral north. This does not mean that all settlement ceased, but that the former economic basis was altered and that hunting and fishing regained their importance.

The Iron Age

At c. 500 A.D., the influence of man on the environment is apparent again in the Umea area, grows, reaching a peak in the Viking period/early Middle Ages, and continues into historical times (Engelmark 1976). This development is similar to the cultivation phases of southern Sweden and common causes, primarily climatic but also cultural, lie behind it (compare for example Welinder 1974: 93-107 and Königsson 1968: 141-62).

Archaeological finds from the Iron Age in Norrland are rather scarce, due largely to lack of excavation. In southern middle Norrland, especially Medelpad, large rectangular house foundations and grave mounds are found. This settlement of permanent and large farmsteads starts in the Roman Iron Age and continues into Viking times. In the interior, so-called Iron Age 'forest cemeteries' are found, often in the same area as Stone Age sites. These have been seen as traces of professional hunters and fur traders whose goods were traded south via the coastal settlers for further transport to Svealand, Gotland and the continent (Hvarfner 1957; Baudou 1973). The interior was also settled and substantial finds come from Dalarna and Jämtland where there was contact with Norway (Tröndelag) (Slomann 1950; Biörnstad 1962). Similar Norwegian contact and possibly settlement can be found in the Arjeplog area in Lappland (Lundholm 1973: 241).

In upper Norrland no established settlements of the south Scandinavian types have yet been found. Most of the artefacts are

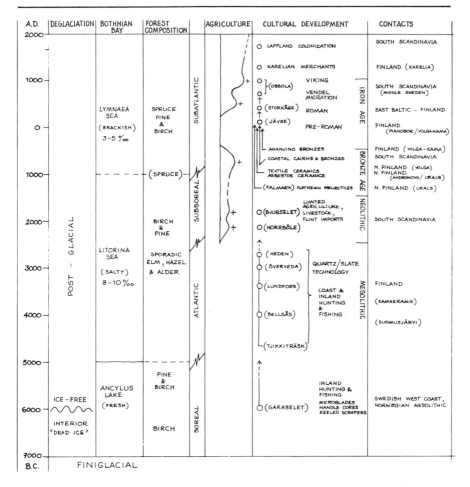

Figure 4. General environmental and cultural development of Upper Norrland. Cultural data refer primarily to the upper Bothnian region.

stray finds. Among the oldest find types are oval Scandinavian strike-a-lights, often picked up along the interior lakes and rivers. They belong for the most part to the Migration period (400-550 A.D.). On the coast, several unusual finds have indicated early foreign contact. A hoard of bronze objects was found at Stor Kage in Västerbotten, dating to around 400 A.D. (Hjärne 1917). These objects are non-Scandinavian and show contact with the east Baltic.

Another interesting find comes from a small cairn at Jävre in Norrbotten. A wheel-shaped bronze ornament dating to 0-500 A.D. was found in the cairn and shows contact with the Russian Pianobor culture, which succeeds the Ananjino culture (Arbman 1933). Two more finds from upper Norrland, also from cairns, were found at Obbola near Umea. A south Scandinavian strap-end from the Vendel period (550-800 A.D.) was recovered from the site and later, two round brooches from the Viking period (800-1050 A.D.), also of south Scandinavian origin (Serning 1960: 30; Christiansson 1969: 197-209).

According to Serning (1960: 88), the material from the Vendel and Viking periods in upper Norrland is almost all south Scandinavian, but during the eleventh century and onward into the twelfth and thirteenth centuries, eastern influence came to dominate. The Karelian culture rises during this period and organised merchants, the *Birkarlar*, from Satakunta in Finland were active in northern Sweden and Lappland, having trading privileges with the Lapps. Lappland does not become permanently colonised by outsiders, however, until the seventeenth and eighteenth centuries.

Very little excavation has so far been carried out on Iron Age sites. Nevertheless, the few finds mentioned here indicate that there was continuous settlement, at least on the coast, throughout most of the period, with the largest break in the first century B.C. Contacts with the east, west and south took place at different times during the whole of the Iron Age.

The picture given here is a very simplified one, but it does give some perspective of the parameters involved. The evidence is taken from a large area and its relevance is therefore limited. Figure 4 gives an overall view of the environmental and cultural development of northern Sweden with the emphasis on upper Norrland, which has also been emphasised in the text.

The major concern of archaeologists working in the north has been chronology, and indeed this is the starting point in any cultural-historical research, but little attempt has been made thus far to analyse more deeply the workings of individual societies within limited chronological, economic and territorial contexts.

For the past few years, the author has concentrated upon such a study. Because of the difficulty of obtaining a stratigraphically limited cultural horizon for study, a settlement was chosen on the Västerbotten coast where shoreline displacement has effectively isolated a shorebound site complex. This complex is called Lundfors.

Lundfors: a case study of a coastal settlement

Lundfors is a small valley located c. 20 km. south-west of the city of Skelleftea on the Västerbotten coast at 64°41′N., 20°40′E. Seven sites located 200 metres apart lie on the north side of the valley at 78 metres above sea level. The sites were formerly shorebound and their exact sea level provenience has been determined through phosphate profiles which indicate high values on the beach below the sites (probably representing butchery areas), and a sharp cut-off at the former shore edge at 77.5 metres. One site, on the more exposed north-west opening of the inlet, had been partially cast up by wave action into a beach ridge.

The Västerbotten coast is at present the epicentre for crustal rebound in Sweden and the landrise equals 0.91 cm. per year. The settlement level has been dated through an exponential landrise curve to c. 3,350 bc (Broadbent 1976). Three uncontaminated radiocarbon dates have confirmed this dating. At the time of settlement, the rate of landrise equalled 2.18 cm. per year. The uniform beach levels for the sites, and the flat topography of the valley show that the area became dry ground after some 100 years and that the sites were not occupied for more than a total of 25-50 years, a fact which helps to establish the homogeneity of the material.

The sites have an even spread along the shore. The average area of the sites is 1,700 square metres, and the shape of the sites is related to their alignment along the shore: they are roughly twice as long as they are deep. The distance between sites is c. 200 metres, with the spread due in part to the form of the bay. The sites were probably not occupied simultaneously, but rather resulted from occupation by one or two groups in a succession of moves. These moves could have been precipitated by the accumulation of stone and organic litter, exhaustion of fuel supplies within a certain radius, or changes in shoreline conditions. The shift of 200 metres evidently represented the ideal 'upwind' adjustment. If this is correct, all suitable shoreline space had been utilised.

No dwelling structures have been found, although some form of tent or hut was probably used. The only small cultural features are pits and rough hearths. The pits, which measure 1-2 metres in diameter and c. 40 cm. in depth, seem to be for cooking and train oil extraction. The hearths are small (c. 1 m.²), and are associated with quartz flakes, suggesting male stone-working areas.

On a higher level of analysis, the location of the settlement was based upon a delicate balance of resource accessibility and exposure (Fig. 5). The sites were situated on the sunny, exposed side of the inlet and at a comfortable distance from the shore, in a belt of trees. They were protected from the sea winds by the mountains behind them. A steady supply of water was provided by several springs, one of which lies immediately behind the sites. Large quantities of good quality quartz could be obtained via a convenient water passage to the south-east. Within the same radius to the north-west, one had access to the Skellefte river estuary and a larger bay area. In the Lundfors inlet itself, and in a nearby narrow lagoon, ideal fishing and seal netting could be practised. Numbers of net weights and even a coarse net fragment (now lost) were found there. One final resource area is a long lake and stream system which extends 35 km. to the south of the settlement area, roughly parallel to the ancient coastline where it opens into a small coastal bay. This beaver-regulated water system offered access to traditional interior hunting and fishing resources of

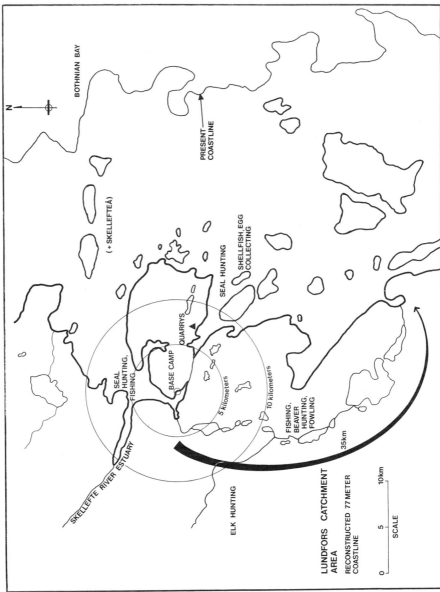

Figure 5. The ancient Lundfors coastline at c. 3,400 bc, and the system of available resources.

great potential within a short distance from the coast.

Faunal analysis has shown that the ringed seal was a major resource on the sites (95 percent), with beaver (1 percent) and elk (1 percent) also represented. The fishes identified are pike and bream, and the smaller game consists of pine marten and hare, all identified from single bones or fragments. At one site fragments of mussel shells and barnacles were identified. Numerous Litorina shell-bank remains are found within the ancient Västerbotten coastal area, and they could have provided an important source of protein.

Taken at their face value, the faunal remains suggest that Lundfors was a seasonal settlement dependent upon seal-hunting. Seal netting of the type in question is best done in the dark autumn months. Faunal assemblages from interior Norrland have been shown in the majority of cases to consist of over 90 percent elk. In other words, the osteological material supports the idea of a coastal-inland seasonal wandering of these people, with perhaps beaver hunting and fishing

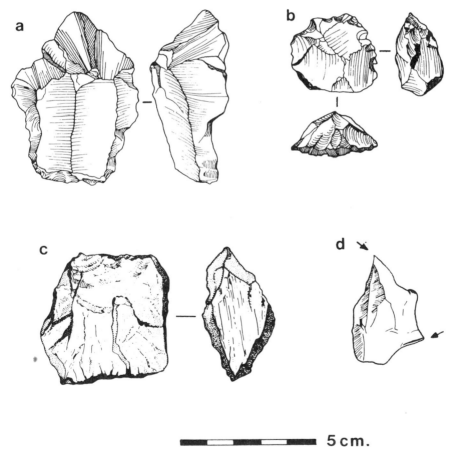

5 cm.

Figure 6. Quartz implements from Lundfors: a – core scraper; b – small end scraper; c – splintered-piece core; d – burin.

playing an intermediate role between the extremes.

Nevertheless, despite the one-sidedness of its faunal material, Lundfors offers an alternative to this pattern. Within the limited coastal range of the sites, forest, lacustrine and coastal resources were accessible. There was absolutely no economic reason for these people to leave the coastal region. I think it would have been entirely possible for a basically permanent population to maintain itself within this zone. It is likely that there were hunting and fishing camps along the local waterways where elk and beaver were hunted and butchered. The scarcity of bones from these animals on the main coastal settlements may reflect the simple fact that these animals were not butchered there. There are many sources of error involved in the interpretation of burnt bone material of this kind, especially when the numbers of individuals cannot be effectively evaluated. Recent research is making this increasingly clear (Higham 1968; Payne 1972). Furthermore, it is misleading to interpret prehistoric settlements 'solely from the point of view of the exploitation of individual species' (Jarman 1972: 125). Lundfors may be taken as a case in point.

A balanced economy of the type proposed would have provided a degree of stability beyond that of migratory hunting. This 'modified maritime' economic basis would have promoted population growth and thus stimulated social and technological development. The role of the specialist would have been enhanced, as would be eventual external contacts and trade beyond the subsistence area of the society (Fitzhugh 1975: 379). Societies of this type were probably central in the development of the slate (and flint) trade throughout the whole Baltic.

The technology of Lundfors

The technology of Lundfors was based on quartz, ground slate and schist, and miscellaneous local rocks. The quartz was obtained from quarries located 7 km. to the south-east of the settlement. The quartz veins were systematically opened by means of fire-setting, and the quartz, both worked and unworked, was transported to the sites via a water passage. It is estimated that 5-7 tons of the largely rose-coloured and smoky quartz from the quarries litter the sites (Broadbent 1973). The quartz was worked using hard hammers on irregular platform and splintered piece (*pièces écaillés*) cores. Tools were made from both cores and flakes. Short end scrapers, flake knives, burins, borers, gravers and even small axes were made (Fig. 6). No projectiles or microliths were found in quartz, and the technique of bifacial (flat-hewn) flaking was not used.

The slate consists of black, green and red varieties. The red and green slate is not local in origin and is certainly derived from the *fjäll* areas. The black slate is found along the nearby Skellefte river. The

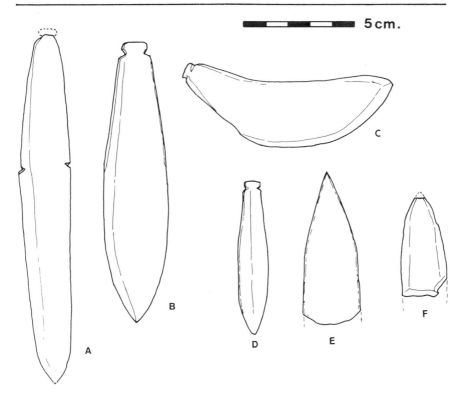

Figure 7. Slate artefacts from Lundfors: A – single-edged knife; B – double-edged knife; C – curved-edged knife; D – pendant; E, F – projectile fragments.

finds consist of knives, projectiles, pendants and flakes and polished schist adzes and chisels (Figs. 7, 9).

The slates and schists are the only non-local raw materials on the sites. The finds are of two kinds: north Swedish slate forms, and adzes of Finnish type. The latter are an early manifestation in northern Sweden, however. Finely-ground and polished slates are typical of northern Sweden. These objects were mass-produced at sites such as Överveda on the Angermanland coast. These slates were very viable trading objects and have been found in Norway, southern Sweden, Aland, Finland and Gotland. The trade probably started as early as the fourth millenium bc and reached a peak during the middle Neolithic (at the same time as flint was being traded to Norrland). This activity continued into the Bronze Age. Distinctive objects from northern Sweden were animal-headed daggers, T-shaped implements, curved knives and tanged projectiles with pointed barbs.

The development of slate technology is closely connected with maritime hunting and fishing and this is where the greatest elaboration of forms has taken place (Fitzhugh 1974). It is also within the coastal regions, around the Gulf of Bothnia for example, that trade has been the most active.

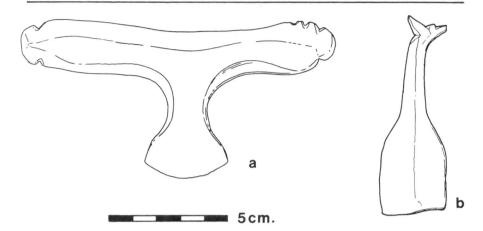

5cm.

Figure 8. a – T-shaped implement of slate from Överveda; b – Animal-headed dagger fragment from Skråmträsk, Västerbotten.

The slate forms from Lundfors are quite similar to those of Överveda. A recent find of a T-shaped implement not far from Lundfors (more than 27 were found at Överveda), and an animal-headed dagger of red slate from the Lundfors site area (Fig. 8a,b) help to confirm the fact that there was contact between coastal upper and middle Norrland.

The flakes and ground adzes and chisels of Finnish type are common finds in northern Sweden, primarily on the coast. These implements, with which one should include the so-called 'North Bothnian Implements', often huge shoe-horn-edged pieces of schist (Fig. 9a) are, as the name implies, especially common on the upper Bothnian coast (Moberg 1955). Northern Österbotten in Finland was also a district with special adze manufacturing centres (Kivikoski 1964: 50). These regions could have been centres for adze production with trade networks to the south and west, perhaps passed on in exchange for Scandinavian slate objects or flint and amber. While basically functional, the slate forms and adzes are sometimes so fine, or large in size, that they can justifiably be considered as purely status, wealth or ceremonial articles. Their distributions reflect extensions and limits of social and cultural communication, not merely trade routes.

Stone cobbles and pebbles were fashioned into many tools at Lundfors: choppers, flakes, whetstones, abraders, and a perforated stone (a digging-stick weight) Fig. 9b). Hundreds of them were made into simple notched net weights, used in sealing (Fig. 9c). Of equal importance was their use as boiling stones. Lundfors shares with the interior sites from the same period the distinction of having many tons of fire-cracked and heat-exfoliated stones. The stones were not found in ring-walls, but were distributed over the sites. As mentioned before,

Figure 9. Stone artefacts from Lundfors: a – 'North Bothnian Implement' (28 cm. long); b – digging-stick weight (maximum diameter 15 cm.); c – notched cobble sinker (weight c. 500 gm.); d – flaked black schist adze (19.6 cm. long).

this is one of the most distinctive features of early north Swedish quartz-slate settlements.

While, as a whole, this technology shares much with the Finnish pre-ceramic Stone Age, the fire-cracked stones indicate a fundamental dissimilarity. In Finland such stones are rarely found and became superfluous with the introduction of pottery at c. 4,200 bc. This difference lies at the root of the question of why comb-impressed pottery never became established in Norrland despite the evidence for continual contact with the east (see for example Christiansson 1969: 51-80). One could even go so far as to suggest that this shows two ethnically and perhaps even racially(?) distinct populations which did not have any form of inter-marriage or wife-exchange. Meinander (1961:16) has commented on the wide distribution of comb-impressed pottery in north-eastern Europe and expressed the opinion that this was due in a large part to exogamy. Interestingly enough, the ceramic type distributions did not correspond with the spread of stone artefact types. In upper Norrland and Finland one has the opposite situation: the stone artefacts are found in both areas, but not the pottery. Pottery did not become established in upper Norrland until the Bronze Age. The cooking and the food preparation in the two areas were based on different principles until this time.

Lundfors and maritime settlement in a wider perspective

The interpretation offered for Lundfors represents an alternative to the coastal-inland, seasonal and migratory way of life. Within a broader time perspective one can study the chronological distribution of other coastal settlements on the Västerbotten. The important point which emerges is that the settlements do not appear to represent a steady growth, but rather tend to occur at specific time horizons, separated by periods of relatively 'findless' levels. There are four main horizons of occupation: two quartz-slate site complexes, one at 78 metres (Lundfors) and one at 65 metres (Heden); a boat axe/flint adze horizon at c. 50 metres (Bjurselet); and a quartzite point/coastal cairn horizon at c. 35 metres. The datings are roughly as follows: Lundfors 3,400 bc; Heden 2,700 bc; Bjurselet 1,900 bc; and the cairn level c. 1,000 bc.

The element that all of these groups have in common (with perhaps the exception of the Bronze Age settlement) is an economy based to a considerable degree on seal hunting. The existence of the settlements was therefore determined by overall maritime conditions and the availability of seals.

As is well known, the Baltic has been subject to variations in salinity, passing from fresh water to salty and brackish conditions and back again. The period of maximum salinity – the Litorina Sea – offered the greatest food resources, and it is during this stage that coastal cultures develop in northern Europe. Upper Bothnia was also involved in this ecological-cultural development. During, for example, the time of Lundfors, the Bothnian Bay had a salinity increase of at least 5 parts per thousand and probably much more. The volume of the Bay was four times greater, the threshold 77 metres deeper (at present 25 metres), and the narrow mouth of the bay (the Kvarken) was no longer a barrier to circulation. These factors had a decisive effect not only on the marine life but also on the land, which had a more maritime climate. This can be seen from the pollen analysis for Lundfors which shows a dominant deciduous forest vegetation with elm, ash, hazel and alder – a biotype with a high vegetable-food potential for man. This forest ran along the coast, with the coniferous forest and its resources only a short distance inland.

Today, when the Bothnian Bay freezes, the weather shifts to more continental conditions. Judging partly from the vegetation spectrum on the Västerbotten coast, it is doubtful whether ice conditions were more extreme during the Litorina period, despite the arguments to the contrary (Pettersson 1914; Ekman 1940: 32). The layering of fresh and salt water in the Baltic today would have been markedly decreased with the increased circulation. The effluence of fresh river water would, on the other hand, have been approximately the same.

Although these arguments make for a richer Bothnian environment than today, it is possible that conditions were not always strong enough to provide a stable maritime influence. This is perhaps reflected by the uneven growth of coastal sites. At various periods, however, 'piston strokes' of salt water enter the Baltic and greatly stimulate marine resources. This happened in 1923 when large quantities of more than 34 parts per thousand salinity were pumped into the southern Baltic, resulting in a haddock fishery in 1925 of 'previously unknown intensity'. Altered wind conditions can also stimulate an increase in salinity for longer periods of time, even in the innermost Baltic, where salinity can rise 10-20 per cent higher than normal (Segerstrale 1957: 757).

In recent years much attention has been given to the study of Litorina transgressions in the Baltic (Berglund 1971; Eronen 1973; Digerfeldt 1975). These transgressions imply increases in water level which have world-wide sea level and climatic connections, perhaps ultimately caused by sun-spot activity (Fairbridge 1963).

Berglund (1971) has obtained evidence for six transgressions of varying intensity at sites in Blekinge, where landrise is near the zero point. These transgressions take place during the following periods: (I) 5,000-4,700; (II) 4,500-4,300; (III) 3,900-3,600; (IV) 3,500-3,300; (V) 2,700-2,500; (VI) 2,100-1,900 bc.

In the upper Bothnian area where isostatic land recovery has been very great, it seems unlikely that any transgressions took place, although certain shore levels could have been stabilised for certain periods by the eustatic rises. The significance of sea-level changes in terms of overall influx of saltwater and the effects on sea-life could, nevertheless, have had great consequences.

On the Västerbotten coast three of the archaeological horizons (Lundfors, Heden and Bjurselet) coincide with transgressions IV, V and VI respectively. As previously stated, seal hunting was central to the economies of the three complexes. While the seal populations could potentially have grown with increased food resources, ice conditions seem to be the key to the distribution and density of the seal species in question, the ringed seal. If ice conditions were decreased rather than increased during Litorina times, the ice that formed would have been concentrated in the northern, coastal-bound areas, and would have been most stable on broken, island-rich coasts such as that of northern Västerbotten. The ringed seal tends to remain throughout the year within such winter, ice-bound, complicated coasts (McLaren 1958; Vibe 1971). This situation might provide one of the reasons for the appearance of coastal settlements within the Bothnian Bay. Settlements of the Lundfors and Heden type could be the result of unusually rich and stable marine and coastal resources which guaranteed a reliable food base for several years. The people of Bjurselet, 800 years later than Heden, may have been obliged to leave the south Baltic for the same reasons – altered ice conditions. Archaeological work on the deeply fjorded coast in Angermanland has revealed the presence of similar coastal settlements (besides Överveda) in the Anunsjön area (Baudou 1973: 161). A shoreline displacement curve is being prepared for the region and distinctive settlement horizons with separating gaps have been found (Urve Miller, personal communication). Two levels dated to 2,700 and 1,900 bc were especially marked. In Finland, Dr Ari Siiriäinen, who has published his thesis on shoreline displacement and prehistoric settlement, has commented on two apparent transgression levels in south Finland at around 3,500/3,600 and 2,900/2,500 bc (Siiriäinen 1974). He states that Berglund's transgression V corresponds exactly to the displacement slowdown in Finland. There is some suggestion that settlements in Finland were especially intensive or clustered at these levels.

Much work remains to be done regarding these transgressions and on the implications they might have had for prehistoric maritime cultures. At present, however, the evidence for marine transgressions and maritime occupation does seem to correlate, having a close relationship to the marine balance of the Baltic and the economic potentials for human culture.

To summarise: there is good reason to believe that basically permanent settlements could have been maintained on the Bothnian coast. These settlements were largely dependent on maritime food resources, but could also utilise forest and lacustrine resources available within the same coastal zone. The Bay of Bothnia was subject to periodic changes in circulation and salinity, and the coastal settlements might have stabilised during periods of optimal maritime conditions. The major settlement horizons have been seen to correspond to transgressions in southern Scandinavia. These occur at c. 3,400, 2,700 and 1,900 bc.

It is clear that the coastal regions of Norrland have been most active in trading and cultural interchange, receiving impulses from and transmitting them to both the south and east. These periods of special contact could have been made possible by increased settlement stability and the development of specialised manufacturing and trading groups. The expansion of the slate trade during late Litorina times might have been due to the presence of these coastal societies.

References

Almgren, O. 1914. *Några svensk-finska stenåldersproblem.* Antikvarisk Tidskrift, 20(1). Stockholm.

Ångström, A. 1968. *Sveriges Klimat.* Stockholm, Generalstabens Litografiska Anstalts Förlag.

Arbman, H. 1945. Jävrefyndet. *Norrbotten*: 111-20.

Atlas över Sverige. 1971. Utgiven av Svenska Sällskapet för Antropologi och Geografi, B1, Stockholm.

Bagge, A. 1937. Stenåldern vid Torne Träsk. *Norrbotten*: 89-106.

Baudou, E. 1968. *Forntida Bebyggelse i Ångermanlands Kustland.* Arkiv för Norrländsk Hembygdsforskning, 17. Härnosand.

Baudou, E. 1970. Forskningsprojektet NTB och Hälla. *Västerbotten* 1: 5 16.

Baudou, E. 1973. Icke bofast och bofast i Norrlands förhistoria. *Tromsö Museums Skrifter*, 14. Tromsö.

Becker, C.J. 1952. Die Nordswedischen Flintdepots. *Acta Archaeologica*, 23: 31-79.

Berglund, B. 1971. The postglacial shore displacement in eastern Blekinge, southeast Sweden. *Sveriges Geologisk Undersökning*, Ser. C, Årsbok, 58, No. 5: 3-47.

Bergstrom, R. 1968. Stratigrafi och isrecession i södra Västerbotten, *Sveriges Geologisk Undersökning*, Ser. C, No. 634.

Biornstad, M. 1966. Forskningsprojektet Norrlands Tidiga bebyggelse. *Fornvännen*, 61: 65-72.

Broadbent, N. 1973. Prehistoric quartz quarrying in Norrland. *Fornvännen*, 68: 129-37.

Broadbent, N. 1976. En Kritisk undersökning av Landhöjning och arkeologi i Västerbotten. *Västerbotten* (in press).

Brögger, A.W. 1909. *Den Arkiske Stenalder i Norge.* Vetenskaps Selskabets Skrifter II. Oslo.

Carpelan, C. 1962. Nellimin löytö. *Suomen Museo*, 69: 5-25.

Christiansson, H. 1969a. Obbolagraven och dess runda spännen. *Nordsvensk Forntid. Skytteanska Samfundets Handlingar*, 6: 197-210.

Christiansson, H. 1969b. Kamkeramiska influenser i Norrland och Norra Svealand. *Nordsvensk Forntid. Skytteanska Samfundets Handlingar*, 6: 51-80.

Christiansson, H. 1970. Nordarkeologi gräver. *Västerbotten* 1: 36-43.

Christiansson, H. 1974. Die Steinzeit Nordschwedens. *Praehistorische Zeitschrift*, 49: 10-37.

Christiansson, H. and Broadbent, N. 1975. Prehistoric coastal settlement on the upper Bothnian coast of northern Sweden. In W. Fitzhugh (ed.), *Prehistoric Maritime Adaptations in the Circumpolar Zone.* The Hague, Mouton: 47-55.

Cullberg, C. 1972. *Förslag till Västsvensk Mesolitisk Kronologi.* Institutionen for Arkeologi, University of Göteborg. (Stencil).

Digerfeldt, G. 1975. A standard profile for Litorina transgressions in Skåne, southern Sweden. *Boreas*, 4: 125-42.

Ekman, S. 1940. Die Biologische Geschichte der Nord- und Ostsee. *Die Tierwelt der Nord- und Ostsee*, Band I. Leipzig.

Engelmark, R. 1976. The vegetational history of the Umeå area during the past 4,000 years. *Early Norrland* 9. Kungl. Vitterhets Historie och Antikvitets Akademien. Stockholm: 75-111.

Eronen, M. 1974. The history of the Litorina sea and associated Holocene events. *Commentationes Physico-Mathematicae*, 44 (No. 4): 80-195.

Erä-Esko, A. 1957. Die Steinzeitlichen forschungen der letzen jahre in Nord-Finnland. *Finska Fornminnestidskrift*, 58: 28-40.

Erä-Esko, A. (ed.) 1975. *Kemijoki 8000*. Stockholm, Statens Historiska Museum.

Fairbridge, R. 1963. Mean sea level related to solar radiation during the last 20,000 years. *Proceedings of the Rome Symposium organized by Unesco* (Liège): 229-42.

Fitzhugh, W. 1974. Ground slates in the Scandinavian younger Stone Age, with reference to circumpolar maritime adaptations. *Proceedings of the Prehistoric Society*, 40: 45-58.

Fitzhugh, W. 1975. A comparative approach to northern maritime adaptations. In W. Fitzhugh (ed.), *Prehistoric Maritime Adaptations in the Circumpolar Zone*. The Hague, Mouton: 339-87.

Florin, S. 1959. Hagtorp. En prekeramisk kvartsförande fångstboplats från tidig Litorinatid. *Tor*, 5: 7-51.

Fransson, S. 1965. The Borderland. In *The Plant Cover of Sweden*. Acta Phytogeographia Suecia, 50: 167-75.

Gaustad, F. 1969. Stone Age investigations in northern Norway. *Norwegian Archaeological Review*, 2: 86-93.

Gjessing, G. 1944. *The Circumpolar Stone Age*. Acta Arctica II. Copenhagen.

Gräslund, B. 1967. Recension av Mesche. (En stenåldersboplats med skärvstensvall). *Fornvannen*, 4: 272-4.

Gräslund, B. 1970. Stenåldersboplatsen vid Ransjön. *Jämten*, 64: 141-6.

Hallström, G. 1942. Norrlands Bebyggelsehistoria och Förhistoriska Utveckling. *Ymer*.

Hallström, G. 1960. *Monumental Art of Northern Sweden from the Stone Age*. Stockholm, Almqvist and Wicksell.

Higham, C.W. 1968. Faunal sampling and economic prehistory. *Zeitschrift for Zaugertierkund*, 33: 297-305.

Hildebrand, H. 1866. *Svenska Folket under Hednatiden*. Stockholm. Seligmanns.

Hjärne, E. 1917. Bronsfyndet fran Stor Kåge. *Fornvannen*, 12: 147-72, 203-25.

Huttunen, P. and Tolonen, M. 1972. Pollen analytical studies of prehistoric agriculture in northern Angermanland. *Early Norrland 1*. Kungl. Vitterhets Historie och Antikvitets Akademien: 9-34.

Hvarfner, H. 1957. *Fångstän och Nybyggare i Ångermanlands Källområden Under Järnåldern*. Arkiv for Norrländsk Hembygdsforskning, 15. Härnosand.

Indrelid, S. 1969. *Kulturhistoriske Undersökelser på Hardangervidda*. Universitetet i Bergen Historiska Museum.

Indrelid, S. 1975. Problems relating to the early Mesolithic settlement of southern Norway. *Norwegian Archaeological Review*, 8: 1-18.

Iregren, E. 1975. Analys av Benmaterialet. *Riksantikvarieämbetet Rapport* 1975, B.65. Stockholm.

Janson, S. and Hvarfner, H. 1960. *Från Norrlandsalvar och Fjallsjoar*. Stockholm, Riksantikvarieämbetet.

Jarman, M.R. 1972. European deer economies and the advent of the Neolithic. In E.S. Higgs (ed.), *Papers in Economic Prehistory*. London, Cambridge University Press: 125-59.

Johansson, A. 1969. Höjfjellsfunn ved Laerdalsvassdraget. *Årbok för Universitetet i Bergen*, Ser. 4: 5-113.

Kivikoski, E. 1964. *Finlands Förhistoria*. Helsinki, Holger Schilds Förlag.

Königsson, L.K. 1968. *The Holocene History of the Great Alvar of Öland*. Acta Phytogeographia Suecica, 55. Uppsala.

Königsson, L.K. 1970. *Traces of Neolithic Human Influence upon the Landscape Development of the Bjurselet Settlement, Västerbotten, Northern Sweden*. Skytteanska Samfundets Handlingar, 7. Umeå.

Lannerbro, R. 1976. Implements of rock material in the prehistory of Upper Dalarna. *Early Norrland 4*. Kungl. Vitterhets Historie Antikvitets Akademien. Stockholm.

Lepiksaar, J. 1975. *The Analysis of the Animal Bones from the Bjurselet Settlement, Västerbotten, Northern Sweden*. Skytteanska Samfundets Handlingar, 8. Umea.

Linder-Rissen, A. 1966. C-14 datering av Norrländsk Asbestkeramik. *Fornvännen*, 61: 140-53.

Lundqvist, J. 1965. South-facing hills and mountains. In *The Plant Cover of Sweden*. *Acta Phytogeographica Suecica*, 50: 216-8.

Martens, I. and Hagen, A. 1961. *Arkeologiske Undersökelser längs elv och vatn*. Norske Oldfunn 10. Oslo.

McLaren, I.A. 1958. *The Biology of the Ringed Seal in the Eastern Canadian Arctic*. Fisheries Research Board of Canada, Bulletin No.118. Ottawa.

Meinander, C.F. 1961. De subneolitiska kulturgrupper i norra Europa. *Societas Scientiarum Fennia Årsbok*, 39 B, No. 4: 1-23.

Meschke, C. 1967. *En Norrländsk Stenåldersboplats med Skärvstensvall*. Antikvarisk Arkiv, 31. Stockholm.

Moberg, C.A. 1955. *Studier i Bottnisk Stenålder I-V*. Antikvariska Serien 3. Stockholm, Almqvist and Wiksel.

Nilsson, A.B. 1969. *Förbindelser mellan Nord- och Sydskandinavien under Mellanneoliticum till Bronsåldern*. Institutionen for Arkeologi, Uppsala (stencil).

Nilsson, S. 1838-43. *Skandinaviska Norden Ur-invånare*. (Stenåldern). Stockholm, Norstedt och Söners Förlag.

Payne, S. 1972. On the interpretation of bone samples from archaeological sites. In E.S. Higgs (ed.), *Papers in Economic Prehistory*. London, Cambridge University Press: 65-81.

Pettersson, O. 1913. *Klimatförandringar i Historisk och Förhistorisk Tid*. Kungl. Vitterhets Historie och Antikvitets Akademien, Band 2, No. 2. Stockholm.

Robertson-Åkerlund, A. 1975. Stenåldersboplatser vid sjön Ockern, Föllinge sn, Jämtland. *Riksantikvarieämbetet Rapport*, 1975, B 65. Stockholm.

Santesson, O.B. 1941. *Magiska Skifferredskap från Norrlands Stenålder*. Arctos Svecia, 1. Uppsala.

Segerstrale, S.G. 1957. The Baltic Sea: treatise on marine ecology and palaeoecology. *Geological Society of America*, Memoir 67 (Vol. 1): 751-99.

Serning, I. 1960. *Övre Norrlands Järnålder*. Skrifter Utgiven av Vetenskapliga Biblioteket i Umeå, 4. Umeå.

Siiriäinen, A. 1974. *Studies Relating to Shore Displacement and Stone Age Chronology in Finland*. University of Helsinki Department of Archaeology, stencil No. 10.

Slomann, W. 1948. *Medelpad och Jämtland i eldre Järnalder*. Universitetet i Bergen Årbok. Historisk Antikvarisk Rekke 2. Bergen.

Stenberger, M. 1964. *Det Forntida Sverige*. Stockholm. Almqvist and Wiksell.

Sundlin, H. 1974. *Fyra Förhistoriska Boplatser från Norra Hälsingland, en Preliminar Analys*. Institutionen för Arkeologi vid Stockholms Universitet (stencil).

Tallgren, A.M. 1949. *The Arctic Bronze Age in Europe*. Eurasia Septintrionalis Antiqua, 11, Helsinki.

Toivonen, Y.A. 1949. *Zum Problem des Protolappischen*. Sitzungsberichte der Finnischen Akademie der Wissenschaften. Helsinki.

Vibe, C. 1970. The arctic ecosystem influenced by fluctuations in sun-spot and drift-ice movements. *International Union for the Conservation of Nature and Natural Resources*, New Series No. 16: 115-20.

Welinder, S. 1973. *The Pre-pottery Stone Age of Eastern Middle Sweden.* Antikvarisk Arkiv, 48, Stockholm.

Welinder, S. 1974a. *Kulturlandskapet i Mälarområdet.* University of Lund Department of Quaternary Geology, Report No. 6. Lund.

Welinder, S. 1974b. Kring västsvensk Mesolitisk kronologi. *Fornvännen,* 4: 147-54.

Westerlund, E. 1969. Okänt folk eller Lappar? *Nordsvensk Forntid. Skytteanska Samfundets Handlingar,* 6: 237-42.

Worsaae, J.J.A., 1872. Ruslands og det Skandinaviske Nordens Bebyggelse og aeldste Kulturforhold. *Aarbøger for Nordhisk Oldkyndighet och Hostorie.* Copenhagen: 309-430.

10

Subsistence and settlement in the north-eastern Baltic

Marek Zvelebil

While the prehistory of western Scandinavia has been described in detail, that of the eastern Baltic has not received such detailed attention. The purpose of this study is to moderate this difference and to make the information that is forthcoming from Estonia, Latvia and south-west Finland more generally available. Settlement and subsistence have been selected as topics particularly needing review, at a time when greater interest than formerly is being taken in subsistence patterns and economic change in prehistory in general. For the sake of a more complete understanding of these aspects of culture, a number of points need to be made about east Baltic ecology and environmental change.

Two geological units are prominent in the north-eastern Baltic: the Russo-Siberian platform and the Fennoscandian Shield. They are separated by Lakes Lagoda and Onega and a belt of Quaternary deposits extending from Lake Onega south-west of the Gulf of Finland. The Fennoscandian Shield is the base of an ancient mountain range formed mainly of crystalline and metamorphic rocks. The retreat of the Fennoscandian glacier and the subsequent isostatic rise of the area has been described by a number of scholars (Sauramo 1958; Donner 1969; Eronen 1974; Clark 1975). The sea washed over the area shaped by glaciers, exposing bare rock on the hilltops and ridges, and depositing finer mineral particles and clays in the valleys and basins. As a result of the gradual isostatic recovery of the land from the weight of the ice sheet, new land was constantly being made available for colonisation by vegetation, fauna and man. This process was temporarily halted and reversed on the southern coast of Finland and in Estonia by a number of marine transgressions, but this paper deals mainly with cultures which are younger than the maximum *Litorina* transgression. Estonia, lying in a more peripheral position to the Fennoscandian glacier, was subjected to a greater deposition of glacial outwash and to an earlier rise from the sea. With the recession of the sea, a large number of lakes was created. In Finland, the Salpausselkä end-moraines effectively impeded drainage of inland water to the sea, thereby contributing to the creation of an environment densely covered with lakes. South and east of the moraines, lake formation took place on a more limited scale and the area is characterised by a 50-100 km. wide coastal plain covered by deposits of *Ancylus* and *Litorina* clays.

Environmental conditions have not been constant in the past. The principal variables have been temperature, precipitation and the distance of any given area from the coastline. Maritime influence has a clearly moderating effect on climate. Over the past 7,000 years the temperate influence of the coastline may be expected to have reached deeper into the interior than it does today. The temperature rise to the Climatic Optimum (4,000-3,000 bc) and subsequent climatic deterioration are indicated in pollen diagrams (Bergelund 1969) and by the distribution of such fossil species as waterchestnut (*Trapa natans*) and the pond tortoise (*Emys orbicularis*) (Vankina 1970; Paaver 1965).

The past vegetational changes are well marked and their zoning has been described by Donner (1963) for Finland, and by Neustadt (1957) for the Baltic area of the U.S.S.R. The changes in forest composition had a pronounced effect on both the fauna and the condition of the soils. Of particular importance during the period covered by this paper was the gradual disappearance of deciduous species and the colonisation of the area by spruce. Advance of spruce across Finland started from the east at c. 2,500 bc and reached the west Finnish coast by c. 1,000 bc (Aartolahti 1966).

The aquatic environment in general and the lacustrine in particular are very important factors in east Baltic geography, ecology and human culture. Although not without exception (Alhonen 1967), a general trend towards eutrophy has been recognised in the north-east Baltic lakes. A general process of development from eutrophic lake to bog has been described by Iversen (1964). As a result of this process, a variety of lake, fen and peat soils were formed which supported vegetation of different productivity and ecological significance (Stålfelt 1960). In south-west Finland, pollen diagrams often indicate the development of bogs through a *Phragmites* stage to a *Carex* stage, which is often replaced by *Sphagnum* type peat. At present, *Carex* and *Sphagnum* peats are still the principal types in south-western Finland. While a number of lake and fen peats with a high water table provided areas suitable for grazing or hay harvesting, most of the peats with a lower water table maintained vegetation in a successional stage dominated by alder and birch, thereby providing a suitable feeding habitat for browsing animals, particularly elk.

This situation was changed to some extent by the immigration of spruce. Spruce is adapted to growing on boggy ground and is often found growing over bogs with a moss undergrowth. Birks and Saarnisto (1975) have described the fall in birch and other deciduous species as a result of spruce immigration, as 'dramatic'. Replacement of broad-leaved forests of both the successional and climax type by spruce had an adverse effect on the grazing and browsing potential of the environment (Mellars 1975).

The fauna of the eastern Baltic has been conveniently sub-divided by Paaver (1965) into 'southern', 'arboreal' and 'ubiquitous' elements. The niche of the 'southern' species is centred on deciduous and forest-steppe environment; the 'arboreal' species are those indigenous to the European Boreal forested zone while the 'ubiquitous' element comprises mainly carnivorous predators. In Estonia and Latvia, the more important 'southern' species were wild horse, wild pig, red deer, roe deer, wild cattle, bison and European hare. The 'arboreal' element comprised the arctic hare (*Lepus timidus*), beaver, bear and elk. In addition, a variety of fur-bearing animals together with seal, fish and waterfowl were hunted. The relative abundance of the two groups fluctuated in time with changing environmental conditions. The representation of the 'southern' species in Finland has been largely restricted to the European hare (*Lepus europeaus*).

The geographic and climatic conditions prevailing between 56° and 62°N. imposed a seasonal regime and a number of other controls on plants, animals and men. In both the Baltic republics and Finland the growing period lasts for around 160 days (i.e. the number of days with a temperature above 5°C.). The length of the photoperiod and of daylight at 60°N. fluctuates from 6-9 hours in January to 18-22 hours in June. The effect of these seasonal fluctuations is seen in a remarkable change of landscape between the winter and summer periods, regulating the mobility patterns of the historic hunting and fishing groups (Hvarfner 1965) and the energy output of the settled farming groups (Mead 1953).

Geographic and climatic controls in north-eastern Europe operate at the expense of stability and predictability of the environment. The area is characterised by a comparatively simple ecological structure and a correspondingly low diversity of both plant and animal species. Grazing herbivores are more limited in their ability to survive winter than browsing ones. Although the length of the growing season in Estonia and Latvia is similar to that in Finland, the reduction in the average thickness of the snow layer in the former areas (10 cm. less than in Finland) makes these areas much more favourable for exploitation by grazing animals.

Subsistence and settlement in Estonia and Latvia

The Kunda Mesolithic

On the basis of the available radiocarbon evidence, settlement belonging to the Mesolithic period can be traced back in these areas to the 8th millennium bc. Radiocarbon dates are available for the sites of

Kunda (Fig. 1, no. 4), Narva-town (no. 2), Osa (no. 17) and Pulli (no. 7) (See Appendix A). Other Mesolithic sites include Siiversti (no. 3), Zveinieki (nos. 15, 16), Lepakoze (no. 8) and hunting and fishing tool kits from Lakes Vyrtsyarv and Lubanas. The associated archaeological assemblages consist of extensive bone tool kits, artefacts made chiefly from poor quality local flint and quartz, slate chisels and stone maceheads. The bone artefacts have been analysed in detail for their cultural affinities (Clark 1936; Indreko 1948, 1964; Loze 1964). In general, they conform to the bone tradition characteristic of the Mesolithic in the Baltic area, though some forms extend as far east as the Urals, while others have a very local distribution (Zagorkis 1963). The abundance and variety of bone harpoons point to a markedly aquatic orientation in the Mesolithic

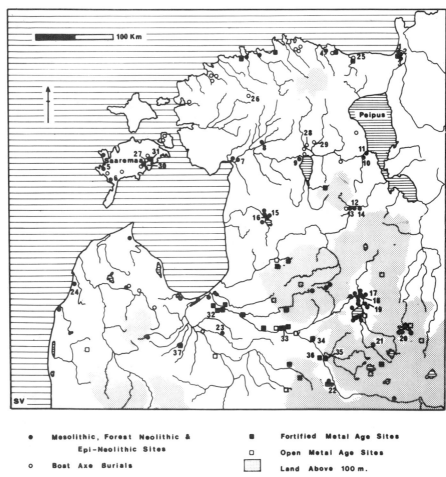

Figure 1. Distribution of prehistoric settlements and burials in Latvia and Estonia prior to 100 A.D. A number of upland hillfort sites in eastern Latvia are not included on the map because their dating to the 1st millennium bc remains equivocal (see LPSRA 1974). For a key to the numbered sites shown on the map see Appendix A.

economy. The location of the sites emphasises this aquatic aspect.

At the time of its Mesolithic occupation Kunda was a lake fed by a small river and separated from the coast by a narrow chain of sand dunes. The surrounding area was covered with pine and birch woodland (Lisytsyna 1958). Faunal material recovered from the Kunda lake shows an overwhelming predominance of elk and beaver (Tables 1 and 2). Relatively few fish bones were found despite the fact that the bone preservation at the site was very good. Seal bones (*Phoca hispida*) accounted for only 12 individuals, despite the proximity of the site to the sea. A similar situation emerges at Narva-town (Fig. 1, no. 2), also near the coast, where Mesolithic layers II and III yielded mainly bones of elk, beaver and wild pig; although many fish bones were preserved, those of seal were extremely rare (Table 1). Other sites, from which faunal remains are lacking, are located without exception either on the coast or closely adjacent to rivers or lakes.

The forest Neolithic

The introduction of pottery brought no abrupt change in either lithic forms or bone tools. New forms which appear at this time include a greater variety of slate tools, a wider range of arrowheads, barbed fish hooks, and a greater differentiation of tree-felling implements. Amber figurines and pendants also make their appearance.

The earliest pottery, belonging to the so-called 'Forest Neolithic', is semi-egg-shaped, with various degrees of pointedness at the base. The principal shape is a wide-mouthed pot, accompanied in some parts of the Baltic by oval-shaped shallow bowls, of which one form (the shoe-shaped pan) has been interpreted as an oil lamp. The most frequent types of decoration are strokes, pits and various kinds of stamps impressed into the unfired surface of the pot. This 'Forest Neolithic' pottery can be divided into a number of local ceramic styles: Narva Ware in Estonia, Osa Ware in east Latvia, and Sarnate Ware in west Latvia. Their absolute dating varies in accordance with preference for a long or short chronology. Jakubovska (in Spang 1975) dates the appearance of pottery to around 4,500 bc, Siiriäinen (1973) to c. 4,000 bc and Timofeev (1975) to c. 3,700 bc. Jakubovska and Timofeev base their claims on radiocarbon dating while Siiriäinen takes into account both radiocarbon dating and the evidence of shoreline displacement.

A more uniform, well-decorated style, the 'typical' Pit-Comb Ware in the east Baltic, or 'Style II' in Finland, appears in the north-eastern Baltic just before 3,000 bc. In Latvia and Estonia it existed alongside Narva and Sarnate pottery for some time, the lower limits of these two types being difficult to determine. Osa-type Ware seems to have gone out of use before the typical Pit-Comb Ware reached the area (Timofeev 1975). By the middle of the 3rd millennium bc more localised groups developed, such as Piestina Ware, existing for at least a millennium before going out of use.

Table 1. Faunal assemblages of principal culled species from East Baltic sites.

	Castor fiber	Ursus arctos	Martes martes	Lutra lutra	Phoca sp.	Equus caball.	Sus scrofa	Cervus elaphus	Alces alces	Bos primig.	Canis famil.	Birds	Fish	Cattle	Ovi-caprids	Horse	Pig	Other species	Total bones	Total animals
														(DOMESTICATED ANIMALS)						
Kunda	1822(117)	74(10)	5(3)	36(13)	73(12)	30(7)	54(13)	7(6)	4512(144)	60(15)	36(15)	204	108					23(13)	6944	365
Narva-town (layers II, III)	152(17)	9(3)	4(2)	2(1)	12(3)		7(1)	35(6)	186(10)	6(2)	27(6)	56	239					13(5)	813	57
Narva-town (layer I)	137(7)	25(4)	5(3)	2(2)	8(3)		140(9)	12(3)	124(4)	20(3)	27(3)	56	75					5(5)	636	46
Kyaepa	3920(296)	613(59)	460(68)	139(36)		282(21)	3214(135)	143(21)	7166(198)	1065(50)	311(39)	421	148					259(63)	19761	986
Narva III	24(3)	13(2)	4(1)	1(1)	178(9)		83(3)	10(2)	226(7)	155(5)	32(3)	2303	10					10(5)	3039	39
Narva I	222(17)	124(112)	93(20)	17(3)	772(29)		1580(43)	1(1)	1725(29)	1125(25)	678(46)	192	292					79(25)	6936	251
Valma	32(9)	4(3)	4(3)	6(5)	3(2)	2	92(16)		59(11)	35(9)	8(3)	2	23					7(5)	273	65
Malmuta	72	21	33	8			173	6	232	82		24	26					31	716	
Piestina	26(5)	7(3)	74(19)	2(2)			151(116)	21(3)	839(9)	17(3)	5(2)	58	20					30(10)	494	72
Kreichi (early phase)	93(15)	29(5)	10(7)	9(4)		2(1)	297(18)	6(5)	285(15)	41(10)	17(5)				3(3)			37(23)	830	111
Leias-ciskas	178	139	6	3			860	no data	no data	1114								348	2648	
Budinka	88	19	15	21			534	11	250	206	4							53	1203	
Akali	61(11)	22(8)	2(2)	7(4)		3(2)	204(12)	3(1)	271(16)	131(7)	12(6)	4	274		1(1)			11(8)	1002	78
Villa	405(26)	12(2)	18(3)	17(4)		2(1)	98(6)	3(2)	572(12)	116(6)	6(3)	114	29		2(1)			22(9)	1304	74
Tamula	4441(293)	168(32)	425(85)	189(51)		1(1)	1671(113)	146(38)	6366(205)	753(75)	163(36)	56	711	1(1)			21(5)	212(96)	15384	1032
Loona			13(8)		935(43)		270(24)	1(1)	9(4)		10(5)		2644				30(9)	32(10)	3990	99
Nakamyae	2(2)	3(2)	8(5)	10(6)	7495(162)		134(11)			4(3)	1(1)	261	54		1(1)		2(2)	19(9)	7991	200
Kreichi (late phase)	89(19)	79(13)	113(25)			5(3)	791(47)	69(14)	1050(51)	167(25)	31(12)							69(36)	2476	254
Silnyupe	1(1)	4(2)	1(1)	1(1)	170(13)	2(1)	16(7)	14(4)	21(5)	27(7)			31						292	46
Rinnyukalns	80(12)	3(1)	5(4)	1(1)		4(2)	52(1)	4(1)	28(1)	36(1)		1	10					4(4)	220	22
Sarnate	2(2)	1(1)			51(10)	3	15(6)	15(15)	9(3)	6(4)					1(1)			3(2)	107	46
Zveinieki	131	19	1				6	6	36	19									221	
Leimanishki	171(119)	9(4)	22(8)	12(8)			79(12)	11(5)	322(17)	137(12)	5(3)	40	21					37(12)	866	100
Kaulenkalns	109(6)	1(1)	1(1)	1(1)			16(1)	2(1)	23(2)	6(2)	1(1)		38					5(5)	204	21
Yurisdika	2(1)	3(3)	1(1)	1(1)			88(16)	29(7)	205(16)	7(3)	1(1)							8(4)	345	53
Asva	8				146		16		36	Bison	14			253	258	74	97	7	909	
Ridala	3(3)	1(1)			89(10)		1(1)		11(3)	Bison	6(2)	17	46	108(7)	160(15)	44(10)	91(11)	2(2)	639	59
Mukukalns	645(94)	38(24)	20(14)	17(13)	1(1)		203(46)	372(62)	308(52)	10(7)	7(6)	28	137	834(93)	385(76)	499(73)	546(87)	84(57)	4134	705
Asote	36(8)	2(1)	3(2)				34(6)	34(6)	28(7)	4(2)	11(2)	4		158(13)	64(11)	70(12)	82(16)	11(6)	541	92
Tervete	12	1					21	5	3	2	5	3		244	147	121	95	19	678	
Klanyukalns							1(1)	1(1)	6(1)										8	3

In each column the first figure indicates the number of bones identified while the second figure (in brackets) indicates the minimum number of individuals. Where only one figure is shown, counts for the minimum numbers of individuals are not available. The figures for 'total animals' do not include fish and birds. The sites are arranged in approximate chronological order. By the first millenium bc Bos primigenius has disappeared from the faunal samples and is replaced by Bison bonasus. Data from Paaver 1965.

Table 2. Percentages of major faunal species represented at six sites in Estonia and Latvia.

	KUNDA (7,000-6,000 bc)	KYAEPA (3,000-2,500 bc)	NARVA III (3,000-2,500 bc)	NARVA I (3,000-2,500 bc)	NAAKA-MYAE (*circa* 2,000 bc)	MUKUK-ALNS (500 bc - 500 AD)
Elk *Alces alces*	65.0	39.9	7.4	25.3	0.1	7.4
Wild cattle *Bos primigenius*	0.9	5.9	5.1	16.2	0.1	—
Horse *Equus caballus*	0.5	1.6	—	—	—	—
Red deer *Cervus elaphus*	0.1	0.8	—	0.1	x	9.0
Roe deer *Capreolus capreolus*	0.1	0.1	0.2	0.4	—	0.4
Wild boar *Sus scrofa*	0.8	17.9	2.7	22.8	1.7	4.9
Brown bear *Ursus arctos*	1.1	3.4	0.4	1.8	x	0.9
Beaver *Castor fiber*	26.2	21.8	0.8	3.2	x	15.6
Otter *Lutra lutra*	0.5	0.8	x	0.2	—	0.4
Pine marten *Martes martes*	0.1	2.6	0.1	1.3	0.1	0.5
Dog *Canis familiaris*	0.5	1.7	1.0	9.8	x	0.2
Seal *Phoca spp.*	1.0	—	5.9	11.1	93.8	
Birds	2.9	1.2	75.8	2.8	3.3	0.7
Fish	1.6	0.8	0.3	4.2	0.7	3.4
Other species	0.3	1.4	0.1	0.8	0.3	1.9
DOMESTICATED FORMS						
Bovids	—	—	—	—	—	20.2
Horse	—	—	—	—	—	12.1
Pig	—	—	—	—	—	13.2
Ovicaprids (sheep/goat)	—	—	—	—	—	9.3
Total identified bones	6,944	17,961	3,039	6,936	7,991	4,134

Owing to incomplete data on numbers of individual animals, the percentages are based on the numbers of identified bones. x indicates a frequency lower than 0.1 percent. More detailed information on the faunas from these sites – including data on numbers of individuals where available – is given in Table 1. Data from Paaver 1965.

Faunal evidence relating to the Forest Neolithic is available from 11 sites. Hunting expanded from a beaver-elk orientation to include the exploitation of wild pig and wild cattle (Tables 1 and 2). According to Paaver (1965) this can be attributed to the expansion of broad-leaf forest in the area during the period of the Climatic Optimum. This view is of course based on the assumption that the hunting activities of the communities in question were essentially unselective, and therefore provide a reliable indication of the available animal resources. An alternative hypothesis – that the change in economy simply reflects changing hunting policies rather than a changing environment – has not as yet been adequately tested. For the present, however, the former interpretation seems more likely, as the kind of changes reflected in the osteological record correspond well with the broader patterns of change in the climatic, edaphic and vegetational aspects of the environment.

Be that as it may, the above form of economy was practised at most sites where bone was preserved. The importance of fishing can be inferred from the finds of net sinkers, bark floats and both single and composite fish hooks, as well as from direct faunal evidence. Identifications from Valma (Jaanits 1959a, 1959b) and Narva (Gurina 1967) suggest that pike and catfish provided the main fishing resources.

The faunal assemblage from Narva site I and III (Fig. 1, no. 1) and Sarnate (no. 24) differed from those described above (Table 2). Perhaps the most interesting point to note in this connection is the exceptionally large numbers of bird bones (principally belonging to adult ducks) in the faunal sample from Narva III. Even allowing for the high proportion of unidentifiable faunal remains from the site of Narva 1, it is impossible to escape the conclusion that the form of exploitation practised at Narva III was significantly different from that at Narva I.

At the time of occupation Narva III was situated on a ridge separating the open sea and a shallow bay, an environment ideally suited for the exploitation of migratory waterfowl. It seems likely in fact that this was a purely seasonal site, probably occupied during the spring. This is suggested by the predominance of the young of harp seal (Bibikova, in Gurina 1967), which must have been hunted from ice flows in the spring, and by the presence of exclusively mature individuals among the duck population, which must have been in the course of their spring or autumn migrations. In addition, waterfowl would not provide a really adequate meat resource for a year-round occupation; an economy based almost entirely on the exploitation of birds over a longer period of time, in the absence of more meat-yielding game, would not seem viable in terms of input and output of energy, even if nets and other devices for seasonal mass hunting were used.

Narva site I differs from site III both in its faunal material and its archaeology. The faunal sample includes several species represented in roughly equal proportions and the site itself consists of several dwellings set amongst large shell middens – suggesting perhaps a settlement of more permanent character. Narva I is situated on the same low ridge as Narva III, but the presence of typical Pit-Comb ware along with Narva pottery would suggest that it dates to a later period. It would seem that at first the location was visited seasonally to cull migratory water-fowl and seal, and that this was followed later by the establishment of a permanent settlement.

The settlements of Narva and Sarnate are the only settlements belonging to the 3rd millennium bc at which bone remains are preserved. Although isolated seal bones have been found at inland sites, the maritime location of Narva and Sarnate is reflected in the sustained exploitation of seal, which, at Sarnate, made up 50 percent of the faunal sample (Vankina 1970).

There is evidence to suggest that the husbanding of waterchestnut (*Trapa natans*) played an important part in the diet during this period. Now a fossil species, it was growing widely on the lakes of north-eastern Europe during the Atlantic and Sub-boreal periods until the beginning of the first millenium bc. At Sarnate, dwellings belonging to the earlier phase of the settlement contained hearths surrounded by lenses of *Trapa* nutshells, several square metres in area and up to 50 cm. thick. Microscopic analysis has suggested that the small wooden hammers found at this site may have been developed especially for breaking the *Trapa* shells. In addition to Sarnate, deposits of waterchestnut were found in cultural layers at Icha (Fig. 1, no. 19), Kreichi (no. 20), Piestina (no. 18), Osa (no. 17) and Liemanishki (no. 21). Bearing in mind the special conditions required for the preservation of these remains, this evidence would seem to indicate exploitation on an extensive scale. There is of course a rich body of historical and ethnographic evidence of the exploitation and indeed for the cultivation of *Trapa natans*. There can be little doubt that the disappearance of this species at the end of the sub-boreal period resulted in a considerable impoverishment in the economic resources available to the human communities.

The location of sites remained unchanged with the introduction of pottery. On a number of sites the Mesolithic levels are overlain by levels of Forest Neolithic – for example at Kunda, Narva-town and Osa. Two Mesolithic sites (Tyrvala and Siivesti) are situated in close proximity to the three Neolithic sites at Narva. The distribution of isolated finds confirms the tendency of sites to cluster around lakes, rivers, or on the coast.

The above description indicates clearly that the appearance of the first pottery in Estonia and Latvia cannot be equated with the introduction of agriculture. The inland sites were involved in the exploitation of beaver, elk, wild pig and, to a lesser degree, wild cattle; on the coast, a greater reliance on seal can be observed in comparison with the coastal sites of the pre-pottery period. This trend towards marine orientation continues into the following Epineolithic period, reaching its peak at the Saaremaa sites where sea mammals accounted for as much as 90 percent of the sample.

Although evidence is sparse, these economic systems probably involved the occupation of both seasonal and permanent settlements. Sarnate, for example, was probably occupied all year round by part of the population at least: occupation during the winter months would seem to be implied by the discovery of a ski fragment, during the spring by the evidence for seal hunting and during the summer by the harvesting of waterchestnut. On the other hand the site of Narva III was almost certainly a seasonal settlement used for the exploitation of wild fowl during their spring or autumn migrations.

The Corded Ware culture and the Epineolithic

Towards the middle of the 3rd millennium bc, traces of Corded Ware (Boat Axe) culture appear in Estonia and Latvia. Its presence is indicated by the characteristic forms of graves and grave goods, and by the appearance of flat-based Corded Ware pottery and associated artefacts alongside late Pit-Comb Ware on the same sites that had earlier contained Neolithic cultures. The distribution of Boat Axe graves differs from that of the earlier Neolithic sites – usually at some distance from water courses or the coast, and on low elevations rather than river basins (Jaanits 1952). However, settlement continuity is clearly shown by the presence of Corded Ware as well as the later Textile Ware on many Pit-Comb Ware settlements: Narva-town (Fig. 1, no. 2), Narva I (no. 1), Valma (no. 9), Kullamyagi (no. 10), Akali (no. 11), Villa (no. 12), Tamula (no. 13), Icha (no. 19), Kreichi (no. 20), Dviete (no. 22), Sarnate (no. 24), and Rutenieki (no. 23) all contained pottery dating to the 2nd millennium bc.

The Corded Ware graves have yielded bones of domesticated animals along with wild species. At Sope (Fig. 1, no. 25), Tika (no. 27), Kunila (no. 29), Kylyaka and Ardu (no. 26), bones of ovicaprids were found, bones of ovicaprids and domesticated pig were found at Sope and Kunila, and the somewhat later burial at Kivisaare (no. 28) yielded bones of domesticated cattle, pig, ovicaprids and horse. Faunal assemblages recovered from dwelling sites dating to the end of the 3rd and the 2nd millennium bc, on the other hand, are composed almost entirely of wild animals. The exceptions are the Saaremaa site of Loona, and isolated bones of ovicaprids, cattle and pig found at Kreichi, Akali and Tamula. At the latter site only 24 of the 14,559 identifiable bones belonged to domestic species.

The faunal samples can be divided into three groups. The first group reveals (as in the Forest Neolithic period) an economy based on the exploitation of beaver, elk, boar and wild cattle. In the second group a greater specialisation can be observed, as at Villa (elk and beaver), Rinnyukalns (beaver forming about 50 percent of the sample) and Yurisdika (elk and wild pig). The third group comprises sites with a maritime economy, such as the island sites of Loona (Fig. 1, no. 5) and Nakamyae (no. 6) in western Saaremaa, where marked specialisation in sea mammal hunting and fishing can be clearly observed, and the coastal site of Silinyupe where, along with seal, terrestrial mammals also played an important role.

It is possible that human subsistence patterns now included the exploitation of the domesticated pig. At Loona, a proportion of the faunal sample belonged to domesticated pigs – that is, to bones that failed to meet the lower limit of size variability of wild boar bones. Paaver (1965) suggested that these individuals might have been in the process of local domestication. It is difficult to believe that the pigs reached Saaremaa on their own account because the island was greatly reduced in size during Boreal and Atlantic times, and thus the distance of the island from the mainland was greater than it is today. Even under present conditions it is unlikely that pigs, whose swimming abilities are very limited, could have reached the island by themselves. A colonisation of the island by wild boar prior to the Boreal period seems unlikely on ecological grounds.

A second feature which can be observed at this time is a relative increase in the reliance on elk and beaver at the expense of the 'southern' type animals (Table 1). This may be due in part to the initial stages of climatic deterioration. It may also be due to the colonisation of the area by spruce. At the same time there is a general decrease in the size of the elk, which may be attributable to the stresses brought about by human exploitation. Paaver (1965) has rejected this possibility on account of the small numbers of the human population at the time – although reliable data on population density are lacking; instead, he attributes the decline in size to a gradual reduction of suitable grazing grounds for elk – a process which, he argues, began with the Climatic Optimum. The size of elk reached its absolute minimum during the 2nd millennium bc, and then increased again during the Sub-atlantic period.

With a decrease in competition from animals of the 'southern' species, an increase in both the population numbers and the body-size of elk might have been expected during the 2nd millenium bc. In view of the almost complete absence of elk from the Saaremaa sites and a general reduction in size on those sites where elk was exploited more intensively than before, it is possible that the elk population was suffering from over-exploitation. Alternatively, the adverse effects of spruce colonisation on the food resources of the elk population may have outweighed the benefits of decreased competition, keeping the elk size low, while the Saaremaa sites may have reached such a degree of economic specialisation that elk hunting was neglected. Nevertheless, it is tempting to see the rationale for bringing the elk population under stress in terms of the withdrawal of the 'southern' species from the area (for example, wild cattle are no longer found on sites dating from the 1st millennium bc) which in turn caused a shift to a greater reliance on elk resources. The later increase in the size of elk in the Sub-atlantic period may be attributable to a combination of factors, including an increase in food supply as a result of greater forest clearance by Man, and at the same time a reduction in the hunting pressure resulting from the adoption of cultivation and husbandry.

While the appearance of the Boat Axe culture resulted in no marked change in settlement location, the character of the finds changes during the 2nd millennium bc, especially in its latter half. The volume of the Epineolithic pottery is greatly diminished and artefact assemblages become relatively impoverished, as compared to the earlier phase of the culture. Good examples of this development can be seen at Akali (Fig. 1, no. 11) and Kullamyagi (no. 10), described by Jaanits (1959a). The first three phases of the settlement at Akali contained Narva pottery, typical Pit-Comb Ware and earlier types of Cord- and Textile-impressed pottery. The thickness of the cultural deposits of these three layers was approximately the same. The fourth period, dated to around 1,500-1,000 bc, was defined by late Corded and Textile pottery. These occurred in much fewer numbers than the earlier types, the cultural layer was thinner, the variety of artefacts diminished, and non-functional objects such as amber figurines disappeared altogether. This trend continued in the fifth and final phase of the settlement, marked by pottery belonging to the early Metal Age, dated to the first half of the 1st millennium bc. The final abandonment of the site may have been caused by the increasing extent of bog formation in the locality. A similar development can be seen at Kullamyagi. The beginning of peat formation on sites previously occupied by hunting and fishing groups is a widespread phenomenon in the eastern Baltic, and must be seen as at least a partial cause of the shift in settlement location around 1,000 bc.

A change in the intensity of settlement, however, can be seen on all sites dating between 1,500 and 1,000 bc. The remains are mostly represented by a thin cultural layer or a scatter of pottery finds. Such is the case at Narva I, Narva-town, Villa, Icha, Leias-ciskas and Sarnate (Jaanits 1959a; Vankina 1970). Occupation of other late Epineolithic sites had either come to an end by this time, or contain Epineolithic sherds whose dating is uncertain. To my mind, these changes indicate a shift in settlement emphasis, at this time, to the effect that former base sites were used only seasonally, probably to carry out specific hunting and fishing activities. The latest pottery at these sites is the same as that of the fortified settlements of the 1st millennium bc that already had a typically Neolithic form of economy. However, settlement evidence is lacking for the time span between the latest permanent Epineolithic sites around the middle of the 2nd millennium bc and the Metal Age dwelling sites.

The Metal Age

The dwelling sites of the 1st millennium bc are either settlements situated in a defensive position on morainic knolls and other elevations and fortified by a bank and ditch, or 'open' settlements. Some of the fortified sites have yielded faunal evidence, the earliest dating to the mid-1st millennium bc. For the crucial period between 500 bc and the latest settlement fauna of the mid-2nd millennium bc, faunal samples come only from the Kivisaare burial dated c. 1,200 bc, containing bones of domesticated animals, and from burials at Reznec and Kalnieski, both dated 1,200-700 bc, where teeth of domesticated horse were found (Graudonis 1967). Some of the fortified settlements contained cultural layers dating to 900-700 bc, as at Mukukalns (Fig. 1, no. 33), Klanyukalns (no. 32) (Graudonis 1967), or Asva (no. 30) (Vassar 1955). Occasionally they also contain pottery dating to the even earlier Epineolithic period. This would seem to have been the case at Kishukalns, Dignaia (no. 36) and Ersika (no. 35) (Paaver 1965). It is probable that with more complete excavation of a greater number of settlements, early cultural layers dating to the early 1st millennium bc or even earlier would become more frequent.

Faunal assemblages are available from six sites dating between the fifth century bc and the first century A.D. (Table 1). Usually, more than half the bones belong to domesticated animals, with ovicaprids predominating on Saaremaa and cattle on the settlements of the Daugava valley. The earliest part of the layer that contained bones at Mukukalns yielded 66 percent of bones of wild animals, more than on any other Metal or Iron Age settlement (Table 2). Taking the Metal Age layer at Mukukalns as a whole, 57 percent of the bones belonged to domesticated animals, while at other sites the corresponding figures were 77 percent for Asva (Fig. 1, no. 30), 79 percent for Ridala (no. 31), 72 percent for Asote (no. 34) and 91 percent for Tervete (no. 37).

The economy of Saaremaa island differs from the mainland firstly because of the predominance of ovicaprids and secondly because of its maritime orientation. Seal remains form more than 80 percent of all hunted animals. Among these, the predominance of the harp seal (*Phoca groenlandica*) is surprising, as this seems to be at variance with data from Finland (Forsten 1975). Intensive fishing is displayed by fish-scale accumulations forming entire layers among the cultural debris at Asva.

Hunting remained an important activity at settlements occupied during the 1st millennium A.D. A hillfort at Ryuge may serve as an example, where 57 percent of all bones belonged to wild animals. The hillfort was dated by radiocarbon to 1,190 ± 230 bp (=760 A.D.) (TA-21). Other settlements of this period, however, yielded faunal samples in which the overall proportion of hunted animals generally falls to less than 20 percent.

The introduction of agriculture into the north-eastern Baltic region had to overcome the two major constraints of poor soil conditions and a severe climatic regime. Although it has been generally accepted that forms of swidden agriculture were employed in the initial stages of cultivation, there is much controversy as to when permanent cultivation systems developed.

Cereal cultivation is first suggested indirectly by the occurrence of bronze sickles in the burials of Kivisaare and Raaziku (c. 1,000 bc). A whole assemblage of agricultural implements developed in the 1st millennium bc, as shown by finds at Mukukalns (Graudonis 1967) and Asva (Vassar 1955). The first direct evidence of cereal cultivation comes in the form of grain impressions on pottery at Asva, indicating knowledge of wheat and (apparently) barley, while knowledge of flax has been postulated by Vassar on artefactual evidence. A layer dating to the end of the 1st millennium bc at Mukukalns yielded grains of barley, wheat and beans. During the first half of the 1st millennium A.D., grain remains come from Kitvy, Daugmale and Sarmukalns, indicating that barley (*Hordeum distichon*) was the principal crop sown, while other cereals were present probably as weeds (Rasniñš 1959). It was not until the eleventh century A.D. that winter-sown rye made its appearance as part of the farming system in the Baltic republics. However, rye was known from at least the fifth century onwards (Rasniñš 1959).

When did cereal cultivation first form a significant element of subsistence economies in Estonia and Latvia? A greater shift towards agriculture has been postulated for the first two centuries A.D. on the basis of a change in burial location, which is thought to have resulted from a general shift in settlement to higher elevations with light soils, and in particular to areas of morainic uplands with pockets of especially fertile soil (Moora 1953; Schmiedehelm 1955). However, such distributions could have been guided by the requirements for pastoral as well as arable farming, and there is some artefactual evidence in support of this view (see below). On the other hand further support for an increase in cultivation at this time is provided by the temporary decline of the population on Saaremaa (whose agricultural potential would have been easily exhausted under swidden agriculture on account of its thin soils) and a corresponding increase of population in north-eastern Estonia, characterised by deeper and more fertile soils (Schmiedehelm 1955).

Widespread adoption of agriculture was probably not synchronous and would have depended on a number of factors, such as the availability of a local iron-making industry, suitable soils, and population pressure. On present evidence it seems clear that the appearance of iron tools gave an impetus at least to the pastoral form of economy. Extension of lowland grave distribution to include upland positions in north-eastern Estonia in the second century A.D. coincides with the appearance of scythes and both perforated and socketed iron axes among the grave finds (Schmiedehelm 1955). The appearance of a novel type of scythe, especially intended for harvesting hay, coincided with an increase in settlement density on Saaremaa in the ninth century A.D. (Kustin 1967). The general importance of iron-made tools for cultivation and animal husbandry in the prehistoric east Baltic has been stressed by Moora (1953) and Krasnov (1971).

It seems clear that the knowledge of both animal husbandry and agriculture existed in these areas for some time before these economic strategies were adopted on a significant scale. On present evidence, the shift to pastoralism must have taken place between 1,500 and 1,000 bc – considerably later than a number of scholars thought. Usually, the earliest pastoralists in the area are thought to have been the Boat Axe people (Briusov 1961; Jaanits 1966; Krasnov 1971). However, while the association of the Boat Axe culture with domesticated animals is beyond doubt, the available samples of faunal material (deriving mainly from graves) are far too limited to provide convincing proof of a pastoral economy. In fact, the available faunal evidence suggests, if anything, that the prevailing form of economy throughout the Epineolithic period continued to be hunting and fishing.

Settlement and subsistence in south-west Finland

As in Estonia and Latvia, discrete chronological and cultural units in the prehistory of Finland have been defined in the past by a series of pottery styles. The associated artefactual assemblages, however, show a remarkable continuity well into the Iron Age, especially in inland

Table 3. Chronology and geographical location of major ceramic and cultural groupings in south-west Finland.

Date bc	Located on shore	Located near coast but not on shoreline	Inland Lake District location
0		Pre-Roman Iron Age	Pre-Roman Iron Age
500		Morby Ware	
1,200		Bronze Age Pottery	
1,300			Sarsa Ware
1,800	Kiukais		
2,300	Pyhensiltä		
2,600		Corded Ware	Combed Ware
2,800	Combed Ware III		III and Corded Ware
3,200	Combed Ware II		Combed Ware II
3,400	Jäkärlä		
4,200	Combed Ware I		Combed Ware I
	Suomusjärvi		Suomusjärvi

Based on Carpelan 1962; Meinander 1969, 1971; Siiriäinen 1974.

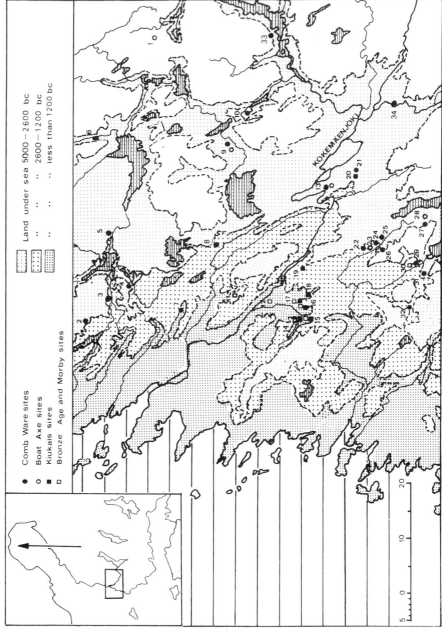

Figure 2. Map to illustrate the distribution of prehistoric sites in relation to shorelines of different periods in the area of the Kokemäenjoki river drainage in Finland. For a key to the numbered sites shown on the map see Appendix B.

areas. In general, the appearance of new artefactual forms does not correlate with the appearance of new ceramic forms. As a result, only a few artefacts can be used for precise relative dating, while the different pottery styles show a considerable degree of chronological overlap.

The chronology and location of pottery groups with well defined distributions, whether regional or extending over large areas, is summarised in Table 3, while the distribution of the individual sites is shown in Figure 2. The sites of the pre-pottery Mesolithic Suomusjärvi culture are not shown on the map, as its remains are frequently very difficult to date in this area. A general discussion of the Mesolithic of Finland has been provided recently by Clark (1975). Sarsa Ware is found on a few sites containing other types of pottery and its presence is not indicated on the map. Sites with Jäkärlä or Pyhensilta Ware have been grouped together with other Combed Ware sites. The absolute chronology follows the dating of Meinander (1971), Siiriäinen (1973) and Carpelan (1973).

Due to the paucity of preserved plant and bone material and to the chronological overlap of cultural groups, this part of the paper dealing with the Finnish evidence will be divided into 'topical' rather than chronological sections. The poor conditions for the preservation of perishable materials increase the relative value of the analysis of site location, which assumes a principal rather than auxiliary position in studies relating to the economy of the prehistoric cultures.

Figure 2 shows the part of south-west Finland that is drained principally by the Kokemäenjoki river. Firstly, the position of the sites must be considered in relation to the contemporary coastlines. Figure 2 shows the maximum *Litorina* coastline, dated to c. 5,000 bc; the *Combed Ware Style III.1* coastline, dated to c. 2,600 bc; and the *Kiukais* coastline, dated to c. 1,200 bc. The coastlines have been drawn following the scheme developed by Siiriäinen (1969, 1972).

The *Litorina* coastline is self explanatory, and of course marks the maximum extent of the postglacial marine transgression in the Baltic area. *Combed Ware Style III.1* is a shore that existed at the end of the Combed Ware period (except for Combed Ware Style III.2 and Pyhensilta); this coastline is nearest in time to the Corded Ware sites. The *Kiukais* coastline is a shore that existed at the end of the Kiukais period; hence the latest Kiukais and the earliest Bronze Age sites would be situated close to this shore.

Site location

It can be seen that Combed Ware sites are located on the coast, and that their distribution extends to the Lake District. The sites of the Corded Ware culture are situated both inland and near the coast, but never actually on the shore. This can be seen particularly clearly in the case of the Corded Ware remains which occur on or near to the sites of the earlier Combed Ware culture in the coastal district; during

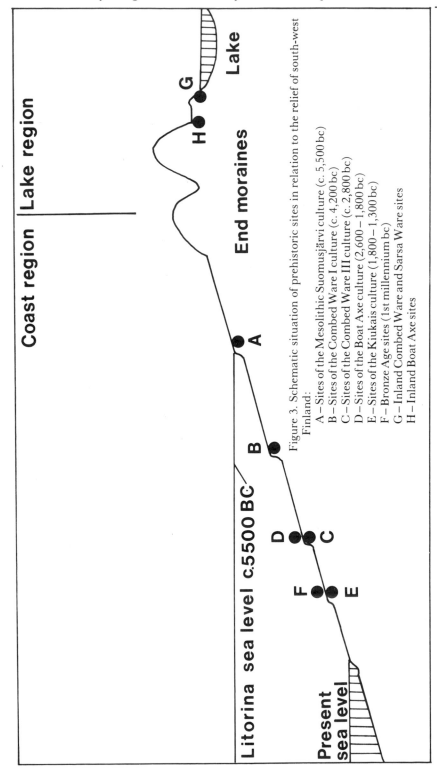

Figure 3. Schematic situation of prehistoric sites in relation to the relief of south-west Finland:

A – Sites of the Mesolithic Suomusjärvi culture (c. 5,500 bc)
B – Sites of the Combed Ware I culture (c. 4,200 bc)
C – Sites of the Combed Ware III culture (c. 2,800 bc)
D – Sites of the Boat Axe culture (2,600 – 1,800 bc)
E – Sites of the Kiukais culture (1,800 – 1,300 bc)
F – Bronze Age sites (1st millennium bc)
G – Inland Combed Ware and Sarsa Ware sites
H – Inland Boat Axe sites

the Combed Ware time these localities were actually on the coast, but by the time of their occupation by Corded Ware groups the shoreline had retreated further west (or further south on the southern coast), leaving a newly-exposed strip of land between the actual sites and the shore (Figs. 3, 4).

Three ceramic groups seem to be represented by sites situated solely on the coast. They are Jäkärlä, a local group of early Combed Ware, Pyhensilta, a late Combed Ware group, and Kiukais, belonging to Epineolithic times, Pyhensilta has a well developed slate technology, while similar artefacts of slate (or metamorphic stone with similar properties) have also been found in Jäkärlä contexts (Edgren 1966). Fitzhugh (1974) linked this slate technocomplex, characterised by projectiles and scraping knives, with a strongly maritime economic adaptation.

During the 1st millennium bc a situation similar to that of the Corded Ware culture developed: settlements of the Bronze Age and the early or pre-Roman Iron Age were situated in the coastal zone, but at some distance from the coast. Hence they are often found in localities which also contain Kiukais Ware. Unlike the Corded Ware sites, however, Bronze and early Iron Age sites are not found in the Lake District, where groups characteristic of the inland Epineolithic had developed not later than 1,300 bc.

Thus, if the location of sites is viewed in terms of exploitation of the environment, the following picture emerges: the Pit-Comb Ware culture groups in general occupied both the littoral and inland environments, with more narrowly defined groups on the coast adopting a strong maritime orientation. The Corded Ware culture also exploited both inland and littoral zones, but the sites were situated away from the shoreline. The Kiukais sites show a return to the occupation of shore locations, while this period also marks the beginning of different groups exploiting inland and coastal resources. The succeeding Bronze and early Iron Age in the littoral zone marks a return to the Corded Ware positions in relation to the shore, while the Lake District continued to be exploited by various Epineolithic groups (Fig. 3).

It is the littoral location of the Corded Ware and later Bronze Age groups that seems anomalous in the context of north-eastern Europe. The location of other groups (using the terminology developed by Fitzhugh 1975) could be described as *modified interior* for Combed Ware groups in general, *modified maritime* for Jäkärlä, Pyhensilta and probably Kiukais groups, and *riverine* for Sarsa and other groups concerned solely with inland resources. A recent survey of archaeological data offered by Fitzhugh (1975) revealed similarities in site location and subsistence patterns within the Boreal region as a whole, corresponding to that of the Combed Ware coastal and inland groups within the area of the Kokemäenjoki catchment.

The location of the Corded Ware sites differs also in terms of microenvironment. Well drained sandy locations were generally preferred for settlement. However, while there is general agreement that Combed Ware sites were situated in sandy locations, there is some controversy as to whether the Corded Ware sites were situated on clay or sandy soils (Äyräpää 1922; Edgren 1970).

The location of Combed Ware hunting and fishing groups must be seen as a function of the distance between suitable site locations and the various points in the landscape where hunting and fishing could be successfully carried out. Thus a site would be situated in a dry place with access to water and from where the largest number of good hunting points were accessible by the shortest route. In south-west Finland, such locations would include a high proportion of morainic soils, and this indeed seems to conform to the observed distribution of Combed Ware sites.

A survey of the Corded Ware sites situated within the region shown in Figure 2 seems to indicate, however, that Corded Ware groups were avoiding morainic soils. While the occupation sites themselves may have sandy locations, the areas defined by a 1 km. radius from the sites were generally occupied by clays and either fine or coarse grained sandy soils. Within a 5 km. radius from the sites, clays were in a much greater proportion in the case of the Corded Ware than in the case of the Combed Ware settlements. The distance of these sites from the coast varies according to the local topographic conditions. The superimposition of the Corded Ware remains over the Combed Ware layers recalls the situation in the Baltic republics. However, there are 106 sites in Finland classified as Corded Ware dwelling places (Edgren 1970) and they include large sites containing almost entirely corded pottery. On the southern coast, where the retreat of the sea took place at a slower rate, sites older than the Combed Ware (i.e. those of the Suomusjärvi culture) were subsequently occupied by the Boat Axe groups.

This would seem to indicate that, unlike the Combed Ware sites, the Corded Ware sites were soil dependent, and that they exploited the catchment areas of their site areally rather than moving to selected points. The preferred soils were light clays and sands, while extensive areas of heavy clays, such as those in Varsinais-Suomi, were avoided.

The economic implications of this change in emphasis are by no means clear. More light would no doubt be thrown on this question by microenvironmental studies which take into account (among other factors) the density of the clay, and by the discovery of Corded Ware sites at which faunal remains are preserved. To my mind, however, the location of the sites would seem to indicate that the Corded Ware groups did not rely solely on a hunting and fishing economy. The areas surrounding the Corded Ware sites are dominated by soils which were most suitable for herbivore grazing and for fodder production, suggesting that pastoral systems may well have been a major component of Corded Ware subsistence in Finland. Neither extensive moraine soils nor hard clay areas are suitable for such exploitation, while soils transitional between the two types are more likely to be suitable for herbivore grazing.

Fauna

Faunal evidence is badly preserved in Finland; existing bone assemblages can only give a rough indication of the kind of animals hunted, while a detailed ennumeration of species (let alone their population structure) is beyond the quality of the bone material. Faunal remains from eight Suomusjärvi (Mesolithic) sites were systematically identified by Forsten (1972). Ringed seal (*Phoca hispida*), beaver and elk were the most commonly occurring species. In addition, numerous fish bones were found at two sites, though remains of waterfowl are rare. Further, bones of fox, bear and domesticated dog were found. One site in central Finland (Saarjavi) yielded bones of reindeer, belonging most likely to the taiga variety which remained abundant in central Finland until the Middle Ages (Nickul 1970). In south-western Finland, however, there is no indication of the presence of reindeer in either prehistoric or historic times.

The above remains are similar to the 'arboreal' type of fauna described for Estonia and Latvia, although with a greater reliance on seal at the Finnish sites. However, while in Estonia and Latvia the onset of the Atlantic period is reflected in a wider range of exploited species, no such trend can be observed in Finland. The fauna remains Boreal in character, and, as Forsten (1972) pointed out, impoverished by comparison with southern Scandinavia. Of course, the low number of species represented and the consistency of their exploitation may reflect economic specialisation. However, it seems likely that if animals of the 'southern' type occurred in any number in Finland during the Atlantic period, the benefit to be derived from culling these species would have outweighed the difficulties inherent in adapting a new hunting strategy. On present evidence, therefore, it would seem that the period of the Climatic Optimum brought no significant change in economic orientation among the hunting and fishing groups in Finland.

Bones from the following Combed Ware period have been identified at Jönsas, Vantaa parish (Forsten and Blomquist 1974) and Hietaniemi (Blomquist, personal communication). At Jönsas the Combed Ware layer contained bones of seal and European hare; at Hietaniemi (where only about 1 percent of the bones were identifiable) beaver and ringed seal formed the majority of the fragments, together with occasional remains of elk, bear, hare, fish and birds. A few other sites yielded bones from mixed deposits containing Combed Ware and later remains; the faunal composition from these sites was of the same kind as that described above. The relative abundance of the ringed seal at Hietaniemi suggests the existence of seals in the lakes of the western Lake District in the 3rd and 2nd millennium bc. The date of their final disappearance from this area is unknown.

A number of sites belonging to the late Combed Ware period and the Epineolithic yielded fauna that suggested intensive specialisation on seal hunting along the coast of the Gulf of Bothnia. Faunal remains from Kierikki (Forsten, personal communication) at the northern end of the Gulf of Bothnia consisted of very abundant remains of ringed seal and fish. At the southern end of the Gulf on the island of Åland, two sites (Jettböle and Otterböle) specialised in seal hunting (Forsten 1975). The occupation of these two sites spans the 2nd millenium bc. During this period some changes took place in the economy: while Jettböle (the older site of the late Combed Ware period) produced remains of exclusively wild animals (including both the ringed seal and harp seal), together with fish and waterfowl, the Bronze Age site of Otterböle showed an association of the remains of grey seal (*Halichoerus grypus*) with those of ovicaprids and domestic pig (Forsten 1974).

The faunal remains from three Corded Ware sites were also made up of wild animals. However, the finds are equivocal: only at Jönsas did seal, beaver, pike and dog bones derive from a distinct Corded Ware layer, while at the other two sites, both preceramic and Boat Axe remains were represented (Forsten and Blomquist 1974).

However, it is only in the 1st millenium bc that there is clear and consistent evidence for stock keeping as a mode of subsistence in Finland. At Rieskaronmäki, the debris of a house with stone foundations revealed bones belonging to domesticated cattle, ovicaprids and dog, along with bones of seal, beaver and hare. The site dates to the Bronze Age period IV-V, but also contains early Iron Age 'Morby' pottery. At other sites, as well as in cairns belonging to this period, isolated bones of horse, pig, ovicaprids and cattle have been found with sufficient frequency to show that during the Bronze Age animal husbandry was an established form of economy at least in south-western Finland (Salo and Lahtiperä 1970). At the same time sealing remained an important activity.

Although bone material continues to be scarce during the 1st millennium A.D., all the available evidence points to the continuing existence of pastoralism and agriculture. Bone samples of the 1st millennium A.D. continue to contain bones of both domesticated and wild animals.

Plant remains

Information relating to vegetable diet is very slight. Fossil finds of waterchestnut (*Trapa natans*) indicate its presence in the southern half of Finland during the Atlantic and early Sub-boreal periods. As in the

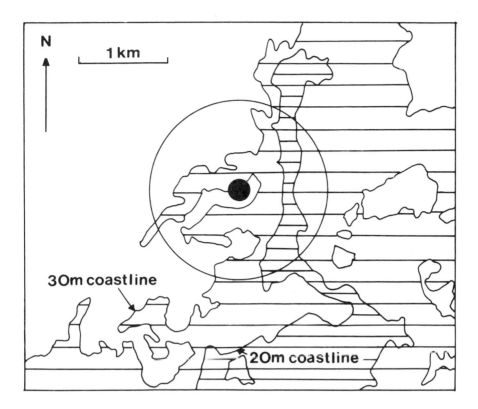

Figure 4. Map showing the location of the Boat Axe site at Jönsas, near Helsinki, in relation to shorelines of different periods. The 30 metre shoreline (single shaded) is contemporary with the early Combed Ware period. The 20 metre shoreline (double shaded) is contemporary with the later Combed Ware (III.1) period. The actual coastline at the time of the Boat Axe/Corded Ware occupation was somewhat less than 20 metres above present sea level. The location of Boat Axe sites in the Helsinki area is generally between 35 metres and 20 metres above sea level. The circle encloses the area within a radius of 1 kilometre from the site.

Baltic republics, it was used as a source of food. At Orimattila, *Trapa* nuts were found among sherds of a Combed Ware pot (style II). Wood from the same level as the pot has been dated to 3,420 ± 140 bc (Hel-12).

Evidence for the beginnings of plant cultivation in Finland has to rely almost entirely on the testimony of pollen analysis. A number of points need to be remembered when dealing with pollen evidence for clearance and cultivation in Finland. Firstly, over-production of pollen of birch, aspen, and to some extent pine tends to obscure landnam phases (Vuorela 1972, 1975) – although correction factors worked out by Donner (1972) for certain species enable some allowance to be made for this. Secondly, pollen-yielding sites tend to be located on bogs which are inherently unsuitable for cultivation and which, furthermore, give a very localised picture of the vegetation. Thirdly, with the exception of *Cerealia* and *Centaurea cyanus*, the non-arboreal-pollen indicators of clearance and cultivation appear naturally in certain open-habitat environments. In densely-forested country such as Finland, these species may occur along the sea coast, on lake and river shores, and on areas of open bog. Since most of the available pollen data derive from precisely these environments, the interpretation of human interference in natural vegetation patterns must depend on the relative strength and variety of the non-arboreal-species encountered in these situations. Fourthly, slash and burn techniques of clearance affect the pollen representation in distinctive ways. Vuorela (1972) considers a decline of deciduous species and spruce followed by a rise in birch and alder, then by hazel and finally by spruce, as the most frequent type of landnam phase, corresponding to the most usual swidden technique. With the establishment of permanent fields and decrease in the shrub and successional vegetation of the forest margins, the curves of birch, alder and hazel fall, while curves for pine and spruce rise (Vuorela 1970). Lastly, among the cereals, only rye is wind pollinated and therefore prone to be better represented than other cereal species in pollen diagrams. However, rye did not reach Finland until the Iron Age, and until then the principal crop was barley which (as a self-pollinating species) tends to be under-represented in pollen diagrams.

Vuorela (1970, 1972, 1975) has surveyed a number of pollen diagrams from south-west Finland for indications of clearance and cultivation. Her diagrams from Katinhännänsuo, Loimansuo, Lehijärvi, Armijärvi and Kirkojärvi provide the most reliable evidence, owing to the large sizes of the pollen samples counted. All the diagrams reflect the regional or local suitability of the environment for cultivation.

On the basis of the existing evidence, the following generalisations can be made. There is a limited amount of evidence in Finland for clearance during the Boat Axe period. This can be seen in the diagrams provided by Simola (BII, Simola 1970) and Alhonen (Kyrösjärvi 5, Jalanti, in Alhonen 1967), while a core taken from the Boat Axe site of Perkiö shows a very distinct clearance phase (Alhonen, in Edgren 1970). The evidence for forest clearance during the Boat Axe period, taken in conjunction with other information referred to earlier, seems to emphasise that pastoralism was part of the Corded Ware economy. While as a whole this is a plausible hypothesis, the evidence for clearance alone cannot be interpreted as a reliable indication of grazing. At present there is no clear indication as to whether forest clearance may have been caused by the Comb Ware groups, and consequently it is impossible to say whether the Boat Axe was the first culture to cause clearances that would be reflected in pollen diagrams. The economic interpretation of clearance must therefore be viewed in this light. From the fifteenth century bc onwards the forest clearance assumed a more permanent character, and pollens of cereals appeared for the first time at Loimansuo and Katinhännäsuo. While culture indicators (Vuorela 1972) and other species indicate the maintenance of an open environment, cereal pollen indicates only sporadic cultivation. Although *Avena* pollen has been noted in a 2nd millennium, it is unlikely, according to the present data at least, that cereal cultivation developed as a regular part of subsistence until the following millennium, when sites like Kirkojärvi (dated c. 1,000-500 bc) attest the cultivation of oats and barley.

The second half of the 1st millennium bc has been described as a period of decline and partial depopulation (Kivikoski 1967). This view has been largely based on a lack of metal ware and datable burials. However, in the last few years continuity of settlement has been demonstrated by the dating of settlements with Morby pottery to this period (Meinander 1969) while the continuation of cereal cultivation and clearance contradict the formerly-held view that the pre-Roman Iron Age economy had been severely disrupted by climatic deterioration.

From the fifth century A.D. a decisive shift towards cultivation takes place. This is indicated by the continual and marked rise of the *cerealia* curve (Vuorela 1975) and the appearance of cultivation in new localities (Kukkonen 1973), while there is some evidence in the tree-pollen data for the establishment of permanent fields. Intensive grazing on abandoned fields is indicated by the frequency of juniper pollen (Bergelund 1969). This implies that cultivation had become well established in some districts, although regional differences in the intensity of cultivation are apparent from Vuorela's work (1970).

Conclusion

The developments in Estonia, Latvia and south-western Finland appear remarkably synchronous in terms of the acceptance of the agricultural economy. In all these areas the period of 1,500-500 bc witnessed the first widespread appearance of domesticated animals and the first indications of cereal cultivation.

At the same time it is apparent that even after cultivation and animal husbandry had become permanently established, the economy of the Iron Age groups remained heavily dependent on hunting and fishing, and continued to do so into Medieval times. This is especially the case in Finland. However, each type of economy had different and sometimes conflicting requirements upon the pattern of life of these groups, and having arrived at the point where cultivation and animal husbandry had become an integral part of their economy – along with hunting and fishing – they had to develop specific adaptations to make the two kinds of subsistence compatible, both in respect to one another and to the surrounding environment.

Final considerations: the case for hunting, fishing and swidden agriculture

Even close to their ecological limits, cultivation and animal husbandry increase productivity per unit area of land. The estimated requirement of land for one elk ranges from 170 to 250 hectares (based on data from the U.S.S.R. and America) while the corresponding figure for one cow in a mixed forest zone with no systematic pasturing is in the region of 5 hectares (Dylis and Sukhachev 1964). However, the number of cattle is limited by the capacity of the herders to gather winter fodder, while in the case of elk the limit is set by the less restricting availability of a browsing layer. Similarly, cultivation greatly increases the yield of edible matter per unit area, although at the expense of ecosystem stability (Colinvaux 1973; Malmer 1969).

It is important to make a distinction between land-extensive swidden agriculture and land-intensive permanent cultivation. There was a wide variety of swidden practices in historical Finland, depending on vegetation, soil, relief, and the crop sown. The average yield for barley – the principal crop in prehistoric times – ranged between 11 and 27 hectolitres per hectare during the eighteenth century (Soininen 1974). The prehistoric figure was probably closer to the higher figure, because the increase in population in historical times resutled in the over-cropping of swidden fields while the practice of *huuhta*, the most profitable form of swiddening, diminished with the disappearance of the virgin forests. The average yield of an indigenous variety of two-rowed barley at the beginning of this century was 15-16 hectolitres per hectare of permanently cultivated field (Mead 1953).

Analogous evidence showing greater yields from *svedjebruk* (swiddening with bush fallow) than from permanent fields on morainic soils in Sweden (Montelius 1953) supports the general conclusion that with the exception of fertile sedimentary plains and valleys, slash and burn cultivation yielded more grain per unit area than permanent farming. It is impossible to calculate actual productivity due to lack of comparative data for settled farming and swidden agriculture in Finland. Boserup's argument (1965) that swidden farming is less labour intensive has been challenged by Bronson (1970). However, even if the effort involved in swidden agriculture equalled that expended on permanent cultivation, the slash and burn yield would be greater on the majority of Finland's soils.

It has often been claimed that cultivation and husbandry provide more reliable and more predictable resources than hunting and fishing. This is not the case in the north of Europe under primitive technological conditions. Due to climatic and soil conditions the cultivation of cereals in this area is close to the limit of its ecological tolerance, and relatively minor fluctuations in temperature, precipitation or frost formation can have drastic consequences.

This is particularly true of permanent cultivation. Here again the case can be demonstrated with reference to barley. Studies relating to the ecology of this crop (Vale and Carder 1962) point to the conclusion that barley is susceptible to poor yields both as a result of early summer drought in the 'sown' to 'headed' phase of its growth, and excessive precipitation in the 'headed' to 'ripe' phase of growth. In addition, night frosts in late summer may destroy the crop just before harvest. The present weather pattern is marked by a drought season in May and early June (with an average precipitation figure of 40 mm. in May) followed by a period of increased precipitation (up to 70 mm. in August) during the later part of the summer. The combined effect of these controls is to produce a diminished safety margin within which barely can be grown.

The incidence of frosts and the occurrence of soils strongly susceptible to drought is greater in locations where permanent cultivation had to take place. The wider range of soils available to swidden agriculture allow for greater manoeuvrability to decrease the effects of the adverse factors just mentioned. Permanent cultivation is further limited by the availability of manure (on which permanent agriculture is largely dependent) and which, in turn, is limited by the number of livestock that can be sustained on available fodder.

By contrast, economic strategies based on the exploitation of native game populations fully adapted to the local environment would appear more reliable. This may be true especially for communities heavily dependent on fish, because fish, with its continuous rate of growth, represents in general a more stable economic resource than either mammals or birds (McCullough 1970). It has been mentioned earlier that highly seasonal environments lean towards instability (Colinvaux 1973). Faunal remains indicate, however, that prehistoric groups concentrated on resources whose energy intake was spent on the maintenance of the existing population (such as elk) rather than on rapid reproduction. The resulting low population densities among animal populations are reflected in the relatively low population densities among hunter-fishers of the region.

There is very little evidence relating to the degree of seasonality and sedentism along the hunting and fishing groups. Vilkuna (1968) described how the hunting activities of the ancient Finns were concentrated on the coast except during the autumn and early winter periods (prior to seal hunting) when inland resources of fish, waterfowl and deer were exploited. A variety of seasonal movements are similarly described by Tegengren (in Hvarfner 1965: 427-92) relating to historical times. From these accounts the winter half of the year emerges as the principal period of seasonal movement. But no direct extrapolation to south-western Finland can be made, because the intensity and direction of the seasonal movements, as well as the distances covered, varied widely depending on local environmental and economic conditions.

Swidden agriculture did not bring about settled conditions of life. Depending on the intensity of the swidden system involved, the same locality could be tended twice a century (in mature mixed or spruce stands), four times a century (in deciduous secondary stands) or even more frequently (in bush fallow). Where forest was abundant the most productive, mature-forest type of swiddening is likely to have been favoured, while a decrease in the availability of land would have favoured the adoption of more intensive systems. The shifting of historical settlements resulting from swidden agriculture has been noted by Teräsvuori (1928) and Vilkuna (1968).

Although a degree of sedentism no doubt existed under both hunting/fishing and swidden cultivation, it was only with permanent agriculture, with the development of various infield-outfield systems and the attendant increase in animal husbandry, that permanent settlement became inevitable. Tegengren (in Hvarfner 1965) linked the acceptance of settled agriculture to the disappearance of game and fish resources. Teräsvuori (1928) described how the loss of *erämaa* – the traditional hunting grounds – in the seventeenth century and the reduction of mature forests for swiddening led to the adoption of settled agriculture and stock-keeping in Savo. It is reasonable to suggest that the combination of the above factors was also responsible for the late development of permanent cultivation in Estonia, Latvia and south-western Finland.

Based on the foregoing, a few tentative conclusions can be drawn:

1. Hunting and fishing, although keeping the population at low density, presented a stable mode of subsistence in the areas considered in this paper.
2. Cultivation and animal husbandry led to an increase in the productivity of the area, but this was achieved at the expense of stability of the environment and predictability of the economic yields.
3. The adoption of permanent cultivation under conditions of primitive technology took place only when extensive agriculture became unproductive through a decrease in forested area.

Acknowledgements

I am deeply grateful to Professor J.G.D. Clark and Dr T. Edgren, my supervisors during this period of research, for their guidance and advice. Dr Edgren has kindly checked the manuscript for the correct forms of Finnish terms. I am indebted to Dr A. Forsten and Mr L. Blomquist who enabled me to include, respectively, their unpublished faunal data from Kierikki and Hietaniemi. I would also like to thank Professor C.F. Meinander, Dr A. Siiriäinen, Mr M. Nunez and Mr C. Carpelan, for many encouraging discussions.

APPENDIX A: CATALOGUE OF SITES SHOWN ON FIGURE 1.

Site	Chronology	Sources
1. Narva I	Typical Pit-Comb Ware, Narva Ware, Cord-impressed Ware	Jaanits 1954a Jaanits 1959a Gurina 1967
Narva II	Pit-Comb Ware and Cord-impressed Ware	*ibid*
Narva III	Narva Ware	*ibid*

2. Narva-town	Mesolithic layer III:
	    5,690 ± 180 bc (Ta-53)
	    5,140 ± 230 bc (Ta-41)
	    5,630 ± 300 bc (Ta-25)
	Mesolithic layer II:
	    5,365 ± 190 bc (Ta-52)
	    4,790 ± 250 bc (Ta-40)
	    4,070 ± 120 bc (Ta-17)
	Mesolithic layer I :
	    3,870 ± 200 bc (Ta-33)
	    3,350 ± 250 (Ta-7)
		Jaanits 1959a
		Jaanits 1966
		Liiva 1966

3. Siiversti	Mesolithic — Boreal/Atlantic transition	Moora 1952 Jaanits 1959a
4. Kunda	Mesolithic layer : 6,390 + 280 bc (Ta-14) Mixed Mesolithic/early Pit-Comb Ware: 4,065 ± 210 bc (Ta-16)	Indreko 1948 Indreko 1962 Jaanits 1959a Liiva 1966
5. Loona	Late Epineolithic, Pit-Comb Ware	Jaanits 1959a
6. Nakamyae	Late Epineolithic, Pit-Comb Ware, Cord-impressed Ware	Jaanits 1959a Jaanits 1966

7. Pulli	Mesolithic :
	    7,350 ± 75 bc (Ta-175)
	    7,625 ± 115 bc (Ta-176)
	    7,650 ± 120 bc (Ta-245)
		Punning 1968
		Punning 1971
		Jaanits 1975a

8. Lepakoze	Mesolithic	Jaanits 1975b
9. Valma	Pit-Comb Ware and Cord-impressed Ware	Jaanits 1959b

Appendix A (continued)

Site	*Chronology*	*Sources*
10. Kullamyagi	Pit-Comb Ware (Typical and Late), Cord-impressed Ware, Textile Ware and early Metal Age Ware	Jaanits 1959a
11. Akali	Narva Ware, Pit-Comb Ware (Typical and Late), Cord-impressed Ware, early Metal Age Ware: 4,305 ± 100 bc (Ta-103) (layer unspecified)	Jaanits 1959a Punning 1968
12. Villa	Pit-Comb Ware, Cord-impressed Ware: 1,620 ± 240 bc (Ta-20) Also early Metal Age Ware	Jaanits 1954a Jaanits 1959a Liiva 1966
13. Tamula	Pit-Comb Ware (Late), Cord-impressed Ware: 2,350 ± 70 bc (Ta-237)⎱ burial 2,230 ± 100 bc (Ta-219)⎰ in early 2,100 ± 180 bc (Ta-28) phase of 1,650 ± 180 bc (Ta-10) settle- ment.	Jaanits 1954b Jaanits 1959a Liiva 1966 Punning 1971 Ilves 1970
14. Kyaepa	Pit-Comb Ware: 2,915 ± 235 bc (Ta-5) 2,530 ± 255 bc (Ta-6) 2,400 ± 220 bc (Ta-4)	Paaver 1965 Liiva 1966 Semyontsev 1972
15. Zveinieki I	Pit-Comb Ware	Jaanits 1959a Zagorska 1970 LPSRA 1974
16. Zveinieki II	Mesolithic settlement and burial	Zagorska 1970 LPSRA 1974
17. Osa	Mesolithic, Osa Ware, Pit-Comb Ware (Late) Mesolithic layer I: 5,010 ± 80 bc (Le-811) 4,810 ± 80 bc (Le-812) 4,630 ± 70 bc (Le-810) Neolithic layer: 3,780 ± 50 bc (Le-850) 2,050 ± 60 bc (Le-758) Osa Ware layer: 3,930 ± 80 bc (Le-961) 3,830 ± 70 bc (Le-962)	Semyontsev 1972 LPSRA 1974 Timofeev 1975 Dolukhanov 1976
18. Piestina	Pit-Comb Ware, Piestina Ware: 2,720 ± 150 bc (Le-750) 2,570 ± 120 bc (Le-748) 2,300 ± 50 bc (Le-867)	Loze 1965 Semyontsev 1972 LPSRA 1974 Dolukhanov 1976
19. Icha	Pit-Comb Ware, Epineolithic Ware	Jaanits 1959a Loze 1965
20. Kreichi	Pit-Comb Ware, Piestina Ware, Textile Ware 2,070 ± 300 bc (Ta-8)	Zagorkis 1963 LPSRA 1974 Liiva 1966
21. Leimanishki	Cord-impressed Ware and Textile Ware:	LPSRA 1974 Liiva 1966

Appendix A (continued)

Site	Chronology	Sources
	2,020 ± 250 bc (Ta-23)	
	1,820 ± 200 bc (Ta-27)	
22. Dviete	Pit-Comb Ware, Piestina Ware	LPSRA 1974
23. Rutenieki	Cord-impressed Ware	Jaanits 1959a
24. Sarnate	Pit-Comb Ware (Typical and Late),	Punning 1971
	Sarnate Ware:	Semyontsev 1972
	2,750 ± 250 bc (Ta-26)	Jaanits 1959a
	2,730 ± 70 bc (Ta-265)	Vankina 1970
	2,690 ± 100 bc (Bln-769)	Liiva 1966
	2,560 ± 110 bc (Le-814)	
	2,548 ± 250 bc (Ta-24)	
25. Sope	Boat-Axe Burial	Jaanits 1952
26. Ardu	Boat Axe burial	*ibid*
27. Tika	Boat Axe burial	*ibid*
28. Kivisaare	Boat Axe burial	*ibid*
29. Kunila	Boat Axe burial	*ibid*
30. Asva	Fortified settlement (1st millennium bc)	Vassar 1955
31. Ridala	Fortfied settlement (1st millennium bc)	Paaver 1965
32. Klangyukalns	Fortfied settlement (1st millennium bc)	Graudonis 1967 LPSRA 1974
33. Mukukalns	Fortified settlement (1st millennium bc)	*ibid*
34. Asote	Fortified settlement (1st millennium bc)	*ibid*
35. Ersika	Fortified settlement (1st millennium bc)	*ibid*
36. Dignaia	Fortified settlement (1st millennium bc)	*ibid*
37. Tervete	Fortified settlement (1st millennium bc)	*ibid*

Additional sites with C14 dates not shown on Figure 1

Lagazha	Pit-Comb Ware:	Loze 1965
	1,290 ± 70 bc (Le-868)	Dolukhanov 1976
Sulka	Osa Ware, Pit-Comb Ware:	Loze 1965
	2,110 ± 60 bc (Le-752)	Semyontsev 1972
Naniekste	Pit-Comb Ware, Cord-impressed	Loze 1965
	Ware: 2,220 ± 130 bc (Le-648)	Dolukhanov 1970
Abora	Cord-impressed Ware and Early	Loze 1965
	Textile Ware:	Semyontsev 1972
	1,920 ± 70 bc (Le-671)	
	1,910 ± 100 bc (Le 749)	
Eyni	Pit-Comb Ware:	Semyontsev 1972
	2,050 ± 60 bc (Le-751)	

APPENDIX B ： CATALOGUE OF SITES SHOWN ON FIGURE 2

Site	Chronology	Sources
1. Santamäki	Corded Ware	
2. Hiidenmäki	Combed Ware	
3. Sauvakoski	Combed Ware	
4. Viitaluoto, Rajasalo	Combed Ware	
5. Anttila-Seppälä, Lassila	Combed Ware	
6. Kukkula	Combed Ware	
7. Tuohimaa	Kiukais Ware	Meinander 1954a
8. Häytiönmaa	Combed Ware	
9. Uusijaara	Combed Ware, Corded Ware	Edgren 1970
10. Koppalainen	Combed Ware	
11. Rieskaronmäki	Bronze Age and Morby Wares	Meinander 1954b, Salo and Lahtiperä 1970
12. Penttala	Morby Ware	Meinander 1954b, Salo and Lahtiperä 1970
13. Pispa	Combed Ware, Corded Ware	Luho 1961, Edgren 1970
14. Kuusisto	Kiukais, Bronze Age Wares	Meinander 1954a, 1954b, Salo and Lahtiperä 1970
15. Uotinmäki	Kiukais, Bronze Age and Morby Wares	Meinander 1954a, 1954b, Salo and Lahtiperä 1970
16. Kaunismäki	Kiukais and Morby Wares	Meinander 1954a, Salo and Lahtiperä 1970
17. Kaasanmäki	Bronze Age and Morby Wares	Salo and Lahtiperä 1970
18. Saamanmäki	Kiukais and Bronze Age Wares	Meinander 1954a, 1954b
19. Lyytikänharju	Combed Ware (Pyhensilta) and Kiukais Ware	Edgren 1956
20. Tolvanmaa	Combed Ware	
21. Ketola	Combed WAre	
22. Sarinmäki	Combed Ware	
23. Paimenenmäki	Corded Ware	
24. Parkkila	Combed Ware (Jäkarlä)	Edgren 1966
25. Kolisoja-Pajusaari	Combed Ware	
26. Eskonkallio	Combed Ware (Jäkarlä)	Edgren 1966
27. Nummi	Combed Ware (Jäkarlä)	Edgren 1966
28. Arpo	Corded Ware	
29. Kauttua (Uusi Kansakoulu)	Combed Ware (Jäkarlä)	Edgren 1966
30. Vähä-Vahe	Morby Ware	Meinander 1970
31. Kauttua (Vanha Kansakoulu)	Combed Ware	

Appendix B (continued)

Site	Chronology	Sources
32. Nummisto	Combed Ware	
33. Happakalio	Combed Ware, inland	Meinander 1954a
	Epineolithic Ware	
34. Vahnkakoski	Combed Ware	Edgren 1966

Where the source is not stated, chronological identifications were based on the archive notes in the National Museum and the artefact assemblages available from the Prehistoric Office. Archaeological remains associated with burials on the above sites are not listed, as it is settlement-landscape relationships that form the primary concern of this paper; information relating to burials will be found in the references cited in the table.

References

Aartolahti, T. 1966. Uber die Einwanderung und die Verhäufigung der Fichte in Finnland. *Annales Botanici Fennici*, 3: 368-79.

Alhonen, P. 1967. Palaeolimnological investigations of three inland lakes in south-western Finland. *Acta Botanica Fennica*, 76: 1-59.

Äyräpää, A. 1922. Forfynd fran Kyrkslätt och Esbo socknar. *Suomen Muinaismuistoyhdistyksen Aikakauskirja – Finska Fornminnesföreningens Tidskrift*, 32: 1-208.

Bergelund, B. 1969. Vegetation and human influence in South Scandinavia during Prehistoric time. *Acta Oecologica Scandinavica Supplementum*, 12: 9-29.

Birks, H.J.B. and Saarnisto, M. 1976. Isopollen maps and principal component analysis of Finnish pollen data for 4000, 6000, and 8000 years ago. *Boreas*, 4: 77-96.

Boserup, E. 1965. *Conditions of Agricultural Growth*. London, Allen and Unwin.

Briusov, A. 1961. Ob ekspansii kultur s voevymi toporami v konce III. Tisyaticheletiya do nashei epokhi. *Sovetskaya Arkheologiya*, 1961, no. 3: 14-34.

Bronson, B. 1970. Farm labour and evolution of food production. In Spooner, B. (ed.), *Population Growth: Anthropological Implications*. Cambridge (Massachusetts), M.I.T. Press: 190-219.

Carpelan, C. 1973. Bofast – icke bofast under förhistorisk tid i Finland. *Tromsø Museum Skrifter*, 14: 190-202.

Clark, J.G.D. 1936. *The Mesolithic Settlement of Northern Europe*. London, Cambridge University Press.

Clark, J.G.D. 1975. *The Earlier Stone Age Settlement of Scandinavia*. London, Cambridge University Press.

Colinvaux, P. 1973. *Introduction to Ecology*. New York, Wiley.

Dolukhanov, P. 1970. Radiocarbon dates of the Institute of Archaeology II. *Radiocarbon*, 12, no. 2: 130-56.

Dolukhanov, P. 1976. Radiocarbon dates of the Institute of Archaeology III. *Radiocarbon*, 18, no. 2: 190-202.

Donner, J. 1963. Zoning of Post-glacial pollen diagrams in Finland and the main changes in the forest composition. *Acta Botanica Fennica*, 65: 1-40.

Donner, J. 1969. Land-sea level changes in southern Finland during the formation of the Salpausselkä end-moraines. *Bulletin of the Geological Society of Finland*, 41: 135-50.

Donner, J. 1972. Pollen frequencies in the Flandrian sediments of Lake Vakojärvi, south Finland. *Societas Scientiarum Fennica Commentationes Biologicae*, 53: 1-19.

Dylis, N. and Sukhachev, V. 1964. *Fundamentals of Forest Biogeocoenology*. Edinburgh, Oliver and Boyd.

Edgren, T. 1956. Stenåldersboplatsen Lyytikänharju i Harjavalta socken. *Finskt Museum*, 63: 30-44 (German summary: Der steinzeitliche Wohnplatz Lyytikänharju im Ksp. Harjavalta).

Edgren, T. 1966. Jäkärlä gruppen. *Suomen Muinaismuistoyhdistyksen Aikakauskirja – Finska Fornminnesföreningens Tidskrift*, 64: 1-159.

Edgren, T. 1970. Studier over den snörkeramiska keramik kulturens i Finland. *Suomen Muinaismuistoyhdistyksen Aikakauskirja – Finska Forminnesföreningens Tidskrift*, 72: 1-118.

Eronen, M. 1974. The history of the Litorina sea and associated Holocene events. *Commentationes Physico-Mathematicae*, 44: 79-195.

Fitzhugh, W. 1974. Ground slates in the Scandinavian Younger Stone Age with reference to circumpolar maritime adaptations. *Proceedings of the Prehistoric Society*, 40: 45-59.

Fitzhugh, W. 1975. A comparative approach to northern Maritime adaptations. In Fitzhugh, W. (ed.), *Prehistoric Maritime Adaptations of the Circumpolar Zone*. The Hague, Mouton: 339-87.

Forsten, A. 1972. The refuse fauna of the Mesolithic Suomusjärvi period in Finland. *Finskt Museum*, 79: 74-85.

Forsten, A. 1974. A Bronze Age refuse fauna from Kökar, Åland. *Finskt Museum*, 81: 56-60.

Forsten, A. and Alhonen, P. 1975. The subfossil seals of Finland. *Boreas*, 4: 143-55.

Forsten, A. and Blomquist, L. 1974. Refuse faunas from the Vantaa Mesolithic and Neolithic periods. *Finskt Museum*, 81: 50-6.

Graudonis, I. 1961. *Pozdnii Bronzovyi i Rannyi Zheleznyi Vek na Territorii Latviiskoi SSR*. Riga, Akademia Nauk Latviiskoi SSR.

Graudonis, I. 1967. *Latvia v Epolkhu Pozdnei Bronzy i Rannego Zheleza*. Riga, Zinatne Publishing House.

Gurina, N.N. 1967. Iz istorii drevnykh plemen zapadnykh oblastei SSSR. *Materialy i Issledovaniya po Arkheologii SSSR*, 144: 1-205.

Hvarfner, H. 1965. *Hunting and Fishing*. Umeå, Norrbotens Museum.

Ilves, E. 1970. Tartu radiocarbon dates IV. *Radiocarbon*, 12, no. 1:238-49.

Indreko, R. 1948. *Die Mittlere Steinzeit in Estland*. Uppsala, Almquist and Wiksell.

Indreko, R. 1964. *Mesolitische und Frühneolitische Kulturen in Osteuropa und West Sibiren*. Stockholm, Almquist and Wiksell.

Iversen, J. and Faegri, K. 1964. *Textbook of Pollen Analysis*. Copenhagen, Munksgaard.

Jaanits, L. 1952. Pozdneneoliticheskyie mogilniki v Estonskoi SSR. *Kratkie Soobshcheniya Instituta Istorii Materialnoi Kultury*, 48: 53-65.

Jaanits, L. 1954a. Neoliticheskyie stoyianki na territorii Estonskoi SSR. *Kratkie Soobshcheniya Instituta Istorii Materialnoi Kultury*, 54: 3-23.

Jaanits, L. 1954b. Novye dannye po neolitu Pribaltiki. *Sovetskaya Arkheologiya*, 19: 159-204.

Jaanits, L. 1959a. *Poselenie Epokhi Neolita i Rannego Metala v Priustye Reky Emaigi*. Tallin, Akademiya Nauk Estonskoi SSR (German summary).

Jaanits, L. 1959b. Neoliticheskoye poselenyie Valma. In Tarakanova, S.A. and Terentseva, N.L. (eds.), *Voprosy Etnicheskoi Istorii Narodov Pribaltiki*. Moskva, Akademiya Nauk SSSR: 32-76.

Jaanits, L. 1966. O poselenyiakh kultury ladyevidnykh toporov v Estonii. In *Ot Epokhi Bronzy do Rannego Feudalisma*. Tallin: 60-66 (German summary: Uber die Siedlungen der Bootaxtkultuur in Estland).

Jaanits, L. 1975a. Frühmesolitische Siedlung in Pulli. *Izvestiya Akademii Nauk Estonskoi SSR, Obshchestvennye Nauki*, 24, No. 1: 64-70.

Jaanits, L. 1975b. Mesoliticheskaya stoyanka v Lepakoze. *Izvestiya Akademii Nauk*

Estonskoi SSR, Obshchestvennye Nauki, 24, no. 1: 70-73 (German summary: Mesolitischer Siedlungplatz im Dorfe Lepakoze in Mittle-estland).

Jutikala, E. 1949. *Suomen Historian Kartasto — Atlas of Finnish History.* Porvoo-Helsinki, Werner, Söderström and Osakeyhtiö.

Kivikoski, E. 1967. *Finland* (Ancient Peoples and Places). London, Thames and Hudson.

Koskimies, M. 1967. Sarsan majavankuviu. *Suomen Museo*, 74: 38-42. (German summary: Ein Biberfigur aus Sarsa).

Krasnov, Y.A. 1971. Ranee zemledelyie i zhivotovodstvo v lesnoi polose vostochnoi Evropy. *Materialy i Issledovaniya po Arkheologii SSSR*, 174: 3-165.

Kukkonen, E. 1973. Sedimentation and typological development in the basin of the Lake Lohjajärvi, south Finland. *Geological Survey of Finland Bulletin*, 261: 1-67.

Kustin, A.E. 1967. Arkheologicheskiye pamyatniki nachala II. Tysiya — chiletiya na ostrovakh Saaremaa i Mukhu. *Sovetskaya Arkheologiya*, 1967, no. 1: 176-87.

Liiva, A. 1966. Tartu radiocarbon dates I. *Radiocarbon*, 8: 430-41.

Lisytsyna, G.N. 1958. K voprosu ob Allerode Pribaltiki i vo vozraste stoyanki Kunda. *Sovetskaya Arkheologiya*, 1958, no. 3: 90-6.

Loze, I. 1964. Mezoliticheskie nakhodki v Lubanskoi nizmennosti. *Izvestiya Akademii Nauk LSR*, 200: 7-21.

Loze, I. 1965. O novykh neoliticheskikh pamyatnikakh Lubanskoi nizmennosti. *Izvestiya Akademii Nauk LSR*, 221: 15-25.

LPSRA. 1974. *Latvijas PSR Arkeologia.* Collective work: responsible editors: Birons, A., Mugurevits E., Stubavs, A., Snore, E. Riga, Zinatne (German summary: Die Archäologie der Lettischen SSR).

Luho, V. 1961. Kokemäen Pispan kivikautinen asuinpaikka. *Suomen Museo*, 68: 5-35 (German summary: Ein steinzeitlicher Wohnplatz auf Pispa in Kokemäki).

Malmer, N. 1969. Organic matter and cycling of minerals in virgin and present ecosystems. *Acta Oecologica Scandinavica: Supplementum*, 12: 79-87

McCullough, D.R. 1970. Secondary production of birds and mammals. In Reiche, E.D. (ed.), *Temperate Forest Ecosystems. Ecological Studies, vol. 1.* Berlin, Springer Verlag: 107-30.

Mead, W.R. 1953. *Farming in Finland.* London, Athlone Press.

Meinander, C.F. 1954a. Die Kiukais Kultur. *Suomen Muinaismuistoyhdystyksen Aikakauskirja — Finska Fornminnesföreningens Tidskrift*, 53: 1-191.

Meinander, C.F. 1954b. Die Bronzezeit in Finnland. *Suomen Muinaismuistoyhdistyksen Aikakauskirja — Finska Fornminnesföreningens Tidskrift*, 54: 1-242.

Meinander, C.F. 1969. Dåvits. En essa om förromersk järnålder. *Finskt Museum*, 76: 27-70.

Meinander, C.F. 1971. Radiokarbon dateringar till Finlands stenalder. *Societas Scientarum Fennica Arsbok — Vuoskirja*, 48 B, no. 5: 1-14.

Mellars, P.A. 1975. Ungulate populations, economic patterns and the Mesolithic landscape. In Evans, J.G., Limbrey, S. and Cleere, H. (eds.), *The Effect of Man on the Landscape: the Highland Zone.* London, Council for British Archaeology (Research Report no. 11): 49-56.

Moberg, C.A. 1968. Spread of agriculture in the North-European periphery. *Nature*, April 1968: 315-19.

Montelius, S. 1953. The burning of forest for the cultivation of crops. *Geografiska Annaler*, 35 (1): 41-56.

Moora, H. 1952. Pamyatniki pozdnego neolita i rannei epokhi metala v Pribaltike. *Kratkie Soobshcheniya Institua Istorii Materialnoi Kultury*, 48: 3-25.

Moora, H. 1953. Voznikovenniye klassovogo obshchestva v Pribaltike. *Sovetskaya Arkheologiya*, 17: 105-33.

Moora, H. 1955. O rezultatakh issledovaniya gorodishch v Estonskoi SSR. *Muistsed Asulad ja Linnused*, 1: 88-95.

Neustadt, M.I. 1957. *Istoriya Lesov i Paleografiya SSSR v Golotsene.* Moscow, Akademiya Nauk SSSR.

Nickul, K. 1970. *Saamelaiset Kansana ja Kansalaisina*. Helsinki, Suomalaisen Kirjallisuuden Seura.

Paaver, K.L. 1965. *Formirovanie Teriofauny i Izmenchivost Mlekopytayushchikh Pribaltiki v Golotsene*. Tartu, Akademiya Nauk Estonskoi SSR (German summary: Die Entstehung der Säugetierfauna und die Varibilität der Säugertiere des Ostbaltikums im Holozän).

Pohjanheimo, O. and Heinonen, R. 1960. The effect of irrigation on root development, water use, nitrogen uptake and yield characteristics of several barley varieties. *Suomen Maataloustieteellisen Seuran – Acta Agralia Fennica*, 95, no. 16: 1-18.

Punning, J.M. 1968. Tartu radiocarbon dates III. *Radiocarbon*, 10, no. 2: 379-83.

Punning, J.M. 1971. Tartu radiocarbon dates V. *Radiocarbon*, 13, no. 1: 78-84.

Rasiňš, A.P. 1959. Kulturnye i sornye rasteniya v materialakh arkheologicheskikh raskopok na teritorii Latvii. In Tarakanova, S.A. and Terentseva, N.L. (eds.), *Voprosy Etnicheskoi Istorii Narodov Pribaltiki*, Moscow, Akademiya Nauk SSSR: 316-40.

Salo, U. and Lahtiperä, P. 1970. Metallikautinen asutus Kokemäenjoen suussa. *Muinaisjäännökset ja muinaislöydöt*. Pori, 1970: 1-219 (German summary: Die metallzeitliche Besiedlung und der Mündung des Flusses Kokemäenjoki).

Sauramo, M. 1958. Die Geschichte der Ostzee. *Annales Academicae Scientiarum Fennicae: Series A*, III, 51: 1-522.

Schmiedehelm, M.H. 1955. *Arkheologicheskie pamyatniki perioda razlozheniya rodovogo sloya na severo-vostoke Estonii*. Tallin, State Publishing House of Estonia.

Semyontsev, A.A. 1972. Radiocarbon dates of the Institute of Archaeology III. *Radiocarbon*, 14, no. 2: 336-68.

Siiriäinen, A. 1969. Über die Chronologie der steinzeitlichen Küstenwohnplätze Finnlands im Lichte der Uferverschiebung. *Suomen Museo*, 76: 40-73.

Siiriäinen, A. 1972. A gradient/time curve for dating Stone Age shorelines in Finland. *Suomen Museo*, 79: 5-18.

Siiriäinen, A. 1973. Studies relating to shore displacement and Stone Age chronology in Finland. *Finskt Museum*, 80: 5-22.

Simola, L.K. 1964. Über die postglazialen Verhältnisse von Vanajavesi, Letensuo und Lehijärvi sowie die Entwickhung ihrer Flora. *Annales Academicae Scientiarum Fennicae: Series A*, III, 70: 1-64.

Soininen, M. 1974. Vanha Maataloutemme. *Historiallisia Tutkimuksia*, 96: 1-459 (English summary: Old traditional agriculture in Finland in the eighteenth and nineteenth centuries).

Spang, K., Welinder, S. and Wyzsomirski, B. 1975. The introduction of the neolithic stone age into the Baltic area. *Dissertationes Archaeologicae Gandenses*, 16: 235-50.

Stålfelt, M.G. 1972. *Plant Ecology*. London, Longman.

Sukachev, V. and Dylis, N. 1964. *Fundamentals of Forest Biogeocoenology*. Edinburgh, Oliver and Boyd.

Teräsvuori, K. 1928. The early settlement and agriculture in Savo. *Suomen Maateloustieteellisen Seuran – Acta Agralia Fennica*, 18, No. 1: 20-30.

Timofeev, V.I. 1975. K voprosu o vremennykh razlichiakh nekotorykh pamyatnikov rannego neolita vostochnoi Pribaltiki. *Kratkie Soobshcheniya Instituta Istorii Materialnoi Kultury*, 141: 18-24.

Valle, O. and Carder, A.C. 1963. Comparison of the climate at Tikkurila, Finland and at Beaverlodge, Alberta, Canada with particular reference to the growth and development of cereal crops. *Suomen Maateloustieteellisen Seuran-Acta Agralia Fennica*, 100, no. 1: 1-30.

Vankina, L.V. 1970. *Torfyannikovaya Stoyanka Sarnate*. Riga, Zinatne (German summary: Die Torfmoorsiedlung von Sarnate).

Vassar, A. 1955. Ukreplennoye poselenie Asva na ostrove Saaremaa. *Muisted Asulad ja Linnused*, 1: 113-34.

Vilkuna, K. 1968. Narodnaya Kultura Finlandii. *Sovetskaya Etnografiya*, 3: 27-36.

Vuorela, I. 1970. The indication of farming in pollen diagrams from southern

Finland. *Acta Botanica Fennica*, 87: 1-40.

Vuorela, I. 1972. Human influence on the vegetation of Katinhäntä bog, southern Finland. *Acta Botanica Fennica*, 98: 1-21.

Vuorela, I. 1975. Pollen analysis as a means of tracing settlement history in south-western Finland. *Acta Botanica Fennica*, 104: 1-48.

Welinder, S. 1975. Agriculture, inland hunting and sea hunting in the western and northern region of the Baltic, 6,000-2,000 B.C. In Fitzhugh, W. (ed.), *Prehistoric Maritime Adaptations of the Circumpolar Zone*. The Hague, Mouton: 21-41.

Zagorkis, F. 1963. Neoliticheskaya stoiyanka Kreichi. *Izvestiya Akademii Nauk Latviiskoi SSR*, 189, no. 4: 23-35.

Zagorska, I. 1970. Orudiya okhoty i rybolova kamennogo veka v mogilnike i poselenyi Zveinieki. *Izvestiya Akademii Nauk Latviiskoi SSR*, 281, no. 12: 51-64.

11
Patterns of Mesolithic land-use in southern England: a geological perspective

Paul Mellars and S.C. Reinhardt

The concept of a significant element of 'geological control' in the patterns of Mesolithic settlement has been current in the literature for over 40 years. In *The Mesolithic Age in Britain*, published in 1932, Grahame Clark made a detailed study of the distribution of Mesolithic sites in relation to the major geological outcrops in the Wealden area of south-east England, and went on to draw some interesting contrasts between the distributional patterns of Mesolithic finds and those of the succeeding Neolithic period (Clark 1932: 88-91). The same theme was pursued further in a number of later publications by Clark (1936: 190-5; Clark and Rankine 1939: 92-4), as well as in papers by Poole (1936), Rankine (1949a, 1956) and Draper (1968). The aim of the present paper is to re-examine this question of 'geological control' over the patterns of Mesolithic activity in southern England and – more importantly – to consider some of the specific ecological mechanisms by which this kind of control might have been achieved.

The main incentive to undertake this study was provided by the comprehensive *Survey of Mesolithic Sites in England and Wales* recently completed by the Council for British Archaeology (cf. Wymer 1977). Although precise figures can hardly be quoted there seems little doubt that this survey has increased the total number of recorded Mesolithic sites in southern Britain by a factor of at least three or four. As an illustration of this change it may be recalled that whereas Clark recorded a total of 32 Mesolithic sites on the areas of the Lower Greensand outcrop (in Clark and Rankine 1939: 93-4), the total number of find-spots recorded on this formation in the course of the recent survey is well over 100; even greater changes are apparent in the distribution of finds on some of the neighbouring geological formations such as the Wealden Clay and the Chalk. Analyses of distributional patterns based on this substantially increased body of data should therefore allow an appreciably more complete and detailed assessment of the patterns of Mesolithic activity in southern England than has been possible hitherto.[1]

One question which is inevitably raised by this kind of study is the utility of the concept of an archaeological 'site'. As Wymer emphasises in his introduction to the recent C.B.A. *Gazetteer* (1977: viii-ix), the extent of documentation associated with many museum and private collections of Mesolithic material is often seriously inadequate, and in a substantial proportion of cases the specific archaeological context and associations of the finds recorded in the recent survey are totally unknown. Partly for this reason, therefore, we have chosen to focus the present study not on the distribution of Mesolithic 'sites' as such, but rather on the distributions of a number of functionally-contrasting implement types. The three types of implement selected for study are (1) microliths, (2) transversely-sharpened axes/adzes, and (3) (so-called) 'pebble mace heads'. Further reasons for adopting this approach will become apparent as the discussion proceeds. It is worth noting at the outset, however, that the significantly different distributions shown by these three implement types indicate that any study of the spatial aspects of Mesolithic settlement or economic patterns which relied on the distribution of a single category of artefacts (for example microliths) could yield potentially misleading results.

The area of southern England considered in the present study is delimited to the north by National Grid line 200 km. North and corresponds essentially with sheet numbers 251 to 359 of the one-inch-to-one-mile map series of the Geological Survey. The only parts of this area not included in the study are the Isle of Wight and the southern parts of the counties of Buckinghamshire and Gloucestershire, for which complete information was not available at the time when the research was undertaken. The task of analysing the distribution of finds over the whole of this area was greatly simplified by a computer program worked out by Mr Gordon Duffus of the Computing Services Department of the University of Sheffield. With the aid of this program it was possible to produce a series of two-dimensional distribution maps of the various findspots recorded in the course of the C.B.A. Survey (defined in each case in terms of a six-figure National Grid Reference) to a number of specified scales.[2] The primary objective of this procedure was to produce a series of maps at a scale of 1:63360 which could be used as overlays for the standard 'one inch' sheets of the Geological Survey. By using a light table it was then possible to observe a direct correlation between the location of each site or find-spot and the particular geological deposit on which it occurred (cf. Table 1).[3]

Before going on to examine the detailed patterns which emerge from this analysis, there are two limitations which underlie the whole of the present study and which should be stated clearly at the outset. In the first place there is the inevitable problem of how far the distributional patterns recorded in the course of the recent survey reflect the true distribution of Mesolithic artefacts in southern Britain

Table 1. Geological units employed in the present study.

Deposit	Estimated area of outcrop in km²	Divisions distinguished on 'one-inch' (1:63360) geological maps
1. Ashdown Sand	455	Ashdown Sand (h') ⎫ Hastings Beds
2. Wadhurst Clay	545	Wadhurst Clay (h'') ⎬ Formation
3. Tunbridge Wells Sand	865	Tunbridge Wells Sand (h''') ⎭
4. Weald Clay	1,690	Weald Clay (h¹)
5. Hythe Beds	405	Hythe Beds (h²') ⎫ Lower Greensand
6. Sandgate Beds	190	Sandgate, Bargate Beds (h²'') ⎬ Formation
7. Folkestone Beds	270	Folkestone Beds (h²''') ⎭
8. Gault Clay (Wealden outcrop)	185	Gault Clay (h³)
9. Upper Greensand (Wealden outcrop)	110	Upper Greensand (h⁴)
10. Gault/Upper Greensand (western outcrops)	1,160	Gault Clay/Upper Greensand (h³⁻⁴)
11. Chalk	7,650	Lower, Middle, Upper Chalk (h⁵)
12. London Clay	3,580	London Clay (i³)
13. Barton Clay etc.	1,910	Barton Clay (i⁴), Bagshot Beds (i⁵), Bracklesham Beds (i⁶)
14. Great Oolite Series	580	Oolitic Limestones (g⁵⁻⁷), Forest Marble (g⁸)
15. Permian deposits	690	Permian Breccia, Sandstone, Conglomerate (e²), Permian Marls (e³)
16. Carboniferous Shale	2,640	Carboniferous Shale (e⁴)
17. Carboniferous Limestone	180	Clifton Down Limestone, Burrington Oolite, Gully Oolite (d⁴)
18. Devonian deposits	4,050	Ladock Beds (c), Dartmouth Beds, Staddon Grits, Meadfoot Beds, Mylor Series, Portscatho Series, Lower Devonian Series (c¹), Devonian Limestone (c²), Middle/Upper Devonian Slates (c³)
19. Granite	1,150	Granite (G)

The areas quoted refer to outcrops of the 'solid' geological formations and exclude areas covered by superficial 'drift' deposits. The Upper Greensand and Gault Clay outcrops have been subdivided geographically into those which form part of the Wealden anticline in south-east England (cf. Fig. 3) and the remaining outcrops of the same deposits in central and western England.

and how far they reflect simply the varying intensities of field work carried out in different areas, varying patterns of erosion, or different types of agricultural activity on different geological formations. Some suggestions as to how these problems might be overcome by means of a systematic programme of field survey will be put forward in the final section of the paper. In the absence of this kind of controlled survey the only point that can usefully be made is that many of the contrasts in the recorded densities of Mesolithic finds on different geological outcrops appear too great — and above all too sharply defined — to be explained entirely in terms of the various distorting factors referred to above. For example, it is difficult to envisage what kind of accidental bias in discovery patterns could be invoked to account for the fact that the density of microliths recorded on the Folkestone Beds division of the Lower Greensand is almost ten times as high as that recorded on the immediately-adjacent areas of the Gault Clay, and over sixty times as high as that on the London Clay (cf. Table 2). Equally if not more difficult to explain in these terms are the striking variations in the *relative* frequencies of the different tool forms on different geological outcrops. Even if some allowance is made for the effects of varying soil conditions on the relative visibility of small artefacts such as microliths, it seems hard to accept that this factor alone can account for the fact that the ratios of axes to microliths recorded on such deposits as the Chalk and London Clay are between ten and twenty times as high as those recorded on the Folkestone Beds or the Tunbridge Wells Sand. On the basis of these and certain other observations, we would suggest that although a number of factors must inevitably have introduced some element of distortion into the recorded distributions of Mesolithic finds, these distortions are not sufficient to mask the existence of very real contrasts in the distributional patterns of different artefact types on different geological formations.

The second limitation concerns the lack of any clear chronological perspective in the distributional data considered here. Any kind of dating of isolated finds of tranchet axes or pebble mace heads is clearly out of the question, and even the separation of associated groups of Mesolithic material into the accepted divisions of 'Early' and 'Later' Mesolithic can be attempted with confidence for only a limited proportion of the recorded sites in southern England. Inevitably, therefore, all of the distributions considered here must be seen as representing essentially 'palimpsests' of human activity extending from the Preboreal to the Atlantic periods. In this connection, however, two points should be made. In the first place it is now clear that vegetational changes were taking place very rapidly during the earlier stages of the postglacial period in southern Britain, and it is likely that most of the changes in vegetational composition that were of major importance to the human communities would have been completed within a space of 1,000 to 1,500 years. According to the evidence from Thatcham (Berkshire) it would appear that substantial proportions of deciduous species were already present in southern England by 7,500 bc (Churchill 1962: 366-9), and it is likely that the transition from predominantly coniferous to predominantly deciduous forest had taken place in these areas by the earlier part of the seventh millennium bc. Secondly, it has been suggested on the basis of a general typological study of the British industries that the number of sites which can be attributed to the earliest stages of the Mesolithic (before c. 7,000 bc) is relatively small (Jacobi 1973: 247).

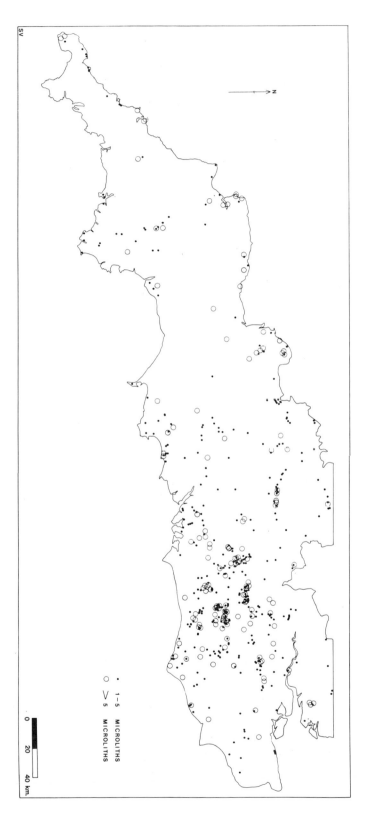

Figure 1. Distribution of microliths in southern England.

If this conclusion is correct, then we should presumably see the major elements in the distributional patterns discussed in the following sections in terms of the human exploitation of an essentially deciduous forest environment, in which varying associations of oak, elm, lime and alder formed the major components (Godwin 1975).

Distribution of microliths

In Table 2 the distribution of microliths on different geological outcrops in southern England has been expressed in two different ways. The first three columns in the Table are based on the numbers of individual *findspots* of microliths on the different geological formations, while the figures in the last three columns relate to the *total numbers* of microliths recovered from these deposits. Although the relative ordering of the various deposits according to these two criteria show a reasonable measure of agreement, it should be emphasised that the figures relating to the total numbers of microliths are particularly sensitive to the occurrence of a single prolific site. For example, the anomalously high density of microliths recorded on the Carboniferous Limestone formation can be attributed entirely to the presence of a single site which contributed 107 of the 111 microliths recovered from this deposit. Similarly, over 3,000 of the 4,551 microliths recorded from the Folkestone Beds deposit derive from the two excavated sites of Oakhanger V and VII. For this reason we would suggest that the numbers of separate findspots of microliths provide a more meaningful and statistically-reliable indication of the distribution of these tools over the different geological outcrops than that provided by the gross totals of implements.

From the data presented in Table 2 two features are immediately apparent. In the first place it will be seen that the densities of both individual find-spots and total numbers of microliths recorded on the different deposits show a remarkable range of variation. Thus the densities of findspots range from as high as 17.5 per 100 square kilometres on the Folkestone Beds to less than 0.4/100 km² on such deposits as the London Clay, Carboniferous Shale and the Permian Marls, while the figures relating to the total numbers of microliths from these deposits exhibit an even wider range of variation (cf. Fig. 2). Perhaps the clearest way of illustrating these contrasts is by means of the 'density index' values, which compare the recorded density of finds on each deposit with the overall or 'average' density of finds recorded over southern England as a whole. This shows that the density of findspots on the Folkestone Beds deposit is over 17 times as high as that recorded for the study-area as a whole, while the densities of finds on the three deposits at the foot of the Table are less than 0.3 of the 'average' figure. As we have already remarked, it seems difficult to accept that variations of this order of magnitude can be attributed

Table 2. Distribution of microliths on different geological outcrops in southern England (cf. Table 1).

DEPOSIT	AREA IN KM2	NUMBERS OF FIND-SPOTS			NUMBERS OF MICROLITHS		
		Numbers of find-spots	Density of find-spots per 100 km2	Density index	Numbers of microliths	Density of microliths per 100 km2	Density index
Folkestone Beds	270	67	24.81	17.47	4,551	1,685.55	46.70
Sandgate Beds	190	17	8.95	6.30	128	67.37	1.87
Hythe Beds	405	35	8.64	6.08	257	63.46	1.76
Tunbridge Wells Sand	865	45	5.20	3.66	1,018	117.69	3.26
Upper Greensand (Wealden outcrop)	110	4	3.64	2.56	9	8.18	0.23
Ashdown Sand	455	16	3.52	2.48	165	36.26	1.01
Weald Clay	1,690	43	2.54	1.79	468	27.69	0.77
Carboniferous Limestone	180	4	2.22	1.56	111	61.67	1.71
Gault Clay (Wealden)	185	4	2.16	1.53	8	4.32	0.12
Wadhurst Clay	545	8	1.47	1.04	20	3.67	0.10
Great Oolite	580	8	1.38	0.97	12	2.07	0.06
Granite	1,150	14	1.22	0.86	166	14.43	0.40
Barton Clay etc.	1,910	22	1.15	0.81	117	6.13	0.17
Gault/Upper Greensand (western outcrops)	1,160	10	0.86	0.61	36	3.10	0.09
Chalk	7,650	57	0.74	0.52	2,126	27.79	0.77
Devonian deposits	4,050	17	0.42	0.30	136	3.36	0.09
London Clay	3,580	14	0.39	0.27	165	4.61	0.13
Carboniferous Shale	2,640	8	0.30	0.21	104	3.94	0.11
Permian deposits	690	1	0.14	0.10	2	0.29	0.01
'Average' density of finds over the study-area as a whole (per 100 km2)			1.42			36.09	

The figures quoted for the 'average' densities of find-spots and implements are based on the total finds from the study-area as a whole, including those from both 'solid' and 'drift' geological formations. The density index values were obtained by dividing the observed density of finds on each deposit by the average density recorded over the study-area as a whole.

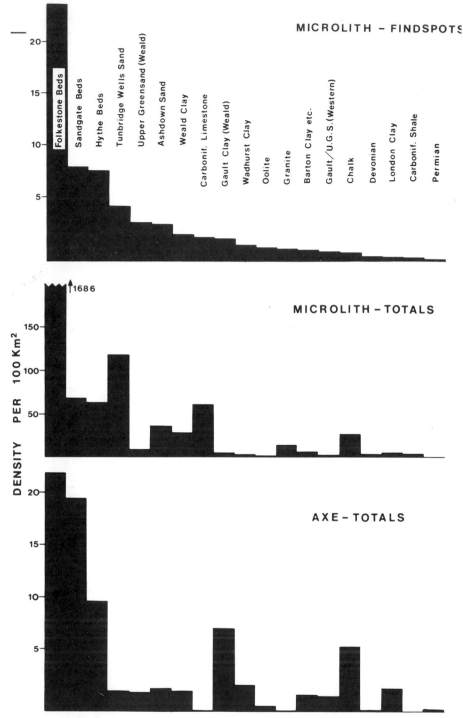

Figure 2. Distribution of microliths and transversely-sharpened flint axes/adzes on the various geological formations listed in Table 1. For microliths, the densities of both individual findspots and total numbers of implements are indicated; for axes/adzes only the overall densities of implements are shown. For data on the actual numbers of finds and surface area of the different geological outcrops see Tables 2 and 4.

entirely to various sources of accidental bias in the patterns of artefact discovery.

The second feature which emerges clearly from Table 2 is the heavy concentration of microliths on deposits which give rise to relatively coarsely-textured sandy soils. Although this point has of course been recognised by many earlier workers (e.g. Clark 1932: 88-9, 1936: 190-2; Childe 1940: 21) the quantitative data assembled here enable this correlation to be demonstrated in a much clearer fashion than has been possible hitherto. Within the areas considered in the present study the close correlation between microlith distributions and areas of sandy soil can be demonstrated in two different ways.

1. The six deposits listed in Table 2 which show the heaviest concentrations of microliths fall clearly into the category of sand-yielding deposits. These include the three major divisions of the Lower Greensand formation (the Folkestone Beds, Hythe Beds and Sandgate Beds), the Upper Greensand, and the two sand-yielding divisions of the 'Hastings Beds' formation (the Tunbridge Wells Sand and Ashdown Sand) in the central Weald. Against this observation may be set the consistently lower densities of finds on the various deposits which give rise to heavy, clay-rich soils – most notably the Gault Clay, the Weald Clay, the Wadhurst Clay and, above all, the London Clay. The extensive areas of the Chalk outcrop in south-east England also show a conspicuously low density of finds. As Clark pointed out in 1932, this contrast between the distribution of sites on areas of sand as opposed to clay-yielding deposits is particularly highlighted in the Wealden area where both kinds of deposit, as well as the Chalk, occur in close juxtaposition. Thus the exceptionally dense concentration of findspots on the Folkestone Beds component of

Table 3. Granulometric composition of soils developed on different geological formations in south-east England.

Deposit	No. of samples analysed	Coarse sand %	Total sand %	Silt %	Clay %
Folkestone Beds	13	55.7	77.6	17.6	4.8
Hythe Beds	18	18.0	57.5	31.7	10.8
Sandgate Beds	4	15.2	49.4	40.2	10.4
Tunbridge Wells Sand	4	6.7	41.5	46.5	12.0
Ashdown Sand	3	2.0	39.9	52.2	7.9
Upper Greensand	5	6.1	37.0	48.5	14.5
Wadhurst Clay	3	2.4	27.0	54.4	18.6
Weald Clay	21	6.7	24.7	55.3	20.0
Gault Clay	5	8.2	22.2	52.8	25.0

Data derived from Hall and Russell (1911). The figures quoted are averages based on the total number of samples analysed from each deposit. Particle sizes are defined as follows: Coarse Sand > 0.2 mm.; Fine Sand 0.2 – 0.04 mm.; Silt 0.04 – 0.002 mm.; Clay < 0.002mm.

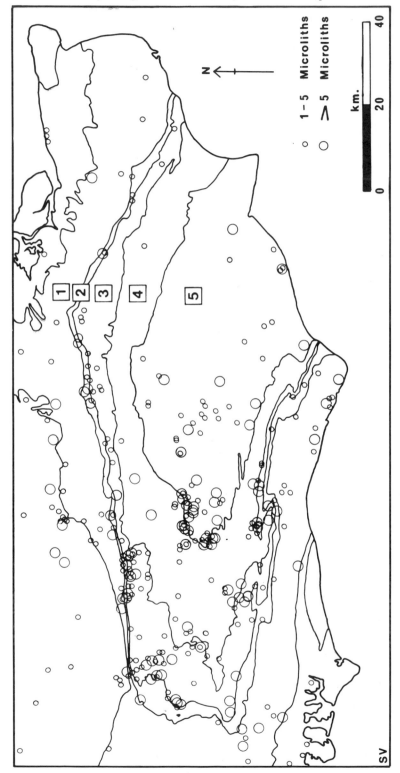

Figure 3. Distribution of microliths on the major geological formations of the Weald and adjacent areas of south-east England. The geological outcrops shown are as follows: 1 – Chalk; 2 – Upper Greensand and Gault Clay; 3 – Lower Greensand (Folkestone, Hythe and Sandgate Beds); 4 – Weald Clay; 5 – Hastings Beds (Tunbridge Wells Sand, Ashdown Sand, Wadhurst Clay).

the Lower Greensand may be contrasted with the relatively sparse distribution of finds on the immediately-adjacent areas of the Gault Clay outcrop. Or again, the conspicuous clustering of sites along the western margin of the Tunbridge Wells Sand may be compared with the much lower density of finds on the neighbouring areas of the Weald Clay (cf. Fig. 3).

2. If attention is now focused on the varying densities of microlith-yielding sites on the six sand-yielding deposits referred to above it is possible to observe a close relationship between the recorded densities of finds and the granulometric composition of the respective deposits. A convenient way of illustrating this point is provided by the detailed sedimentological analyses published by A.D. Hall and E.J. Russell in *The Agriculture and Soils of Kent, Surrey and Sussex* (1911). From the data supplied by Hall and Russell it can be seen that the various sand-yielding formations of the Wealden area can be divided into three major groupings (Table 3). At the head of the Table comes the Folkestone Beds division of the Lower Greensand which shows a clear predominance of sediments (usually between 50 and 70 percent) in the 'coarse sand' category, and a combined fraction of both coarse and fine-grained sand in the region of 70-85 percent. The next grouping is represented by the two remaining divisions of the Lower Greensand – the Hythe Beds and Sandgate Beds – in which the percentages of coarse sand are consistently lower than those in the Folkestone Beds (c. 10-30 percent), and in which the average component of both coarse and fine sand is in the region of 50-60 percent. The third grouping comprises the Upper Greensand and the two sandstone formations of the central Weald – the Tunbridge Wells Sand and Ashdown Sand. In these deposits the percentage of coarse sand is frequently almost negligible, while the overall sand fraction falls to around 40 percent. All of these deposits stand clearly apart from the true clay-yielding formations of south-east England (the Gault Clay, Weald Clay, Wadhurst Clay and London Clay) in which the total proportion of sand particles rarely exceeds 20-25 percent, and in which the bulk of the sediments fall into either the clay or fine silt grades.

It will be immediately apparent from Table 2 that the relative ordering of these deposits in terms of predominant grain size corresponds closely with the ordering of the deposits in terms of microlith densities. As we have already seen, the Folkestone Beds outcrop shows by far the heaviest concentration of microlith-yielding sites in southern England, while the Hythe Beds and Sandgate Beds on the one hand, and the Upper Greensand, Tunbridge Wells Sand and Ashdown Sand on the other hand, form groupings of progressively lower microlith densities (cf. Fig. 2). All of these deposits show significantly heavier concentrations of finds than those recorded on any of the major clay formations. Of course, all of these deposits exhibit a good deal of variation in sedimentological composition from one point to another (even the clay formations incorporating occasional seams of sand) and it might perhaps be more meaningful to think of these correlations in terms of the *relative areas* of the different geological outcrops which are characterised by the more coarsely-textured sediments than in terms of the 'average' grain-size of the deposits. Unfortunately, in the absence of much more detailed geological mapping it is hardly possible to test this suggestion in any systematic way. But whichever way the situation is envisaged, the fact remains that the empirical correlation between the recorded distribution of microliths and the overall sedimentological composition of these particular geological formations is remarkably close.

Several explanations might be offered to account for the concentration of microliths on areas of sandy soil. The obvious attractions of highly permeable, freely drained soils for the location of occupation sites have been commented on by several earlier workers (e.g. Clark 1932: 88; Draper 1968: 110), and have been noted frequently by ethnographers as a major factor in controlling the choice of camp sites among modern hunter-gatherer groups. In Australia, for example, the attraction of sandy locations has been attributed not only to the relative dryness of these sites, but also to the impression of 'warmth' created by the heat-insulating properties of the loose, porous soils (Tindale 1974: 11, 53, 73). Other authors (e.g. Bradley 1972: 194) have drawn attention to the advantages of sandy sub-soils for the construction of 'pit-dwellings' and analogous features of the kind which have now been recorded from over a dozen Mesolithic settlements in southern England. If some of these features were used for the storage of food resources over the winter season, rather than as foundations for living structures, then the properties of unimpeded drainage and heat insulation offered by sandy soils would have assumed even greater importance.

Although the importance of the various factors discussed above should not be minimised (especially in the case of settlements located close to the boundary between contrasting geological outcrops) we would suggest that the primary attraction of areas of sandy soil to Mesolithic communities lay rather in the character of the vegetation developed on these deposits. The close relationships between subsoil conditions and the structure and composition of the modern oak-dominated woodlands growing on different geological formations in lowland Britain were discussed at considerable length by A.G. Tansley in *The British Islands and their Vegetation* (1949: 267-357; see also Tansley and Proctor 1968: 86-113). In this book Tansley drew a basic distinction between what he referred to as the 'damp' and 'dry' types of oakwood community. According to Tansley the 'damp' type of oakwood is developed most characteristically on deposits which give rise to finely-textured clay and silt-dominated soils, of which he cites the London Clay and the various clay-yielding formations of the Wealden area (the Weald Clay, Gault Clay and Wadhurst Clay) as typical examples. The 'dry' type of oakwood on the other hand is regarded as the characteristic woodland community of the major sand-yielding formations, represented by such deposits as the Bunter Sandstone of Nottinghamshire, the Bagshot Sands of the London and Hampshire Basins, and the Lower Greensand, Tunbridge Wells Sand and Ashdown Sand of the Weald (Tansley 1949: 111-13, 271-4, 286-7, 304, 350-2). Several features are quoted as serving to differentiate these two types of woodland; these include a richer variety of floristic composition in the 'damp' than in the 'dry' type of oakwood, and a general tendency in the latter woodlands towards a replacement of the pedunculate (*Quercus robur*) by the sessile (*Quercus petreae*) species of oak. A feature to which Tansley makes repeated reference, however, is the marked contrast in the density of the understorey shrub vegetation in the two types of woodland. Thus he points out that whereas the damp oakwoods are generally characterised by an exceptionally heavy growth of shrubs (principally hazel but also including such species as hawthorn, blackthorn, dogwood and willow) the development of the shrub layer in the dry oakwoods growing on sandy soils is usually either sparse or, in some cases, almost totally lacking (Tansley 1949: 271, 286-7, 304-6; Tansley and Proctor 1968: 106-7). As an illustration of the latter situation Tansley refers to the surviving remnants of Sherwood Forest growing on the Bunter Sandstone formation in Nottinghamshire – a deposit which shows a close resemblance in its overall sedimentological composition to the Folkestone Beds component of the Lower Greensand (Tansley 1949: 352): 'The fragments of old forest still extant are very simple in structure, consisting of two layers only, the tree canopy and the field layer. The tree layer consists of the two species of oaks (with hybrids) in varying proportions, together with *Betula pubescens* where the light is sufficient ... There is no shrub layer, shrubs being practically absent from most of the woods' (Tansley 1949: 352-3). Throughout this discussion Tansley leaves no doubt that he regards the weak development of shrubs in the woodlands growing on areas of sandy soil as an essentially 'natural' feature of the vegetational communities in these areas, which cannot be attributed merely to the impact of modern biotic factors such as varying intensities of grazing pressure or different patterns of woodland management. The reasons for the weak development of shrubs in these woodlands are unfortunately not discussed in detail by Tansley, but the explanation most probably lies in the varying abilities of trees and shrubs to compete for the limited supplies of mineral nutrients and (perhaps more importantly) water, available in the parent soils. In this situation, of course, the deep and extensive rooting systems of mature trees give them a strong competitive advantage over the shallower rooting systems characteristic of most understorey shrubs species (H. Godwin, personal communication; see also Tansley 1949: 214, 369).

The potential importance of these variations in vegetational structure to hunting and gathering communities has been discussed in detail elsewhere (Mellars 1976b: 31-3). Essentially, two points are relevant. In the first place it has been argued that it is the density of the understorey vegetation – rather than the density of tree growth as such – that poses the major obstacle to the *mobility* of human groups in forested areas, and that this factor must have had a significant bearing on the amount of time and energy expended in almost all kinds of economic activities in these environments. Secondly, and perhaps more significantly, the density of the understorey vegetation is known to have a particularly important bearing on the efficiency and productivity of hunting activities in forested areas. The important factors in this context are not simply the mobility and visibility of the hunters themselves, but also the amount of escape cover available to hunted animals. The importance attached to this factor amongst modern hunting groups is clearly reflected in the ethnographic literature (cf. Stewart 1956; Day 1953). For example, Stewart writes:

Klamath Indians in forested southern Oregon and Pomo Indians in the redwood country of northern California complained to me that modern forestry, which allows brush and trees to grow rank and uncontrolled, was depriving the Indians of much hunting territory. The Klamath Indian said: 'Now I just hear the deer running through the brush at places we used to kill many deer. When the brush got as thick as it is now we would burn it off.' (Stewart 1956: 119)

A similar motivation for setting fire to vegetation was reported by an early explorer in the Massachusetts Bay area of New England:

There is no underwood saving in swamps and low grounds that are wet ... for it being the custom of the indians to burne the wood in November, when the grasse is withered, and leaves dryed, it consumes all the underwood and rubbish, which otherwise would overgrow the country, making it unpassable, and spoil their much affected hunting; so that by this means in those places where the Indians inhabit there is scarce a brush or bramble, or any combersome underwood to be seene in the more champion ground. (Wood 1634, quoted in Day 1953: 335)

The reference to the deliberate burning of woodland in these quotations raises a number of important issues which will be pursued further at a later point in the discussion. The essential point to note here is simply that the density of the understorey vegetation should probably be seen as the most important single factor controlling the overall productivity and economic efficiency of hunting procedures in different types of woodland. Indeed, it may well be that in forests characterised by exceptionally heavy shrub growth the exploitation of widely dispersed and fast-moving animals virtually ceased to be a viable economic pursuit. Whether or not this is the case it seems clear that the hunting of all kinds of game must have been significantly easier and more profitable in the woodlands which supported the most open type of undergrowth, and it is reasonable to assume that it is in these areas that the major emphasis on hunting as a subsistence activity would have been placed.

How far Tansley's observations on the structure of present-day woodlands can be applied to the various forms of 'mixed oak forest' which developed in southern Britain during the later stages of the Boreal and the Atlantic periods must inevitably remain a matter for debate. In the first place recent work on the differential pollen production of different tree species (Andersen 1973) has cast doubt on the traditional idea that oak formed the dominant element in the forests of the Atlantic period, and suggests that over large areas of southern England the 'climax' forest at this time may have consisted of a more or less co-dominant association of both oak and lime (Godwin 1975: 59-61; Birks *et al.* 1975). To what extent these large amounts of lime in the zone VIIa forests may have influenced the development of the understorey vegetation is difficult to assess, although it could be argued that since lime is known to cast a deeper shade than oak this might have had the effect of reducing to some extent the density of the shrub growth in the woodlands developed on all types of sub-soil. The other important question is how far the contrasts in vegetational structure documented by Tansley in the modern woodlands growing on different geological formations represent essentially 'natural' features of the forests developed on these deposits, and how far they reflect the cumulative effects of various processes of soil deterioration extending over the past 5,000-10,000 years. The work of Dimbleby (1962) and others has provided convincing evidence of the ways in which even brief episodes of deforestation can lead to a rapid decline in soil fertility in areas of naturally impoverished soils, and it could no doubt be argued from this that the structure of the present-day woodlands growing on areas of sandy soil provides an unreliable guide to the character of the forests that would have developed on the same areas during Mesolithic times. It would be easy, however, to exaggerate the implications of this reasoning. In the first place it must be remembered that many coarsely-textured sandy geological formations are known to be naturally deficient in many of the chemical nutrients that are important for plant growth (Tansley 1949: 90, 97; Dimbleby 1962: 35), and it is reasonable to assume that this would have had a significant influence on the fertility of the soils developed on these deposits throughout the whole of the postglacial period. Again, the same deposits are inevitably more vulnerable to the effects of leaching than deposits which contain a high proportion of clay and silt particles, and are therefore inherently more susceptible to a progressive loss of nutrients from the upper levels of the soil profile. Thirdly it is clear that the soils developed on areas of highly permeable sub-soil must be more sensitive to the effects of drought than those developed on the more finely-textured geological formations (Limbrey 1975: 149, 240); as we have already suggested, it is likely that the latter factor would have played a particularly important role in the competitive relationships between different plant species in the low-lying areas of south and east England, where a combination of low rainfall and high temperatures can lead to serious deficiencies of soil moisture during the summer months (Smith 1976).

In considering the character of the soils on which the original deciduous forests of lowland Britain developed, some allowance must presumably also be made for the processes of soil development that were in operation during the immediately preceding periods. A factor which may have had an important bearing in this context is the heavy predominance of pine which is known to have characterised the earlier stages of the postglacial in south-eastern England. Pollen diagrams from five separate localities in Surrey, Hampshire and Dorset reveal a very consistent picture in which pine normally accounts for between 60 and 90 percent of the total arboreal pollen in samples from zones IV, V and VIa of the vegetational succession (Seagrief 1959, 1960; Seagrief and Godwin 1961). It could be argued that under these conditions of heavily pine-dominated forest soil deterioration would be likely to take place rapidly on areas of sandy soil, since pine is generally recognised as a species that has little capacity to maintain soil fertility, and in fact tends to intensify the effects of leaching by increasing the levels of acidity at the soil surface (Butzer 1964: 80; Pearsall 1968: 90; Limbrey 1975: 146). If – as we shall argue later – fire was a relatively frequent occurrence in these early postglacial coniferous forests, then the deterioration in soil conditions during this period might have been especially marked. However, the picture is complicated by the appearance of hazel as a major component of the forests during the later stages of the Boreal, and it may be that the presence of this species did much to counteract the harmful effects of the pine on the overall processes of soil development (G. Dimbleby, personal communication).

Leaving aside these theoretical considerations, there would appear to be a good deal of empirical evidence to suggest that the existence of impoverished soil conditions in areas of sandy sub-soil can be traced back to an early stage of the postglacial period. At the site of Elstead in Surrey, situated on the Folkestone Beds deposit, Seagrief and Godwin found evidence that substantial areas of heath vegetation were already present in this area at the end of the late-glacial period, and suggested that other indications of acidic soil conditions could be traced throughout zones IV, V and VI of the vegetational succession (Seagrief and Godwin 1961: 87, 90). Equally significant in this context are the results of soil pollen analysis undertaken by Dimbley (1962: 75-8) at the sites of High Rocks and Keston Camp in Kent. Both of these sites are located on areas of sandy or gravelly soil (the Tunbridge Wells Sand and Blackheath Pebble Beds respectively) and both sites appear to show that heavily podzolised soil profiles had developed on these deposits under conditions of apparently undisturbed deciduous forest. Dimbleby's comments on these two sites are worth quoting directly:

A section through the ramparts (at Keston Camp) revealed a buried soil, which was a humus-iron podzol. However, in contrast to other lowland sites, pollen analysis showed that this site had never been occupied by heathland but was in fact under oak forest at the time of construction of the ramparts. There was nothing to suggest that this forest was secondary; on the contrary, its rich woodland flora confirmed its primary nature.

Other indications have been found that the deciduous forest climax may have been associated with a podzolised soil in some places. At High Rocks, for instance, though no soil profile was observed, a Mesolithic site was overwhelmed by sand which was rich in forest pollen and which was intensively bleached. At Portesham a Bronze Age barrow covered a well-developed podzol, although there was no evidence of earlier heathland conditions (Dimbleby 1962: 16).

In discussing the composition of the pollen spectra from the Keston site, Dimbleby observed:

Quercus was the absolute dominant, but was accompanied by a surprisingly large amount of *Ilex*. *Corylus* and *Betula* were the only other noteworthy woody species. The remarkable thing about this list is that *Ilex*, *Corylus* and *Betula* are all species which have been described as soil improvers, yet here they are associated with a well-developed podzol. Their influence in this direction may have been counteracted by the nature of the *Quercus* litter and probably even more by the properties of the soil parent material. It is clear that one cannot postulate the existence of a brown forest soil merely on the evidence that such species were present, without taking into account the nature of the parent material (Dimbleby 1962: 21).

As Dimbleby points out, it is possible to quote many other instances in which processes of soil deterioration leading towards podzolisation can be shown to have occurred under a covering of mature deciduous forest, and in all these cases the overriding control of the parent material over the general processes of soil development would seem beyond dispute (Dimbleby 1962: 15-16, 21, 35-7; Limbrey 1975: 147-9). Moreover, it could be argued that these processes would have been likely to operate at an even faster rate during the Atlantic period, when increased precipitation would have tended to accelerate the effects of leaching on the more permeable sandy soils. Whether or not this was the case, there are clearly strong grounds for believing that the existence of impoverished soil conditions on areas of sandy sub-soil cannot be attributed exclusively to the effects of various forms of human interference on the natural patterns of soil development, and that significant variations in the fertility of soils developed on different geological outcrops can probably be traced back throughout the greater part of the postglacial period. If this conclusion is correct, then the existence of corresponding variations in the composition of the original vegetational communities growing on these deposits must be regarded as at least a reasonable working hypothesis.

The effects of forest fires on settlement and subsistence strategies

In the final analysis, of course, the character of the undisturbed 'climax' vegetation of southern England may be of only limited relevance in considering the settlement patterns and economic strategies of Mesolithic populations. Over the past fifteen years evidence has been accumulating to show that in many areas of Britain the 'natural' vegetational communities were influenced to a substantial extent by the activities of the Mesolithic communities themselves, and the evidence points strongly to the conclusion that this modification was brought about largely if not entirely by the action of fire. The empirical evidence for the impact of burning on the Mesolithic landscape has been set out fully in the publications of Dimbleby (1961, 1962 etc.), Simmons (1969), Smith (1970) and several other workers, and the potential importance of these environmental changes for the economic and social organisation of Mesolithic groups has been discussed in two recent papers by one of the present authors (Mellars 1975, 1976b). Without attempting to summarise all of the relevant considerations here, it can be said that a sysematic and carefully-controlled policy of burning in many types of forest and woodland habitats would have yielded substantial benefits to Mesolithic communities in at least six major respects:

1. By increasing the *mobility* of the human groups, thereby reducing the amount of time and energy expended in most types of economic activity:
2. By improving conditions for the hunting of game – principally by reducing the amount of escape cover available to hunted animals, but perhaps also by allowing the use of more efficient and productive forms of communal hunting strategies;
3. By increasing the total numbers and population density of animal populations, through improvements in both the total quantity and nutritional quality of the available forage resources:
4. By increasing the relative growth-rate of young animals, the maximum size attained by mature animals, and the reproductive capacity of females;
5. By controlling the distribution of the animals, thereby making the movements of the animals more predictable and accordingly more accessible to the hunters; and,
6. By increasing the yields of certain kinds of vegetable food resources.

The benefits might perhaps be summed up by saying that burning has the capacity to increase both the total *productivity* of the environment in terms of the production of basic food resources, and also the relative *efficiency* with which these resources could be exploited. Some indication of the potential importance of these changes to the Mesolithic economy may be gauged by the fact that the occurrence of fire in at least certain types of woodland is likely to have increased the overall productivity of the environment in terms of the yields of animal protein by as much as 500-900 percent (Mellars 1976b: 22-6). The effects of burning on the productivity of plant foods is more difficult to estimate, but in the case of certain vegetable resources (for example hazelnuts) it is likely that the improvements in the level of annual yields were no less impressive than those achieved in the production of animal food supplies (cf. Rawitscher 1945; Smith 1970: 82-3; Lewis 1973).

The suggestion that the deliberate burning of vegetation may have played a central role in the economic strategies of Mesolithic populations has a number of important implications for any discussion of the distribution of Mesolithic settlement and subsistence activities in different ecological zones. The first and most obvious consideration is the relative ease with which different types of woodland could be set on fire. In this context it can be said at once that at least two features of the woodlands developed on areas of coarsely-textured sandy soils must have rendered them especially susceptible to the occurrence and spread of fires (cf. Dimbleby 1962: 27). On the one hand the combination of highly permeable, freely-drained soils and relatively open vegetational structure would have provided the optimal opportunities for the lower levels of vegetation to dry out thoroughly during the drier months of the year. On the other hand, the woodlands developed on these areas were almost certainly well endowed in rich and continuous growths of various kinds of ground vegetation (grasses, bracken, dwarf shrubs etc.) which are known to act as the principal agencies for spreading fires through forested environments (Tansley 1949: 276-7, 280, 353; Tansley and Proctor 1968: 106-7; Biswell 1972: 78-9). By contrast the 'damp' types of woodland growing on the various clay and silt-dominated soils of lowland Britain must have been far more resistant to the occurrence of fire. As Simmons has pointed out (1969: 111), the periods when these woodlands became sufficiently dry to support an extensive fire must have been few and far between, whilst the heavy development of the understorey shrub vegetation would have tended to suppress the growth of most kinds of fuel-producing ground vegetation on the forest floor (Tansley 1949: 277). Indeed, the combination of perpetually damp soil conditions and limited fuel supplies may well have rendered the woodlands developed on the more fertile soils of southern England virtually fire-proof, except during periods of exceptionally dry climatic conditions.

But the role of soil conditions in controlling the ecological impact of forest fires is likely to have extended further than this. It is generally acknowledged that the rate at which ecological succession proceeds following any kind of disturbance is controlled by a variety of environmental factors, of which the fertility of local soil conditions is certainly one of the most important. In other words, the length of time required for the re-establishment of the original 'climax' vegetation following disturbances such as burning tends to be appreciably shorter in areas where the natural fertility of the soil is high than in areas where inherent deficiencies in either soil nutrients or soil moisture serve to slow down the rates of plant growth. It would seem to follow from this, therefore, that fires would not only be more frequent and widespread in the woodlands growing on areas of impoverished sandy soil, but also that the ecological consequences of any individual episode of burning would be more prolonged in these areas than in the forests developed on more fertile clay and silt-dominated soils (cf. Mellars 1976b: 29-30).

So far we have considered only the short-term effects of fire on the development of forest vegetation. Equally if not more important in the present context are the effects of *recurrent* burning on the development of the ecosystem as a whole. The mechanisms by which the repeated occurrence of fires can lead to a rapid deterioration in soil fertility in areas of naturally impoverished soils have been set out clearly by Dimbleby in *The Development of British Heathlands and their Soils* (1962: 27-34). As Dimbleby points out, even if a single fire is not sufficiently intense to result in the complete destruction of tree cover, the inevitable effect of repeated burning is to prevent the regeneration of tree seedlings, so that the end result of this process is a situation in which the natural regeneration of mature forest is largely if not entirely suppressed. Dimbleby goes on to point out that any reduction in the extent or density of the tree cover would have important implications for the development of local soil conditions. In the absence of a continuous tree canopy the amount of precipitation reaching the ground is increased, leading to a significant increase in the rate at which chemical nutrients are removed by leaching from the upper levels of the soil. At the same time, the loss of the deep-rooting systems of mature trees removes the principal agency by which the recycling of nutrients from the lower levels of the soil profile is maintained. In addition, of course, the occurrence of fires can contribute to the loss of nutrients from the ecosystem in a more direct way by exposing the surface of the soil to various forms of erosion and by releasing a small but significant fraction of the available nutrients to the atmosphere in the form of smoke; moreover, many of the chemicals which are returned to the surface of the soil in the form of ash are readily dissolved by rain water and are therefore especially vulnerable to removal by leaching (Limbrey 1975: 118-19). In the case of naturally fertile soils developed on top of poorly drained geological formations the combined effects of these factors on the overall processes of soil development may be very slight. But in the case of soils developed on more coarse-grained deposits, where the original nutrient content of the parent material is relatively low and where the high permeability of the sub-soil encourages rapid leaching, the effects of any kind of deforestation on the fertility of local soil conditions could be dramatic.

To sum up therefore it can be said that the effects of repeated burning on areas of naturally impoverished, sandy soils would be greatly to accelerate the inherent tendencies of these areas towards soil degradation. From the standpoint of the vegetational cover, this would have three major consequences. First, it can be assumed (for reasons explained above) that vegetational succession would proceed at a progressively slower rate as the fertility of soil conditions declined, so that the ecological consequences of each successive episode of burning would become increasingly prolonged as time went by. Secondly, if we follow the suggestions of Tansley it is likely that the woodlands which did succeed in re-establishing themselves on the areas of partially degraded soils would be significantly more 'open' in character (particularly as regards the density of the shrub vegetation) than those developed on the original, undisturbed forest soils. Thirdly, it has been pointed out by Dimbleby and others that the processes of soil deterioration which served to retard the spread of trees into areas of burned-over ground would at the same time tend to encourage the spread of other types of vegetation (most notably heather and associated heathland species) which are themselves especially susceptible to the occurrence of fires (Dimbleby 1962: 27, 34; Evans 1975: 96). In other words, the occurrence of fires in these habitats would tend to establish a self-perpetuating cycle of ecological developments in which the damaging effects of burning on the processes of soil development would serve to encourage the spread of vegetational communities which became progressively more susceptible to the incidence – and therefore to the ecological consequences – of fire. Seen from the standpoint of the human communities, this would have the effect of producing vegetational conditions which were increasingly more open in character, and accordingly more favourable to at least certain types of economic exploitation.

It remains to ask whether any kind of empirical evidence can be quoted to support the suggestion that the vegetation developed on sandy geological formations was in fact modified substantially by the action of fire during Mesolithic times. The answer, of course, must be in the affirmative. The clearest evidence is provided by three sites investigated by Dimbleby – Iping Common in Sussex and Oakhanger sites VII and VIII in Hampshire – all located on the Folkestone Beds division of the Lower Greensand and all associated with evidence of Mesolithic occupation (Keef *et al.* 1965; Rankine and Dimbleby 1960,

1961). At the site of Iping Common, for example, Dimbleby found evidence of an apparently rapid replacement of dense hazel woodland by open heath communities in a vegetational context which points strongly to a date within the Boreal period. Commenting on this transition, Dimbleby wrote:

The replacement of hazel woodland by heath is a change which could hardly occur without some biotic influence such as fire or grazing, though the latter process would rather have favoured the grasses, which in fact showed no parallel increase in pollen percentage. We have here clear evidence of a change of vegetation of the sort which human influence would produce. There is also the archaeological evidence of intensive occupation by man. Complete proof of the association of these two events cannot be produced, but it is not unreasonable to infer that they are associated. (Keef *et al.* 1965: 88)

After this initial attack on the woodland, hazel showed a temporary recovery, but the continued predominance of heather in all of the subsequent pollen spectra suggested that some kind of continous pressure by biotic factors (either by fire or just conceivably by heavy grazing) prevented the regeneration of closed woodland on this site throughout the whole of the Mesolithic and later prehistoric periods.

At the two sites investigated by Rankine on Oakhanger Warren (sites VII and VIII) the vegetational changes were less dramatic but in each case the pollen evidence indicated a progressive opening up of the local forest canopy (marked by an expansion of heather and grasses) during the later stages of the Mesolithic occupation – in this case attributable on botanical grounds to pollen zone VIIa (Rankine and Dimbleby 1960: 255-62; 1961: 7-8). Hardly less significant than the palaeobotanical evidence, however, is the fact that at all three of the sites examined by Dimbleby there was evidence that large-scale erosion and redeposition of sediments had taken place during the Mesolithic period, which led to the burial of the Mesolithic occupation levels under thick deposits of either wind- or water-transported sand. At Oakhanger site VII the initial phase of erosion can be dated to a relatively early stage of the Boreal period, while at both this site and the sites of Oakhanger VIII and Iping Common there is evidence that similar movements were taking place during the Atlantic period. As Dimbleby points out (1960: 260) erosion of sediments on this scale could hardly occur without some kind of 'drastic local interference with the surrounding vegetation', and by far the most likely cause of such interference would be the action of fire. The fact that the erosion and transportation of sediments occurred on at least two separate occasions at Oakhanger VII provides a further indication that some form of disturbance in the local vegetational cover was a recurrent phenomenon on the Lower Greensand areas throughout a substantial part of the Mesolithic period.

Although the present discussion has focused primarily on the effects of burning within the context of an essentially deciduous forested environment, it should be emphasised that the same observations could be applied with equal if not greater force to the heavily pine-dominated forests which are known to have characterised the earlier stages of the post-glacial (zones IV, V and VIa) in south-eastern England (cf. Seagrief 1959, 1960; Seagrief and Godwin 1961). Coniferous forests are notoriously prone to the occurrence of fires, partly because of the relative inflammability of the coniferous trees themselves, but also because of the accumulation of thick deposits of resinous and highly inflammable needle 'litter' on the forest floor. Under these conditions of predominantly pine forests it could no doubt be argued that fires would be relatively frequent and widespread over all the major geological formations in southern England, regardless of the character of local soil conditions. Whether or not this is true remains debatable, but the important point to be recognised (as emphasised above) is that the ecological impact of burning on the development of local soil conditions would be much greater on the areas of relatively impoverished and freely-drained soils than on the more fertile and leach-resistant soils of the various clay and loam-yielding geological formations. If we are correct, therefore, in assuming that fires would have been particularly frequent in the early postglacial pine forests of south-east England it follows that the cycle of ecological developments leading to the emergence of increasingly podzolised soil conditions and progressively more open, heath-like vegetational communities can probably be traced back on areas of coarsely-textured sandy soils to a relatively early stage of the Mesolithic period. As we have just seen, empirical support for this suggestion is provided by the pollen record at Iping Common, which seems to indicate the initial establishment of open heath vegetation at this particular locality in a clearly pre-Atlantic vegetational context (Keef *et al.* 1965). Similarly the stratigraphic sequence at Oakhanger site VII points to the occurrence of some kind of major disturbance in the local vegetational cover at an apparently early stage of the Boreal period. If the implications of this evidence are accepted, therefore, we should presumably see the later Mesolithic occupation of the Lower Greensand and ecologically similar areas of southern Britain not in terms of the exploitation of an essentially virgin deciduous forest environment, but in terms of the exploitation – and perhaps even deliberate management – of an environment that had been to a large extent 'pre-adapted' for human settlement by 1,000 years or more of humanly-induced disturbance in both vegetation and soils.

Mesolithic exploitation of the Chalk outcrop

One of the major features of microlith distributions which remains to be considered is the relative scarcity of finds over the extensive areas of the Chalk outcrop. Clark's original suggestion (1932: 88) that Mesolithic sites may be entirely lacking from these areas has not been borne out by more recent research (Rankine 1956: 8, 31-40; Draper 1968), but the sparsity of well documented occupation sites over the greater part of the Chalk formation remains one of the more striking features of Mesolithic distributions in southern England (cf. Table 2, Fig. 2). Viewed in ecological terms, two possible explanations for this pattern may be suggested. One possibility is that the exploitation of these areas as hunting territories was inhibited by essentially the same factors as those which are thought to have inhibited the exploitation of the various clay-yielding formations – in other words by the development of an exceptionally heavy growth of shrubs in the under-storey vegetation of the original forests. It must be remembered, of course, that the predominance of beech which is characteristic of the present-day woodlands growing on the Chalk outcrop is a comparatively recent phenomenon (probably dating from the Sub-atlantic period) and that the character of the original deciduous forests which would have developed on these areas during later Boreal and Atlantic times must remain to a large extent hypothetical (Godwin 1975: 60-1; Tansley 1949: 358-72). Nevertheless it is known that calcareous soils provide favourable growing conditions for many of the species of understorey shrubs which are typical of deciduous forests, and indeed the total range of species encountered on these soils tends to be greater than that found on areas of more acidic or neutral soils (Tansley 1949: 264-6, 288-9, 373). It may well be therefore that the density of the shrub vegetation presented as much of an obstacle to human exploitation in the original deciduous forests growing on the Chalk outcrop as in the contemporary woodlands developed on areas of heavier clay soils.

A second factor which must have played a critical role in the Mesolithic exploitation of the Chalk outcrop was the difficulty of gaining access to fresh water supplies. Over large areas of the Chalk formation surface supplies of water (in the form of springs, streams etc.) are virtually non-existent, and the only dependable water-resources available to the human groups would have been provided by the major rivers which traverse the Chalk, together with perhaps a number of small ponds supported on the overlying deposits of Clay-with-flints (Wooldridge and Goldring 1953: 124-5; Hall and Russell 1911: 97-9). Perhaps the most important point to emphasise is not merely that this pattern of water supplies would have allowed Mesolithic communities very little freedom in their choice of potential occupation sites, but that by limiting the number of separate points at which base camps could be established the human groups would have been forced to travel over greater distances in order to exploit the full range of available economic resources. Whether or not there were any areas of the Chalk outcrop from which economic exploitation was effectively excluded by the absence of water supplies must remain an open question, but it seems clear that any factor which has the effect of increasing the amount of movement (and therefore energy expenditure) entailed in the exploitation of a particular range of economic resources must inevitably have a significant bearing on the extent to which these resources are utilised. In these circumstances, therefore, it may be that many areas of the Chalk outcrop were reduced to the status of 'marginal zones' in an economic sense, which were only exploited on a significant scale when some kind of fluctuation in the subsistence resources available in the ecologically more favourable areas of southern England (or alternatively an increased pressure on these resources as a result of a build-up in human population numbers) threatened the economic security of the human groups. In any event, it seems significant that all of the major occupation sites that have so far been recorded on the Chalk formation (most notably at Iwerne Minster in Dorset, Downton and Cherhill in Wiltshire, and Butser Hill in Hampshire) are located close to the edges of the outcrop in locations which would have had ready access both to fresh water supplies and to the economic resources available on the neighbouring geological formations.

Distribution of axes

The distribution of transversely-sharpened flint axes/adzes in southern England is summarized in Table 4 and Figure 2 and 4. Since the great majority of axes have been recovered as isolated surface finds, and rarely make up more than one or two percent of any individual assemblage (cf. Mellars 1976a: 387), it seemed more meaningful to express the distribution of these tools in terms of the total numbers of implements, rather than in terms of the numbers of individual find-spots. As in the case of microliths, the Table records: (1) the total number of finds from each geological outcrop; (2) the density of the finds in terms of the numbers of axes per 100 square kilometres; and (3) the 'density index' of the finds on each deposit.

Before going on to discuss the detailed patterns which emerge from this analysis, there are two general features of axe distributions in southern England which should be commented on at the outset. In the first place it will be apparent immediately from Figure 4 that the overall distribution of Mesolithic axes is heavily concentrated in the eastern half of southern England and shows a very sparse distribution over the whole of the western half of the country. We would suggest that the explanation of this pattern lies largely if not entirely in the question of raw material supplies. Thus it will be seen from Figure 4 that the western limit of the area of concentrated finds is remarkably abrupt and coincides closely with the westernmost limit of the major Chalk outcrop. In other words, the area of concentrated axe

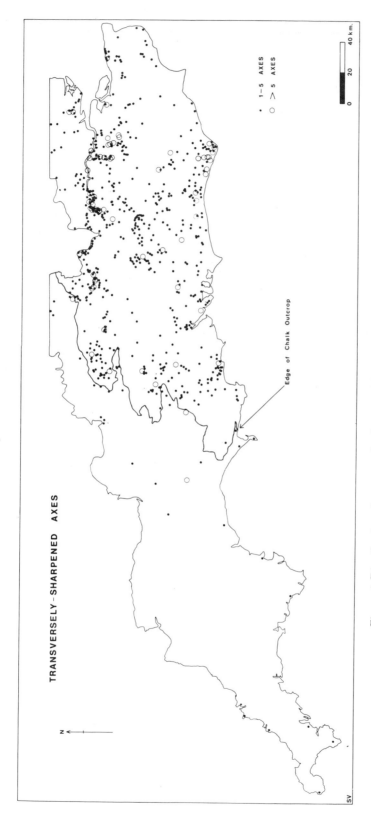

Figure 4. Distribution of transversely-sharpened flint axes/adzes in southern England. The line drawn across the centre of the area marks the western limit of the main Chalk outcrop.

distribution coincides precisely with the areas of southern England in which suitable flint supplies for axe manufacture would have been most readily available. As several authors have pointed out (e.g. Sieveking *et al.* 1972: 164) the successful manufacture of flint axes is dependent not only on access to relatively large nodules of raw material, but also to flint which has been obtained in a reasonably fresh condition from the parent Chalk. Even when sufficiently large nodules can be obtained from secondary geological sources, such as river gravels or beach deposits, these are almost invariably affected by incipient fractures due to battering and thermal action which makes them totally unsuitable for the manufacture of relatively large implements. Moreover it should be recalled that secondary sources of flint in alluvial formations are effectively confined to the deposits of rivers whose catchment areas include some part of the Chalk outcrop itself. Beyond the limits of the Chalk outcrop therefore, the acquisition of adequate supplies of flint for axe manufacture have been dependent

Table 4. Distribution of transversely-sharpened flint axes/adzes on different geological outcrops in southern England.

Deposit	Area of deposit in km^2	Total number of axes	Density of axes per $100\ km^2$	Density index
Folkestone Beds	270	62	22.96	4.84
Sandgate Beds	190	39	20.53	4.33
Hythe Beds	405	43	10.62	2.24
Gault Clay (Wealden (outcrop)	185	15	8.11	1.71
Chalk	7,650	478	6.25	1.32
Wadhurst Clay	545	14	2.57	0.54
Ashdown Sand	455	10	2.20	0.46
London Clay	3,580	77	2.15	0.45
Tunbridge Wells Sand	865	17	1.97	0.42
Weald Clay	1,690	33	1.95	0.41
Upper Greensand (Wealden outcrop)	110	2	1.82	0.38
Barton Clay etc.	1,910	30	1.57	0.33
Gault/Upper Greensand (western outcrops)	1,160	17	1.47	0.31
Great Oolite	580	3	0.52	0.11
Permian deposits	690	1	0.14	0.03
Granite	1,150	1	0.09	0.02
Devonian deposits	4,050	3	0.07	0.15
Carboniferous Limestone	180	—	—	—
Carboniferous Shale	2,640	—	—	—
'Average' density of axes over the study-area as a whole (per 100 km^2)			4.74	

The 'average' density of finds and density index values were calculated as explained in Table 2.

either on extensive movements on the part of individual Mesolithic groups (or perhaps individual craftsmen), or alternatively on the operation of some form of exchange network between communities occupying adjacent territories. The sparse distribution of axes over the whole of the northern and western areas of Britain would seem to imply that if such exchange networks did exist amongst Mesolithic communities they were much less effective than those which developed (for example) during the Neolithic period.

The second feature which emerges clearly from Figure 4 is the heavy concentration of Mesolithic axes along many of the major river valleys in southern England. This shows up particularly clearly along the valley of the Thames but can also be detected along certain stretches of the Darent, the Kennet, the Wey and the Hampshire Stour. The explanation of this riverine pattern of distribution is inevitably more speculative, although one should perhaps not overlook the obvious possibility that one of the primary functions of axes in Mesolithic contexts lay in the manufacture of dugout canoes. Whether or not this was the case, the distribution points unambiguously to the fact that river valley environments played an important role in at least certain aspects of the economic and/or settlement strategies of Mesolithic communities, a feature which emerges far more clearly from the distribution of these tools than from the distribution of microliths (cf. Fig. 1). Perhaps the main point which needs to be reemphasised in this connection is that the particular ways in which the economic resources of any region are exploited must necessarily be influenced not only by the spatial distribution of the resources themselves, but also by the relative efficiency with which the methods of exploitation can be organised. When viewed in these terms the potential importance of water transportation amongst communities occupying a heavily forested environment is easy to visualise. By locating settlements along the course of large and easily navigable rivers, Mesolithic communities would have been able to travel over relatively long distances with the minimum expenditure of time and energy, and thereby to expand considerably the size of the 'catchment areas' which could be exploited efficiently and economically from a single settlement location. In stressing the economic efficiency of water transport we must of course think not only in terms of the amount of time and energy expended by human individuals and groups in gaining access to economic resources, but also in terms of the far more significant element of energy-expenditure involved in transporting these resources (for example, heavy and bulky animal carcases) from the point of supply to the point of consumption. The use of water transport may also have played a critical role in the social organisation of Mesolithic populations by allowing local groups to maintain an extensive and effective network of communications with other communities occupying the same river system. An alignment of

Mesolithic settlements along the major river valleys of lowland Britain may therefore have been favoured both by economic considerations and also by the equally important social requirements of the human groups.

If we turn now to the detailed distribution of axes on the various geological outcrops listed in Table 4 it is possible to observe certain basic similarities with the distributional patterns of microliths, together with a number of significant differences. In the first place it will be seen that the three deposits which exhibited the heaviest concentrations of microlith-yielding sites – the Folkestone Beds, Sandgate Beds and Hythe Beds divisions of the Lower Greensand formation – also emerge clearly at the head of the table of axe densities. While this fact tends to underscore the particular importance of the Lower Greensand areas in the settlement and subsistence strategies of Mesolithic communities, however, it should be noted that the *relative concentration* of axes on these deposits is appreciably less than that shown by the distribution of microliths. Thus it will be seen that the density index values recorded for axes on the Folkestone, Sandgate and Hythe Beds are only 4.8, 4.3 and 2.2 respectively, as compared with values of 17.5, 6.3 and 6.1 for the distribution of microliths on the same deposits. It would appear from this therefore that whatever factors were responsible for inducing a concentration of microliths over the Lower Greensand outcrop were somewhat less effective in controlling the distribution of axes over the same areas.

Leaving aside the Lower Greensand formation, the relative ordering of the various deposits in the lower part of Table 4 reveals some interesting contrasts with the distributional patterns of microliths (cf. Fig. 2). Perhaps the most striking feature is the relatively heavy concentration of axes on the Chalk outcrop. Thus it will be seen that this deposit occupies the fifth position in the rank ordering of axe densities, as compared with a position close to the bottom of the Table (fifteenth in rank order) in the ordering of microlith densities. Similar if less conspicuous differences can be seen in the relative ordering of the various sand and clay-yielding formations. For example, three of the major sandy geological formations which showed relatively high densities of microlith sites (the Tunbridge Wells Sand, Upper Greensand and Ashdown Sand) can be seen to occupy consistently lower positions in the table of axe densities. Thus by comparing Tables 2 and 4 it will be seen that the Tunbridge Wells Sand falls from rank order 4 to 9, the Upper Greensand from rank order 5 to 11, and the Ashdown Sand from rank order 6 to 7. By contrast three of the principal clay-yielding formations which occupied relatively low positions in the table of microlith densities (the Gault Clay, Wadhurst Clay and, above all, the London Clay) can be seen to occupy much higher positions in the table of axe densities; in this case the relative positions in the two tables change respectively from 9 to 4, 10 to 6 and 17 to 8. As a generalisation therefore we can say that with the exception of the three deposits at the head of the table (i.e. the three divisions of the Lower Greensand), the relative ordering of the various sand and clay deposits in the table of axe densities is effectively the reverse of that to be seen in the ordering of microlith densities. The one deposit which is anomalous in this regard is the Weald Clay, which in fact shows a slightly higher position in the table of microlith densities than in that of axe densities.

Perhaps the most interesting general feature which emerges from the preceding analysis is that the distribution of axes appears to be appreciably less 'selective' with regard to different geological formations than that of microliths. This point can be illustrated in two ways. In the first place we have already noted that the maximum density index recorded for the distribution of axes is only 4.8 as compared to a maximum value of 17.5 for the distribution of microliths. Secondly, and more to the point, there is a much weaker contrast in the recorded densities of axes on deposits which differ radically in their general sedimentological, mineralogical and soil-forming properties. For example, if we compare the maximum and minimum densities of axes recorded on the various geological outcrops in the eastern half of southern England (i.e. within the areas bounded by the main flint-bearing Chalk outcrop) we find that these differ by a factor of approximately 12 (from a maximum on the Folkestone Beds to a minimum on the Weald Clay). By contrast, the maximum and minimum densities of microliths recorded over the same areas (comparing in this case the Folkestone Beds with the London Clay) differ by a factor of over 60. A possible explanation of this pattern may lie in the relative degree of functional specialisation of the two tool forms. Despite some recent controversy over the functional interpretation of microliths (cf. Clarke 1976) there is nevertheless widespread agreement that these represent relatively specialised tools which functioned primarily as armatures for various forms of hunting projectiles. If this interpretation is correct, then we would expect the distribution of microliths to be controlled chiefly by the extent to which hunting was carried out in different ecological zones. By contrast it is fairly easy to visualise how axes might have been employed in one form or another in virtually the whole range of economic activities engaged in by Mesolithic communities. In fact, it seems probable that the major functions of axes lay not in any primary subsistence activities, but rather in various types of 'maintenance' activities, such as the clearance of trees and shrubs from the vicinity of living sites, the collection of fuel supplies or the shaping of wooden supports for the construction of living structures, food drying racks and so forth. If so, then the distribution of axes over different geological outcrops in south-east England may well provide a more accurate reflection of the true distribution of Mesolithic activity over these areas than that provided by the distribution of microliths.

The relatively heavy concentration of axes on the Chalk outcrop must inevitably reflect to some degree the influence of raw material supplies. The point has already been made that the manufacture of flint axes requires not only relatively large nodules of raw material but also flint which has been obtained more or less directly from the parent Chalk. Regardless of whether the production of Mesolithic axes was ever organised along fully 'industrial' lines, therefore, it is to be expected that the manufacture of axes should have been concentrated to some extent on the Chalk outcrop itself. The other obvious way in which raw material supplies can influence the distribution of implements lies in the rate at which tools are discarded as a result of wear or breakage. In areas where flint supplies are scarce and difficult (or costly) to obtain there must inevitably be a strong incentive to economise on the available resources, either by resharpening or reworking of heavily-worn implements, or alternatively by working them down into smaller implement forms; thus broken axes might be employed, for example, as cores for the manufacture of microliths. Where raw material supplies are plentiful, on the other hand, there will be a greater temptation to discard heavily worn or damaged implements and to replace them with newly-manufactured tools.

The third feature in which the distribution of axes contrasts with that of microliths is in the relative concentration of these types on sand and clay deposits. As we have seen, there appears to be a general tendency for microliths to be *relatively* more heavily concentrated than axes on the major sand-yielding geological formations, whilst axes are correspondingly better represented on the various clay and loam-yielding deposits. One possible explanation of this pattern has already been suggested – namely, that axes were employed in a variety of economic activities not connected directly with the hunting of game, and therefore not concentrated to the same extent – if at all – on areas of sandy soil. The other possible explanation relates more directly to the need for woodland clearance on soils of differing texture and fertility. On the areas of coarsely-textured sandy soils, as we have seen, the forests are likely to have been relatively open in character, and substantial areas of entirely treeless vegetation may well have existed, either as a result of deliberate clearance of the woodland by the repeated use of fire or (less probably) as a result of heavily podzolised soil conditions. In the forests developed on the more fertile clay and loam soils, on the other hand, the development of both the tree growth and the understorey vegetation is likely to have been relatively dense, posing an obstacle to all forms of economic exploitation in these areas. Whatever the particular economic activities engaged in by Mesolithic groups on the heavier clay soils of lowland Britain, therefore, it is easy to visualise that the requirements for some form of mechanical (as opposed to fire-induced) forest clearance would have been significantly greater in these areas than in the woodlands developed on areas of impoverished sandy soils.

Distribution of pebble mace heads

Our knowledge of the detailed morphology and cultural associations of so-called 'pebble mace heads' derives largely from a series of papers published by the late W.F. Rankine (1949b; 1951; 1953; 1956: 58-61). Rankine was able to show that these implements had been found in close association with Mesolithic artefacts in at least three sites in southern England (Southampton Dock, Blackdown and Addington), while more 'inferential' Mesolithic association could be claimed from a further five or six sites (Rankine 1949b; 1956: 58; Rankine and Dimbleby 1960: 251-2). Similar associations are of course well documented from Mesolithic contexts on the continent, where mace heads identical to the British specimens have been recovered from both Maglemosian and Ertebølle settlements in Scandinavia (Clark 1936: 105-6, 145-7; 1975: 112-13). To what extent these tools may have continued into use into later prehistoric periods is at present open to debate, but there seems little reason to doubt that the greater

Table 5. Distribution of 'Pebble mace-heads' on the major geological formations in southern England.

Deposit	Area of deposit in km^2	Total of mace-heads	Density of mace-heads per 100 km^2	Density index
Lower Greensand	1,080	21	1.94	5.16
Chalk	7,650	47	0.61	1.62
London Clay	3,580	21	0.59	1.57
Upper Greensand/ Gault Clay	1,460	7	0.48	1.28
Weald Clay	1,690	6	0.36	0.96
Barton Clay etc.	1,910	6	0.31	0.82
Granite	1,150	3	0.26	0.69
Devonian deposits	4,050	8	0.20	0.53
Great Oolite	580	1	0.17	0.45
Hastings Beds	1,870	3	0.16	0.43
Carboniferous Shale	2,640	1	0.04	0.11
Carboniferous Limestone	180	–	–	–
Permian deposits	690	–	–	–

'Average' density of mace-heads over the study-area as a whole (per 100 km^2)	0.38

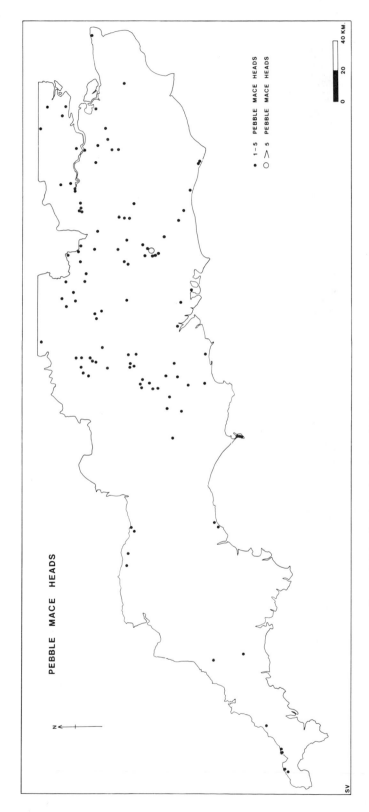

Figure 5. Distribution of perforated 'pebble mace heads' in southern England.

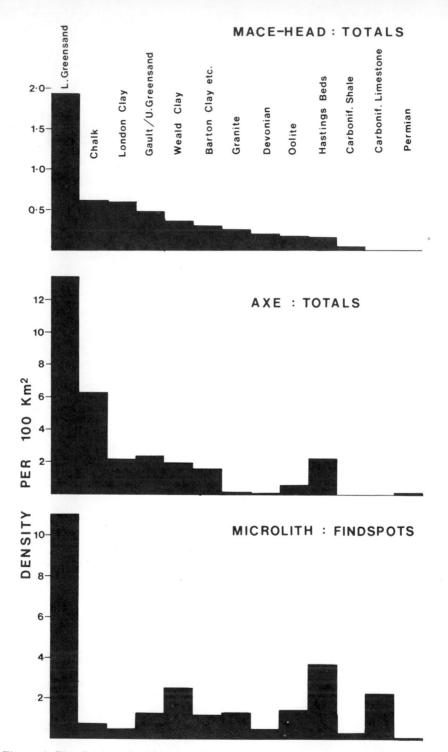

Figure 6. Distribution of pebble mace heads, flint axes/adzes and microliths on the major geological divisions shown on the 1:625,000 geological maps. For reasons explained in the text the distribution of microliths is expressed in terms of numbers of findspots rather than total numbers of implements. For data on the actual numbers of finds on each deposit see Tables 2, 4 and 5.

proportion of the specimens recorded from the areas considered in the present study are in fact of Mesolithic date.

Pebble mace heads are comparatively rare finds in all areas of Britain and for this reason we have chosen to analyse the distribution of these tools in terms of the broad geological divisions shown on the 'ten mile' (1:625,000) geological maps; to have analysed the distributions in terms of the finer divisions shown on the one inch maps would have yielded sample sizes which were too small in most cases to have any statistical validity. The main effect of this procedure has been to group together the three divisions of the Lower Greensand (the Folkestone Beds, Hythe Beds and Sandgate Beds), the Upper Greensand and Gault Clay formations, and the Tunbridge Wells Sand, Ashdown Sand and Wadhurst Clay components of the Hastings Beds formation in the central Weald. The remaining divisions correspond with those employed in analysing the distributions of microliths and axes (Table 5).

As Rankine himself pointed out (1956: 59) the general distribution of pebble mace heads in southern Britain is strikingly similar in many respects to that of tranchet axes (Table 5; Figs. 5, 6). The main points to be noted are as follows:

1. By far the heaviest concentration of finds is apparent once again on the areas of the Lower Greensand outcrop, which shows an overall density of mace heads over five times as high as that recorded for southern England as a whole. In view of the relatively sparse evidence for later prehistoric occupation over these areas, this observation could no doubt be seen as a further argument in favour of the primarily Mesolithic associations of this tool form. As we have already noted in the case of axes, however, the *relative concentration* of mace heads on the Lower Greensand outcrop (as reflected in the density index value) is very much less than that shown by the distribution of microliths, which would seem to indicate that the particular economic and/or environmental factors which controlled the distribution of mace heads over this formation were somewhat different from those controlling the distribution of microlithic forms.

2. The most striking similarity between the distributional patterns of mace heads and axes can be seen in the relatively heavy concentration of both of these types on the Chalk outcrop. To some extent the same observation might be made with regard to the densities recorded on the London Clay, although it may be noted that the relative concentration of mace heads on this formation is appreciably greater than that of axes. It will be recalled that both of these deposits were characterised by exceptionally low densities of microliths (cf. Table 2).

3. Lastly, the very sparse distribution of both mace heads and axes on the Hastings Beds formation (Tunbridge Wells Sand/Ashdown Sand/Wadhurst Clay) may be contrasted with the relatively heavy densities of microliths on these deposits.

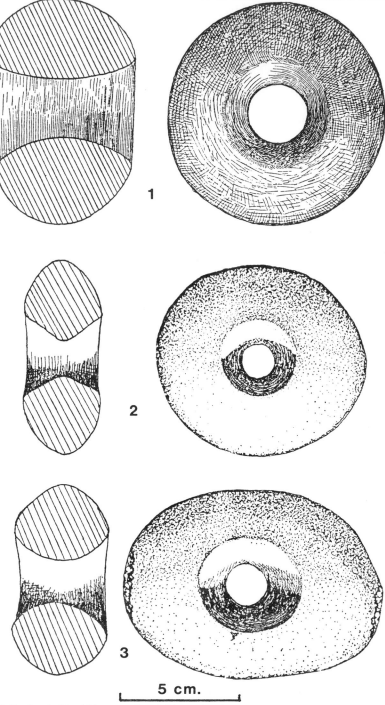

Figure 7. Perforated 'pebble mace-heads' from Southampton Dock, Hampshire (no. 1) and Blackdown, Sussex (nos. 2, 3). No. 1 is of sarsen stone; nos. 2 and 3 are of quartzite. From Rankine 1949b.

Any attempt to formulate a plausible explanation for the distribution of mace heads is of course hampered by the lack of any general agreement as to the intended functions of these tools (cf. Rankine 1953: 186). Here we shall simply explore two alternative possibilities, either of which might help to explain at least the broad features of the distributional patterns discussed above. One suggestion which has cropped up recurrently in the literature is that mace heads served as weights for digging sticks employed in the harvesting of various kinds of vegetable roots, tubers etc. A strong case for this interpretation could be made out on the basis of ethnographic parallels (Schapera 1930: 141; Kroeber 1925: 503; Oswalt 1976: 56-9) and would certainly accord well with the almost inevitable importance of vegetable food resources in the diet of communities occupying a temperate forested environment (cf. Lee 1968: 41-3; Mellars 1976a: 375-6; Clarke 1976). Against this interpretation might be set the small size of the perforation recorded in certain mace heads, but there is no reason to doubt that implements with a perforation greater than 1 cm. in diameter (which according to Rankine (1953: 188) would account for around 90 percent of the recorded examples) could have been used very efficiently for this purpose, especially if the digging sticks themselves were manufactured from the harder kinds of wood. The virtue of this interpretation is that it would help to explain the relatively heavy densities of mace heads recorded on both the chalk outcrop and the major clay-yielding formations of southern England. As we have already noted, the soils developed on both of these types of deposit tend to be more fertile than those developed on the various sand and sandstone formations, and this is reflected in a richer variety of floral composition. Thus Tansley (1949: 286-9) records a list of 103 species which are said to be characteristic of the ground-flora of the 'damp' type of oak-wood growing on areas of clay and loam soils, as compared to a range of only 42 species in the 'dry' type of woodland on areas of sandy or gravelly soil. No full range of species is quoted for the woodlands growing on calcareous soils, but it is stated that these include an 'abundance of several calcicolous species in addition to those (characteristic) of the damp oak-wood' (Tansley 1949: 289). From these observations it would seem reasonable to infer that the maximum range and variety of vegetable foods would be available in the woodlands developed on areas of clayey and calcareous soils, and that this would serve as a strong incentive for Mesolithic communities to exploit these areas for the specific purpose of obtaining plant food supplies.

The second hypothesis is less specific and is based on the premise that mace heads were not employed directly in any primary food-procurement activities but were used instead in certain activities connected with the general 'maintenance' requirements of the human groups (cf. Binford and Binford 1966). For example, Rankine has argued that mace heads served primarily as 'hafted percussion tools'

(1953: 186; 1956: 60) while Roger Jacobi has suggested in conversation that they might have functioned as centrifugal weights for hand-operated rotary drills. If either of these suggestions is correct then we might adopt a similar explanation for the distribution of mace heads to that suggested for the distribution of axes – in other words that the occurrence of these tools was not related directly to the distribution of any specific subsistence resources, but reflects in a more general way the full range of habitats exploited in one form or another by Mesolithic groups. The implications of this interpretation – as in the case of axes – would be that the distribution of these tools provides a more accurate indication of the true distribution of Mesolithic activity in different ecological zones than that provided by the occurrence of more economically specialised forms such as microliths.

Discussion

While the discussion in the preceding sections may help to account for the major features of Mesolithic distributions in southern England there are certain aspects of these distributional patterns which remain to be explained. Why is it, for example, that the density of Mesolithic sites is so much greater on the various divisions of the Lower Greensand than on the geologically-similar deposits of the Bagshot Sands of the London and Hampshire basins (cf. Tansley 1949: 111)? Or again, why should the density of sites be significantly higher on the heavy clay soils of the Wealden Beds or the Gault Clay than on the closely analogous soils of the London Clay (Burnham 1972)? The point which seems to emerge from these and certain other observations is that the various geological outcrops which make up the classic Wealden region reflect an intensity and concentration of Mesolithic exploitation which cannot be accounted for entirely in terms of any inherent ecological properties of the deposits themselves. In other words, the overall attraction of the Wealden area for Mesolithic populations would appear to be greater in some way than the sum of the individual geological parts.

A possible solution to this problem may lie not so much in the particular character of the various geological outcrops which comprise the Weald, but rather in the distinctive arrangement of these deposits in space. The peculiar dome-shaped structure of the Wealden area is reflected in a broadly concentric arrangement of the major rock outcrops, each of which emerges as a relatively narrow but continuous belt of land extending around the northern, western and southern margins of the central dome (Gallois and Edmunds 1965). The important corollary of this arrangement from the standpoint of the human communities was that by establishing a settlement at almost any point towards the periphery of the Wealden region the groups would have been able to gain access to a comparatively wide variety of distinct habitats with only a limited amount of movement. By establishing a base camp almost anywhere over the area of the Lower Greensand formation, for example, it would have been possible to gain access to at least four other geological outcrops (the Weald Clay, Gault Clay, Upper Greensand and Chalk) by travelling a maximum distance of no more than four or five miles – well within the conventional 'catchment area' of hunter-gatherer settlements (cf. Fig. 3). The extent to which these different environmental zones were in fact exploited by Mesolithic groups remains to a large extent hypothetical, but it is likely that all of the zones would have contributed something in the way of either food resources or raw materials to the Mesolithic economy. The hunting of large animals may well have been concentrated primarily on areas of sandy soil (for reasons already discussed), but it is likely that the richest and most varied supplies of plant foods would have been available on the more fertile soils of the adjacent clay and loam-yielding deposits. The Chalk outcrop may also have contributed important supplies of certain varieties of vegetable foods, and would in any case have provided the primary sources of flint for tool manufacture. Additional to these resources, of course, would have been the economic resources of rivers and the associated riverside environments with which the Wealden region is particularly well endowed. Perhaps the most important point to emphasise in this context is that the ability to exploit a wide range of ecological habitats would have benefited Mesolithic communities not only by providing the most varied – and therefore presumably the most attractive – subsistence resources, but also by adding a greater element of stability to the food quest. Economic strategies which are dependent on the exploitation of a relatively wide variety of food resources are inevitably less vulnerable to short-term fluctuations in one or more basic commodities, and therefore tend to be more viable on a long term basis (cf. Harris 1969: 8-9). The other important advantage of ecological diversity is that it helps to reduce to a minimum the amount of movement necessary to maintain adequate supplies of both food and raw materials throughout the annual cycle. Unlike communities in many other areas of Britain therefore (cf. Clark 1972: 31-7; Mellars 1976a: 380-4) the Mesolithic occupants of the Weald may have been able to practice economic and settlement strategies which, if not entirely sedentary, were dependent upon only a limited degree of territorial movement in response to seasonal and annual variations in the distribution of essential resources.

An alternative way of expressing the environmental situation in the Weald is to visualise the area in terms of a succession of closely-spaced 'ecotones' – i.e. transition or contact zones between separate ecological communities. The particular importance of these ecotone situations to many forms of both plant and animal life has been summarized by Odum as follows:

What may not be so evident from casual observation is the fact that the transition zone often supports a community with characteristics additional to those of the communities which adjoin the ecotone. Thus, unless the ecotone is very narrow, some habitats and, therefore, some organisms are likely to be found in the region of the overlap which are not present in either community alone. Since well-developed ecotonal communities may contain organisms characteristic of each of the overlapping communities plus species living only in the ecotone region, we would not be surprised to find the variety and density of life greater in the ecotone ... Furthermore, some species actually require as part of the habitat, or as part of their life history, two or more adjacent communities that differ greatly in structure. Organisms which occur primarily or most abundantly or spend the greatest amount of time in junctions between communities are often called 'edge' species (Odum 1971: 158)

A significant point brought out in this description is that ecotone situations are often characterised not only by a much greater *variety* of both plant and animal life, but also by a significantly increased *density* of certain specifically edge-adapted forms.

That Mesolithic populations were well aware of the advantages to be gained from exploiting these ecological contact zones is strongly suggested by the distribution of sites in certain areas of the Weald. In the neighbourhood of Horsham in the central Weald, for example, it is possible to detect a very marked concentration of sites along the boundary between the Tunbridge Wells Sand and the Weald Clay formations (cf. Fig. 3). A similar concentration of sites can be seen along the junction of the Lower Greensand and Gault Clay in the area between Guildford and Reigate, or again along the western margins of the Lower Greensand outcrop in parts of both Hampshire and Sussex. These distributions would seem to indicate that the ability to exploit the economic resources of two or more contrasting geological outcrops was an important factor in the location of at least certain types of Mesolithic settlements in the areas under review.

Summary and test implications

This study has had two major objectives: first, to analyse the distributions of three functionally-contrasting forms of Mesolithic artefacts in terms of the principal geological formations on which the artefacts occur; and second, to employ some of the more significant patterns which emerge from this analysis as a basis for advancing a number of hypotheses concerning the behaviour of Mesolithic communities, and the ways in which these behavioural patterns related to contemporary environmental conditions. The major hypotheses that have been put forward may be summarised briefly as follows:

1. A concentration of Mesolithic settlements on areas of coarsely-textured, sandy soils must be attributed at least in part to the inherent

advantages offered by these well drained, well insulated soils for the location of occupation sites.

2. The exploitation of sandy areas was favoured in economic terms by two principal factors: on the one hand by the relative openness of the vegetation in these areas (marked especially by a reduction in the density of the under-storey shrub vegetation) which made these environments especially favourable for the hunting of game; and on the other hand by the particular susceptibility of these 'dry' habitats to the occurrence and ecological consequences of forest fires. We have suggested that the modification of these habitats by the action of fire can be traced back to an early stage of the postglacial period, and that this should probably be seen as the most important single factor in explaining the concentration of Mesolithic activity on the various sand-yielding geological formations of lowland Britain.

3. The exploitation of other economic resources (for example plant foods) was not concentrated to the same degree as hunting on areas of sandy soil, and that these activities were distributed more evenly over most of the major geological formations in southern England.

4. The economic exploitation of many areas of the Chalk outcrop was inhibited by the difficulty of obtaining fresh-water supplies.

5. The manufacture of flint axes was strongly concentrated on the Chalk outcrop, owing to both the abundance and the superior quality of the flint supplies available in these areas.

6. Beyond the limits of the main flint-bearing Chalk deposits Mesolithic communities paid particular attention to the problems of economising on the available supplies of raw material. In the case of axes this would have taken the form of repeated resharpening and reworking of heavily worn or damaged implements, and most probably also the re-utilisation of worn-out or broken axes as cores for the production of smaller implement types.

7. A concentration of Mesolithic settlements along the course of major river valleys in southern England reflects the important role played by water transportation among communities occupying a heavily forested environment. Use of water transport would have allowed the human groups to increase substantially the size of the 'catchment areas' that could be exploited efficiently and economically from a single settlement location, and at the same time to maintain an extensive network of social communications with other groups occupying the same river system.

8. The particular attraction of the Wealden region to Mesolithic populations can be attributed in part to the distinctive arrangement of the various geological formations which make up this area. This was reflected in a relatively close spacing of the various 'ecotone' situations between the contrasting geological outcrops and a corresponding increase in the variety – and perhaps also the density – of the economic resources which could be exploited from a single settlement location.

The point has been emphasised in numerous recent works on archaeology that the formulation of hypotheses should never be regarded as an end in itself, and that the ultimate success of any programme of scientific investigation must depend on the extent to which the various hypotheses that have been formulated are capable of being systematically tested in the course of subsequent research. In concluding the present study, therefore, it may be useful to identify which of the various hypotheses listed above appear most readily amenable to at least some measure of testing against existing or readily accessible sources of archaeological data, and to suggest some of the specific lines along which future research might proceed.

1. Perhaps the most obvious and immediate requirement is for some kind of systematic programme of field survey to test the validity of the basic distributional patterns employed in the present study. As we emphasised in the Introduction, the artefact distributions recorded in the course of the recent C.B.A. survey are potentially susceptible to various sources of accidental distortion, of which variations in the extent and intensity of the fieldwork carried out in different areas are probably the most significant. Systematic campaigns of exploration designed to overcome these sources of bias in archaeological distributions have recently been undertaken in several areas of North America and the kind of work carried out in such regions as the Reese River Valley in Nevada (Thomas 1974: 36-40) or the Hay Hollow Valley in Arizona (Plog 1974: 82-4) provide excellent models of the kind of statistically-controlled surveys which can be organised with these objectives in mind (see also Plog and Hill 1971). The opportunities for organising a completely random pattern of field survey in southern England are of course limited by the need to confine exploration either to areas of cultivated land or to localities where natural erosion has exposed substantial areas of the ground surface; but there seems no doubt that some form of effective 'stratified' sampling procedures could be devised to meet these circumstances. There are of course certain other potential sources of distortion which are more difficult to control, such as variations in the relative visibility of small artefact forms such as microliths under varying soil conditions (e.g. sand versus clay), or the effects of post-Mesolithic erosion and sedimentation in different topographical situations. On the whole it seems unlikely that these factors have played more than a minor role in determining the broad distributional patterns discussed in the present study, but even these variables should be amenable to a certain amount of empirical control. For example the effects of varying soil conditions on the relative discovery potential of different artefact categories could be investigated by means of repeated, intensive surveys over the same areas of ground – or even by means of artificially controlled experiments – and if necessary a series of approximate correction factors worked out for the different artefact types under differing field conditions. Similarly, it

should be recalled that the occurrence of post-mesolithic erosion and sedimentation on a scale sufficient to lead to the complete obliteration of Mesolithic sites is likely to have been a comparatively localised phenomenon (largely confined to the steeper escarpment slopes and the flood-plains of river valleys) and is unlikely to have influenced the distribution of finds over the outcrops of the major geological formations considered in the present survey to more than a limited degree. If the survey were to be extended to the distribution of finds on certain kinds of 'drift' formations – for example, river-valley alluvial deposits – then this factor would of course need to be given more serious consideration.

2. If we now consider ways in which more information could be derived from the existing distributional data, one useful approach would be to analyse the distribution of Mesolithic sites not merely in terms of the *immediate* ecological setting of the sites but also in terms of the broader environmental resources that could be exploited from the different settlement locations. In other words we would need to develop an approach along the lines of what Higgs and Vita Finzi (1972) have termed 'site catchment analysis'.

The problems of formulating a meaningful definition of what constitutes the 'catchment area' of a hunter-gatherer settlement are perhaps more complicated than some earlier workers have recognised. Leaving aside these problems, however, it is fairly easy to see how an analysis of Mesolithic settlement locations in these terms could be used to test at least two of the hypotheses that have been advanced here. In the first place it is clear that a marked tendency for Mesolithic settlements to occur close to the boundary between contrasting geological formations would provide strong support for the view that the ability to exploit the resources of at least two ecological zones was important in the economy of the societies in question. Conversely, a tendency for sites to be located at some distance from these ecological contact zones would suggest that the primary reliance at these settlements was placed on the resources of only a single type of habitat. As we have already seen, a distinct tendency for Mesolithic sites to cluster along the interface between contrasting geological outcrops does seem to be apparent in at least certain areas of southern England (notably along the boundary between the Lower Greensand and the Gault Clay, and at the junction of the Tunbridge Wells Sand and the Weald Clay) but a more systematic analysis of site locations in these terms is clearly required.

A second hypothesis which could be tested effectively by means of this approach is the proposition that the concentration of Mesolithic settlements on areas of sandy soil can be attributed at least in part to the inherent advantages of these well drained, well insulated soils for the location of camping sites. Two separate approaches to this question might be suggested. In the first place attention could be focused on the *precise* location of settlements which occur close to the

L

boundary between sand- and non-sand-yielding (especially clay) formations. In these situations a logical prediction from our hypothesis would be that the sites should exhibit a strong tendency to occur on the sandy side of the geological boundary. A tendency for sites to be distributed in more or less equal numbers on either side of the boundary would suggest that the character of local soil conditions was largely irrelevant in determining the choice of camp-site location. A second approach would be to examine the distribution of sites in areas where relatively small, localised patches of sand occur in areas otherwise dominated by contrasting geological formations. In this case the prediction would be that the sites should occur preferentially on these sandy areas rather than on the surrounding deposits. In this context it might be recalled that a certain amount of evidence for precisely this pattern of site location was recognised by Clark in *The Mesolithic Age in Britain* over forty years ago. Thus Clark pointed out that at a number of points in the neighbourhood of Peacehaven and Seaford in Sussex concentrations of Mesolithic material had been recovered from small areas of Woolwich Beds Sand which occurred as isolated patches within the area of the extensive Chalk outcrop of the South Downs (Clark 1932: 82-3, 88, Figs. 52, 55). A similar phenomenon was noted at Chiddingford in Surrey, where a single Mesolithic site was located on a localised patch of sand in the middle of the Weald Clay formation (*ibid*: 86-8). If Clark's observation that some of these sandy deposits were only 'a few acres in extent' (1936: 190) is to be taken literally, then we are probably justified in assuming that the choice of these particular locations was determined not by the economic resources available on the sand deposits themselves, but rather by the more immediate attractions of these areas for the location of camp sites.

3. Thirdly, and perhaps most important, future research into the distributional aspects of the Mesolithic will need to take into account not only the *overall* distribution of specific artefact types, but also the varying *composition* of discrete artefact assemblages recovered from well defined and well documented occupation sites (cf. Clark 1972; Mellars 1976a; Price, this volume). One important advantage of this line of evidence is that data on the composition of such assemblages (assuming that methods of recovery have been adequate to ensure the unbiassed representation of all the major artefact forms) should be less susceptible to various sources of accidental distortion than are the broad distributional patterns of the individual implement types.

Perhaps the most obvious application of this approach would be to test the extent to which hunting activities were concentrated in different environmental zones. For example, if our hypothesis that the hunting of game was concentrated chiefly on areas of sandy soils is correct, a reasonable prediction from this hypothesis would appear to be that artefacts associated specifically with hunting activities should make up a significantly higher proportion of the individual tool assemblages recovered from these areas than those recovered from areas of contrasting soil type. The relevant artefacts in this context might include not only microliths (on the assumption that these do indeed represent the armatures of hunting projectiles) but also artefacts associated specifically with the manufacture of microliths – for example, micro-burins, or micro-blade forms clearly intended for microlith production. In theory artefacts associated with the butchering of animal carcases might also be considered in this context, but in practice it is doubtful whether any of the currently-recognised forms of Mesolithic implements can be interpreted confidently in these terms. It should perhaps be recalled that this emphasis on hunting equipment should not necessarily be apparent at every site located on areas of sandy soil. There is of course every reason to assume that many other economic activities in addition to hunting were carried out over these areas, and certain kinds of 'limited activity' sites (cf. Plog and Hill 1971: 8-9) devoted largely or entirely to these non-hunting activities would be no less likely to occur on areas of sandy soil than on other types of geological formation. Nevertheless, the logical prediction from the hypothesis that we have advanced here should be that when examined *in toto*, the individual tool assemblages recovered from the major sand-yielding geological formations of lowland Britain should reflect a significantly greater emphasis on hunting equipment than those recovered from areas of clay or silt-yielding formations. In the assemblages from the latter areas one would expect to find a quantitatively weaker representation of hunting equipment, and a correspondingly stronger emphasis on tools associated with other economic activities – for example, the collection and processing of plant foods, or activities connected with the general 'maintenance' requirements of the human groups.

A rather simple illustration of the potential application of this approach is shown in Table 6, in which the assemblages from five sites located on the major sand-yielding formations of the Wealden area (the Lower Greensand and Tunbridge Wells Sand) are compared with those from three sites located within the general areas of the Chalk outcrop. The data of course are limited, and it is debatable whether the methods of recovery employed on any of the sites were adequate to ensure the completely unbiassed representation of all the relevant implement types. Nevertheless it is interesting to see that in the case of four out of the five sites located on the sand deposits the overall percentages of microliths in the tool assemblages are in fact very much higher than those recorded at any of the three sites located on the Chalk. As far as the assemblages from these particular sites are concerned, therefore, the data are in good agreement with the theoretical prediction made above. The second fact which emerges very strikingly from these figures is the very much stronger representation of flint axes at all three of the sites located on the Chalk outcrop than at any of the sites located on the sand. As we have seen, a number of possible explanations might be offered to account for a concentration of Mesolithic axes on the Chalk outcrop, including a concentration of axe manufacture in the areas adjacent to the main centres of flint supply, a less 'curative' approach towards the utilisation of raw material resources in these areas than in the areas where flint supplies were more difficult to obtain, and a possibly greater need for various kinds of forest clearance on the comparatively fertile soils of the Chalk lands than on the more acidic and nutrient-deficient soils of the sand formations. Whatever the explanation, it is interesting to see that the sharp contrasts which we have already noted in the overall distributional patterns of axes and microliths on the Chalk versus sand deposits appear to be reflected equally in the composition of the individual artefact assemblages recovered from these two types of deposit.

4. Finally, the hypothesis which links the distribution of Mesolithic axes with the distribution of raw material supplies offers perhaps the best opportunities of all for systematic testing on the basis of the existing archaeological material. Two separate approaches to this question might be suggested. The first one hinges on the fact that the occurrence of flint is not in fact common to the whole of the Chalk

Table 6. Comparison of tool assemblages from 5 sites located on sand-yielding deposits in the Wealden area with those from 3 sites located on the Chalk outcrop.

Site	Micro-liths	Scrapers/ Burins/ Saws	Axes/ Adzes	Total tools
	%	%	%	
Sites on Sand				
High Rocks (Kent)	96.4	3.6	0	56
Iping Common (Sussex)	90.8	9.2	0	119
Abinger Common (Surrey)	76.4	22.8	0.8	127
Selmeston (Sussex)	71.0	29.0	0 (?)	183
Oakhanger V/VII (Hants.)	41.0	59.0	0.04	6,678
Sites on Chalk				
Downton (Wiltshire)	47.4	49.1	3.5	287
Peacehaven (Sussex)	39.4	54.9	5.7	175
Iwerne Minster (Dorset)	39.2	53.2	7.6	421

The sites of Iping Common, Abinger, Selmeston and Oakhanger are located on the Folkestone Beds division of the Lower Greensand, while High Rocks is situated on the Tunbridge Wells Sand. The tool percentages are calculated as described in Mellars 1976a. Data from Mellars 1976a and Money 1960. Only fully-published assemblages with more than 50 retouched tools are included.

formation in southern England but is effectively confined to the deposits classified by the Geological Survey as the 'Upper Chalk' (Gallois and Edmunds 1965: 38-44; Wooldridge and Goldring 1953: 16-18). A logical prediction from our hypothesis should therefore be that when the distribution of axes is examined over the Chalk outcrop as a whole, they should show a significantly heavier concentration over the areas of the Upper Chalk outcrop than over the exposures of the underlying Middle and Lower Chalk. Unfortunately, the way in which the distributional data were analysed during the present study makes it impossible to test this prediction with the data immediately to hand, but further processing of the material recorded in the course of the original C.B.A. survey should enable this point to be pursued without too much difficulty.

The second approach is based on the more specific hypothesis that beyond the limits of the main flint-bearing Chalk deposits Mesolithic communities would have gone to particular lengths to economise on the available supplies of raw material. We have suggested that in the case of axes this 'curative' approach to flint technology would have taken the form of repeated resharpening or reworking of heavily worn or damaged implements, and also the conversion of axes which became too small for further resharpening into cores for the manufacture of small implement types. If this inference is correct, it should presumably be reflected in at least two features of the surviving archaeological material: on the one hand by an increase in the ratio of axe-sharpening flakes to axes in the areas remote from the main centres of flint supply; and on the other hand by a significant reduction in the *average size* of the axes recovered from these areas as compared with those from areas in which raw material supplies were readily available. Testing of both of these predictions will clearly require more work on the original sources, but should prove perfectly feasible with the material at present available in museum collections.

Acknowledgements

We are indebted to Mr J. Wymer for providing access to the records of the Council for British Archaeology Mesolithic Survey prior to the publication of the recent *Gazetteer*, and to Mr G. Duffus for supplying the computer program on which the analysis of the distributional data was based. We are also indebted to Dr F. Roe and Dr I.F. Smith for discussions of some of the archaeological problems raised by the Survey, and to Professor G.W. Dimbleby, Sir Harry Godwin, Dr A. Hibbert, Dr M.C.F. Proctor, Dr O. Rackham and Professor A.J. Willis for valuable comments on the interpretation of the botanical data. Needless to say, none of these people should be held responsible for the particular interpretations and opinions expressed here.

Notes

[1] The initial analyses on which this study is based were carried out as an M.A. project at the University of Sheffield in 1973-74 (Reinhardt 1974). Subsequent additions and corrections to the data collected in the course of the Council for British Archaeology Survey since that date have required a number of corrections to the original figures published in this thesis, which have been incorporated into the present study. Similarly, the areas occupied by the different geological outcrops have been recalculated and differ in some cases from those quoted in the earlier study.

[2] Since the location of many of the finds in the C.B.A. *Gazetteer* could only be defined in approximate terms it is probable that a certain proportion of the sites located close to the boundaries between different geological outcrops will have been attributed to the wrong deposits (cf. Wymer 1977: viii-ix). In terms of the present analysis this must be seen as a 'background noise' effect which will in some cases have tended to *reduce* the contrasts in the apparent densities of finds on adjacent geological formations. The important point to recognise is that there is no way in which these uncertainties in site locations can produce contrasts in the distributional patterns of finds where no such contrasts exist. The only significant distortion which might arise from these uncertainties would be an apparent increase in the density of finds on deposits which are immediately adjacent to areas of very heavy Mesolithic concentrations. For example, it is conceivable that the recorded densities of finds on both the Gault Clay and Wealden Clay formations have been increased to some extent by a mis-identification of sites located close to the margins of the Lower Greensand deposits. The empirical data presented here (cf. Table 2) suggests that the quantitative extent of any distortions of this kind is relatively slight.

[3] The present study is confined entirely to sites which occur on outcrops of 'solid' (i.e. bedrock) geological formations. There is little doubt that an analysis of sites which occur on various types of 'drift' deposits, such as river valley alluvium or 'plateau gravel' deposits could yield potentially interesting results, but for a number of both theoretical and practical reasons these have been excluded from the present survey. The analysis was further simplified by omitting some of the more localised geological formations distinguished on the 'one inch' geological maps (chiefly in the western half of southern England) and by grouping together certain other deposits into the broader units adopted on the 'ten mile' (1:625,000) geological maps. A full list of the deposits considered in the study is given in Table 1.

References

Andersen, S.T. 1973. The differential pollen productivity of trees and its significance for the interpretation of a pollen diagram from a forested region. In H.J.B. Birks and R.G. West (eds.), *Quaternary Plant Ecology*. Oxford, Blackwell Scientific Publications: 109-14.

Binford, L.R. and Binford, S.R. 1966. A preliminary analysis of functional variability in the Mousterian of Levallois facies. *American Anthropologist* 68, No. 2, Pt. 2: 238-95.

Birks, H.J.B., Deacon, J. and Peglar, S. 1975. Pollen maps for the British Isles 5000 years ago. *Proceedings of the Royal Society of London*, Ser. B, 189: 87-105.

Biswell, H.H. 1972. Fire ecology in Ponderosa pine-grassland. *Proceedings of the Annual Tall Timbers Fire Ecology Conference*, 12: 69-96.

Bradley, R. 1972. Prehistorians and pastoralists in Neolithic and Bronze Age England. *World Archaeology*, 4: 192-204.

Burnham, C.P. 1972. The soils of Kent. *Cantium*, 4: 61-8.

Butzer, K.W. 1964. *Environment and Archaeology*. Chicago, Aldine.

Childe, V.G. 1940. *Prehistoric Communities of the British Isles*. London, Chambers.

Churchill, D.M. 1962. The stratigraphy of the Mesolithic sites III and V at Thatcham, Berkshire, England. *Proceedings of the Prehistoric Society*, 28: 362-70.

Clark, J.G.D. 1932. *The Mesolithic Age in Britain*. London, Cambridge University Press.

Clark, J.G.D. 1936. *The Mesolithic Settlement of Northern Europe*. London, Cambridge University Press.

Clark, J.G.D. 1972. *Star Carr, a Case Study in Bioarcheology.* Addison-Wesley Modular Publications, 10. Reading (Massachussetts).

Clark, J.G.D. 1975. *The Earlier Stone Age Settlement of Scandinavia.* London, Cambridge University Press.

Clarke, J.G.D. and Rankine, W.F. 1939. Excavations at Farnham, Surrey (1937-38). *Proceedings of the Prehistoric Society,* 5: 61-118.

Clarke, D.L. 1976. Mesolithic Europe: the economic basis. In G. de G. Sieveking, I.H. Longworth and K.E. Wilson (eds.), *Problems in Economic and Social Archaeology.* London, Duckworth: 449-81.

Day, G.M. 1953. The Indian as an ecological factor in the northeastern forest. *Ecology,* 34: 329-46.

Dimbleby, G.W. 1961. The ancient forest of Blackamore. *Antiquity,* 35: 123-8.

Dimbleby, G.W. 1962. *The Development of British Heathlands and their Soils.* London, Oxford University Press.

Draper, J.C. 1968. Mesolithic distribution in south-east Hampshire. *Proceedings of the Hampshire Field Club,* 110-19.

Evans, J.G. 1975. *The Environment of Early Man in the British Isles.* London, Elek.

Gallois, R.W. and Edmunds, F.H. 1965. *British Regional Geology: the Wealden District* (4th edition). London, Her Majesty's Stationery Office.

Godwin, H. 1975. History of the natural forests of Britain: establishment, dominance and destruction. *Philosophical Transactions of the Royal Society of London* (Ser. B), 171: 47-67.

Hall, A.D. and Russell, E.J. 1911. *A Report on the Agriculture and Soils of Kent, Surrey and Sussex.* London, His Majesty's Stationery Office.

Harris, D.R. 1969. Agricultural systems, ecosystems and the origins of agriculture. In P.J. Ucko and G.W. Dimbleby (eds.) *The Domestication and Exploitation of Plants and Animals.* London, Duckworth: 3-15.

Higgs, E.S. and Vita-Finzi, C. 1972. Prehistoric economies: a territorial approach. In E.S. Higgs (ed.) *Papers in Economic Prehistory.* London, Cambridge University Press: 27-36.

Jacobi, R.M. 1973. Aspects of the 'Mesolithic Age' in Great Britain. In S.K. Kozlowski (ed.) *The Mesolithic in Europe.* Warsaw, University Press: 237-65.

Keef, P.A.M., Wymer, J.J. and Dimbleby, G.W. 1965. A Mesolithic site on Iping Common, Sussex, England. *Proceedings of the Prehistoric Society,* 31: 85-92.

Kroeber, A.L. 1925. *Handbook of the Indians of California.* Bureau of American Ethnology Bulletin 78.

Lee, R.B. 1968. What hunters do for a living, or, how to make out on scarce resources. In R.B. Lee and I. DeVore (eds.), *Man the Hunter.* Chicago, Aldine: 30-48.

Lewis, H.T. 1973. *Patterns of Indian Burning in California.* Ballena Press Anthropological Papers No. 1.

Limbrey, S. 1975. *Soil Science and Archaeology.* New York and London, Academic Press.

Mellars, P. 1975, Ungulate populations, economic patterns and the Mesolithic landscape. In J.G. Evans, S. Limbrey and H. Cleere (eds.), *The Effect of Man on the Landscape: The Highland Zone.* London, Council for British Archaeology Research Report No 11: 49-56.

Mellars, P. 1976a. Settlement patterns and industrial variability in the British Mesolithic. In G. de G. Sieveking, I.H. Longworth and K.E. Wilson (eds.) *Problems in Economic and Social Archaeology.* London, Duckworth: 375-99.

Mellars, P. 1976b. Fire ecology, animal populations and man: a study of some ecological relationships in prehistory. *Proceedings of the Prehistoric Society,* 42: 15-45.

Money, J.H. 1960. Excavations at High Rocks, Tunbridge Wells. *Surrey Archaeological Collections,* 98: 173-221.

Odum, E.P. 1971. *Fundamentals of Ecology* (3rd. edition). London, Saunders.

Oswalt, W.H. 1976. *An Anthropological Analysis of Food-Getting Technology.* New York and London, Wiley.

Pearsall, W.H. 1968. *Mountains and Moorlands*. London, Fontana.

Plog, F.T. 1974. *The Study of the Prehistoric Change*. New York and London, Academic Press.

Plog, F.T. and Hill, J.N. 1971. Explaining variability in the distribution of sites. In G.J. Gumerman (ed.) *The Distribution of Prehistoric Population Aggregates*. Prescott (Arizona), College Press.

Poole, H.F. 1936. An outline of the Mesolithic flint cultures of the Isle of Wight. *Proceedings of the Isle of Wight Natural History and Archaeological Society*, 2 (pt. 7): 551-81.

Rankine, W.F. 1949a. *Mesolithic Survey of the West Surrey Greensand*. Research Papers of the Surrey Archaeological Society, No. 2.

Rankine, W.F. 1949b. Stone 'maceheads' with Mesolithic associations from south-eastern England. *Proceedings of the Prehistoric Society*, 15: 70-6.

Rankine, W.F. 1951. Quartzite pebble maceheads with hour-glass perforation: their distribution in England. *Archaeological News Letter*, 4(4): 53-5.

Rankine, W.F. 1953. A study of quartzite maceheads: functional interpretation and perforation technique. *Archaeological News Letter*, 4(12): 186-8.

Rankine, W.F. 1956. *The Mesolithic of Southern England*. Research Papers of the Surrey Archaeological Society, No. 4.

Rankine, W.F. and Dimbleby, G.W. 1960. Further investigations at a Mesolithic site at Oakhanger, Selborne, Hants. *Proceedings of the Prehistoric Society*, 26: 246-62.

Rankine, W.F. and Dimbleby, G.W. 1961. *Further excavations at Oakhanger, Selborne, Hants. Site VIII*. Wealden Mesolithic Research Bulletin.

Rawitscher, F. 1945. The hazel period in the postglacial development of forests. *Nature*, 156: 302-3.

Reinhardt, S.C. 1974. *Patterns of Mesolithic Settlement in Southern England*. M.A. dissertation, University of Sheffield.

Schapera, I. 1930. *The Khoisan Peoples of South Africa*. London, Routledge and Kegan Paul.

Seagrief, S.C. 1959. Pollen diagrams from southern England: Wareham, Dorset and Nursling, Hampshire. *New Phytologist*, 58: 316-25.

Seagrief, S.C. 1960. Pollen diagrams from southern England: Crane's Moor, Hampshire. *New Phytologist*, 59: 73-83.

Seagrief, S.C. and Godwin, H. 1961. Pollen diagrams from southern England: Elstead, Surrey. *New Phytologist*, 60: 84-91.

Sieveking, G. de G., Bush, P., Ferguson, J., Craddock, P.T., Hughes, M.J. and Cowell, M.R. 1972. Prehistoric flint mines and their identification as sources of raw material. *Archaeometry* 14: 151-76.

Simmons, I.G. 1969. Evidence for vegetation changes associated with Mesolithic man in Britain. In P.J. Ucko and G.W. Dimbleby (eds.), *The Domestication and Exploitation of Plants and Animals*. London, Duckworth: 113-19.

Smith, A.G. 1970. The influence of Mesolithic and Neolithic man on British vegetation: a discussion. In D. Walker and R.G. West (eds.), *Studies in the Vegetational History of the British Isles*. London, Cambridge University Press: 81-96.

Smith, L.P. 1976. *The Agricultural Climate of England and Wales*. Ministry of Agriculture, Fisheries and Food Technical Bulletin 35. London, Her Majesty's Stationery Office.

Stewart, O.C. 1956. Fire as the first great force employed by man. In W.L. Thomas (ed.), *Man's Role in Changing the Face of the Earth*. Chicago, Aldine: 115-33.

Tansley, A.G. 1949. *The British Islands and their Vegetation*. London, Cambridge University Press.

Tansley, A.G. and Proctor, M.C.F. 1968. *Britain's Green Mantle*. London, Allen and Unwin.

Thomas, D.H. 1974. *Predicting the Past*. New York and London, Holt, Rinehart and Winston.

Tindale, N.B. 1974. *The Aboriginal Tribes of Australia.* Canberra, Australian National University.

Wooldridge, S.W. and Goldring, F. 1953. *The Weald.* London, Collins.

Wymer, J.J. (ed.) 1977. *Gazetteer of Mesolithic Sites in England and Wales.* London, Council for British Archaeology.

12

Northern England in the eighth millennium bc: an essay

R. M. Jacobi

It is possible to recognise from 8th millennium contexts in England a series of microlith industries characterised by broad, obliquely blunted points, isosceles triangles, short or elongated bitruncated blades and, on the majority of sites, convex backed points also. With this range of archery equipment (Petersson 1961) may be found core-axes, end-scrapers, burins and truncated blades, the whole being closely associated with the birch and pine-hazel woodland of the early postglacial and with the exploitation of a wide range of forest-living ungulates, including red deer, pig, roe deer, elk and aurochs. In addition to these there is a limited spectrum of fur-bearing animals: beaver, pine-marten, fox, wild cat and badger, the latter three of which are nocturnal or burrow-dwelling carnivores and may have been taken by self-acting traps (Freeman 1973), or with the aid of dogs (Degerbøl 1961). Dogs which appear only in our Early Mesolithic would clearly serve to follow the blood trail left by cutting arrows of Loshult type, approximating in function to that of the *Dornpfeilspitzen* of the later European Bronze Age (Mercer 1970: Fig. 3).

Collectively, the stone industries connected with this pattern of exploitation could be described as 'Early Mesolithic' or, more specifically, as belonging to the north European 'Maglemosian technocomplex', stretching from Mecklenburg to west Cornwall, and from south Sweden to northern France. If we were to map the British sites now recognised as belonging to this technocomplex our map would differ radically from earlier attempts (Clark in Warren *et al.* 1934: Fig. 10; Wainwright 1960: Fig. 1) not only in the vastly inflated total of sites now recognised – in the region of 230 – but in the high proportion of sites represented in the northern half of England (Fig. 1). Following on the work of Radley and Mellars (1964), it is possible to recognise 116 find-spots on the Pennine uplands and their foothills and, from the crests of the North York Moors, some 33. In other words, not only are well over half of our recognised Early Mesolithic sites northern

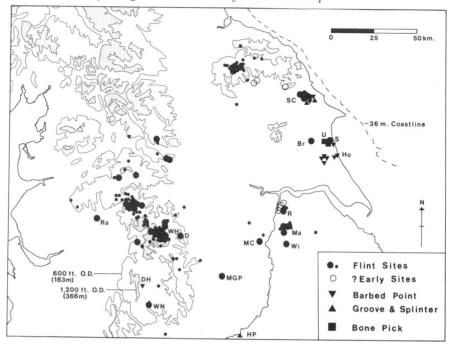

Figure 1. Distribution of Early Mesolithic sites in northern England: Br –Brigham; D –
Deepcar; DH – Dowel Hall Cave; Ho – Hornsea; HP – Holme Pierrepoint; Ma –
Manton Warren; MC – Misterton Carr; MGP – Mother Grundy's Parlour; Ra –
Radcliffe Ees; R – Risby Warren; S – Skipsea; SC – Star Carr; U – Ulrome; WH
Warcock Hill; Wi – Willoughton Site A; WN – Wetton Mill Minor Rock-shelter.

in distribution, but they also lie above 200 metres, the bulk over 300
metres. The change is thus dramatic. To the north of these areas early
finds are few: a core-axe and an obliquely blunted point from
Monkwearmouth near Jarrow, small groups of obliquely blunted
points in grey or white flint from Sheddon's Hill near Gateshead
(Coupland 1925), and an enigmatic assemblage with apparently early
microlith   shapes   excavated   from   a   site   at   Spindleston,
Northumberland (Buckley 1925). The purpose of the present paper is
to review the evidence for this Early Mesolithic occupation in northern
England and, in particular, to discuss the evidence which has been
obtained from recent excavations of a number of newly-discovered sites
belonging to this period on the North York Moors.

The earliest postglacial occupation of northern England

The dating of these Early Mesolithic assemblages in northern
England raises a number of interesting issues which are worth
examining in more detail. At the outset it should be pointed out that
although radiocarbon dates for these assemblages have been obtained

Table 1. Radiocarbon dates for Early Mesolithic sites in northern England.

Sites of 'Deepcar' Type		*Date bc*	*Lab. No.*
Lominot Site III	West Yorkshire (Pennines)	7,615 ± 470	Q-1187
Money Howe Site I	North Yorkshire (North York Moors)	7,480 ± 390	Q-1560
Waystone Edge	North Yorkshire (North York Moors)	7,446 ± 210	Q-1300
Sites of 'Star Carr' Type			
Star Carr	East Yorkshire	7,607 ± 210	Q-14
Star Carr	East Yorkshire	7,538 ± 350	C-353
Warcock Hill South	West Yorkshire (Pennines)	7,260 ± 340	Q-1185

from five separate sites, all of the determinations are subject to certain limitations (Table 1). The measurements for Star Carr were carried out over twenty years ago, while the remainder (samples processed in the course of a current Cambridge University Research Programme: Switsur and Jacobi 1975) all possess standard deviations which are too large to make any but the most general discussion possible. In the case of upland sites, these large standard deviations reflect how little hearth material has escaped rapid dispersion by gales or sheet erosion; what charcoal has survived has done so only by virtue of lying at the base of shallow artificial 'fire pits', usually infilled by knapping debris within the lifetime of the site itself.

Even allowing for the qualifications already made, the dates are sufficiently cohesive as to make it clear that the exploitation of both the southern Pennines and the North York Moors had been achieved by groups using the material equipment associated with postglacial woodland hunting and trapping by the middle of the 8th millennium bc. If one accepts the sites from Gateshead and Monkwearmouth at their face value, colonisation along the east coast might have been successful as far as 55° North. A hundred miles to the north – north of 56°N – the earliest radiocarbon dates associated with a microlithic industry of postglacial type are still those of 6,100 ± 225 bc for Morton Tayport in Fifeshire (R-2826/1: Coles 1971: 320-1) and 6,244 ± 350 bc for Lussa Wood site I on the island of Jura (SSR-160, Mercer 1974).[1]

The scale of the standard deviations for the radiocarbon dates listed in Table 1 must clearly be kept in mind. Taken as a group, however, all of the dates could be seen as relating to the middle or later parts of the 8th millennium bc. The important point to be noted here is that none of these dates is comparable to the earliest C14 determinations for Mesolithic assemblages from south-eastern England. Thus at

Thatcham site III a typical Early Mesolithic industry has been dated to 8,415 $\pm$ 170 bc (Q-659) and 8,080 $\pm$ 170 bc (Q-658), while occupation debris from site I had already begun to enter the accumulating adjacent 'algal marl' by 7,890 $\pm$ 160 bc (Q-651: Churchill 1962). While Thatcham site III consists of a series of hearths and flint concentrations spanning a millennium, the fauna (as isolated from squares G5, 3-5, 7 and 8 and associated with the determination of 8,415 bc), consists of *Bos* (not *Bison*), red deer and pig – a woodland or woodland-margin fauna. Roe deer, a species primarily of the deciduous woodland, is absent, as are reindeer, elk, giant deer (*Megaloceros*) and horse. The associated artefacts are identical to those from the Early Mesolithic sites in northern England that we have so far discussed, consisting entirely of slender obliquely blunted points, end scrapers and an axe-sharpening flake. Even allowing for a minus error of two standard deviations – giving a 95.4 percent probability that the true age lies within this range – this occupation at Thatcham must date from before 8,000 bc. In other words, this occupation would appear to be earlier by a factor of at least 500-700 years than that of the earliest *dated* Mesolithic sites in the northern half of England.

If we turn back to northern England, there are several dates of immediate relevance to this apparently unrepresented half to three-quarters of a millennium. Almost identical to Q-659 at Thatcham is a determination of 8,440 $\pm$ 90 bc (BM-603: Burleigh *et al.* 1976) on horse bone from the upper part of a brecciated scree in Robin Hood's Cave, Creswell. Whatever interpretation one places on the stratigraphy in view of the obviously intrusive faunal elements in this scree (Burleigh *et al.* 1976; also probably Campbell 1969: Table 1) and mixture within it of Earlier and Later Upper Palaeolithic artefacts (Garrod 1926: Fig. 29, nos. 9, 10; also Fig. 30, nos. 1, 2) the date *is* quite clearly directly relevant to the hunting, and to the butchery on the site, of horse and the extinct giant deer *Megaloceros*, both of which are notably absent from the faunal assemblage at Star Carr. Associated with this activity were backed blades and shouldered points of late-glacial 'Creswellian' type.

More critical to the discussions as a whole, and to the possible interpretation of economic strategies to be detected within northern England in the first centuries of the 8th millennium, is the series of three dates (Table 2) from the Anston Cave in south Yorkshire (Mellars 1969; White 1971). The associated artefacts are all of types known from late Devensian Creswellian contexts, including angle-backed blades, a shouldered point, and four large forms of straight-backed blades (Mellars 1969: Fig. 1). Also associated with the radiocarbon determinations were a number of firmly identified bones of both reindeer and arctic hare. While the dates suggest that the Anston site is the contemporary of such southern Mesolithic sites as Thatcham sites III and V and Marsh Benham, initial examination of

Table 2. Radiocarbon dates for the Anston Cave, South Yorkshire. From Mellars 1969.

Material	Date bc	Lab. No.
Bone collagen	7,990 ± 115	BM-440A
Bone collagen	7,900 ± 115	BM-439
Reindeer antler	7,800 ± 110	BM-440B

the pollen spectra associated with and above the artefacts has been taken to suggest that the dates, while impressive in their internal consistency, may be too young (Mellars 1974: 74-5). Indeed, it has been suggested that the occupation may have occurred 'well back into the late-glacial period'. These spectra thus demand further consideration.

The problems involved in any discussion of these pollen spectra are not ones of attempting to assign the counts to a particular pollen zone (Godwin 1940), but rather one of whether the vegetational environments represented can be matched in any other pollen diagrams from northern England which can be shown on independent evidence to be their precise contemporaries. Immediately relevant, then, are only two securely dated diagrams: Scaleby Moss, Cumbria (Godwin *et al.* 1957) and Red Moss, Lancashire (Hibbert *et al.* 1971).

The characteristic features of the four Anston Cave pollen counts are, firstly, the low representation of arboreal pollen, 17-29 percent of the total pollen, the greater part being willow (either tree or shrub), but with some birch and pine. The actual numbers of tree pollen grains per sample (10-39) are however so low as to make detailed interpretation impossible. Secondly the counts are characterised by the very high values of non-arboreal pollen (52-66 percent) of which some 50 percent is composed of grasses or sedges (White 1971: 5).

At Scaleby Moss comparable pollen spectra must be sought *midway* between determinations of 8,210 ± 193 bc (Q-152) at 70 cm. and a pair just above 50 cm. of 7,614 ± 209 (Q-154) and 7,797 ± 183 bc (Q-155), while at Red Moss similar spectra are associated with a date of 7,848 ± 200 bc (Q-924). At 60 cm., or from 10 cm. below this level on the Scaleby Moss diagram, tree pollen makes up just under 25 percent of the total pollen, with near-equal representation of birch and willow; some 60 percent of the residue consists of grasses and sedges. At Red Moss, the diagram shows some 20 percent tree pollen (mainly birch) and 60 percent grasses and sedges. In short, there is a close similarity between these pollen spectra and those from the Anston cave, both in the relative proportions of the main vegetational components, and also in the range of plant species represented. The values for juniper and *Empetrum* at the Anston site are broadly similar to those of the other pair of diagrams, while, with the exception of *Armeria*, all of the plants interpreted by Campbell (in White 1971: 5) as suggesting a tundra or alpine environment can be documented from other early 8th millennium contexts in northern Britain. There would thus be no *prima facie* evidence against accepting an early 8th millennium date for both the pollen counts and the associated artefacts at Anston, and, with this, the evidence for the exploitation of reindeer.

Contemporary pollen data from southern England are effectively lacking, and the few dated absolute counts for the period which concerns us were undertaken for purely chronological rather than ecological reasons. However, when we can begin to pick up the botanical record at Thatcham close to 7,890 $\pm$ 160 bc (Q-651) – a date identical to those for the use of the Anston Cave – the associated spectrum (recalculated as percentages of the total pollen from Churchill 1962: 368) contains 29 percent birch, 19 percent pine and 14 percent willow. Recent pollen studies (Goddard 1971; Tinsley and Smith 1974) suggest that values of tree pollen greater than 50 percent of the total land pollen might be expected only below a tree or shrub canopy. Even if we interpret the 14 percent willow pollen together with that of the *Cyperaceae* (10.5 percent) as reflecting purely lakeside communities, the fact that birch and pine pollen could contribute 48 percent of the grains counted, even after filtering through this zone, would seem to indicate the probability of a continuous woodland canopy around the collecting basin, rather than isolated stands. Associated with this count were macroscopic remains of birch and pine, while similar fossil records of pine at both Elstead, Surrey (Seagrief and Godwin 1960) and Nursling, Hampshire (Seagrief 1959), and of birch at Elstead, have been taken to indicate such woodland in southern Britain in zone III, i.e. before 8,300 bc. However, these diagrams are without absolute dating and, at Croydon an organic lens dated 8,180 $\pm$ 120 bc (Birm-101) yielded only twigs of tree willow (Osborne 1971). In the absence of charcoal identifications from the relevant sectors of Thatcham site III, vegetation patterns before 7,900 bc remain equivocal.

Slightly later counts from Thatcham (7,750 $\pm$ 160 bc) and Broxbourne site 104 (7,657 $\pm$ 200 bc: Q-1096) give totals for pine and birch pollen combined of 58 percent and 78 percent respectively, the two trees being represented by more or less equal percentages at Broxbourne, while at Thatcham the high proportion of pine pollen (43 percent) quite clearly indicates the changing character of the woodland cover. In northern England, the high birch values found in contemporary diagrams must represent the initial birch period in the forest succession there (Birks and Saarnisto 1975). Thus, at 35 cm. in the Scaleby Moss diagram, some 15 cm. above 7,797 $\pm$ 183 bc (Q-155), not only has the tree pollen risen to 80 percent of the total pollen, but some 75 percent is birch, the significant increase in tree pollen from 40 to 70 percent taking place between 40 and 45 cm. Similar marked increases take place for the first time at Red Moss slightly before 7,636 $\pm$ 200 bc (Q-923), while the birch woodland surrounding Star Carr (c.7,500 bc) is abundantly documented in both the pollen and macrofossil record.

To summarise, pollen spectra from northern and southern Britain indicate a closed woodland environment for both areas by 7,600 bc with a rather greater proportion of pine in the south. In terms of tree cover, these counts resemble those for the succeeding Boreal period, and associated in both areas with this woodland are groups using a Maglemosian technology. In the north there is the suggestion not only that this technology appeared *later* than in the south, but that it was specifically linked with the rather later establishment of this woodland cover. Contemporary with the earliest Maglemosian in southern England we find, in the markedly more open environment of the north, the maintenance of a characteristically late-glacial form of technology, still associated with the hunting of reindeer.

Settlement patterns and social groupings in the Early Mesolithic of northern England

Seasonal movements

As we have already noted, one of the most striking features of the distribution of Early Mesolithic sites in northern England is the high proportion of sites which occur at high elevations on both the central and southern Pennines and the North York Moors, in some cases reaching an altitude of almost 500 metres. As several authors have pointed out, there can be little doubt that the economic exploitation of these upland areas by Mesolithic communities must have been largely confined to the summer months, and that this pattern of exploitation was determined to at least some extent by the seasonal migration patterns of such species as red deer (cf. Clark 1972). In brief, the length of the snowlie above 350 metres (up to 50 days), combined with driving rains, mists, and a resultant foreshortening of the growing season for grazing plants, must have rendered these uplands in the highest degree unfavourable for ungulates during the winter months. Conversely, the degree of insect irritation, particularly by the headfly (*Hydrotea irritans*), in the early summer would tend to drive animals away from the areas of lowest topography and lightest snowfall which had proved so ideal for winter yarding back up onto the highest ground – now an area of fresh growth, longer hours of sunshine, and where diurnal temperature range would be at its minimum. The length of movements made by individual herds would of course have varied with the abruptness (or rather, in northern England, the relative gentleness) of the transition between areas of highest and lowest ground. Working from topographic arguments alone, it may be necessary to envisage, at least for the groups exploiting the southern

Pennine upland, annual territories of up to 80 km. in length. A point, however, which deserves emphasis here is that the proportion of any ungulate population to leave the uplands with the onset of winter, their date of departure and even the occurrence of such a departure, would have depended on the severity of winter conditions *from year to year*. John Leland, writing in the second quarter of the sixteenth century, is quite specific in his comments on the behaviour of red deer in Bishopsdale in the mid-Pennines. Thus he noted that 'yn the hilles about hir be redde deer. In faire winters the deere keepe theere; in sharp winters they forsake the extreme colde and barrenes of them' (Smith 1909).

If one accepts the ecological reasoning outlined above it is immediately pertinent to look for evidence of Early Mesolithic settlements on lower ground with an identical microlithic tool-kit and which could be considered complementary to the sites on the uplands. Most spectacular, of course, of these potential winter sites is Star Carr (Clark 1954), situated like Flixton site I (Moore 1950) on the northern edge of the contemporary Lake Pickering and at the southern foot of the North York Moors. In addition to these two sites, however, it is possible to recognise isolated sites in lowland Lancashire to the west of the Pennines (Spencer 1953) and – of more significance to the discussion later in this paper – two small groups of sites to their east. Firstly we have such sites as Misterton Carr (Buckland and Dolby 1973) or the two sites at Cloud's Lane, Beltoft, and Cove Farm, Haxey, both on the Isle of Axholme, and all three situated to exploit the low-lying ground of the present Hatfield Chase. Secondly, there is the rich group of sites in northern Lincolnshire, including Bagmoor (Dudley 1949), Sheffield's Hill (Armstrong 1931), Manton Warren (Gatty's site), Risby Warren site I and Willoughton site A (Armstrong 1932). These sites form part of a larger complex of 79 Mesolithic find spots stretching along the Lincolnshire Edge from Roxby, north of Scunthorpe, to Willoughton and Laughton Common to the south, and are closely tied (like the Domesday Villages: Darby 1952), to the springline at the junction of the limestone and the underlying clays. The distribution of these sites forms a chain roughly parallel to the southern Pennine uplands and some 60-80 km. to the east of sites on Pike Lowe and Mickleden Edge at 390 metres O.D. (Radley and Marshall 1965) or Warcock Hill at 380 metres (Radley and Mellars 1964). Within the home ranges of these sites – taken here to be a radius of 10 km. – would lie the flood plains of the Trent and Ancholme and, in the case of Sheffield's Hill, the Humber also. In their low altitudes and short periods of snowlie, these areas would provide ideal winter ranges.

Social groupings

The most complete description of the typology of the north British

N.W. LINCS. : COMPARISON OF RAW MATERIAL CONTENT
FOR EARLY AND LATER MESOLITHIC SITES

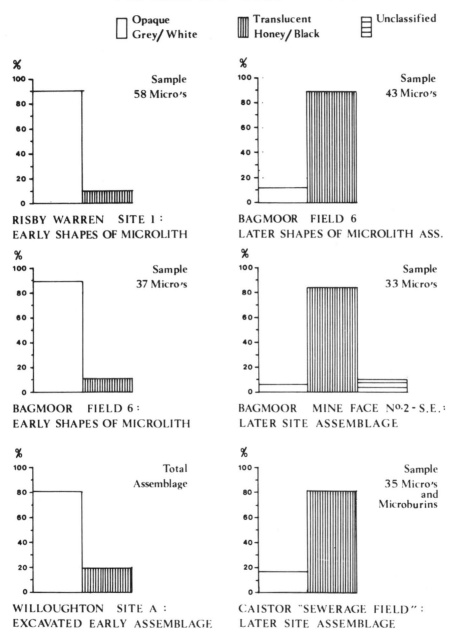

Figure 2. Lincolnshire Edge sites; raw material composition of Early and Later Mesolithic microlith groups.

Early Mesolithic must be that offered by Radley and Mellars (1964) for the site of Deepcar in the east Pennine Foothills, and for sites excavated by Francis Buckley on the Pennine crests of Warcock Hill North site, Lominot sites II and III and Windy Hill site IIIa. The comments made then are still applicable to all the sites known on the Pennines – with one notable exception – and to all those on lower ground to the east, for example, along the Lincolnshire Edge. The microliths are all of simple forms and only two observations need to be made. Firstly, a varying proportion of the obliquely blunted points show added retouch on the leading edge, while some points possess convex blunting down the whole of one margin. These traits serve to link this microlithic component to that from such more southerly sites as Thatcham, Oakhanger V and VII and Kelling Heath, a visual impression confirmed by computer cluster analysis (Jacobi, forthcoming).

Secondly, these sites are rendered distinct by their reliance on a white flint originating in the Wolds of north Lincolnshire and east Yorkshire for the production of their complete stone equipment from microliths to core-axes. Proportions of this white flint recorded at sites above 300 metres on the Pennines (80-99 percent) are as high as those encountered on sites immediately adjacent to the flint sources 80 km. to the east (cf. Fig. 2). Given this reliance, movement of this flint type must be seen in a completely different social context to that of Portland chert in southern England which, it has been suggested (Jacobi 1976b), circulated largely as an item in a gift exchange system; thus there is only a single small blade of the latter material among 186,000 pieces excavated at Oakhanger sites V and VII (Rankine 1961) and only a pair of microliths among 10,709 worked pieces from Farnham pit 4 (Rankine 1951). By contrast, what we may be witnessing in the case of this white flint is its direct collection by groups exploiting the Pennine uplands in summer from established quarries or exposures in precisely the same areas which we have suggested could have served as optimum wintering grounds. The presence of isolated flakes of Pennine chert on sites along the Lincolnshire Edge and in Hatfield Chase might be seen as confirmation of such annual movements.

Perhaps the most interesting point brought out in the paper by Radley and Mellars, however, is that the type of industry represented at Deepcar and the other sites described above appears to represent only one facet of the Early Mesolithic occupation of northern England. The existence of a significantly different industrial tradition was first suggested by the assemblage excavated by Francis Buckley from what he referred to as the 'South' site on Warcock Hill. As Radley and Mellars point out (1964: 20-1), the microlithic component of this assemblage differs in several respects from that recovered from the other Pennine localities, and can be compared closely with the range of microlithic forms represented in the assemblage from Star

Carr. Of particular significance is the fact that the 'broad obliquely blunted points ... [are] never retouched on the leading edge', and the presence of isolated examples of broad isosceles triangles and trapezes – a combination still without parallel on any other Pennine site. Convex backed points are completely absent. With this comparison this paper is completely in accord. Equally if not more significant, however, was their recognition that the site differed radically also in the raw materials employed. While some 10 percent of opaque white flint and 5 percent of black chert identical to that used on other Pennine sites could be identified, the balance was made up of 'a variety of translucent flints ranging in colour from mottled yellow to brown or black' (Radley and Mellars 1964: 21).

Re-examination of the original material showed that this balance (85 percent) was made up of precisely the same semi-translucent speckled grey flint and transparent honey-coloured flint which had been employed by the groups at Star Carr and Flixton. There was also the same low representation of the speckled yellow and brown flint. As to the remaining 15 percent of white flint and chert reported from this site, there may well be grounds for questioning the provenance of this material. Thus Buckley, writing in 1924 (when he had excavated an area of 80 square yards) noted specifically that the artefacts were of 'clear brown and grey flint, without patina and no chert' (1924: 3). The presence of both white flint and chert in the collection as it now survives could be due to subsequent mixing in the museum.

The same two subdivisions of the Early Mesolithic industries can also be distinguished on the Cleveland Hills of north Yorkshire, where industries incorporating much white flint and with a microlithic repertoire identical to Deepcar are found on the same moors as sites with a restricted range of microlith shapes made, as at Star Carr and Warcock Hill South, on semi-translucent and speckled flints (see below). Finally, it was a deliberate over-simplification when it was suggested that all of the early sites along the Lincolnshire Edge resembled Deepcar and were manufactured very largely of white flint. From Manton Warren sites I and V (Clark 1932: 35-6) and also from Manton Pond, opposite Greetwell Hall, come groups of short obliquely blunted points, lacking retouch on their leading edges and associated with broad isosceles triangles and trapezes. Differing in outline and angularity from other local Early Mesolithic industries, it comes as no surprise to find that these microliths, which resemble so closely those from Star Carr and Warcock Hill South, are also made from semi-translucent speckled grey flint, or translucent black or honey-coloured material.

To summarise, it is possible to recognise for each of the three areas from which we have adequate samples of material (i.e. the Pennines, North York Moors and Lincolnshire) a consistently recurring pattern indicative of a pair of Early Mesolithic microlithic traditions. The scant radiocarbon evidence (Table 1) suggests their contemporaneity.

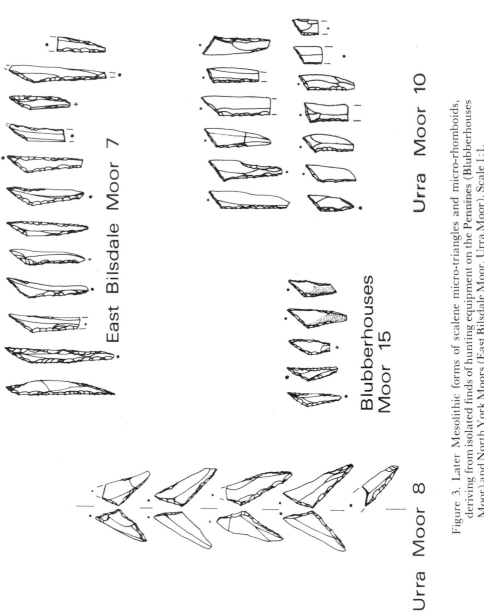

Figure 3. Later Mesolithic forms of scalene micro-triangles and micro-rhomboids, deriving from isolated finds of hunting equipment on the Pennines (Blubberhouses Moor) and North York Moors (East Bilsdale Moor, Urra Moor). Scale 1:1.

Translated into social terms, we may be detecting the activities of a pair of 'social groupings' (cf. Clark 1975: 69) exploiting, apparently close in time, identical territorial ranges.

For a possible explanation of this pattern we may perhaps turn to Thompson's (1939) frequently-quoted study of the Wik Monkan groups of north-eastern Australia, however remote the extrapolation. Here, the *ownership* of particular areas of land is invested in a relatively small social unit (the 'clan'), but the right to *hunt* over these individually-owned areas may extend to members of several different clans by recognition of certain bonds of relationship, such as kinship ties. Thus a man is invariably permitted to hunt in the 'clan territory' of his mother. The actual group found at any one time within such a clan territory is referred to as the 'horde'. It is, of course, impossible to identify such groupings as clans and hordes in Mesolithic archaeology. It would likewise be realistic to admit that we can make only potential estimates of population and with it the degree of packing of annual territories (Clark 1972: 37-9). If, however, we make the *assumption* of equating peculiarities of behaviour, as mirrored in the stone equipment, with specific clans or groups of clans, then extension of their individual hunting ranges over those of other clans by ties of kinship (i.e. incorporation into hordes) might explain these observed distributions.

Discussion in this paper is deliberately restricted to the 8th millennium bc, since within the first few centuries of the 7th millennium the microlithic technologies discussed above – and with them the pair of social groupings proposed – apparently disappear. Projectiles of the 'Loshult' type are replaced by points set with micro-triangles and related forms (cf. Figure 3; Radley *et al.* 1974; Jacobi 1976a) while apparently synchronous with this change are abrupt changes in the selection of preferred raw materials. In the Pennines for example there is a virtual replacement of flint for tool manufacture by a variety of locally-occurring cherts (accounting for between 84 and 100 percent of the lithic assemblages), while in the proposed wintering areas of the Lincolnshire Edge there is a corresponding change from the rich sources of local white flint to a transparent, honey-coloured flint of unknown origin (Fig. 2). This evidence, combined with that for major functional changes in the macrolithic tool kits around this time, is suggestive of a significant change in both social organisation and behavioural patterns shortly after 7,000 bc.

Early mesolithic exploitation patterns in north-east Yorkshire

In his 1972 paper, *Star Carr: A Case Study in Bio-archaeology*, Clark suggested that the annual territory of the groups using this site may have included the higher parts of the North York Moors in the

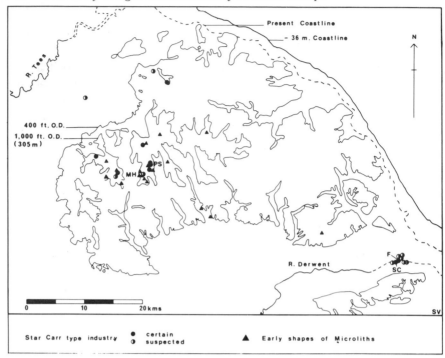

Figure 4. Distribution of Early Mesolithic sites on the North York Moors and adjacent
areas: PS – Pointed Stone; MH – Money Howe; SC – Star Carr; F – Flixton.

summer months. As he sadly noted, there were 'no records of scientific
excavations' in this area. While it was possible for Clark to map nine
sites on these moorlands, all of these belonged to one or other of
Buckley's 'Narrow Blade' industries – in other words, the sites were of
Later Mesolithic age (Clark 1972: Fig. 12). There was, therefore, a
clear incentive to make a detailed study of all the available material
from this region and attempt from this to select sites which appeared
worthwhile to excavate, particularly any site which might relate
directly to Star Carr and the problems as outlined by Clark.

　　Analysis of the material held in both public and private collections
revealed some 30 find-spots which could be attributed with some
degree of confidence to the Early Mesolithic, including two dozen
which lay above 300 metres and nearly all the discoveries of Mr and
Mrs G.V. Taylor of Bradford (Fig. 4). As on the Pennines, microlith
typology again suggested a broad division of these finds into two
groups: (1) the first with numerous distinctly elongated, narrow,
obliquely blunted points, frequently retouched along the leading edge,
and a proportion of points with convex blunting down the whole of
one margin, the total assemblage resembling Deepcar; (2) the second
group (with some ten find-spots) characterised by shorter, more
angular, obliquely blunted points, with retouch on the leading edge in
only one instance, and accompanied by isosceles triangles and

trapezes; a limited range, but one identical to Star Carr.

Again, remarkably, the typological differences between the two microlithic tool kits are enhanced by a subtle variation in the raw materials employed. Thus, the sites of the Deepcar type are characterised by a significant proportion of the same opaque grey to white flint which had proved the distinguishing characteristic of such sites on the Pennines. In this case, however, there is not the same total reliance on this material, primary dependence being placed on what are obviously more local sources. Even so, if this opaque flint proves, as visual inspection suggests it may, to be from the same source as that used on the Pennines, then we may be seeing represented in the relatively constant proportions of this raw material the maintenance of strong social connections between what could be interpreted as a colonising group, and an already established system of raw material procurement in the areas further to the south. In this situation the white flint may perhaps have resembled the 'Gerri of Arnhem Land' described by Thomson (1949), which are known to have been traded over considerable distances as an item of ceremonial exchange, despite the existence of more easily accessible local resources.

During 1974 and 1975 excavations were carried out on three of these Early Mesolithic sites, the first pair of which appeared from the surface collections of microliths and flint waste (eroding from below the thin raw humus) to show the closest similarities to Star Carr. These two sites – Pointed Stone sites 2 and 3 – lie 20 metres apart, close to one of the highest points of the hills, at 410 metres on the eastern flank of Bilsdale East Moor, above Bransdale. It was felt that these sites, over 60 percent of whose home range at a 10 km. radius lay over 800 ft. (244 m.) O.D., might yield evidence for the summer activities of groups who had spent at least a portion of the winter on the northern margins of Lake Pickering, using sites, 60 percent of whose home ranges lay, by contrast, below 200 ft. (61 m.). Apart from some overlap between 400 and 600 ft., the ranges of the two groups of sites could be regarded as strictly complementary (Fig. 5).

Both sites were completely stripped, particular care being taken to define the limits of each flint scatter. Every piece was plotted and the position of boulders recorded. The latter made no clear pattern and only on site 3 was it possible to pinpoint occasional stones which, overlying worked flints, had been moved during or *after* the occupation. These detailed plans will be published elsewhere, and only general comments are offered here, with a smaller breakdown of each site simply in terms of numbers of flints per square metre (Fig. 6).

The immediately striking feature of the flint scatter on site 3, with 4,557 struck flints, is that far from their forming a single concentration thinning towards its edges, there are quite clearly three clusterings, each associated with areas of burnt flint. This burnt flint shows a tendency to lie within the comparatively 'empty' centre of the scatter.

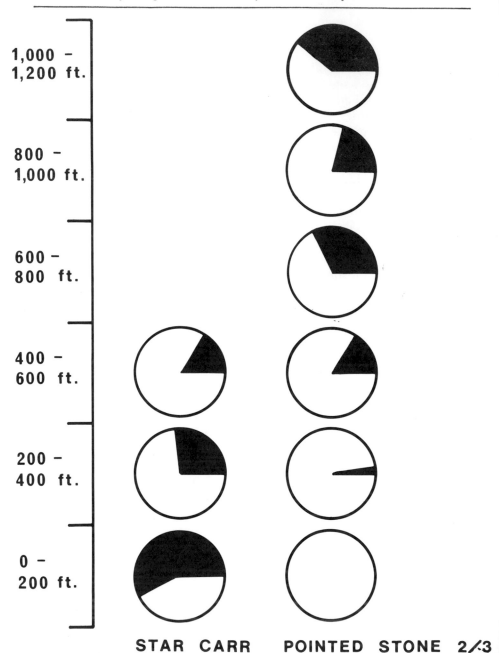

Figure 5. Comparison of the altitudinal ranges exploited (at a 10 km. radius) from Star Carr and Pointed Stone sites 2 and 3.

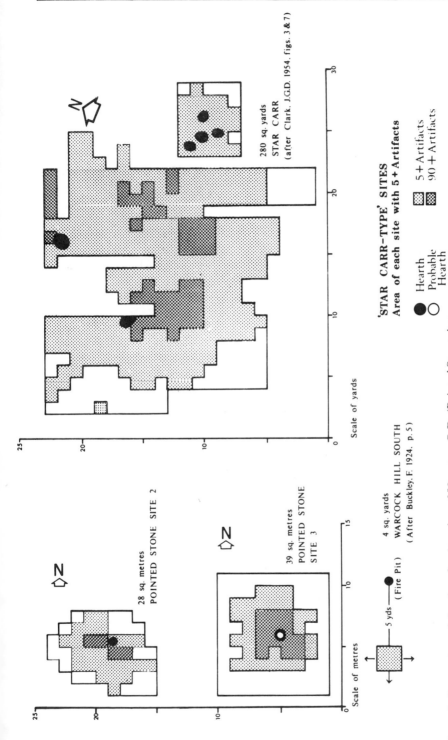

Figure 6. Comparison of site plans for sites above 350 metres O.D. (Pointed Stone sites 2 and 3 and Warcock Hill South site) with Star Carr.

Whether one or even three (conflated) hearths could be represented in this zone is now impossible to determine. The possibility, however, exists that rather than representing a single tent or shelter with a single hearth in the centre (as the breakdown in Figure 6 might suggest), the site could equally well represent a cluster of perhaps three inward-facing shelters. No stakeholes, however, could be identified, and it must be assumed that if shelters are implied these resembled that from Frainslake, Pembrokeshire (Gordon Williams 1926), or that reported by Buckley (1923) from the Later Mesolithic site of Badger Slacks II, which consisted of an oval scatter of 604 flints with a 'scattering of burnt wood' (identified as birch and ling) concentrated at one end (Clark and Rankine 1939: 104).

The plan of site 2 is more complex, and shows no obvious patterning beyond a sharp cut-off in flint to the east and north-east into the direction of prevailing winds. The flint distribution is ambiguous, with a possibility of a pair of clusters, one to the north, the other to the south-west of a patch of reddened clay marking the position of a hearth (Fig. 6).

The areas recorded for these two sites – 28 and 39 square metres respectively – are of course far below that recorded for the excavated portion of Star Carr, some 250 square metres. It must however be immediately admitted that, in attempting to compute the size of the occupying group from the area of flint debris, we cannot (1) recognise whether what has been excavated represents the *inside* contents of the structure or simply a midden deposit associated with hearth(s) outside; or (2) estimate the limits of physical contact tolerable among a group now simply represented by their stone artefacts (Draper 1973). It is thus hazardous to attempt an estimation of the group sizes involved. Certainly inappropriate are calculations based on floor area under roof as attempted by Naroll (1962), Casselbury (1974) or Le Blanc (1971) for multi-family dwellings; it is unrealistic to apply such 'indoor' calculations to groups who must have carried out the majority of their tasks outside. There is again no flexibility in Naroll's constant of 10 square metres per person as applied to villages of 75 and cities of 200,000, and not surprisingly the results obtained fit his predictions badly. If an estimate is demanded, most relevant to our situation may be Weissner's regression of the logarithm of the area of !Kung Bushman camp sites (defined by 'all of the space within a continuous border that encircles huts and major concentrations of bone, charcoal, vegetable remains etc.'), against the logarithm of the camp population (Weissner 1974: 348, Fig. 4). Extrapolation from this regression would suggest a group of 4 people for Pointed Stone site 2 and of 6 people for the rather larger site 3. The ground area, it should be remembered, is arbitrarily defined by flint waste alone. Application of this same regression to the *excavated area* of Star Carr, assuming the whole of this to be in use at any one moment, suggests a group-size of 20-21, an estimate close to that suggested by Clark

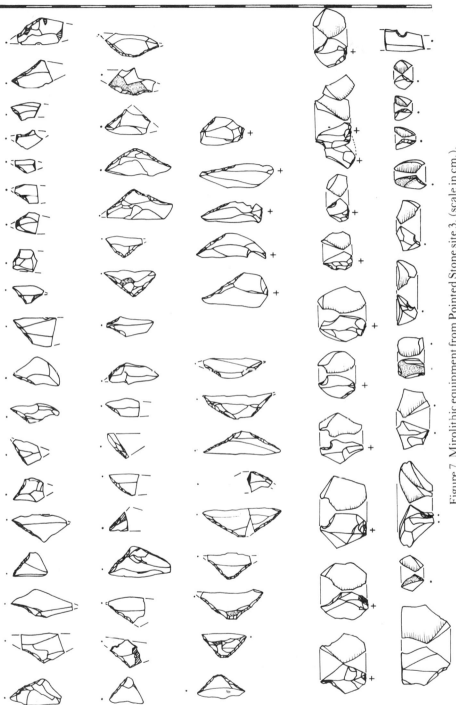

Figure 7. Mirolithic equipment from Pointed Stone site 3. (scale in cm.).

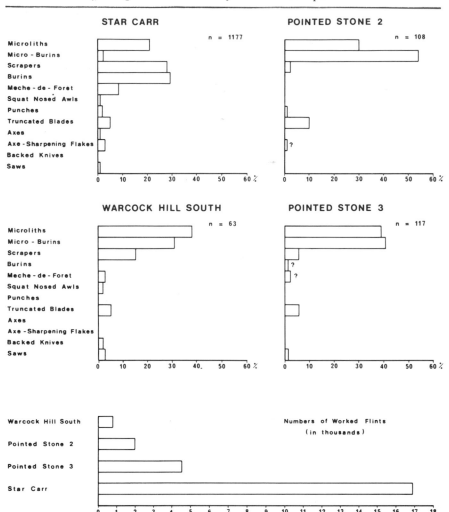

Figure 8. Comparison of tool assemblages from three sites above 350 metres O.D. (Pointed Stone sites 2 and 3, Warcock Hill South Site) with that from Star Carr.

himself. It would, of course, be tempting to interpret Star Carr as the base camp for group hunting at a time when red deer would have been congregated into their yards, perhaps with the use of traps (Noe Nygaard 1973), while the smaller upland sites could represent activity when the animals would be at their most dispersed and wary. To the social aspects of this hunting we shall return at the end of this paper.

In the windswept environment of the North York Moors no charcoal has survived to allow independent dating, and the recognition of a direct relationship between this pair of sites and Star Carr is based entirely upon the close similarities of the microlithic equipment (see Figure 7 for Pointed Stone site 3). The range of short obliquely blunted points, isosceles triangles and trapezes may be compared also with that from Flixton site I (Moore 1950). Identical in the extreme angularity of their outlines, the only difference may be the slightly smaller size of the points from the two upland sites. Even this is scarcely significant, while the most highly idiosyncratic forms are trapezes retouched on all three angles of their backs, immediately linking Star Carr to Pointed Stone site 3 (Clark 1954: Fig. 35, no. 53; our Fig. 7, nos. 37-41). Effectively there is nothing to choose between the four microlith collections.

It is only when one comes to examine the tool kits as a whole and attempt a functional analysis that significant contrasts between the sites become apparent (Fig. 8). While microliths made up only 20 percent of the *finished tools* at Star Carr, at Pointed Stone sites 2 and 3 they make up 60 and 70 percent respectively. In addition, while at Star Carr there were only 27 microburins to 248 microliths – a ratio of 1:9 – on the upland sites this ratio is sharply adjusted to approximately 2:1 and 1.1:1. Thus, at both of the upland sites microliths together with microburins make up the bulk of retouched pieces (80 and 85 percent respectively), while at the comparable Pennine site of Warcock Hill South, their combined contribution is 70 percent – figures to be contrasted with 25 percent at Star Carr. None of the microburins from the upland sites fits any of the (often broken) microliths, which would seem to imply preparation for hunting in the future, the microliths found deriving from broken equipment, being themselves broken or arriving in the carcasses of hunted animals.

Pursuing this observation further, one could stress the low and erratic representation of processing equipment on the sites above 350 metres. None of these sites possess core-axes or unequivocal sharpening flakes; *Mèches de Foret* can be recognised with certainty only from Warcock Hill South site (Radley and Mellars 1964: Fig. 9, nos. 82-3), and there is only a single 'punch' or 'strike-a-light' (cf. Clark 1954: Fig. 44) from Pointed Stone site 2. Scrapers are present on all three sites in relatively low proportions (2-15 percent) while truncated blades (cf. Clark 1954: Fig. 38, nos. 73-9) would appear to represent an ubiquitous element on Mesolithic sites of all ages. Finally, and most significantly, we can record only a *single* possible burin from Pointed Stone site 3. To this unique flint we shall return.

In short, as compared to Star Carr where some 60 percent of retouched pieces are either end scrapers or burins (Fig. 8), the processing of skins at sites above 350 metres appears to have been relatively unimportant, perhaps suggesting that the animals were being hunted before the skins had reached their optimum condition in autumn. Similarly, evidence for the working of bone and antler is either absent or minimal. At Star Carr, on the other hand, the sort of intensive preparation of archery equipment represented so clearly on the upland sites was obviously not a primary activity. Instead, it was the working of skins and, more importantly, antlers, which occupied the group at Star Carr, although simple analysis of the faunal elements present on the site suggests that the animals which provided these resources *had been killed elsewhere*. This last realisation is essential to an understanding of the role played by Star Carr in the annual cycle.

Two general rules apply to butchery practices past and present: (1) the larger the animal the more likely it is to be butchered at the kill-site; and (2) the greater the distance of the kill from the living site, the greater will be the economy in what is transferred back to the living site. To conserve energy, the heavier, non-useful parts, such as the vertebrae, pelvic areas and skull (other than the mandible, antlers and horns) will be discarded on the kill-site. While the fauna from Star Carr is in need of intensive re-study, it is apparent from the statistics presented by Fraser and King (1954) that the distribution of parts is such as to indicate both selectivity in the portions brought to the site (particularly attached antlers) and the intensive fragmentation of meat-bearing and marrow-rich long-bones. Thus there is: (1) a greater representation of lower jaws detached at the ramus either brought onto the site with the tongue, or to be split longitudinally for the marrow, than of the maxillary regions; (2) a scarcity of vertebrae, inferring that the axial muscles. had been cut away and the vertebrae left at the kill site; (3) a higher representation of unworked scapulae than articular ends of humeri, radii, ulnae and metacarpals, suggesting that the forelimbs were cut loose from the trunk and brought onto the site for further cutting and fragmentation to obtain bone grease, while (4) the scarcity of pelvic fragments is again indicative of abandonment at the kill site, though the extreme fragmentation of the attached rear limb-bones (particularly the proximal femora) makes further discussion of the actual butchery difficult. In short, so much of the skeletal material is 'missing' as to suggest within the home range of Star Carr the existence of a series of (1) specialised *hunting sites* with preparation of arrow equipment, precisely as on the upland sites; and (2) *butchery sites* with all the faunal components which are *absent* from Star Carr. Thus, at least two categories of site can already be seen to be missing from the Vale of Pickering.[2]

If the butchery patterns for the post-cranial regions of animals represented at Star Carr are themselves interesting, it is even more illuminating to make a direct comparison of the number of red deer represented by antlers as contrasted to those represented by the post-cranial skeleton. In addition to the 21 stag antler 'frontlets' (all of which had almost certainly been 'worked down' by groove-and-splinter technique prior to the final shaping and lightening processes), there are also present on site the left-hand 'massacred' antlers of a further 29 stags (Fraser and King 1954: 79) – already implying a total kill of at least 50 animals. In addition, there are: a male cranium with a single unshed antler broken above the brow point; a pair of frontlets with 'prickets' (from animals lesss than 1½ years old); two half frontlets, possibly from the same animal, with the pedicels represented by mere outgrowths below the skin (?8 months old); 5 cranial frontals with shed antlers, and two female crania. Cumulatively, this material represents a kill of at least 61 deer.

On the evidence of skeletal parts other than skulls or antlers, a maximum of only 25 deer would appear to be represented on the site. Thus, there are 25 left mandibles, 25 left and right scapulae, 25 right metatarsals and 19 right distal radii – impressively consistent highest scores. Very simply, it could be argued that 60 percent of the 59 stags represented by antler and skull material at Star Carr had been butchered, processed and presumably consumed, on sites away from Star Carr, only the antlers broken out at the pedicels being brought back in 29 cases. Of the 30 male crania/frontals represented, 25 carried antlers, and in 22 of these cases they had developed brow tines.

Of the antlers themselves, 84 percent of those which are sufficiently complete for analysis had developed brow and bez tines and 91 percent brow tines. In many cases, however, potential bez tines had been 'worked away'. It is impossible to age deer simply on the appearance of individual tines (*Pace* Fraser and King 1954: 79-80). Certainly the presence of the bez tine cannot be taken as indicative of an animal in its 'fourth year or over'; in reality, this tine can have appeared by the second year, and its absence from many heads of this, or a greater age, is associated with purely genetic factors, being perhaps the commonest point of variation within the antlers of any deer population (B. Mitchell, personal communication). What the high proportion (91 percent) of brow tines among the unshed antlers (and 96 percent among the *shed* and unshed combined) *does* indicate, is the harvesting of antlers with beams sufficiently well-developed to be capable of producing antler splinters suitable for conversion into barbed points. Thus there appears to be a clear selection against the cropping of the 12-25 cm. long spikes (or 'prickets') characteristic of animals in their second year, i.e. animals with antlers too small for this purpose. Modern experience of autumn hunting in Iowa and Missouri suggests that where cropping is unrestricted, some 55-65 percent of the kill may be made up precisely of animals entering their first or second winter (Elder 1965). It must remain debatable, however, whether the conspicuous under-representation of deer within this age range at Star Carr – if not an artefact of the difficulties in making confident age estimates on highly fragmented bones (Noe-Nygaard 1975) – is a reflection of (1) a deliberate cropping policy which avoids the culling of calves, (2) selectivity in the size of winter antler taken back to the site for industrial purposes, or (3) simply the naturally poor preservation of juvenile bone.

During the summer months, growing antlers will be without value for tool making since they retain their velvet (that is to say, their

M

covering of living skin) until this is killed by increasing values of testosterone in August/September (Goss 1970). The dead antler then becomes more compact, and hence valuable as a raw material through the winter, when falling testosterone values lead to resorbtion of the bone at the base of the old antler and finally to shedding in the following April. It was this shed antler with its maximum compactness which was so particularly sought-after in the later Mesolithic and Neolithic for the manufacture of perforated axes, and in the Neolithic and later periods, picks. We would expect then, in a technology where red deer antler only served as a source for splinters, that burins would be rarest or absent from sites occupied in the summer, and most numerous on sites used at the end of winter. This expectation would appear to be fulfilled.

Thus, precisely as Clark (1972) predicted, the upland sites, which have been interpreted for biological reasons as summer red deer hunting sites (see above), and which showed so positively the renewal of archery equipment, have provided only a *single* possible burin. Moreover, the piece in question was a thin thermal fragment of flint with blows struck down each side from a prepared platform, and might well represent an attempt to produce micro-blades rather than a burin.

By contrast, the occupation at Star Carr, known to have fallen to a minimum during the last four months of winter (January to April), would correlate with the full development and maximum compactness of these antlers. As Clark (1954: 21) has so neatly expressed it: 'Star Carr was a scene of intense activity', with the removal from a total of 104 antlers and frontlets of around 360 splinters for conversion into barbed points (1954: 118). In accordance with this observation is the extremely high percentage of burins represented on the site (almost 30 percent of the retouched tools) which, as Clark has pointed out, were essential for isolating the individual splinters of antlers by means of the groove and splinter technique. In every respect, the stone equipment present on the individual sites, the observed patterns of industrial activity and the seasonal predictions made, correlate exceptionally well. However, certain features of the evidence remain to be discussed.

While the group using Star Carr may have produced 360 splinters of antler, only four such unworked pieces were identified in the original report (Clark 1954: 118-19). Re-examination of the excavated material revealed a *few* more, of which one was almost two feet in length (52.8 cm.), and thus clearly capable of producing a pair of barbed points. Amazingly, there are no half-made points, no splinters in the initial stages of grinding down into an oval section, nor any of the hundreds of minute lozenges to be expected as a by-product of the notching out of the barbs. One must, therefore, wonder whether the points for which these splinters were being prepared were actually manufactured on the site or whether (exactly as on such late-glacial sites as Meiendorf) the reduction of the antlers to splinter form was simply a stage in the reduction of a natural commodity into its most portable form – in other words, blanks for working-up elsewhere, quite possibly later in the summer, when suitable supplies of antler for tool manufacture would not be immediately available. If so, then this must lead to further speculation on their function.

A point to which Clark drew particular attention was the absence of fish bones at Star Carr. Especially noteworthy is the absence of pike which, at the contemporary site of Hohen Viecheln and the later Danish Maglemosian settlements was the subject of specialised fishery – from the ?7th millennium bc onwards by 'trolling' with a bone hook, and concurrently and earlier by spearing. This absence may seem particularly surprising given the clear indications that some at least of the occupations at Star Carr were continued into early summer. Thus, new-born calves of both elk and roe deer must have been taken in May or June (Noe Nygaard 1975), while the fact that all of the roe deer antlers were unshed indicates use of the site from April/May onwards (Fraser and King 1954: 93). Indeed, the consistent presence of unshed roe deer antlers on Danish Maglemosian sites has long been a part of the classic arguments for their summer use. Star Carr could thus have been in use over precisely the months when, after spawning in March/April, pike had begun their period of intensive summer feeding, thus being capable of capture by line fishery or, when sunning themselves in shallows, by spearing. That pike and perch were absent from a settlement occupied so early in the postglacial might be interpreted as a direct function of the distance of Lake Pickering (at the very head of the Hartford and Derwent river systems) from the contemporary freshwater bodies and river systems of mainland western Europe from which these populations must have originated (A. Wheeler, personal communication) – a situation in complete contrast to the lakes of Zealand and north Germany which were in immediate contact with the freshwater Baltic. On the other hand it must be acknowledged that there is at present remarkably little evidence for *any* kind of freshwater fishing in Britain throughout the whole of the Mesolithic period, and it might be argued from this that the absence of fish bones from Star Carr and other inland locations reflects an attitude of conscious economic selectivity with regard to the exploitation of these resources.[3]

With no evidence for fishery and given the high proportion of anciently broken points at Star Carr, their use must surely be associated with the hunting of land mammals – a use already documented by Lubbock (1865: 515-16) for closely similar ethnographic examples collected on the voyages of the *Adventure* and *Beagle* between 1826 and 1836 (Fitzroy 1839: 186-7). Direct support for this interpretation is provided by the discovery of two very similar barbed points in association with a complete elk skeleton at Poultonle-Fylde in west Lancashire (Hallam *et al.* 1973). This find however remains unique, since the barbed points from Skottemarke were unassociated with the elks from the same site, while the tang fragment found with the much later Taaderup elk (Ødum 1920) is not, despite confusion in the literature, obviously from a barbed point.

If the use of these barbed points can be demonstrated from the low lakeside environment of Star Carr and Flixton, there is, for simple reasons of preservation, no direct evidence as to whether they were used also on our upland sites above 400 metres. That the requisite blanks for barbed-point manufacture were not themselves *produced* on these upland sites has, I hope, been adequately demonstrated by both biological and archaeological lines of evidence. But what we *cannot* show is that the blanks, prefabricated from full-grown compacted winter antler elsewhere and reduced to their most portable form, were not being worked up into finished points on these summer sites.

The apparent prominence of flint archery equipment on these upland sites is, we have just suggested, an artefact of preservation, although in the open environment of the Preboreal moors where approach by stealth would be particularly difficult, bows with their greater range and relative silence could be expected to have been preferred to spear heads for the initial 'wounding' stages of the hunt. Shot at *distance*, however, their accuracy and impact would be in all probability erratic. The barbed antler points, on the other hand, are clearly intended to achieve the deepest possible penetration and not (as with the shorter Azilian spear heads) to 'toggle' in the wound and, with a dragging shaft, to impede the prey. The barbs on these antler points resemble finely-polished blades facilitating unimpeded entry, but with minimal retentive properties. Their function – if not projected from traps set along traditional deer paths or preferred wallows (cf. Darling 1969) – may, as with Medieval hunting daggers, have been linked specifically to the final despatch of animals exhausted by the 'blood-letting' arrow-heads employed in the preliminary stages of the hunt and run to ground with dogs. Alternatively they may have served as the equipment of stationary 'posted' marksmen upon whom the game would be driven down – in both cases the points being intended to penetrate the heart or lungs. At this stage in the discussion we are making the assumption to be pursued at the end of the paper that summer hunting on these uplands was carried out by cooperating groups of hunters and *was not an individual activity*.

In the winter months when the herds of elk and red deer, already more tightly concentrated, could be manoeuvered into the natural traps formed by drifting snow or boggy ground, such spear points could be expected to have been used to greater effect at closer range. In late winter the thin ice cover over the shallows of Lake Pickering may have acted as just such a trap, and the recovery of a paddle from Star Carr, as from other continental lake-side sites, may be suggestive of the use of boats in the final *battue*. Such winter herd hunting might frequently lead to an 'overkill' of the type so frequently described for the Canadian buffalo in strictly non-European contexts (Roe 1951). Characteristically in such situations, the bulk of the meat will go unconsumed, only that portion which can be immediately glutted being removed to the actual settlement, together with those parts of the animals which would have had an obvious long-term value as raw materials. Part of the explanation of Star Carr may lie in the processing of the substantial by-products of just such an overkill, carried out while the red deer stags were concentrated within their winter yards.

Relative to other categories of hunting equipment, these north European fine-barbed points have a markedly limited range in time. If we are correct in linking them specifically to the 'kill' stages of group hunting, or the massacre of trapped game, then in both situations, it could be argued, their roles could have been fulfilled equally well by flint-tipped archery equipment. This would be particularly true when in the former case (as so regularly shown in the Spanish rock art: cf. Fig. 10) the game had been brought to lie close to and directly facing the marksmen – their bodies in this position giving the minimal natural obstacle to penetration. In much the same way the effectiveness of bows used at short range with maximum impact on 'trapped' game is shown by the evidence from the late-glacial site of Stellmoor. Given the reality of a choice in this portion of the kill equipment, it is perhaps not surprising to find contemporary and later Mesolithic societies where such specialised antler points are absent, and their roles filled by more simply replicated arrows (see below).

Having discussed in some detail, and contrasted the functional aspects of, the tool kits represented at Star Carr and its upland counterparts, it is instructive to attempt a similar exercise for topographically complementary sites of the Deepcar type, taking the third recently excavated site on the North York Moors as representative of the upland range. This site, Money Howe site I, excavated by Mr and Mrs Taylor in 1975, lies at 340 metres on the south-western end of Bilsdale Moor, 3 km. south-southeast of Pointed Stone. The site consists of a roughly circular scatter of worked flint some 7 metres across, which was completely excavated, its edges being defined all round. Two or possibly three marked concentrations of knapping debris were recognisable, while the liberal distribution of fire-cracked flint over the whole of the central part of the site is suggestive of shifting hearth spots. To the north, a sharp 'cut-off' in the flint distribution is indicative of an artificial boundary. Since recovery is considered total down to 2 mm., the flint work is regarded as the best sample at present available for a site of this type above 300 metres. Its date of 7,480 $\pm$ 390 bc (Q-1560) has already been commented on (Table 1).

Perhaps the most fully documented Early Mesolithic sites of the

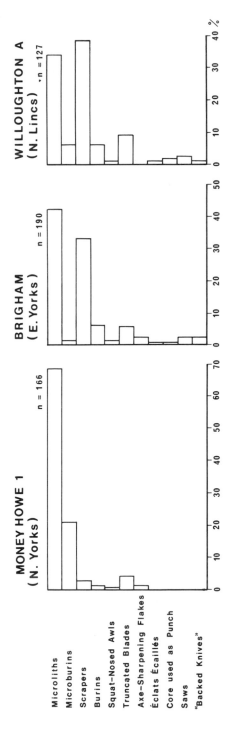

Figure 9. Comparison of tool assemblages from the upland site of Money Howe Site I with those from lowland sites of Brigham (east Yorkshire) and Willoughton site A (north Lincolnshire).

Deepcar type in the lowland areas of northern England are those of Brigham near Driffield (situated at 15 metres O.D. overlooking Brigham Carr: Manby 1966), and Willoughton, near Scunthorpe (situated at 45 metres O.D.: Armstrong 1932). The striking contrast between the material equipment recovered from these sites and that recovered from Money Howe can be seen once again in the much heavier emphasis on hunting equipment at the upland site. Thus microliths comprised 67 percent of the tool-kit at Money Howe as compared to only 42 and 34 percent respectively at the two lowland sites. Of the remaining 33 percent at Money Howe, 21 percent is made up of microburins (Fig. 9). By contrast, not only are microburins far rarer at Brigham and Willoughton but, microliths apart, the commonest retouched shape is the convex scraper: 33 and 39 percent respectively, while at Money Howe these have a value of only 4 percent. In short, precisely as at Star Carr, processing equipment in the form of end scrapers is of enormously increased importance on the lower-lying sites. Truncated blades, nosed awls and burins are common to all three sites. Of particular interest, however, is the much weaker representation of burins at Brigham and Willoughton (reaching a maximum of 8 percent at Brigham) as compared with the remarkably high burin percentage recorded at Star Carr.

Clearly, the last observation calls for comment. It was suggested earlier that sites of Deepcar type show a close resemblance to many of the major Early Mesolithic sites in southern England, including, for example, Kelling, Oakhanger and Thatcham. We possess complete or adequately representative samples of tool kits from 26 such sites. Apart from microliths, scrapers tend to be the most common tool represented, with a consistent suggestion that these are more numerous on lowland than on upland sites. Burins are markedly less common on all of the sites; their maximum value is only 9 percent at Thatcham site III, while at all except six of the sites (of which Brigham is one) frequencies of this tool are below 5 percent. At Star Carr, it would, I think, be generally agreed that there is a direct correlation between the uniquely high proportion of burins and the preparation of antler splinters for the specific purpose of manufacturing barbed points. Examination of all the bone and antler available from sites resembling Thatcham has, however, failed to produce any evidence for the use of barbed points: it has also failed to produce any evidence of groove-and-splinter work.

It is perhaps worthwhile then to summarise precisely what we *do* know of the bone and antler technology of these Thatcham-type sites. There is clear evidence that antler beams were divided into lengths by the classic technique of nibbling through the hard outer wall of the antler and then snapping (see, for example, the detached crowns from Thatcham site II: Wymer 1962: Plate XLVIII lower left). Similarly, tines could be removed by the same process (Wymer 1962: Plate I lower, 3rd from left). Both beams (Wymer 1962: Plate I upper left, Fig. 13, no. 6) and brow tines (Sheridan *et al.* 1967: Fig. II, no. 21) could be converted by bevelling on one or both faces into 'chisels' or, more probably, skin stretchers and smoothers (Deffarges *et al.* 1974). Plain points were made of either bone or antler, the longest (a bone point from Thatcham site III) being 18.3 cm. long. If not produced by *grooving*, the splinters for these points must necessarily have been obtained, as in the much later Obanian sites of Scotland (Clark 1956), by the vertical *splitting* of metapodials or lengths of antler (Wymer 1962: Plate I lower, 4th from left), these being ground or scraped to an oval or rounded section. In the Obanian sites, splinters over 19 cm. in length could be obtained by this method (Clark 1956: Fig. 7c) for use either as limpet scoops or as blanks for harpoon heads. One of the harpoon heads from McArthur's Cave at Oban attains a length of 15.2 cm., while that from Shewalton, Ayrshire (even in its damaged condition) has a length of 19.2 cm. (Lacaille 1939). Thus blanks of sufficient size for the longest of the Thatcham points could have been obtained by vertical splitting, and it is therefore significant that it is possible to recognise suitable vertically, rather than spirally, broken splinters of red deer metapodials from Thatcham, and other early sites of Thatcham type. If these suggestions on the processes involved in the preliminary stages of splinter production are accepted, then we have also an immediate explanation for the scarcity of burins not only on the pair of northern lowland sites which we have considered (Brigham and Willoughton) but also on sites of the Thatcham-type in general. As a corollary to this argument it may be noted that well over half of the burins examined from these sites have working edges far wider than those of the burins at Star Carr and Flixton, and must surely have served as chisels or gouges rather than as grooving tools.

Residential patterns and hunting strategies in the upland Mesolithic

It has long been customary to stress the small size of upland sites such as those discussed above, and to contrast the seeming flimsiness of any associated structures with the more substantial features found on vastly larger sites in lowland Britain. More detailed study, however, reveals not only that equally small *isolated* sites of Early Mesolithic date have been excavated in south-eastern England, but also that analysis of density plots for some at the apparently larger sites – for example, Thatcham sites II and III – shows them to break down into individual clusters of artefacts, frequently associated with hearth spots, each covering only a few square yards. Conversely, not only do separate concentrations of tools and waste similarly cluster on sites above 300 metres – for example, Buckley's excavations at Warcock

Hill North which disclosed four contiguous circular concentrations of material (Radley and Mellars 1964) – but the surface areas of artefact scatters of Later Mesolithic date on both upland sites (for example, Cock Heads, Ecton Moor or White Gill on the Clevelands: Radley 1970) are equivalent in area to the largest lowland surface sites. They likewise represent the conflation of unnumbered residential units.

To be blunt, it is unfortunately impossible to draw conclusions on group size as opposed to specific activities from the excavation of such isolated upland flint scatters. Indeed, it may be emphasised that such scatters rarely, if ever, occur singly, the same Pennine sites which attracted antiquaries to them a century ago still producing, as the peat weathers back, an abundance of new material in fresh locations. On both the Pennines and North York Moors, these sites are significantly clustered on certain ridges, hills, 'edges', valley heads or eminences, each one controlling the maximum possible local view. Significantly, recent work in the Pennines would seem to indicate (Jacobi, Tallis and Mellars 1976) that, during at least the later stages of the Mesolithic, closed tree cover above 360 metres was suppressed by regular burning of the upland vegetation, a suppression which, it might be suggested, represents the deliberate stabilisation of the vegetation patterns of the earlier post-glacial. Such burning of forest or scrub communities can, by providing areas of maximum browse and forage, not only impose a degree of predictability on the movements of ungulate herds, but also lead to an increase in their productivity (Mellars 1976). As Mellars points out, maximum concentrations of animals may be achieved by a patchwork of burning, creating distinct ecotones between open burnt-over ground and undisturbed vegetation which would provide cover. It is notable then that not only do upland sites in northern England cluster at or slightly above 1,200 ft. (365 metres) but many of the sites, particularly on the Pennines, over-look natural basins, reservoirs within which such artificial concentrations of deer, once established, could most successfully be supervised.

Summarised, sites cluster at or slightly above the ecotone between wooded and more open ground, precisely where the maximum aggregations of animals might be expected to form. The sites are so situated also as to take into view the largest areas possible. Away from these concentrations of sites, large areas of the moors are, beyond discoveries of microliths from isolated arrow-shafts (Fig. 3), without evidence of human settlement.

Finally, do we have any evidence relating to the hunting patterns which may have been used over the summer months in such situations? Extrapolating from the small size and often *apparent* isolation of upland flint scatters, there has been a natural tendency to infer a pattern of individual stalking similar to that familiar to us from the Scottish deer 'forests'. Such stalking without dogs is of totally recent origin, the product of more reliable and more accurate rifles –

Figure 10. Scene depicting red deer hunting 'drive' from the Cueva de los Caballos (Spain). After Obermaier and Wernert 1919.

the express rifle of 1865 and the small-bore rifle with nitro-powder of 1894. Even stalking dependent on the strength and wind of hunting dogs is a phenomenon largely of the earlier nineteenth century, and appears to have been first practised no earlier than the middle of the eighteenth century (Millais 1906).

Traditional to Scotland before the nineteenth century and still practised up to 1860 in such large 'forests' as Glen Tilt and Blackmount, was the practice of driving deer to posted rifles, a method of hunting described by Pennant (1771: 98, 1041) for the forests of Atholl and, working from earlier sources, Braemar. It is thus of peculiar significance that the sole *complete* scene of a summer hunt of red deer to survive for us, that from Cueva de los Caballos in eastern Spain (Obermaier and Wernert 1919), shows some twelve hunters, eight acting as beaters driving a herd of twelve deer towards a line of four waiting archers (Fig. 10). All carry bows and both parties have released arrows, the waiting marksmen aiming for the throat and lungs, their arrows penetrating the front of the rib cage. That the hunt is a summer one (i.e. while the herd is still in its summer ranges) can immediately be grasped from the detailed representation of the deer themselves. The animals comprise seven or eight hinds and a pair of fawns, the latter distinguished by their size and spotting. Clearly we have here the depiction of a female herd with its attendant fawns, the latter, when male, staying with their mothers until their second year. Intruding into this group is a carefully depicted male, a twelve pointer. Stags will normally only enter the territory of a female herd in October for the rut, retiring again on completion to their own territories. The month to which the hunt shown at the Cueva de los Caballos refers can thus, it is suggested, be determined with particular accuracy.

In Britain, it is on the high moors, within the deer's summer ranges, that the rut takes place. If we extrapolate from the Spanish evidence, then, far from such summer hunting being the activity of *individuals*, it is potentially that of a dozen men. If then we ask what is the size of the social unit which worked in concert to exploit the herds of the Pennines or North York Moors, it is to such evidence as this scene that we must appeal, since calculations of population from areas of flint waste will, as discussed above, never reveal the common enterprise which linked groups dispersed in apparently unconnected shelters on a hillslope or spaced out on separate vantage points around a grazing area. Further, there is, of course, no reason why the material culture of the participating groups should be identical. We can only work within strict limitations and it is as well to be aware of these. Even if the hunts of Mesolithic northern England had been of the magnitude and complexity of those of the seventeenth century forest of Braemar, it is totally improbable that we could now either appreciate or detect these dimensions.

Acknowledgements

In concluding this paper it should be emphasised once again that the discovery of the Maglemosian sites on the North York Moors is entirely the result of individual survey – in this case that of Mr and Mrs G.V. Taylor. Their work underlines the degree to which pre-Neolithic studies in the British Isles can still rely on private initiative to undertake critical fieldwork, often in highly unattractive environments.

Notes

[1] Possible evidence of an earlier penetration of Scotland (north of 57°N) is provided by the barbed antler point from Glenavon in Banffshire (Lacaille 1954: 184-5). This is clearly the re-utilised fore-part of a once-longer 'fine-barbed' antler point (cf. the re-use of points P63 and P129 at Star Carr) of the type which disappeared from west European contexts around 6,800 bc (Jacobi 1976a). In addition there is the sea-rolled tanged flint point recovered by Mercer from beach gravels at 16.2 metres O.D. at Lussa Wood I, which is demonstrably earlier by an unknown factor than 6,000 bc (see above) and quite possibly of late-glacial age (Mercer 1974: 65-6). A point which must be emphasised, however, is that the patterns of economic exploitation associated with this early penetration of Scotland – and even the species of animal exploited – remain for the present strictly speculative; the earliest direct evidence of any kind for the economic activities of Scottish Mesolithic groups is that provided by the shell-midden accumulations of Morton Tayport in Fifeshire (Coles 1971: 341-50) and the west Scottish 'Obanian' sites (Lacaille 1954: 196-245) dated respectively to the 5th and 4th millennia bc.

[2] It may be suggested that three of the bovids which are represented by substantial portions of the skulls and pelves could have been killed closest to the site. Skulls represent the part of the animal which provides the least amount of usable meat (White 1953) and are therefore most likely to be abandoned at, or close to, the actual location of the kill.

[3] There is at present very little convincing evidence from England for the exploitation of fresh-water fish resources in the Mesolithic – to be precise a pike jaw (dentary) from Dowel Hall Cave, Derbyshire (D. Bramwell, personal communication), while isolated centra from several other sites (for example Thatcham) could as easily have been regurgitated by birds of prey. While, as in the final Mesolithic of Denmark (Andersen 1971) harpoons appear during the 4th millennium bc in northern British coastal and estuarine zones, there is no obvious group of British bone or antler equipment which can be directly compared to the one-to four-barbed bone 'spears' of the later Danish Maglemosian. While the hafting evidence quoted for such spears suggests a variety of functions, it is generally conceded that one of their roles lay in pike fishery. Even, however, when as at Svaerdborg pike were represented by the apparently impressive total of some 64 left lower jaws (Clark 1975: 143) their contribution to the total diet must have been relatively minor – given that some 42 pike (employing a meat weight of some 2.5 kg.; cf. Hohen Viecheln: Schuldt 1961) would be needed to make the same contribution as a red deer stag of Star Carr size (c. 114.5 kg. clean carcase weight, according to Clark 1954: 15, recalculated at 60 percent dead weight). A clear reconsideration of the point at which large scale exploitation of fresh-water resources might be likely to become of significance to economies operating within the environment of a northern Boreal woodland is clearly necessary, particularly in situations where considerable freedom of choice existed as to the precise mechanisms of calorie extraction. Not only is formal evidence for fishery absent from most Mesolithic sites in England, but even where sites are situated in proximity to water sources they are rarely located so as to take the best advantage of fish runs or lake populations.

Interestingly, fish bones are also absent from the coastal middens on the isle of Portland, Dorset (Palmer 1972) and at Westward Ho!, Devon – a sharp contrast to the *deep-water* marine fishing attested for the east Scottish coast (Coles 1971) and the intensive *inshore* fishing of the west coast (Lacaille 1954; Mellars and Payne 1971). Since voyaging clearly lay within the technology of the latter groups (on the islands of Oronsay and Risga) their failure to exploit a potentially extremely rich *deep-water* fishery must again represent conscious economic selectivity.

References

Andersen, S.H. 1971. Ertebøllekulturens Harpuner. *Kuml*: 73-125.

Armstrong, A.L. 1925. Excavations at Mother Grundy's Parlour, Creswell Crags, Derbyshire. *Journal of the Royal Anthropological Institute*, 55: 146-78.

Armstrong, A.L. 1931. A late Upper Aurignacian station in north Lincolnshire. *Proceedings of the Prehistoric Society of East Anglia*, 6: 335-9.

Armstrong, A.L. 1932. North of England notes: Upper Palaeolithic and Mesolithic stations in north Lincolnshire. *Proceedings of the Prehistoric Society of East Anglia*, 7: 130.

Birks, H.J.B. and Saarnisto, M. 1975. Isopollen maps and principal component analysis of Finnish pollen data for 4,000, 6,000 and 8,000 years ago. *Boreas*, 4: 77-96.

Buckland, P.C. and Dolby, M.J. 1973. Mesolithic and later material from Miserton Carr, Notts.: an interim report. *Transactions of the Thoroton Society*, 77: 5-33.

Buckley, F. 1923. In the *Oldham Chronicle*, 15th December, 1923.

Buckley, F. 1924. *A Microlithic Industry of the Pennine Chain*. Marsden, privately printed.

Buckley, F. 1925. The microlithic industries of Northumberland. *Archaeologia Aeliana*, 4th series, 1: 42-7.

Burleigh, R., Hewson, A. and Meeks, N. 1976. British Museum natural radiocarbon measurements VIII. *Radiocarbon*, 18: 16-42.

Campbell, J.B. 1969. Excavations at Creswell Crags. *Derbyshire Archaeological Journal*, 89: 47-57.

Casselbury, S.E. 1974. Further refinement of formulae for defining population from floor area. *World Archaeology*, 6: 117-22.

Churchill, D.M. 1962. The stratigraphy of the Mesolithic sites III and V at Thatcham, Berkshire, England. *Proceedings of the Prehistoric Society*, 28: 362-70.

Clark, J.G.D. 1932. *The Mesolithic Age in Britain*, London, Cambridge University Press.

Clark, J.G.D. 1954. *Excavations at Star Carr*. London, Cambridge University Press.

Clark, J.G.D. 1956. Notes on the Obanian, with special reference to antler and bone work. *Proceedings of the Society of Antiquaries of Scotland*, 89: 91-106.

Clark, J.G.D. 1972. *Star Carr: A Case Study in Bio-archaeology*. Addison Wesley Modular Publications, 10, Reading (Massachussetts).

Clark, J.G.D. 1975. *The Earlier Stone Age Settlement of Scandinavia*. London, Cambridge University Press.

Clark, J.G.D. and Rankine, W.F. 1939. Excavations at Farnham, Surrey (1937-38). The Horsham culture and the question of Mesolithic dwellings. *Proceedings of the Prehistoric Society*, 5: 61-118.

Coles, J.M. 1971. The early settlement of Scotland: excavations at Morton, Fife. *Proceedings of the Prehistoric Society*, 37: 284-366.

Coupland, G. 1925. A microlithic industry, Durham. *Proceedings of the Prehistoric Society of East Anglia*, 5: 62-4.

Darby, H.C. 1952. *The Domesday Geography of Eastern England*. London, Cambridge University Press (3rd edition).

Darling, F.F. 1969. *A Herd of Red Deer*. London, Oxford University Press.

Deffarges, R., Laurent, P. and Sonneville-Bordes, D. de. 1974. Ciseaux ou lissoirs magdaléniens. *Bulletin de la Société Préhistorique Française*, 71: 85-96.

Degerbøl, M. 1961. On a find of a pre-Boreal domestic dog (*Canis familiaris L.*) from Star Carr, Yorkshire, with remarks on the other Mesolithic dogs. *Proceedings of the Prehistoric Society*, 27: 35-65.

Draper, P. 1973. Crowding among hunter/gatherers: the !Kung bushmen. *Science*, 182: 301-3.

Dudley, H. 1949. *Early Days in North-West Lincolnshire*. Scunthorpe, W.H. and C.H. Coldicott.

Elder, W.H. 1965. Primeval deer hunting pressures revealed by remains from American Indian middens. *Journal of Wildlife Management*, 29: 366-70.

Fitzroy, R. 1839. *Narrative of the surveying Voyages of His Majesty's Ships Adventure and Beagle between the years 1826 and 1836* ..., Vol. 2. London, Henry Colburn.

Fraser, F.C. and King, J.E. 1954. Faunal remains. In J.G.D. Clark, *Star Carr*, London, Cambridge University Press: 70-95.

Freeman, L.G. 1973. The significance of mammalian faunas from Paleolithic occupations in Cantabrian Spain. *American Antiquity*, 38: 3-44.

Garrod, D.A.E. 1926. *The Upper Palaeolithic Age in Britain*, Oxford, Clarendon Press.

Goddard, A.A. 1971. *Studies of the Vegetational Changes associated with the Initiation of Blanket Peat Accumulation in North-East Ireland*. Unpublished Ph.D. thesis, the Queen's University, Belfast.

Godwin, H. 1940. Pollen analysis and forest history of England and Wales. *New Phytologist*, 39: 370-400.

Godwin, H., Walker, D. and Willis, E.H. 1957. Radiocarbon dating and postglacial vegetational history: Scaleby Moss. *Proceedings of the Royal Society*, Series B, 147: 352-66.

Gordon Williams, J.P. 1926. The Nab Head chipping floor. *Archaeologia Cambrensis*, 81: 86-110.

Goss, R.J. 1970. Problems of antlerogenesis. *Clinical Orthopaedics*, 69: 227-38.

Hallam, J.S., Edwards, B.J.N., Barnes, B. and Stuart, A.J. 1973. The remains of a late-glacial elk associated with barbed points from High Furlong, near Blackpool, Lancashire. *Proceedings of the Prehistoric Society*, 39: 100-28.

Hibbert, F.A., Switsur, V.R. and West, R.G. 1971. Radiocarbon datings of Flandrian pollen zones at red Moss, Lancashire, *Proceedings of the Royal Society*, Series B, 177: 161-76.

Jacobi, R.M. 1976a. Britain inside and outside Mesolithic Europe. *Proceedings of the Prehistoric Society*, 42: 67-84.

Jacobi, R.M. 1976b. Population and landscape in Mesolithic lowland Britain. In *The Effect of Man on the Landscape: The Lowland Zone*. Council for British Archaeology Research Report (in press).

Jacobi, R.M., Tallis, J.H. and Mellars, P.A. 1976. The southern Pennine Mesolithic and the ecological record. *Journal of Archaeological Science*, 3: 307-20.

Lacaille, A.D. 1939. A barbed point of deer antler from Shewalton, Ayrshire. *Proceedings of the Society of Antiquaries of Scotland*, 73: 48-50.

Lacaille, A.D. 1954. *The Stone Age in Scotland*. London, Oxford University Press, for the Wellcome Historical Medical Museum.

Le Blanc, S. 1971. An addition to Naroll's suggested floor area and settlement population relationship. *American Antiquity*, 36: 210-11.

Lubbock, Sir J. 1865. *Prehistoric Times*. London, Bell and Daldy.

Manby, T.G. 1966. A Creswellian site at Brigham, east Yorkshire. *Antiquaries Journal*, 46: 211-28.

Mellars, P.A. 1969. Radiocarbon dates for a new Creswellian site. *Antiquity*, 43: 308-10.

Mellars, P.A. 1974. The Palaeolithic and Mesolithic. In C. Renfrew (ed.), *British Prehistory: a New Outline*. London, Duckworth: 41-99.

Mellars, P.A. 1976. Fire ecology, animal populations and Man: a study of some ecological relationships in prehistory. *Proceedings of the Prehistoric Society*, 42: 15-45.

Mellars, P.A. and Payne, S. 1971. Excavation of two Mesolithic shell middens on the island of Oronsay (Inner Hebrides). *Nature*, 231: 397-8.

Mercer, J. 1974. New C-14 dates from the isle of Jura, Argyll. *Antiquity*, 48: 65-6.

Mercer, R.J. 1970. Metal arrowheads in the European Bronze and early Iron Ages. *Proceedings of the Prehistoric Society*, 36: 171-213.

Millais, J.G. 1906. *The Mammals of Great Britain and Ireland*, Vol. 3. London, Longmans, Green and Co. Ltd.

Moore, J.W. 1950. Mesolithic sites in the neighbourhood of Flixton, north-east Yorkshire. *Proceedings of the Prehistoric Society*, 16: 101-8.

Moore, J.W. 1954. Excavations at Flixton Site 2. In J.G.D. Clark, *Star Carr*, London, Cambridge University Press: 192-4.

Naroll, R. 1962. Floor area and settlement population. *American Antiquity*, 27: 210-11.

Noe-Nygaard, N. 1973. The Vig Bull: new information on the final hunt. *Bulletin of the Geological Society of Denmark*, 22: 244-8.

Noe-Nygaard, N. 1975. Two shoulder blades with healed lesions from Star Carr. *Proceedings of the Prehistoric Society*, 41: 10-16.

Obermaier, H. and Wernert, P. 1919. *Las Pinturas Rupestres del Barranco de Vall torta (Castellón)*. Madrid, Museo Nacional de Ciencias Naturales.

Ødum, 1920. Et elsdyrfund fra taaderup paa falster. *Danmarks Geologiske Undersogelse*, 4 Raekke, 1: 3-10.

Osborne, P.J. 1971. The insect faunas of the organic deposits within the Wandle Gravels. *Proceedings and Transactions of the Croydon Natural History and Science Society Ltd.*, 14: 162-75.

Palmer, S. 1972. Excavations at the Culverwell Mesolithic site, Portland, 1971. *Proceedings of the Dorset Natural History and Archaeological Society*, 93: 132.

Pennant, T. 1771. *A Tour of Scotland, 1769*. Chester, John Monk.

Petersson, M. 1951. Microlithen als Pfeilspitzen. Ein fund aus dem Lilla-Loshult Moor: Ksp. Loshult, Skåne. *Meddelanden fran Lunds Universitets Historiska Museum*, 123-37.

Radley, J. 1970. The Mesolithic period in north-east Yorkshire. *Yorkshire Archaeological Journal*, 42: 314-27.

Radley, J. and Marshall, G. 1965. Maglemosian sites in the Pennines. *Yorkshire Archaeological Journal*, 41: 394-402.

Radley, J. and Mellars, P.A. 1964. A Mesolithic structure at Deepcar, Yorkshire, England, and the affinities of its associated flint industries. *Proceedings of the Prehistoric Society*, 30: 1-24.

Radley, J., Switsur, V.R. and Tallis, J.H. 1974. The excavation of three 'Narrow Blade' Mesolithic sites in the southern Pennines, England. *Proceedings of the Prehistoric Society*, 40: 1-19.

Rankine, W.F. 1951. Artefacts of Portland chert in southern England. *Proceedings of the Prehistoric Society*, 17: 93-4.

Rankine, W.F. 1961. *A Mesolithic Flaking Floor at Oakhanger, Selborne, Hants: Epitomized Supplement to the Abstract of the Report Published in the Proceedings of the Prehistoric Society 1960*. Privately circulated, 4pp.

Roe, F.G. 1951. *The North American Buffalo: A Critical Study of the Species in its Wild State*. Toronto, University Press.

Schuldt, E. 1961. Hohen Viecheln, ein Mittel Steinzeitliche Wohnplatz in Mecklenburg. *Deutsche Akademie der Wissenschaftenzu Berlin Schriften der Sektion für Vor-und Frühgeschichte*, 105.

Seagrief, S.C. 1959. Pollen diagrams from southern England: Wareham, Dorset and Nursling, Hampshire. *New Phytologist*, 58: 316-25.

Seagrief, S.C. and Godwin, H. 1960. Pollen diagrams from southern England: Elstead, Surrey. *New Phytologist*, 59: 84-91.

Sheridan, R., Sheridan, D. and Hassell, P. 1967. Rescue excavation of a Mesolithic site at Greenham Dairy Farm, Newbury, 1963. *Transactions of the Newbury and District Field Club*, 11: 66-73.

Smith, L.T. (ed.) 1909. *The Itinerary of John Leland in or about the Years 1535-1543*. London, George Bell and Sons.

Spencer, A. 1953. Preliminary report on archaeological investigations near Radcliffe, Lancashire. *Transactions of the Lancashire and Cheshire Archaeological Society*, 62: 196-200.

Switsur, V.R. and Jacobi, R.M. 1975. Radiocarbon dates for the Pennine Mesolithic. *Nature*, 256: 32-4.

Thompson, D.F. 1939. The seasonal factor in human culture, illustrated from the life of a contemporary nomadic group. *Proceedings of the Prehistoric Society*, 5: 209-21.

Thompson, D.F. 1949. *Economic Structure and the Ceremonial Exchange Cycle in Arnhem Land*. Melbourne, MacMillan and Co.

Tinsley, H.M. and Smith, R.T. 1974. Surface pollen studies across a woodland/heath transition and their application to the interpretation of pollen diagrams. *New Phytologist*, 73: 574-66.

Wainwright, G.J. 1960. Three microlithic industries from south-west England and their affinities. *Proceedings of the Prehistoric Society*, 26: 193-201.

Warren, S.H., Clark, J.G.D., Godwin, H., Godwin, M.E. and MacFadyen, W.A. 1934. An early Mesolithic site at Broxbourne sealed under Boreal peat. *Journal of the Royal Anthropological Institute*, 64: 101-28.

White, G.F. 1971. *Excavation of the Dead Man's Cave, North Anston*, Worksop, Borough

Library and Museum.

White, T.E. 1953. Observations on the butchering technique of some aboriginal peoples. *American Antiquity*, 19: 160-4.

Wiessner, P. 1974. A functional estimator of population from floor area. *American Antiquity*, 39: 343-50.

Wymer, J.J. 1962. Excavations at the Maglemosian sites at Thatcham, Berkshire, England. *Proceedings of the Prehistoric Society*, 28: 329-54.

13

The chronology and economy of the Irish Mesolithic: some working hypotheses

Peter C. Woodman

Ireland has the distinction of being one of the few parts of Europe which is not known to have been inhabited during the Palaeolithic. While occasionally some evidence has been found which is claimed to indicate the presence of Man in Ireland at this date, little has yet been found that would confirm these indications of an Irish Palaeolithic. The best documented discovery would appear to be the Palaeolithic flake from the Boyne Valley recently described by Mitchell and Sieveking (1972), but for the present this remains an isolated find.

Equally significant is the lack of any industries in Ireland which can be compared to the Early Mesolithic, or 'Maglemosian', assemblages of the British mainland. Inferences based on negative evidence must always be treated with caution, but research has so far failed to reveal any collections of microliths which can be compared to the distinctive 'Broad Blade' microlithic forms recovered from a number of sites in England dated to the 8th millennium bc (see Jacobi, this volume). The earliest clear indications of the presence of Man in Ireland are provided by a series of radiocarbon dates recently obtained for a Mesolithic occupation site at Mount Sandel, County Derry (Table 1, Fig. 1). The dates range between 7,010 and 6,490 bc and were obtained on samples of hazel-nut shells removed from various features on the site, including hearths associated with one of the structures recovered. The industry from the site may indicate that at the time of the first occupation at Mount Sandel Man had already been present in Ireland for a small but significant length of time, since a number of distinctively local characteristics had already appeared in certain groups of implement types.[1]

On the basis of radiocarbon determinations obtained over the past five years it is now clear that the Mesolithic occupation of Ireland can be divided into two principal stages, of which the industry recovered from Mount Sandel can be regarded as typical of the earlier phase. The later phase is best represented by the succession of industries recovered in the course of recent excavations at the site of Newferry (County Antrim) in the Bann Valley (Woodman 1977).

Table 1. Radiocarbon dates for Irish Mesolithic sites. All the dates are uncalibrated (in years bc) and based on the conventional half-life of 5,568 years.

Site	Material	Lab. No.	Date bc
Mount Sandel (Upper Site)	Hazel-nut shells	UB-952	7,010 ± 70
Mount Sandel (Upper Site)	Hazel-nut shells	UB-951	6,840 ± 185
Mount Sandel (Upper Site)	Hazel-nut shells	UB-912	6,775 ± 115
Mount Sandel (Upper Site)	Hazel-nut shells	UB-913	6,605 ± 70
Mount Sandel (Upper Site)	Hazel-nut shells	UB-2008	6,490 ± 65
Mount Sandel (Lower Site)	Charcoal	UB-532	6,520 ± 200
Cushendun (Lower Lagoon silts)	Charcoal	I-5134	5,720 ± 140
Cushendun (Lower Lagoon silts)	Wood	UB-689	5,445 ± 65
Toome	Charcoal	Y-95	5,730 ± 110
Newferry Site 3 : zone 9	Wood	UB-487	6,240 ± 120
zone 9	Organic mud	UB-888	6,225 ± 145
zone 8	Wood	UB-641	5,680 ± 195
zone 7(M)	Charcoal	UB-496	5,535 ± 115
zone 7(M)	Charcoal	UB-517	5,240 ± 110
zone 7(M)	Charcoal	UB-887	5,030 ± 115
zone 7(M)	Charcoal	UB-516	5,005 ± 60
zone 7(M)	Charcoal	UB-886	4,965 ± 60
zone 7(M)	Charcoal	UB-636	6,945 ± 125
zone 7(U)	Charcoal	UB-885	5,125 ± 125
zone 6	Charcoal	UB-514	5,195 ± 105
zone 6	Charcoal	UB-890	4,640 ± 60
zone 5	Charcoal	UB-505	4,655 ± 170
zone 5	Charcoal	UB-653	4,490 ± 185
zone 4	Charcoal	UB-490	4,265 ± 100
zone 3	Charcoal	UB-630	3,755 ± 90
zone 3	Charcoal	UB-489	3,465 ± 95
Rockmarshall (Midden I)	Charcoal	I-5323	3,520 ± 110
Derravarragh	Charcoal	I-4234	3,410 ± 110
Dalkey Island Site V	Charcoal	D-38	3,350 ± 170
Newferry Site 4	Charcoal	D-34	3,340 ± 170
Sutton (hearth under midden)	Charcoal	I-5067	3,300 ± 110

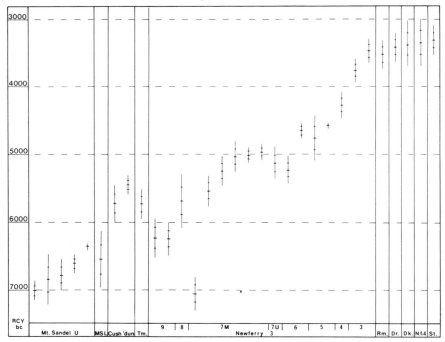

Figure 1. Distribution of available radiocarbon dates for the Irish Mesolithic. Abbreviated site names are as follows: MS(L) – Mount Sandel Lower site; Tm. – Toome; Rm. Rockmarshall; Dr. – Derravaragh, Dk. – Dalkey; Nf. – Newferry site 4; St. – Sutton. The actual dates for these sites are given in Table 1.

Detailed accounts of both of these sites are given below, but it may be noted at the outset that one of the most striking points of contrast between the earlier and later stages of the Mesolithic lies in the almost total lack of typical microlithic forms in the later Mesolithic assemblages. The problems associated with this transition from the earlier to the later Mesolithic will be discussed in a later section of the paper.

Early Mesolithic occupation

Sites which can be attributed with certainty to the earlier phase of the Irish Mesolithic are still rather limited (Fig. 2), although this undoubtedly reflects to some extent the inadequacies of previous field work. Perhaps the major problem in this connection has been the lack of awareness among collectors of the need to collect material from discrete sites which could be re-located later. Most Irish collectors relied heavily on the purchase of their specimens from travelling tinkers or, in the case of the Bann Valley, from diatomite cutters. The situation has been further complicated by the tendency of many workers to attribute a *Neolithic* date to discoveries of microliths, and

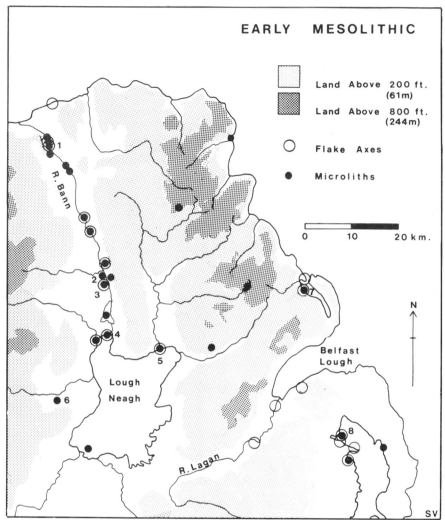

Figure 2. Distribution map of Early Mesolithic sites in Ireland. The numbered sites are as follows: 1 Mount Sandel; 2 Glenone; 3 Culbane; 4 Maddens; 5 River Maine/Lough Neagh; 6 Tullywigan; 7 Glynn; 8 Rough Island.

indeed to deny the existence of any form of true Mesolithic occupation in Ireland! When these factors are combined with the low chances of recovery from heavy plough soils, river beds and raised beach deposits, it is perhaps not surprising that so little is known about this aspect of the Irish Mesolithic.

Apart from the material recovered from the recent excavations at Mount Sandel, the most instructive assemblage of early Mesolithic material derives from a surface site at Glenone in the Bann Valley. A further, small collection of microliths was found during the excavation of a late Neolithic occupation site at Tullywiggan, County Tyrone (N.

Bamford and C.S. Briggs, personal communication) but the remainder of the early Mesolithic material derives to a large extent from geologically disturbed contexts. For example, groups of material have been recovered from the shores of Lough Neagh at the mouth of the river Maine and at the Maddens site, Toome. Similarly, on the coast there is material in large quantities from a disturbed context at Glynn, where numerous Mesolithic axes were recovered, but where few microliths had survived. Further south in the Strangford Lough area there are occasional signs of the presence of these early Mesolithic industries, but the quantities of material are often rather small – as for example at Ardmillan.

The excavations at Mount Sandel

In the present state of evidence our knowledge of the early Mesolithic occupation of Ireland must inevitably depend very heavily on the material recovered from the recent excavations at Mount Sandel, County Derry. Over the past few years excavations have been carried out at two separate sites in the Mount Sandel area, referred to respectively as the 'lower' and 'upper' sites. The excavations at the lower site were commenced by Mr A.E.P. Collins of the Historic Monuments Branch of the Department of the Environment and are still continuing. This site has recently been dated by radiocarbon to 6,520 ± 200 bc (UB-532). The excavations of the upper site were begun by the writer in 1973. As already noted, this site has now been dated by five C14 determinations ranging from 7,010 to 6,490 bc (Table 1).

The excavations of the upper site at Mount Sandel are still in progress, and therefore many of the details given here should be regarded as provisional. The site is located in a commanding position on top of a 30-metre high bluff overlooking the river Bann. There would seem to have been numerous occupations of the site in the early Mesolithic, but in many areas the traces of these events have been partially destroyed by extensive ploughing. The best-preserved area of the site occupies a natural depression in the ground which appears to have been artificially enlarged during Mesolithic times. This depression was filled with Mesolithic occupation soil, beneath which were found well preserved traces of several huts. The archaeological material was found in the pits, post holes and hearths of these huts, as well as in the overlying occupation soil, and in a number of partially preserved features around the margins of the hollow.

Essentially, the assemblage from Mount Sandel represents a narrow bladed industry which is made on flint imported from several miles away. The blades would seem to have been removed from the cores with a controlled indirect percussion technique. Their mean length is only 4.3 cm. Over 1,000 of these small blades were recovered from a small area of occupation soil, perhaps suggesting that some may have been used as parts of composite implements without further alteration. The major retouched tool forms are as follows (Fig. 3):

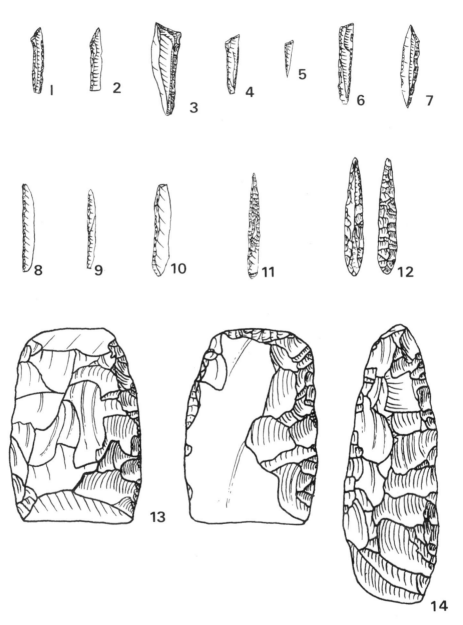

Figure 3. Early Mesolithic flint implements from Mount Sandel. 1 – 12 microliths; 13 flake axe; 14 core axe.

Microliths

These are by far the most common type of implement found on the site. During the first season alone almost 700 were recovered. As there are so few large assemblages of microliths from Ireland it has been decided to keep to a relatively simple microlith typology for the moment.

Scalene triangles. These represent the dominant microlith type at Mount Sandel, although their relative frequency varies in different parts of the site. In the occupation soil they are present in considerable numbers but do not dominate the range of microlithic shapes, while in certain pits they are almost the only form present. The usual form of triangle is rather elongated and narrow as shown in Figure 3: 6 while small examples such as Figure 3: 5 are rare. Pieces recovered from different features appear to differ in the extent of retouching on the leading edge. One common characteristic is a concave short edge.

Rods. In Ireland this term has been confined to microliths with retouch along a single edge (Fig. 3: 8-10). These vary between rather broad forms (which might be described as 'backed blades' rather than microliths) and exceptionally narrow forms, very steeply trimmed, with retouch from both dorsal and ventral surfaces. They are particularly common in the occupation soil.

Points. These are perhaps the most distinctive type of microlith found in Ireland. The normal form is made on a blade trimmed to a point with the usual abrupt retouch, but with the addition of a certain amount of surface retouch on the ventral surface. Normally this retouch is confined to the tip and base (Fig. 3: 11), but occasionally forms with more extensive surface retouch have been found (Fig. 3: 12). There is no evidence that these types are in any way later than the other forms on the site.

Other forms. All other types of microliths are rare. A small number of 'non-geometric' points from the site should probably be regarded as unfinished triangles. Certain of the more distinctive 'geometric' forms which have been reported from other areas of Britain (such as rhomboids, trapezoids and isosceles triangles) are unknown at Mount Sandel and other sites in Ireland.

Axes

Two types of axe are found at this site. The most common type is the small face-trimmed core axe. All are trimmed to a narrow cutting edge, while some are shaped to a pointed butt (Fig. 3: 14). The other form is the flake axe which is made from a large flake and has a broad, rather splayed cutting edge (Fig. 3: 13). The edge is formed from the original edge of the flake, and would appear to reflect some kind of deliberate prepared-core technique (Woodman, forthcoming). In general terms the flake axes in Ireland resemble those from Ertebølle sites in Denmark, although there is of course a significant difference in date. Functionally, these tools would seem to represent adzes, and were presumably intended for rather different purposes from the more narrow-edged core axes.

Micro-awls

These are usually rather small examples, not unlike those found in the Early Mesolithic of Britain at sites such as Star Carr and Flixton site I (Clark 1954: Fig. 39). Some are made with simple dorsal retouch down the whole length of both lateral edges, while others are trimmed alternately.

Scrapers

During the first season of excavation at Mount Sandel (upper site) only five typical scrapers were recovered, although 15 axes and more than 600 microliths were found. Some of the scrapers would seem to be made on blades or blade fragments.

Burins

No burins have so far been recovered from either the upper or lower site at Mount Sandel.

Perhaps the most striking feature which emerges from this study of the Mount Sandel industry is that despite the relatively early date assigned to it by radiocarbon, the industry already reveals features which serve to distinguish it very clearly from any of the industries so far known from other parts of Britain. Probably the most distinctive industrial element is the flake axe which appears to be completely unknown on the mainland areas of Britain. The microlithic needle points would also appear to represent a distinctively local element, although possible examples of this type have been found on one site in southern England (R.M. Jacobi, personal communication). If we assume that the population responsible for the Mount Sandel industry reached Northern Ireland via the mainland areas of Britain, we must therefore presumably allow for a certain length of time for these local features to develop. But of course this proposition raises even more interesting problems, since the overall affinities of the Mount Sandel industry are clearly with the later Mesolithic, 'Narrow Blade' industries of Britain, for which the earliest available radiocarbon dates (c. 6,600-6,800 bc) are closely comparable to those for the Mount Sandel site itself. Certainly there is no reason to see any contact at this stage with Scotland (which shows the closest geographical connections with Northern Ireland) where the industries dated to the 7th millennium bc would seem to be dominated by large trapezes and isosceles triangles (Mercer 1974). At the same time, however, there are certain elements in the Irish assemblages (most notably the core axes and micro-awls) for which the closest parallels can be found in the earlier Mesolithic 'Maglemosian' industries of Britain. Hence the whole question of the origins of the earliest Mesolithic industries in Ireland presents a number of interesting problems which are difficult at present to resolve.

Despite the limitations of field work, there are a number of other sites in Ireland which have produced assemblages essentially similar to that described above (Fig. 2). The industry from the lower site at Mount Sandel differs from that recovered from the upper site in a rather higher proportion of flake axes (apparently more 'evolved' in type) and an apparent absence of the more leaf-shaped microlithic forms. At Tullywiggan there were at least 12 elongated triangles along with some fragments with slightly invasive retouch; as no other

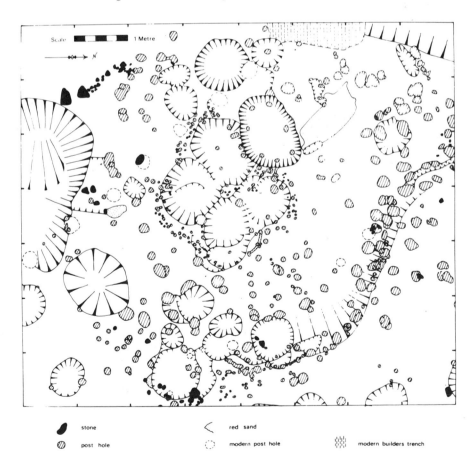

Figure 4. Plan of Mesolithic hut at Mount Sandel (Upper Site).

implements were present on the site, this might represent a hunters' camp at which several composite implements were left (H. Bamford and C.S. Briggs, personal communication). With the exception of the Glenone assemblage, which has the same types of microliths and axes as Mount Sandel, the remainder of the material belonging to this phase of the Mesolithic has been collected in circumstances in which the scarcity of microliths could be attributed as easily to collecting bias as to a genuine absence of these forms. The only notable fact which emerges from the assemblages recovered from sites such as Maddens and the River Maine is that at both sites axes were associated with a number of flake scrapers and, at Maddens, with a few micro-awls and burins. Since burins have also been found in certain other early Mesolithic contexts, this suggests that their absence at Mount Sandel might well be related to the specific function of that site. Numerous other stray finds of microliths have been made, particularly at sites in the Bann Valley. These include numerous examples of microlithic points, which are somewhat larger than the forms found at Mount Sandel.

The structures at Mount Sandel

Perhaps the most important feature revealed by the Mount Sandel excavations was the existence of a series of well preserved structural features on the site. The presence of the artificially-enlarged hollow which preserved these features has already been mentioned. As can be seen from Figure 4, this area was found to contain an exceptionally large number of post-holes, some of which were over 20 cm. deep. Some of these, particularly along the south-eastern edge of the hollow, were sloping inwards at a slight angle from the vertical. Some were cut away by hearths in the centre of this area, while another hearth cuts across post-holes associated with the same huts, suggesting that there had been extensive re-occupation of the site and that the huts preserved in the hollow were only a small part of a long series which were built on the site (Fig. 5).

In spite of the apparently random scatter of post-holes shown in Figure 4 it was possible by following the arrangement of the post-holes on the eastern lip of the hollow to suggest that at least one of the huts had been built with its edge around the rim of the hollow. To the north, this arc of post-holes was interrupted by other arcs cutting across it, but from the areas where the post-holes were best preserved it is possible to suggest that the huts were built with large structural posts driven into the ground, and that the spaces between them were filled in with smaller stakes. Even allowing for differential preservation, there is no doubt that the walls of the huts were more substantial on the northern and eastern edges, as the post-holes in that area would seem to have been placed quite close together.

Figure 5. Vertical photograph of Mesolithic hut and associated features at Mount Sandel (Upper Site).

Unfortunately, a large portion of the southern edge of the huts was destroyed by a massive tree root hole. In the centre of the hollow was a group of four large hearths, and to the north-west of the hearths and partially cutting across one was a pit over 60 cm. deep. Another pit of slightly smaller size lies to the west of the group of hearths. In addition, there are numerous smaller pits within this hollow, as well as a number of outlying hearths around its eastern and western edge. The hearths are distinguished by being relatively broad (one metre or more in diameter) and rather shallow. Some have a line of burnt earth around their edge. Besides containing layers of occupation soil, some of these features also contain layers rich in burnt hazel-nut shells, and often in association with the hazel-nut layers were lenses of light-coloured soil which contained large numbers of burnt bone fragments. This array of features could be interpreted in the following manner. If the arc of post-holes referred to above is taken to represent the edge of one hut, then the most easterly of the four hearths would seem to be the central hearth of that hut. There is no evidence that any of the post-holes inside that arc represent structural posts intended to support the roof of the same hut. Instead, these may well represent the edges of other huts which in turn relate to other hearths in the central group. Of course, there is no reason to assume that the cutting of a new hearth automatically implies the building of a new structure, so that the presence of four hearths should not necessarily be taken to imply the construction of four separate huts within the hollow.

The other pits on the site belong to separate phases of occupation when the huts were presumably built elsewhere. These pits consist of large, deep hollows which most probably represent storage pits, together with a large number of smaller pits usually less than 50 cm. in diameter. It can be assumed that these were dug outside the huts rather than within them.

The occurrence of faunal remains in several of these features is clearly of particular importance, and great care was taken to ensure as complete recovery of this faunal material as possible. The bone-rich layers were removed as bulk samples and sieved carefully under laboratory conditions through mesh sizes of 1.5 and 0.85 mm. (All other material from features and occupation features and occupation soil was wet-sieved on site through a 3 mm. mesh.) As a result of this careful sieving large numbers of identifiable bones have been recovered which are at present being studied by M. Van Wyjngaarden Bakker of the Van Giffin Institute, Amsterdam. She reports that amongst the bones are substantial numbers of phalangeal bones of young pig. Bones of hare (*Lepus* sp.) are also present, whilst remains of red deer appear to be rare. Besides mammal bones there are exceptionally large numbers of fish bones on the site, although the diagnostic fragments are usually only the vertebrae. Bird bones, including at least one species of duck, have also been identified. As the excavation has not yet been completed, and the sieving process is rather time-consuming, it will be some time before a definitive list of the faunal remains is available. However, certain significant features are already apparent. As noted above, fish bones are exceptionally common, and pig would appear to have played a more important role in the diet than red deer. As the fauna consists of material taken from numerous features belonging to different stages of occupation of the site, the picture presented by the fauna is a general one rather than the result of one single short occupation of the site. So far it has not been possible to relate either the presence or absence of fauna or the particular types of fauna represented to any specific type of feature; this suggests (as one might expect) that the filling of the various features is a secondary phenomenon which does not relate directly to the original functions for which the features themselves were intended.

The final problem posed by this site concerns the total duration of the Mesolithic occupation and the season, or seasons, of the year when this occupation took place. The occurrence of abundant remains of hazel-nut shells on the site would suggest that the site was occupied at least by the late autumn months, while several other features (notably the size of the huts, the presence of storage pits and the location of the site well above the winter season floodwaters of the river Bann) may indicate that the site served as a winter-season base camp. The question of the total duration of the occupation is more difficult to answer, but the range of the radiocarbon determinations would suggest that the occupation spanned a period of several hundred years. Whether or not there were any major gaps within this period of occupation is of course much more difficult to assess.

The transition from the earlier to the later Mesolithic

On the basis of the existing radiocarbon determinations from Mount Sandel and Newferry there would appear to be a gap in the chronological sequence of material in the Irish Mesolithic (Table 1, Fig. 1). The occupation of the former site would appear to have come to an end around 6,500 bc, while the occupation sequence at the latter site commences around 5,500 bc. There is a single date of $5,730 \pm 110$ bc for the site of Toome, but the associated archaeological material is too sparse to provide any reliable indication of the character of the industry involved. There is therefore a gap of nearly a millennium between the material from Mount Sandel on the one hand and that from the lower lagoon silts at Cushendun or zone 8 at Newferry on the other.

Within the rather limited assemblages belonging to the early Mesolithic it is not possible to detect any clear typological development, and it is therefore difficult to assess the total duration of the early narrow blade industries in Ireland. The later Mesolithic industries are represented by a series of rather specialised localised implement types which will be described in more detail below. When it was thought that these two industrial traditions might be contemporaneous (Woodman 1974a) the possibility of some kind of 'functional' differentiation between the two industries was examined. As most of the material seemed to come from similar locations, and both groups were found on both coastal and inland sites, it was felt that this was not a reasonable explanation. The recent radiocarbon dates for the Mount Sandel site offer a much more straightforward explanation of these technological differences in terms of a simple chronological succession.

The arguments advanced in an earlier publication in favour of a chronological overlap between the earlier, Mount Sandel-type material and the so-called 'Larnian' or 'heavy bladed' Mesolithic were based primarily on a number of sites where the former type of material had been found in deposits which were approximately contemporary with the maximum of the postglacial marine

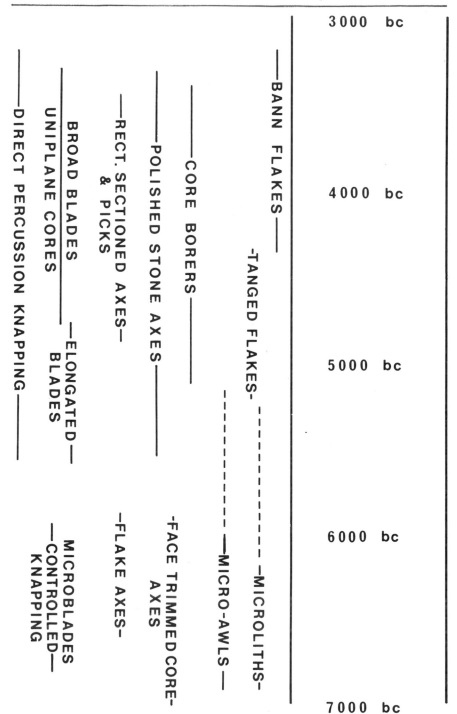

Figure 6. Chronological distribution of implement types and flaking techniques in the Irish Mesolithic.

transgression (Woodman 1974b). However, although these deposits are late, the material in them – being derived – could be considerably earlier in date. Certainly in the Bann Valley, where material can be found in undisturbed geological contexts, there is nothing in a late context which resembles the early Mesolithic microblade industries from Mount Sandel. The only other feature which might be used to argue for a late date for the narrow blade industries is the presence of the flake axe, which is typologically rather similar to the flake axes of the continental Ertebølle and Campignian cultures, both dated to the 4th millennium bc. However, other elements found in the latter cultures are not present in Ireland, and at the moment it would seem preferable to accept the radiocarbon dates as indicating that the Mount Sandel-type industries predate the 'heavy bladed' Mesolithic, and that the Irish flake axe developed independently from those on the continent.

Later Mesolithic occupation

The later Mesolithic industries of Ireland are those which have been referred to as 'Larnian' by Movius (1953). While this term will be retained as having some meaning in a technological sense (see below) it will be abandoned as a general descriptive term for the Irish Mesolithic. Both the range of implement types and the way in which they are made can be used to distinguish between the earlier and later Mesolithic industries in Ireland. The earlier industries were produced with a controlled knapping technique, probably with the aid of a punch. (There is no evidence that the striking platforms of the blades in these early industries was prepared in the fashion needed to use pressure: cf. Semenov 1964; Crabtree 1968). The use of this technique is reflected not only in the small size of the blades produced, but also in the occurrence of very small striking platforms – usually less than 2 mm. deep. In the later industries, on the other hand, the striking platforms can have a depth ranging from less than 2 mm. to over 12 mm., while the mean depth of the platform is usually between 7 and 8 mm. This would seem to be the result of a change from a controlled flaking technique to a method of direct percussion, in which the size of the striking platform would be much more difficult to control. The change in the technique of flint knapping can be paralleled by an increase in the size of the blades produced and, apparently, by the disappearance of microliths.

The major problem in understanding how and why this transition took place is posed by the lack of industries from the critical intervening period between c. 6,500 and 5,500 bc. Certainly, by the time of the earliest occupation at Newferry the industries would appear to have passed any transitional stage. Mitchell (1976) has suggested that the change may reflect the arrival of a new population in Ireland, but as will be seen from a description of the implement types which characterise the later Mesolithic, this interpretation presents a number of problems. The distinctive implement types of the later Mesolithic – or at least the particular forms which they take – are in fact peculiar to Ireland, and are accordingly difficult to interpret as intrusive elements into the Irish succession.

The earliest assemblages of later Mesolithic material at present available are those from the lower lagoon silts at Cushendun (Movius 1940) and from zone 8 at Newferry, County Antrim. At the latter site new excavations have yielded a series of large blades produced by direct, uncontrolled percussion in deposits dated to around 5,500 bc (Table 1). At the former site similar material was found in deposits which could be dated to some point after 5,500 bc and which were sealed by deposits dated to around 5,000 bc. Newferry zone 8 also produced a number of implements, including blades trimmed at the butt and a polished stone axe. All we can say at the moment, therefore, is that the major distinguishing features of the later Mesolithic industries would seem to have evolved some time before 5,000 bc.

A detailed sequence of these later Mesolithic industries was recovered during excavations by the writer at the Newferry site (referred to here as 'site 3'). This site is adjacent to the site excavated by Smith and Collins (1971) and on the opposite side of the river to the original Newferry site excavated by the Harvard expedition in the 1930s (Movius 1936). The site consists of a sequence of occupation levels resting on a series of sand banks in the middle of the flood plain of the river Bann, where it flowed out of Lough Beg. This location has inevitably resulted in considerable disturbance of the occupation horizons caused at least in part by annual fluctuations in the river level. The only way in which the occupation material could be divided into meaningful groups was to subdivide the sequence on the basis of changes in the geology of the site, and to accept that the material in each of the zones might include material derived from several discrete occupations (Fig. 7). While there was some trace of human activity in the lowest of the zones (zone 9) the first significant concentration of archaeological material was that referred to above in zone 8. Occupation continued until after the end of zone 3, which would seem to date from some time after 3,500 bc (cf. Table 1; Figs. 1 and 8). The only substantial traces of structural remains were found in zone 7, where stones and wood had been thrown down to stabilize the lip of the sand bank. Occasional traces of hearths and pits were recorded in other levels, but these were rare. The lower occupation levels (zones 7-5) consisted either of occupation horizons on top of sand banks, or of silts which had accumulated around their edges. During this period the level of the river was rising, so that the deposits were gradually accumulating at a higher level. However another type of deposit began to accumulate in the Bann Valley during this period, which

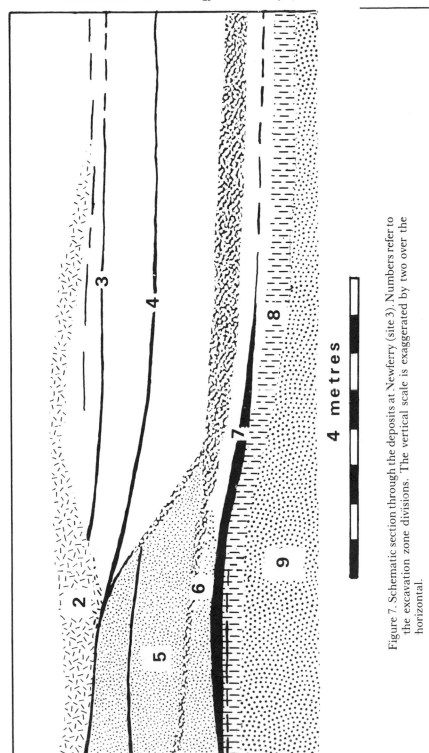

Figure 7. Schematic section through the deposits at Newferry (site 3). Numbers refer to the excavation zone divisions. The vertical scale is exaggerated by two over the horizontal.

N

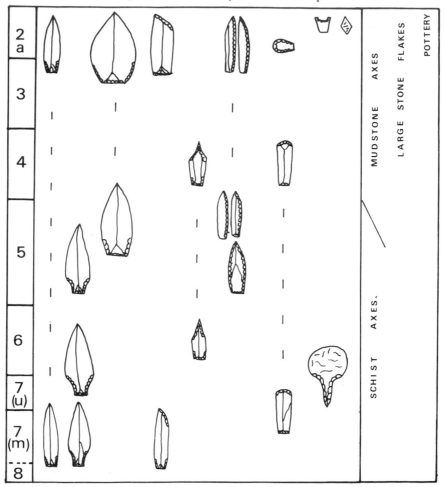

Figure 8. Schematic sequence of major implement types at Newferry.

eventually began to inundate many parts of the flood plain. This is diatomite, or *Kieselguhr*, which was probably formed during the winter floods when the shells of diatoms were washed up onto the edges of the flood plains. These deposits gradually accumulated around the sand banks and eventually buried them some time in the 4th millennium bc. Therefore the later part of the Newferry sequence in zones 4 and 3 represents a period of gradually deteriorating conditions as the tops of the sand banks were progressively inundated, turning the area from one of braided streams into a wide diatomite flat. Finally, an erosion channel was formed which cut through the top of these deposits, removing traces of the final level of occupation in which both Mesolithic and Neolithic artefacts (including pottery) were present. Unfortunately, this event cannot be accurately dated.

Perhaps the most significant feature revealed by this excavation was that the type of industry found during the Harvard excavations at

Newferry (Movius 1936) represents only the *final* phase of a long series of industries which extend over a period of approximately 2,000 years. Since this is the only sequence of material from the later part of the Irish Mesolithic which can be independently dated, it must inevitably provide the primary basis for comparison with other sites. Space does not permit a detailed discussion of the Newferry succession, but the major features of this sequence are summarised in Figure 8. No hard lines have been drawn between the zones, and the dates given in Table 1 and Figure 1 can provide only a general time calibration for this succession; clearly, too much reliance should not be placed on any individual date. Similarly, it must be remembered that implements could have been washed into later zones, and so no hard and fast divisions can be used to indicate points of typological change within the Newferry sequence.

Within this sequence, the first major concentration of archaeological material was recovered from zone 7, which can be dated to around 5,000 bc. Here there is some evidence that the working of flint was being carried out on the site itself – a feature which is apparently lacking from other zones on the site. The industry recovered from this level is characterised by numerous narrow, elongated blades which exhibit the large, direct-percussion platform typical of the later Mesolithic.

The range of implements found in this and all of the other zones at Newferry differs completely from that found at Mount Sandel. The only possible point of overlap is provided by a single micro-awl and one questionable microlith recovered from zone 7. The most common implement type is the butt-trimmed flake, which shows only minor changes throughout the Newferry sequence (Fig. 9). In zone 7 these vary from rather narrow, laminar forms with little restriction of the butt to forms with very definitely restricted or tanged butts. Other forms include rather broad, single-edged backed knives and distally-trimmed forms which usually have oblique retouch across the distal end. The latter type may also be trimmed at the butt. This group, including the fragmentary forms, usually accounts for more than 50 percent of the total number of implements in any zone. Other flint implements are remarkably rare. Apart from a small number of scrapers and burins, the only other flint implement type of any consequence is the large, crude, notched spokeshave.

Turning to the heavier equipment, there are only two flakes from the site which can be identified (apparently) as coming from flint axes. By contrast there are large numbers of polished stone axes. For the most part these are relatively small, few being more than 15 cm. in length. In general they are made from chlorite schist or mudstone and show little sign of having been flaked into shape. Most of them were probably made from pebbles of approximately the right shape which were simply ground into axes. Two types can be recognised: those with symmetrically placed cutting edges which can probably be

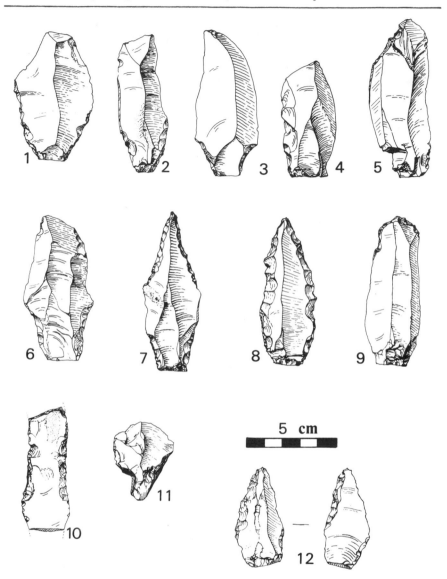

Figure 9. Implements from zone 5 at Newferry. 1, 2 simple butt-trimmed forms; 3
    tanged flake; 4 backed knife; 5, 6 distally-trimmed forms; 7, 8 blade points; 9 blade
    scraper; 10 heavily worked blade; 11 flint axe manufacturing flake; 12 bar form.

regarded as axes in the true sense, and others with assymetric edges
which should probably be regarded as adzes. The other notable group
of stone implements are the polishing or grinding stones, made from
carboniferous sandstone.

As can be seen from Figure 8, the same general range of implement
types is found throughout the Newferry sequence. There are some
minor alterations at various points, but there is no point at which a
major change can be said to have taken place. For example, there is

some variation in different levels in the extent to which some of the butt-trimmed forms are constricted. But this may reflect nothing more than an attempt to maintain the same width of butt applied to blades of varying dimensions; thus an increase in blade width necessitates an increase in butt constriction. In the upper part of the sequence these constricted forms are replaced by rather broader-butted forms which may have served the same purpose but which would have been hafted in a slightly different manner. These gradually evolve into the types which can be found at the end of the Mesolithic sequence – as, for example, at the site on the other side of the Bann river excavated by the Harvard expedition (Movius 1936). The narrow laminar forms and the other types would appear to exist at all points in the sequence with very little alteration. Similarly, the burins, where they occur, tend to be crude angle forms, while most of the scrapers are made from blades.

One of the few marked changes which can be detected within the sequence is the appearance of what are referred to here as 'blade points' and 'bar' forms. The former type appears in zone 6 and persists through to zone 3. These are large blades or flakes which have been trimmed at the distal end to a reasonably strong point. The 'bar' forms appear in zone 5 and similarly occur throughout the rest of the sequence (Fig. 9: 12). They are made by trimming both lateral edges of a flake along their total length; this retouch leaves a slightly irregular edge, and usually a rather poor, weak point.

There are certain other minor changes in the way the implements were made but these do not seem to have any functional importance. Two examples of this are the change in the upper part of the sequence to axes made of baked mudstone or shale, and the appearance of large flakes of chert and other poorly silicified rock.

As stated earlier, all of these changes, both stylistic and functional, would seem to take place at different points in the sequence, suggesting that we are dealing with a relatively stable population.

Clearly, one of the major questions which must be considered in relation to the Newferry succession is how far this sequence can be regarded as truly representative of the later Mesolithic in Ireland. The main problem in attempting to test this is of course posed by the scarcity of comparable collections of well dated material. However, while it is impossible to create a totally independent sequence of material which can be used to parallel the Newferry sequence, there is sufficient evidence available to suggest that the latter site is in fact reasonably representative of this period.

The first aspect of the Newferry succession which can be paralleled elsewhere is the method of blade production. In the upper part of the Newferry sequence it is possible to detect a shift from an elongated, laminar-type of industry to an industry characterised by rather broader blades. Material from the lower gravels at Cushenden (Movius 1940), besides having a narrow blade element, also has a

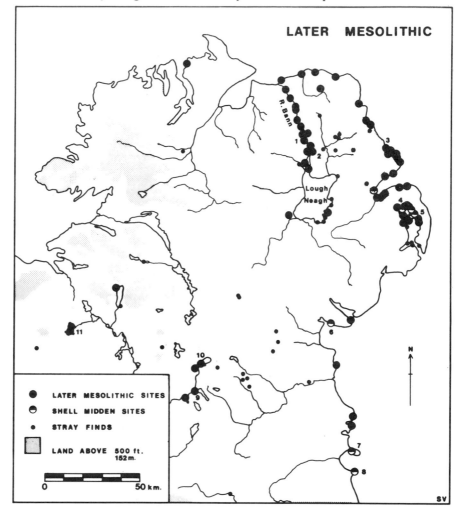

Figure 10. Distribution map of later Mesolithic sites in Ireland. The numbered sites are
as follows: 1 Culbane; 2 Newferry; 3 Larne; 4 Rough Island; 5 Goldsmith's; 6
Rockmarshall; 7 Sutton; 8 Dalkey Island; 9 Lough Derravarragh; 10 Lough
Kinale; 11 Lough G'ara.

heavy but elongated laminar industry in layers sealed below late
Boreal silts – i.e. dating from before 5,000 bc. A similar industry has
also been found just below the high water mark at Sydenham, near
Belfast (Fig. 12: 6), a site which must similarly have been inhabited
prior to about 5,000 bc. At the other end of the chronological scale
there is material from post-Maximum Transgression contexts (i.e.
after 3,500 bc: Woodman 1974b) such as Sutton, County Dublin,
where the blades are significantly broader. At the Curran Point,
Larne, in contexts which predate the Maximum Transgression but
which are not particularly early, there is a flake/blade industry
associated with flat, uniplane cores (Fig. 11: Woodman 1974b). It

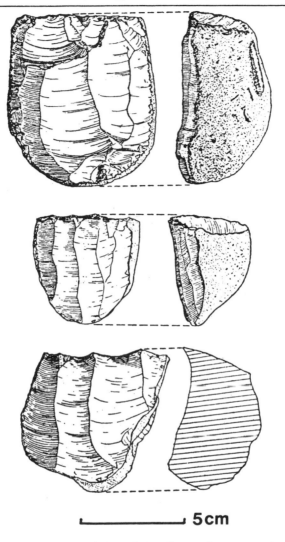

5cm

Figure 11. Uniplane cores from Curran Point, Larne, County Antrim. After Movius (1953).

would seem to be this change to a flat uniplane core which brings about the change to the broader type of flake/blade industry. This can also be seen in the Lough Beg hoard (Parker 1938; also Woodman, forthcoming). Here, flat uniplane cores were reconstructed by joining together blades from a cache of 158 artefacts found during peat cutting. These were associated with a number of end-of-blade scrapers. In the writer's opinion, it would be best to restrict the term 'Larnian' to this particular method of flint working – that is, to industries which have predominantly single platformed cores, tending to be worked on a single plane and which use direct percussion technique. The best examples of this technique are in fact to be found at the site of Curran Point, Larne, which served as the original type-site for the 'Larnian culture' (Movius 1953).

The disappearance of tanged forms from the latest stages of the Mesolithic can be confirmed by their absence in the various sites on the Leinster coast – for example, Rockmarshall, Sutton and Dalkey. Some of these sites can be dated to the transition between the Mesolithic and Neolithic, but the equipment is essentially the same as that found in the uppermost levels of the Newferry sequence. Unfortunately, there is little evidence apart from Newferry itself to confirm the age of the various tanged and 'constricted' implement types. The only clear indication is provided by material from Toome (Whelan 1930), where a cache of flakes with rather restricted butts was found under 1.5 metres of diatomite, strongly suggesting that these forms predate the typical, broader-butted 'Bann Flake' types which were found in the *upper* part of the diatomite around Toome.

It is even more difficult to corroborate the dating of the ground stone axes, as there is at present no way of distinguishing between Mesolithic and Neolithic examples of this type (though it should be pointed out that there is no evidence that Tievebulliagh was being exploited as a source of raw material in the Mesolithic). Among other types which may belong in a late Mesolithic context are the large numbers of heavy flint core axes and picks recovered from Larne Lough. These appear to come from the same contexts as numerous stray finds of later Mesolithic material and are almost certainly of the same date. In the upper part of zone 7 at Newferry was found an example of a heavy-duty boring tool of the type which has been found in apparent association with later Mesolithic material at various surface sites in Ireland. Bar forms and points which have been recovered as stray finds in the Bann Valley would appear to have a very specific function as they are not found in large numbers elsewhere. Other simple forms such as blade scrapers cannot be distinguished from earlier or later specimens on an individual basis.

There is, therefore, sufficient evidence to show that the sequence of implement types recorded at Newferry can probably be accepted as generally representative of the later stages of the Irish Mesolithic. However, the question of 'functional variability' – both between sites and between regions – will require more excavation to replace the evidence from the rather poor and often selectively-collected surface collections. The other major problem concerns the question of assigning functions to the different implement types. For example, the 'Bann Flake' and other butt-trimmed forms have often been regarded as tips for spears, but in view of the fact that the distally-trimmed forms are worked in the same fashion, the existence of butt trimming can only be considered as a method of hafting, and not as a reliable indicator of function. There is reason to believe that many of these implements could have served several functions. Similarly, many of the blades in the Lough Beg hoard show signs of use without any indication of trimming into formal implement types. Indeed, there are many groups of Late Mesolithic material in Ireland where there are no apparent 'implements' in the traditional archaeological sense.

Finally, there are a number of other small groups of material which would seem to belong to this phase of the Irish Mesolithic. Several fragments of bone points were found in zone 5 at Newferry. These suggest that some of the bone points found by Whelan (1952) might well be Mesolithic. Elongated pebbles were found in several zones during the recent Newferry excavations and also in the adjacent site excavated by Smith and Collins (1971). Similar elongated pebbles have been recovered from coastal sites, along with bevelled forms often referred to as 'limpet scoops'. The smaller type of 'limpet scoop' found in the Scottish 'Obanian' sites does not, however, occur in Ireland. Finally, although no really typical examples were found at Newferry, it is possible that Mahr's so-called 'salmon clubs' could belong to this period. But of course, this should not be taken to imply that the whole of Mahr's (1937) 'Riverford Culture' can be assigned to the Mesolithic!

Typologically, the Irish Mesolithic can be seen as a period in which little apparent contact existed between Ireland and Britain – including, rather surprisingly, western Scotland. At its beginning the Irish Mesolithic did not differ significantly from that in the rest of Europe, but after this initial period of colonisation there is little evidence of any contact. Even the west Scottish Obanian, with its distinctive *éclats écaillés* forms, cannot be paralleled in Ireland.

Site distribution

This aspect of the Mesolithic can be examined at various levels. As can be seen from Figures 2 and 10, the known distribution of Mesolithic sites is rather limited. How far does this reflect the true extent of colonisation of Ireland in the Mesolithic, and how far does it reflect a bias caused by uneven collecting?

Certainly, the concentration of material in the north east of Ireland must be attributed at least in part to the large numbers of collectors in this area, but collectors in turn are commonest where the material is available. In the northern Midlands, where there is a scatter of sites, the collectors have tended to concentrate on the crannogs and other later aspects of archaeology; but even so, from the few inadvertent discoveries made, we may suggest that an extensive series of sites exists in this area. To the south, the almost complete absence of material away from the Leinster coast suggests that Mesolithic occupation may have been very slight. The most enigmatic area is that which lies between the north Midlands and the north-east of Ireland. There is no material from Lough Erne in spite of the fact that there were many collectors of antiquities on the crannogs in the lakes, where

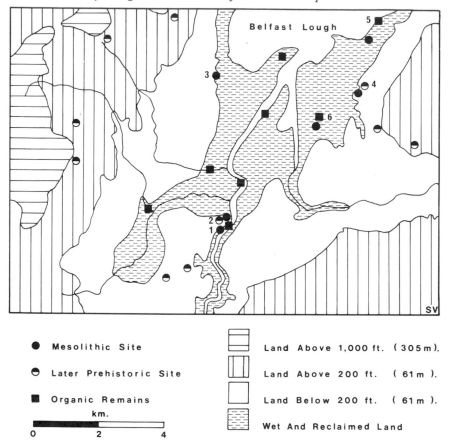

● Mesolithic Site	▢ Land Above 1,000 ft. (305m).
◐ Later Prehistoric Site	▥ Land Above 200 ft. (61m).
■ Organic Remains	▢ Land Below 200 ft. (61m).
km.	▤ Wet And Reclaimed Land

0   2   4

Figure 12. Mesolithic and later prehistoric sites in the Belfast area. The numbered sites are as follows: 1 Ormeau Bridge; 2 North Sports Ground; 3 Ringans Point; 4 Knockagoney; 5 Kinnegar; 6 Sydenham.

Mesolithic material might be expected to occur. The Blackwater Valley is another empty area, yet this provides the obvious route from the Midlands northwards to the Bann Valley.[2]

The fact that two early Mesolithic sites have been found by excavation in the south-western portion of the Lough Neagh area suggests that there may be a more extensive area of settlement in the early Mesolithic than is indicated by the present maps. So far all the southern material belongs to the later Mesolithic, and nearly all of that to the final stages of the Mesolithic. The use of various rock types which are not immediately available in the Newferry area indicates that even in the later Mesolithic settlement may have extended over a considerably larger area than is indicated in Figure 10. Flint would have to be brought either from the Antrim coast or from the closer flint sources on the western edges of Lough Neagh. Carboniferous sandstones (used for polishing stones) are available in an area further to the south or west of Lough Neagh, while the festooned chert and mudstone flakes would have to come from either the same areas, parts of Fermanagh, or the Carboniferous deposits in the Midlands. These areas could also provide the sources for the mudstone used for manufacturing axes. Since this material appears at Newferry in zone 4 (i.e. before 4,000 bc) it is possible that Mesolithic communities had penetrated into the Midlands long before the end of the later Mesolithic. Unfortunately there are at present no assemblages from the Midlands that can be shown to be earlier than the latest phases of the Mesolithic, although there are occasional finds which could possibly be early.

The significance of the distribution pattern of sites within the north-east has already been considered elsewhere (Woodman 1974a). A significant feature in this region is the lack of any evidence for extensive Mesolithic occupation in the upland areas. This can be seen from the distribution of sites and finds in Figure 10. As there were numerous collectors in the Belfast and mid-Antrim areas who found later prehistoric material on the uplands, the absence of Mesolithic material from these areas cannot be due simply to a lack of investigation.

Within the areas where Mesolithic material is relatively common, certain types of location would seem to have been preferred. Along the coast many of the sites are located on offshore islands where middens are often preserved (for example Dalkey and Rough Island) or on river estuaries where the human groups could have taken advantage of several juxtaposed environments. Inland, the main concentration of material is along the course of the river Bann. Here, material is not quite so easily available as is traditionally supposed. Although large quantities can be found at several different locations, there are large areas of diatomite flats where very little can be found. There are two main types of sites in the Bann Valley. The first type is similar to those in the Newferry area where the sites would seem to be associated with sand ridges in the centre of the valley. The other type of site is often in the areas of modern eel fisheries or salmon leaps, and is associated with an area of higher ground at a point where the valley narrows. The general distribution of sites in Ireland is typified by that found in the Belfast area (Fig. 12). Later prehistoric sites can be found in both low-lying situations close to the river Lagan and up as far as the 1,000 ft. (305 m.) contour. By contrast, no Mesolithic material has been found in the uplands, and similarly no organic remains have been found away from the areas covered by marine deposits. Sites number 1 and 2 on the map (the Ormeau Bridge and North Sports Ground sites) and site 6 (Sydenham) are located on river estuaries. Sites 3 and 4 (Ringnans Point and Knocknagoney respectively) are situated on bluffs overlooking the washing limit of the Maximum Transgression, while site 5 (Kinnegar) is a typical raised beach site. One of the factors which controls the distribution of sites in the coastal area is of course the high sea level of the Maximum Transgression. In north-east Antrim this rises as high as 36 ft. (11 m.) above Irish Ordnance Datum and possibly dates from slightly earlier than the beaches in the Dublin Bay area which are only 20 ft. (6 m.) I.O.D. (Synge and Stephens 1966). On present evidence it would seem that the beaches in the latter area can be dated to before 3,000 bc (Woodman 1974b), while around the north-east coast of Ireland there would appear to have been a high sea level – prior to the maximum transgression itself – from before 4,000 bc. As a result, there is a tendency to find mostly late sites around the coast, and it must be assumed that many early sites have been either submerged or destroyed by the rising sea. The pattern of site distribution shown in Figure 12 is therefore partially a product of this high sea level. Where sites are placed on islands, it should be remembered that this maximum sea level must have reduced considerably the size of the island, and similarly that certain sites which are located on coastal drumlins would have appeared as islands during later Mesolithic times.

The economy of the Irish Mesolithic

When considering the question of food procurement in the Irish Mesolithic, we should remember that there were certain factors which conditioned or limited the choice of economic strategies. Perhaps the most important stems from the fact that Ireland had already become separated from Britain by the time of the first Mesolithic occupation. Indeed, there is at present no really convincing evidence for any kind of postglacial land-bridge between Britain and Ireland.

Prior (1966) has noted that there are higher strandlines on the east coast of Antrim than there are inside the line of the latest ice-sheets of the Armoy ice (Line D in Synge 1970), which suggested to him that even in pollen zone 1 the sea had penetrated from the south up the Irish Sea basin. To postulate the existence of a later land-bridge would necessitate the withdrawal of the sea from the Irish Sea basin at a time when, according to Donner (1970), there was comparatively little drop in the eustatic sea level. It is just possible that a slight drop in eustatic sea level combined with a possible isostatic raising of land in the south may have allowed the formation of a short-lived southern land-bridge, or at least some form of partial land-bridge. However, this is more likely to have been a late-glacial feature dating from zone II at the latest, rather than a postglacial phenomenon. Certainly there is no evidence for any form of postglacial land-bridge in the north.

The early insulation of Ireland inevitably served as an obstacle to the immigration of both plants and animals, and as a result of this the fauna and flora of Ireland is rather restricted. Savage (1966) has pointed out that the number of mammalian species which are native to Ireland is extremely limited. Ungulates such as wild cattle, elk and roe deer are not represented amongst the native fauna of the island.

Table 2. Faunal remains from Irish Mesolithic sites.

Mammals	Mount Sandel	Newferry	Cushendun	Ormeau Bridge	Sydenham	Sutton	Rockmarshall	Dalkey II	Dalkey V
Red deer	x	—	—	x	x	x	—	—	—
Pig	xx	—	x	—	x	xx	—	x	xx
Wolf or fox	—	—	—	—	—	x	x	—	—
Bear	—	—	—	—	—	—	—	x	x
Hare	x	—	—	—	—	x	—	—	—
Unspecific	—	x	—	—	—	—	—	—	—
Domesticated forms	—	—	—	—	—	—	x?	x	xx
Birds									
Auks	—	--	—	—	—	x	—	x	—
White-tailed eagle	—	—	—	—	—	—	—	x	—
Goshawk	—	—	—	—	—	—	—	x	—
Blackbird	—	—	—	—	—	—	—	x	x
Duck	x	—	—	—	—	—	—	—	x
Freshwater fish									
Eels	—	x	—	—	—	—	—	—	—
Unspecific	xxx	x	—	—	—	—	—	—	—
Sea fish									
Unspecific	—	—	x	—	—	x	x	x	x
Sea Mammals									
Seal	—	—	—	—	—	—	—	xx	x
Dolphin	—	—	—	—	—	—	—	x	—
Porpoise	—	—	—	—	—	—	x?	—	—
Shellfish	—	—	—	xxx	—	xxx	xxx	xxx	xxx

Key: x = Present   xx = Common   xxx = Exceptionally Common

Information is taken from the following sources: Cushendun – Movius 1940; Ormeau Bridge – Adams 1899; Sydenham – Patterson 1892; Sutton, Rockmarshall and Dalkey – Liversage 1968 (Appendix by T. Hatting); Mount Sandel and Newferry – L. Van Wyjngaarden-Bakker (personal communication). The sites of Ormeau Bridge, Sutton, Rockmarshall, and Dalkey II and V are shell middens.

Fairley (1975) has pointed out that of the few species which are known to be native to Ireland, several (such as the pygmy shrew and the stoat) are able to survive in very cold conditions. Therefore, the Irish fauna could be made up of an element which survived from late-glacial times, since after 14,000 bc most of Ireland would have been free of ice (Mitchell *et al.* 1973). Other species, such as red deer and pig, may have been present in the extreme south of Ireland at the very end of the late-glacial period, or alternatively may have been introduced at some point during the early stages of the postglacial. Even greater difficulties are encountered in trying to establish which species of fresh water fish are native to Ireland. Several species, such as the pike and roach, are known to have been introduced during historical times, and the assumption that certain other species are native rests largely on the absence of any positive evidence that they were introduced. There is at the moment little evidence that fish such as tench or bream are really native to Ireland. Certainly in historical times the fish which seem to have been exploited most were the eels and the salmon, neither of which are totally fresh-water species, and both of which are migratory forms.

It is unfortunate that the majority of Mesolithic material in Ireland has been found in areas where soil conditions are particularly unfavourable to the preservation of bone. A few fragments of bone were recovered from the sandy deposits at Newferry, but both these and the more abundant material from Mount Sandel consisted mostly of burnt fragments. Apart from the material from the late Mesolithic shell midden sites (Sutton, Rock Marshall, Dalkey and Ormeau Bridge), there are only a few other sites where bones have been found. All of the available faunal material has been listed in Table 2, where an attempt has been made as far as possible to indicate the relative abundance of the different species. Unfortunately, the existing information is far too limited to allow any quantitative estimates of either the numbers of individuals or total weights of meat represented by the different species.

From this table several facts emerge. Perhaps the most striking feature is that red deer appears to have played a far less important role in the Mesolithic economy of Ireland than it did in Britain and most other parts of Europe. The presence of settlements in the upland areas of England has been attributed to a movement of Mesolithic groups into these areas during the summer months in direct response to the seasonal migrations of red deer (Clark 1972). This kind of movement is clearly absent in Ireland, and indeed there is some reason to suspect that lowland sites such as Newferry were occupied during the summer months. The absence of sites away from the rivers and the absence of evidence for extensive burning of deciduous forests to attract game would seem to indicate that mammal hunting played a secondary role in the Irish economy. One possibility is that red deer was a relatively late arrival in Ireland, and for some reason was never present in sufficiently large numbers to be worthwhile exploiting as a staple element in the food supply.

In many areas the choice was between small game (which could have been trapped), wild pig and fish. At Mount Sandel and Newferry fishing would seem to have played an important part in the economy, and certainly if the location of sites in the Bann Valley is taken into consideration, where there are so few sites away from the river, it would seem that the choice of site location was at least partially conditioned by the need to be near good fishing grounds. The insular position of Ireland may have restricted the range of mammalian species but this was probably compensated for by an abundance of migratory fish – most notably, eels and salmon. Salmon run upstream in Ireland during the spring and early summer and are available inland on the lakes until the autumn, when they spawn. During the winter they then move back down stream, but are not normally caught at this time of the year. Eels on the other hand are available inland in the lakes throughout most of the year, but are best caught when they are moving as shoals downstream to the sea. This occurs in the second half of the year at roughly monthly intervals. The complementary runs of salmon and eels may therefore have provided a unique combination of subsistence resources in Ireland, which allowed the Irish Mesolithic to develop on a rather different economic basis from that in Britain and the rest of Europe.

Seasonality and site function

At the moment it is unfortunately very difficult to attempt to ascribe particular functions to different sites other than on the basis of site location. Certainly if fishing played an important role in the economy of the Irish Mesolithic, this would pose difficulties in attempting to ascribe correctly functions to specific implement types. If nets or stone weirs were used, there may be no implements related to their manufacture which would usually be preserved in the archaeological record, while if wooden weirs with fish traps were used (as may well have been the case in Ireland) much of the equipment would consist of heavy woodworking equipment employed in the building and maintenance of the weirs, rather than fishing equipment as such. As we shall see, similar problems are encountered in attempting to explain the range of microlith-dominated equipment recovered from sites such as Mount Sandel. There are too many implements whose primary purpose is to produce the means of production (i.e. hunting equipment) and too many whose function is unknown, to use simple typological categories as absolute functional divisions. Therefore in the discussion which follows the location of sites, together with certain other indications where available, has been used as the main basis for attributing specific functions to particular sites, and the possible seasons and duration of occupation of these settlements.

Early Mesolithic

Many of the early Mesolithic sites have been either eroded away by rising sea or river levels or alternatively buried under later deposits.

We therefore have access to relatively few sites which can be placed together into a seasonal pattern. Nevertheless a strong case can be made out for regarding some of the sites in the Bann Valley as winter season 'base camps'. As we have seen, sites such as Culbane and Mount Sandel are located well above the winter flood levels of the river, and at the latter site the evidence of a very substantial living structure and of large, deep pits which were probably employed for food storage, could be used as an argument for winter occupation. The presence of large numbers of burnt hazel nuts on the site may indicate that occupation commenced during the autumn, although it has been suggested that in many contexts hazel nuts may have been collected and stored deliberately as a source of winter food (Mellars 1976: 376). Against this interpretation might be set the poor representation of 'maintenance' tools (notably scrapers and burins) at these sites, but it is plainly debatable how much significance can be attached to this kind of evidence. If red deer was never an important element in the Irish fauna, then the lack of burins (and perhaps also scrapers) might be explained in these terms (cf. Clark 1972: 34-5). Indeed, the only early Mesolithic site which has produced substantial numbers of scrapers and burins (at Maddens, on the shore line of Lough Neagh) seems much more likely to have a summer than a winter settlement. For reasons which will be given below, it is likely that some of the coastal settlements would have been occupied during the spring.

Later Mesolithic

In the later Mesolithic, sites are known from a wider range of locations, but unfortunately none has produced the same range of evidence as that recovered from Mount Sandel. Geographically, the sites can be divided into three groups: coastal sites; sites in the Bann Valley and in the neighbourhood of Lough Neagh; and sites in the Midlands.

Outside County Antrim, some of the coastal sites are associated with shell-middens, most of which have been destroyed in the last few years. Apart from the Sutton midden, all of these are rather small and are often situated on what at the time of the Maximum Transgression would have been small islands. On the basis of the limited faunal information available, it seems clear that these are not winter settlements, and that the most likely period of occupation would be during the spring (cf. Table 2). For example, most of the northern sites are oyster middens. The oysters would need to be collected mostly from below low tide level, which in winter would not have been an easy source of food. On the southern middens the presence of bones of auk and other sea birds would also argue against winter-season occupation. This is certainly true of the puffin (recorded from at least one site) which remains off-shore throughout most of the autumn and winter months. The easiest time for catching all of these birds would be during the spring, when the birds are nesting. The fact that many of the sites are situated on small islands, together with the small size of the sites themselves, could be invoked as further arguments against their interpretation as winter settlements. Taking into account all of this evidence, the midden sites are therefore interpreted most easily as specialised 'procurement' sites, most probably occupied for a relatively brief period during the spring months. It is possible that some of the estuarine sites may have been occupied for slightly longer as base camps, but it is equally likely that these sites were similarly occupied for a relatively short period during the spring months, when the migratory fish were beginning their runs upstream.

There is some evidence that most of the summer and part of the rest of the year would have been spent inland. At many riverside locations fish could have been caught during their runs upstream to the lakes, while during the second half of the year eels could have been exploited in a similar way as they made their way downstream to the sea. Certainly the very low-lying position of the Newferry site – within the flood-plain of the Bann river – would argue in favour of occupation during the summer months, while the discovery of seeds of the wild raspberry during the Harvard excavations at Newferry would provide further support for this interpretation. However, it is likely that additional visits to sites such as Newferry would also be made throughout the autumn, and perhaps even part of the winter when reduced levels of the river made this occupation possible. With the possible exception of fishing camps it is at present difficult to identify any later Mesolithic sites which are likely to have been occupied during the winter months.

Perhaps the major problem posed by the Later Mesolithic centres on the identification of sites which can be regarded in the conventional sense as base camps. As we have seen, the coastal midden sites would appear to represent rather specialised 'procurement' sites which were probably occupied for only a brief period, while the heavy emphasis on fishing at most of the inland sites such as Newferry would similarly suggest the existence of economically-specialised 'procurement' or 'extraction' sites. Other sites, such as Curran Point, Larne, would seem to represent sites of specialised industrial activity (Movius 1953). It would appear, therefore, that sites occupied for several months, or 'home bases', of the Later Mesolithic communities in Ireland remain as yet to be found.

To summarise, there is sufficient evidence available to suggest a tentative working hypothesis for the Irish Mesolithic economy, and for a seasonal cycle of movements. As in many temperate, non-agricultural communities, fishing would appear to have played an important role (cf. Lee 1968). However, there would also be a tendency to exploit different resources at different seasons of the year. Maritime resources were probably exploited primarily during the

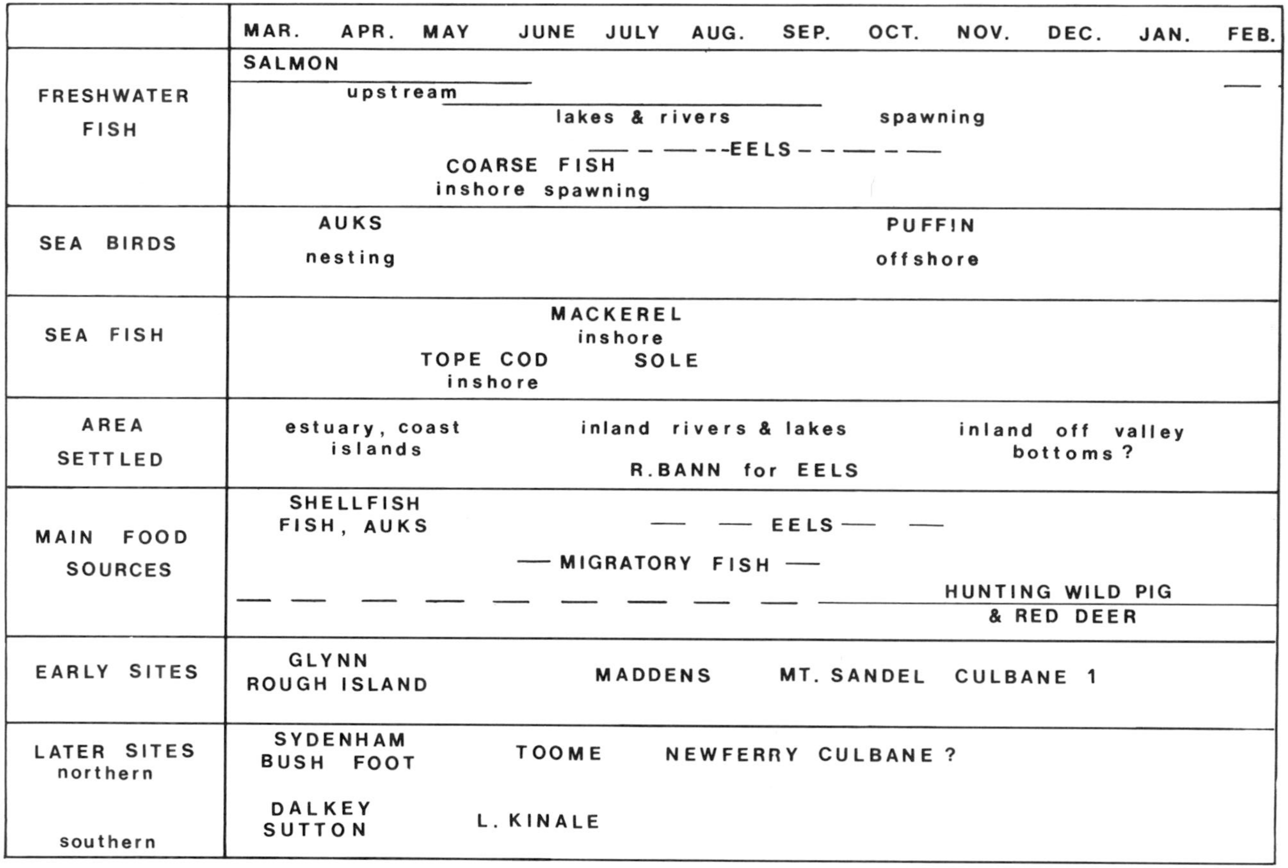

	MAR.	APR.	MAY	JUNE	JULY	AUG.	SEP.	OCT.	NOV.	DEC.	JAN.	FEB.
FRESHWATER FISH	SALMON		upstream		lakes & rivers				spawning			
				COARSE FISH inshore spawning		– –EELS– – –	– – –	–				
SEA BIRDS			AUKS nesting					PUFFIN offshore				
SEA FISH			TOPE COD inshore		MACKEREL inshore SOLE							
AREA SETTLED			estuary, coast islands		inland rivers & lakes R.BANN for EELS				inland off valley bottoms?			
MAIN FOOD SOURCES			SHELLFISH FISH, AUKS			– – MIGRATORY FISH – – EELS – –			HUNTING WILD PIG & RED DEER			
EARLY SITES			GLYNN ROUGH ISLAND			MADDENS		MT. SANDEL CULBANE 1				
LATER SITES northern			SYDENHAM BUSH FOOT		TOOME NEWFERRY CULBANE ?							
southern			DALKEY SUTTON		L. KINALE							

Figure 13. Summary of possible seasonal pattern of movements and economic exploitation in the Irish Mesolithic.

spring months, whilst it has been suggested that the runs of migratory fish would have encouraged the human groups to move inland into river-side locations during the summer and autumn months. The most difficult period – when the law of minimum resources would apply – would occur during the winter months, after the down-stream migration of the eels. No doubt some fish would still be available in the lakes at this time of year – for example, those mature and near-mature eels which had not migrated. But apart from the winter shoaling of pollan, most kinds of fish would not have been so easily available at this time of year. On the whole, therefore, it seems likely that fishing played a less important role during the winter months and that the hunting of animals such as pig, perhaps combined with a certain amount of trapping, would have become more important at this time of year. Additional sources of food during the winter may have been provided by the storage of certain resources such as hazel nuts, and perhaps also eels, which can be preserved by smoking.

Obviously, these are only tentative suggestions of how food could be procured during the annual cycle. It is reasonable to assume that while many different sources were available and exploited throughout the year, there would be a tendency to catch or track certain animals when they would be either most vulnerable or present in large numbers, and thus easily available. Thus there might be a tendency to concentrate on the exploitation of birds when nesting, fish when shoaling, and so on (cf. Price, this volume). An attempt to indicate the probable availability and exploitation of these different economic resources throughout the annual cycle is shown in Figure 13.

In conclusion, it is possible to identify two major problem areas within the Irish Mesolithic on which future research will need to be concentrated. The first one hinges on the general problems of the origins of the Irish Mesolithic and (perhaps more particularly) on the character of the technological transition from the early to the later Mesolithic. What kind of forces brought about this change in the form of implements, and how were the morphological changes in the shapes of the implements related to changes in the basic technology of flake production? The second group of problems concerns questions such as the total geographical extent of Mesolithic colonisation in Ireland, and the specific economic and social systems which characterised different stages of the Mesolithic occupation. In this regard there is clearly a need to locate and excavate sites which can throw light not only on the detailed chronology of the Irish Mesolithic, but also on the ways of life practised during this period.

Notes

[1] Since this article was written radiocarbon dates have become available for two more Early Mesolithic sites. These are:

Castleroe, County Derry:
    6,805 ± 135 bc (UB-2171)
    6,610 ± 75 bc (UB-2172)
Lough Boora, County Offally:
    6,525 ± 75 bc (UB-2199)
    6,400 ± 70 bc (UB-2200)

[2] Within the last year it has been possible to extend the distribution pattern of early Mesolithic material much further south. M. Ryan's excavation at Lough Boora, County Offally, has produced a significant concentration of microliths on the shores of a fossil lake, and a small scatter of microliths has been found along the River Dee to the north of Drogheda, County Louth. It was implicit in this article that the concept of a movement of Mesolithic groups from Argyll (western Scotland) to Ireland was no longer acceptable. A movement from northern England to the east coast of Ireland was regarded as a more likely alternative. This extended distribution of Early Mesolithic material further to the south would be more in keeping with an initial movement of man into the east, rather than the extreme north of Ireland.

References

Adams, W.A. 1899. Prehistoric sites near the Ormeau Bridge, Belfast. *Ulster Journal of Archaeology* (2nd series), 5: 5-8.

Clark, J.G.D. 1954. *Excavations at Star Carr*. London, Cambridge University Press.

Clark, J.G.D. 1972. *Star Carr: A Case Study in Bio-archaeology*. Addison Wesley Modules in Anthropology, 10. Reading, Massachussetts.

Crabtree, D.E. 1968. Mesoamerican polyhedral cores and prismatic blades. *American Antiquity*, 33: 446-79.

Donner, J.J. 1970. Land/sea level changes in Scotland. In D. Walker and R.G. West (eds.), *Studies in the Vegetational History of the British Isles*. Cambridge University Press: 23-39.

Fairley, J.S. 1975. *An Irish Beast Book*. Belfast, Blackstaff Press.

Fitzhugh, W.W. 1972. *Environmental Archaeology and Cultural Systems in Hamilton Inlet, Labrador*. Smithsonian Contribution to Anthropology, 16. Washington, Smithsonian Institute Press.

Lee, R.B. 1968. What hunters do for a living, or how to make out on scarce resources. In R.B. Lee and I. DeVore (eds.), *Man the Hunter*. Chicago, Aldine: 30-48.

Liversage, D.L. 1968. Excavations at Dalkey Island. *Proceedings of the Royal Irish Academy*, 66, C: 52-233.

Mahr, A. 1937. New aspects and problems in Irish prehistory. *Proceedings of the Prehistoric Society*, 3: 262-336.

Mellars, P.A. 1976. Settlement patterns and industrial variability in the British Mesolithic. In G. de G. Sieveking, I.H. Longworth and K.E. Wilson (eds.), *Problems in Economic and Social Archaeology*. London, Duckworth: 375-99.

Mercer, J. 1974. New C14 dates from the Isle of Jura, Argyll. *Antiquity*, 48: 65-6.

Mitchell, G.F. 1976. *The Irish Landscape*. London, Collins.

Mitchell, G.F. and Sieveking, G. de G. 1972. A flint flake probably of Palaeolithic age, from Mell Townland, new Drogheda, County Louth, Ireland. *Journal of the Royal Society of Antiquaries of Ireland*, 102: 174-7.

Mitchell, G.F., Penny, L.F., Shotton, F.W. and West, R.G. (eds.), 1973. *A Correlation of Quaternary Deposits in the British Isles*. Geological Society of London, Special Report no. 4. Edinburgh, Scottish Academic Press.

Movius, H.L. 1936. A Neolithic site on the River Bann. *Proceedings of the Royal Irish Academy*, 43, C: 17-40.

Movius, H.L. 1940. An early postglacial archaeological site at Cushendun, Co. Antrim. *Proceedings of the Royal Irish Academy*, 46, C: 1-48.

Movius, H.L. 1953. Curran Point Larne, Co. Antrim, the type site of the Irish Mesolithic. *Proceedings of the Royal Irish Academy*, 56, C: 1-95.

Parker, D. 1938. Flints from the shore of Lough Beg. *Ulster Journal of Archaeology*, 2: 107.

Patterson, L. 1892. On a newly discovered site for worked flints in the County of Down. *Journal of the Royal Society of Antiquaries of Ireland*, 22: 154-5.

Prior, D.B. 1966. Late-glacial and postglacial shorelines in north-east Antrim. *Irish Geography*, 5: 173-87.

Savage, R.J.G. 1966. Irish Pleistocene mammals. *Irish Naturalists Journal*, 15(5): 117-30.

Semenov, S. 1964. *Prehistoric Technology*. London, Cory, Adams and Mackay (English translation by M.W. Thompson).

Smith, A.G. and Collins, A.E.P. 1971. The stratigraphy, palynology and archaeology of diatomite deposits at Newferry. Co. Antrim, Northern Ireland. *Ulster Journal of Archaeology*, 34: 3-25.

Synge, F.M. 1970. The Irish Quaternary: a review. In N. Stephens and R.E. Glassock (eds.), *Irish Geographical Studies*. Belfast, Queen University: 244-58.

Synge, F.M. and Stephens, N. 1966. Late and postglacial shorelines and ice limits in Argyll and north-east Ulster. *Transactions of the Institute of British Geographers*, 39: 101-25.

Whelan, C.B. 1930. The tanged flake industry of the River Bann, Co. Antrim. *Antiquaries Journal*, 10: 134-8.

Whelan, C.B. 1952. *A Bone Industry from the River Bann*, Archaeological Research Publications (Northern Ireland), no. 1. Belfast, Stationery Office.

Woodman, P.C. 1974a. Settlement patterns of the Irish Mesolithic. *Ulster Journal of Archaeology*, 37: 1-16.

Woodman, P.C. 1974b. The chronological position of the latest phases of the Larnian. *Proceedings of the Royal Irish Academy*, 74, C: 237-58.

Woodman, P.C. 1977. Recent excavations at Newferry, County Antrim. *Proceedings of the Prehistoric Society*, 43: 155-99.

14

Excavation and economic analysis of Mesolithic shell middens on the Island of Oronsay (Inner Hebrides)

Paul Mellars

The small island of Oronsay in the Inner Hebrides lies approximately 30 kilometres to the west of the Scottish mainland at a latitude of 56° North. At present the island has a total land area of only 5.8 square kilometres, much of which is covered by thick accumulations of wind-blown sand. As a result of the delayed recovery of the land from the effects of isostatic depression during the last ice age it is likely that the area of the island would have been reduced to less than 4 square kilometres during later Mesolithic times (cf. Jardine 1977). Immediately to the north of Oronsay lies the larger island of Colonsay, while some 10-12 kilometres to the east – between Oronsay and the mainland – are the islands of Islay and Jura (Fig. 1).

The chief archaeological interest of Oronsay lies in the occurrence of a series of six Mesolithic shell middens, of which all except one are located along the south-east facing coast of the island (Fig. 2). Three of these middens (Caisteal nan Gillean I, Cnoc Sligeach and Cnoc Riach) were identified in the nineteenth century, and were excavated on various occasions between 1879 and 1913 (Grieve 1885, Anderson 1898, Bishop 1914). The three remaining sites (Caisteal nan Gillean II, Cnoc Coig and the Priory Midden) were identified in the course of the current programme of excavations which commenced in 1970. This remarkable concentration of Mesolithic shell middens on Oronsay is unique within the context of the British Mesolithic, and can be paralleled from only two or three other localities in Europe as a whole (cf. Bailey, this volume).

The general aims and orientation of the current work on Oronsay have been summarised in an earlier paper (Mellars and Payne 1971) and will therefore not be discussed in detail here. The present report is intended to provide a brief, interim account of the progress of the Oronsay investigations, and to indicate some of the principal results of the work achieved so far.

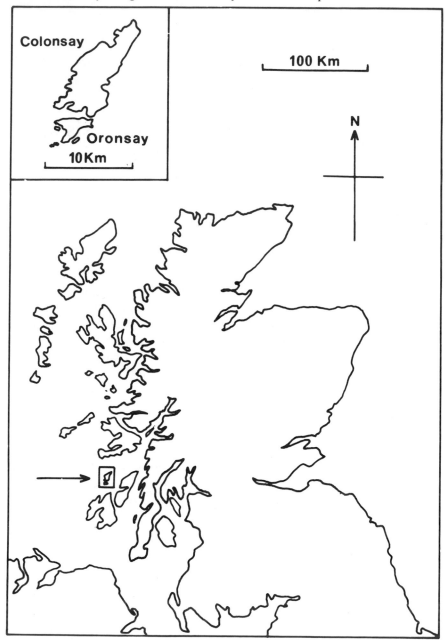

Figure 1. Map showing the position of Oronsay.

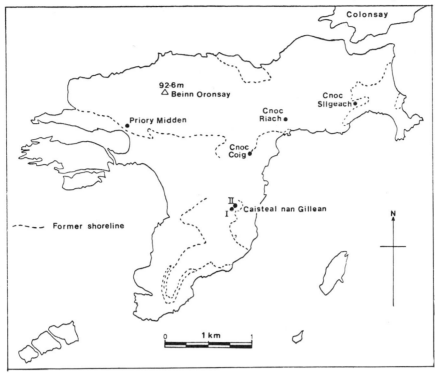

Figure 2. Map showing the location of Mesolithic shell middens on Oronsay in relation to raised shore-line features associated with the maximum postglacial marine transgression on the island. The position of the raised shoreline is based on Jardine 1977, Fig. 1.

Excavation and sampling procedures

In practical terms, the excavations on Oronsay have focused on two major objectives: firstly, to obtain representative samples of midden material from each of the middens on the island to provide a basis for radiocarbon dating, economic and seasonal interpretations, palaeoenvironmental studies and so on; and, secondly, to excavate larger areas of at least one of the sites in order to throw light on the overall stratigraphy of the midden deposits and to search for any traces of structural features associated with the Mesolithic occupations.

In the course of five field seasons detailed samples of shell-midden material have been excavated from four of the six middens on the island (Cnoc Sligeach, Caisteal nan Gillean II, Cnoc Coig and the Priory Midden) and it is hoped to obtain further samples from the two remaining sites during a further season of field-work planned for the summer of 1978. The most extensive sampling operations have been carried out on the Cnoc Coig midden. During the 1975 season

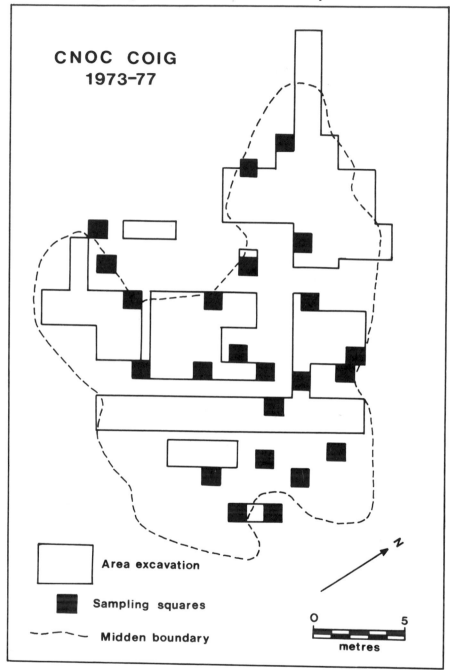

Figure 3. Plan of the Cnoc Coig midden, showing the position of probabilistic sampling squares and the total extent of areas excavated in 1973, 1975 and 1977.

stratified samples of midden material were excavated from 23 separate points distributed over the entire area of the site and selected on the basis of statistically-controlled 'probabilistic' sampling procedures (Fig. 3). The general theory and strategic problems underlying these sampling procedures have been discussed in a recent paper by Will Peacock (1978), and the analysis of the large quantities of material recovered in the course of this work will form the major component of a Ph.D. dissertation at present being prepared at the University of Cambridge. The objectives of this work are to obtain data not only on the *overall* composition of the midden deposits, but also on the extent to which the composition of the midden deposits varies both vertically (i.e. through time) and horizontally. In addition to providing valuable information on the general patterning of human activities over the site as a whole, the analysis of multiple samples of midden material should provide a firm basis for assessing any significant patterns of association, or 'covariation', in the different elements (both artefacts and food refuse) represented in the middens. Equipped with this information it should then be possible to make some assessment of how much reliance can be placed on the smaller samples of material recovered from the more limited sampling procedures applied to the other Oronsay sites.

The detailed sampling procedures applied to the Cnoc Coig midden have been supplemented during the past three seasons by extensive area excavations on this site. In all, 156 square metres of the midden deposits have now been totally excavated, which is estimated to represent approximately 60 percent of the total area of the site. Large-scale excavations of shell midden deposits have rarely been attempted in the past because of the depth and stratigraphic complexity of the deposits involved, but in the present case this policy has been amply justified by the recovery of a varied series of structural features preserved in the wind-blown sand deposits which underlie the midden. Further excavations to shed additional light on these features, and to provide a more complete picture of the overall stratigraphy of the midden deposits, are planned for 1978.

Dating evidence

Prior to the current excavations the only evidence bearing directly on the age of the Oronsay middens was provided by their relationship to raised beach deposits associated with the maximum of the postglacial marine transgression on the island. In general terms the sites can be seen to lie close to or slightly above the maximum extent of this transgression (Fig. 2), and during the early excavations at Cnoc Sligeach, Bishop claimed to have found evidence of an interstratification of occupation material and raised beach deposits in the lowermost levels of the site (Bishop 1914: 67-71). From these

Table 1. Radiocarbon dates for Oronsay shell middens.

CNOC COIG

Q-1351	Upper part of midden	Charcoal	3,545 ± 75 bc
Q-1352	Upper part of midden	Charcoal	3,480 ± 130 bc
Q-1353	Lower part of midden	Charcoal	3,695 ± 80 bc
Q-1354	Lower part of midden	Charcoal	3,585 ± 140 bc

CAISTEAL NAN GILLEAN II

Birm-346	Upper part of midden	Charcoal	3,200 ± 380 bc
Birm-347	Lower part of midden	Charcoal	3,500 ± 140 bc
Q-1355	Lower part of midden	Charcoal	3,510 ± 65 bc
Birm-348(a)	Lower part of midden	Limpet shells: (inner fraction)	3,900 ± 310 bc
Birm-348(b)		(middle fraction)	3,770 ± 140 bc
Birm-348(c)		(outer fraction)	3,620 ± 140 bc

CNOC SLIGEACH

GX-1903	Position unknown	Oyster shell	3,065 ± 210 bc
GX-1904	Position unknown	Bone	3,805 ± 180 bc
BM-670	Upper part of midden	Charcoal	3,476 ± 159 bc

observations it has been recognised for some time that the middens must belong to a relatively late stage of the Mesolithic period, but the uncertainties over the precise dating of this phase of marine transgression – and in particular the date at which the sea began to retreat from this level – have precluded any firm dating of the sites from this evidence alone. In the course of the current work a detailed survey of the relationships between the shell middens and raised shoreline features around the coasts of Oronsay has been undertaken by Dr W.G. Jardine; a preliminary account of the results of this work has been published recently in *Nature* (Jardine 1977).

At present a total of twelve radiocarbon dates are available from the middens themselves (Table 1). Of these, two were obtained by Dr E. MacKie (1972) on the basis of material collected during the excavations of Henderson Bishop at Cnoc Sligeach, while the remainder are based on samples collected during the current work. A detailed discussion of the results of these measurements will be published elsewhere, but perhaps the main point to note here is that all of the dates so far obtained from samples of charcoal (comprising eight separate samples from the sites of Caisteal nan Gillean II, Cnoc Coig and Cnoc Sligeach) fall within a relatively narrow range of time. between 3,695 ± 80 and 3,200 ± 380 bc ('uncalibrated' measurements). A rather earlier range of dates was obtained from samples of limpet shells collected from the lower levels of the Caisteal nan Gillean II midden (3,900 ± 310, 3,770 ± 140 and 3,620 ± 140 bc, for the 'inner', 'middle' and 'outer' fractions of the shells) but these dates are in direct conflict with those obtained from two samples of charcoal from the same level in the midden (3,500 ± 140 and 3,510 ± 65 bc) and evidently reflect the effects of hard-water error or some other anomaly in the isotopic composition of the shells (Shotton and Williams 1973: 456). Further dates of 3,805 ± 180 and 3,065 ± 210 bc were obtained for samples of animal bone and shell respectively collected during the 1913 excavations at Cnoc Sligeach, but the stratigraphic provenance of these samples within the midden deposits is unknown (MacKie 1972). Further samples of charcoal from Cnoc Coig and the (as yet undated) Priory Midden are at present being processed, and it is hoped to collect additional samples for C14 dating from at least one of the remaining Oronsay sites during the forthcoming excavations. As the evidence stands at present it would seem to point to an intensive and relatively short-lived exploitation of the island by Mesolithic communities centred around the middle of the fourth millennium bc. However, when the results of the new measurements are available we shall clearly be in a better position to make a firm assessment of both the total duration of the Mesolithic occupation on Oronsay, and on the extent to which the occupation of the different middens can be regarded as essentially synchronous.

Economic data

One of the main objectives of the current work has been to obtain data on the total range and relative importance of the different food resources exploited by the Mesolithic communities on Oronsay. More work will be needed before a detailed quantitative analysis of all the categories of food refuse represented in the different middens can be provided, but already a number of interesting facts have emerged. Perhaps the most significant feature which has emerged so far is the major importance of fish in the diet of the Oronsay communities. A preliminary attempt to estimate the relative importance of fish and shell-fish in a series of stratified midden samples from three of the sites (Cnoc Sligeach, Caisteal nan Gillean II and the Priory Midden) is shown in Figure 4. How much significance should be attached to the fluctuating frequencies of fish as opposed to shell-fish remains in different levels of the middens is clearly open to debate, but from the data presented in Figure 4 there can be little doubt that the systematic exploitation of marine fish resources played a major role in the subsistence activities of the Mesolithic groups on Oronsay during at least certain seasons of the year.

The most striking feature which has emerged from the analysis of the fish bones themselves is the overwhelming proportion of the remains which belong to a single species – the saithe or coalfish (*Pollachius virens*). In almost all of the midden samples analysed so far this species accounts for over 90 percent of the total fish-bone material, and in many of the samples it is the only species represented.

FISH/SHELL MEAT RATIOS

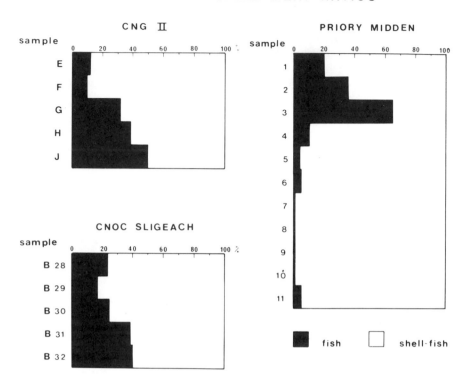

Figure 4. Relative contributions of fish and shellfish in a series of stratified midden samples from Caisteal nan Gillean II ('CNG II'), Cnoc Sligeach, and the Priory Midden. The figures are based on the fresh (i.e. uncooked) meat weights contributed by the two resources and assume that only 50 percent of the total body weight of the fish was used as food. Calculations of the meat weight of the fish are based on data collected by M. Wilkinson. Further data on the meat weights of shell-fish are taken from Fowler (1974) and Sloan (1976).

In environmental terms, of course, this is by no means surprising, since the saithe is by far the most common species encountered in the immediately inshore waters around the coasts of western and northern Scotland at the present day, and is known to have formed a staple element in the diet of many coastal communities in these areas until relatively recent times (Darling and Boyd 1969: 243; Barry 1808: 300). What is perhaps more surprising is that no reference whatever to this species appears in the accounts of the earlier excavations on Oronsay, presumably because the bones are too small to have been recognised with the methods of excavation employed. It is salutary to recall that without the use of fine-scale sieving and sorting techniques one of the major economic resources exploited by the Mesolithic communities on Oronsay – and conceivably one of the most important factors controlling the location of the Oronsay sites – might well have been completely overlooked.

Accurate assessments of the quantitative importance of the other food elements represented in the middens pose more difficult problems which have still to be satisfactorily resolved. Remains of at least two species of crabs are relatively abundant in all of the Oronsay middens, and it is likely that these resources made a major contribution to the diet during at least the summer and autumn months. Other significant results which have emerged from recent work include the wide range of birds exploited from the sites (of which over 30 different species have so far been identified), and the occurrence of large numbers of seal bones in the Cnoc Coig midden. The samples of mammalian bones so far recovered from the other sites are too small to provide a reliable basis for generalisations, but in the case of the Cnoc Coig midden at least there is a conspicuous scarcity of bones representing the larger species of land mammals. Indeed, if one is to judge by the Cnoc Coig fauna it seems very doubtful whether any of the larger land mammals were being hunted on the island itself. In the case of red deer, for example, there is a heavy over-representation of antlers as compared to other parts of the skeleton, suggesting that the bulk of the remains were brought on to the site not in the form of food but as sources of raw material for tool manufacture. Whether or not this is true of the other Oronsay middens remains to be established, but it would seem open to question on purely ecological grounds whether native populations of red deer or any other ungulate species were ever present on either Oronsay itself or on the larger adjacent island of Colonsay. If this were the case, then the presence of red deer antlers and other ungulate remains in the Oronsay middens would have to be seen as evidence of some kind of regular contact between Oronsay itself and either the Scottish mainland or (more probably) the larger islands of Islay and Jura which lie some 10-12 kilometres to the east.

Inevitably, the major uncertainty concerns the role of plant foods in the economy of the Oronsay communities. The only positive evidence in this direction is provided by the recovery of large numbers of burnt and broken hazel-nut shells from almost all of the occupation levels of the Cnoc Coig midden, but any kind of estimate of the quantitative importance of this resource in the total food supply is clearly out of the question. Other samples of carbonised plant remains recovered by the use of froth flotation techniques are at present awaiting identification. In view of the very small land area of Oronsay in late Mesolithic times it could no doubt be argued that any kind of terrestrial plant resources are unlikely to have made more than a limited contribution to the food supply. The potential exploitation of various species of edible seaweed, on the other hand, should perhaps be seen in a rather different light, especially in view of the relative breadth of the inter-tidal zone around the greater part of the coastline of the island, and the high proportion of this zone which would have been occupied by outcrops of seaweed-bearing rock. The use of such species as 'dulse' (*Rhodymenia palmata*),

'Irish moss' (*Chondrus crispus*) and 'laver' (*Porphyra umbilicalis*) has continued down to modern times along many parts of the western coastline of Britain, and it would be surprising if these resources did not make at least some contribution to the human food supply during Mesolithic times (cf. Mabey 1975: 116-20; Yonge 1963: 322-3). As Clarke has recently emphasised (1976), until we can find some means of evaluating the importance of these and other plant-food resources, our ability to reconstruct the overall subsistence strategies of Mesolithic communities will remain at best incomplete, and at worst potentially misleading.

Evidence for seasonal occupation

Information on the seasons of the year during which the different shell middens on Oronsay were occupied is clearly critical to an understanding of the patterns of Mesolithic exploitation on the island. The most instructive data in this direction have so far been provided by studies of the otoliths of saithe, of which large numbers have been recovered from all four of the middens investigated (**Fig. 5**). The use of these bones for seasonal interpretations depends on the fact that during the first 2-3 years of life the growth of the young saithe is very rapid (Wheeler 1969: 274; Bertelsen 1942). So long as we can assume a close relationship between the growth of the otoliths and the growth of the fish as a whole, therefore (cf. Fig 6), it should be possible to use data on the size distribution of the otoliths as an indication of the approximate *age* of the fish, and hence of the seasons of the year in which the fish were caught.

The detailed results of these analyses will be published elsewhere (Mellars and Wilkinson, in press) but the essential data relating to the four Oronsay middens are summarised in Figure 7. Perhaps the most immediately striking feature of these diagrams is that in the case of two of the sites, Cnoc Sligeach and Cnoc Coig, the length distributions of the otoliths exhibit a sharply bimodal pattern, in which the two modes can be shown to correspond respectively with fish in the first and second years of life. This of course is precisely the pattern one would expect to find if the fishing activities at the two sites were carried out over a relatively short span of time (say 2-3 months of the year) and if the fishing techniques employed resulted in the more or less simultaneous capture of fish belonging to the first two year groupings. A sharp contrast to this pattern is provided by the otolith samples from the Priory Midden, which show a strongly unimodal distribution, apparently representing fish belonging almost exclusively to the first-year group. The fourth histogram, from Caisteal nan Gillean II, shows a more or less intermediate pattern in which the otoliths are distributed more evenly over the whole of the length range. The main point to be emphasised here, however,

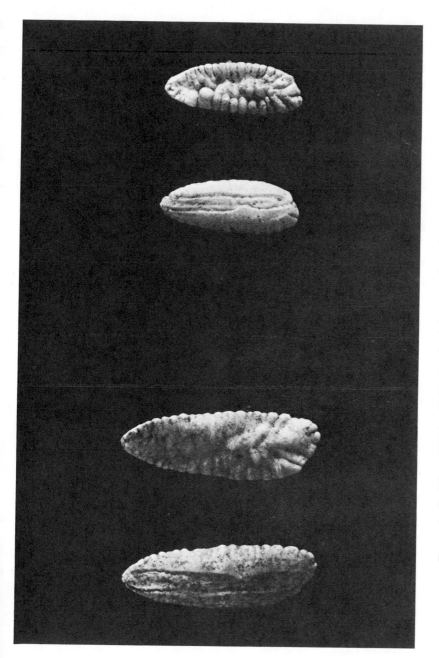

Figure 5. Otoliths of Saithe (*Pollachius virens*) from the Cnoc Coig midden. The two otoliths on the left (showing the upper and lower faces respectively) derive from fish belonging to the second-year age group while those on the right are from fish belonging to the first-year group. The otolith on the extreme left is 10.5 mm. long.

o

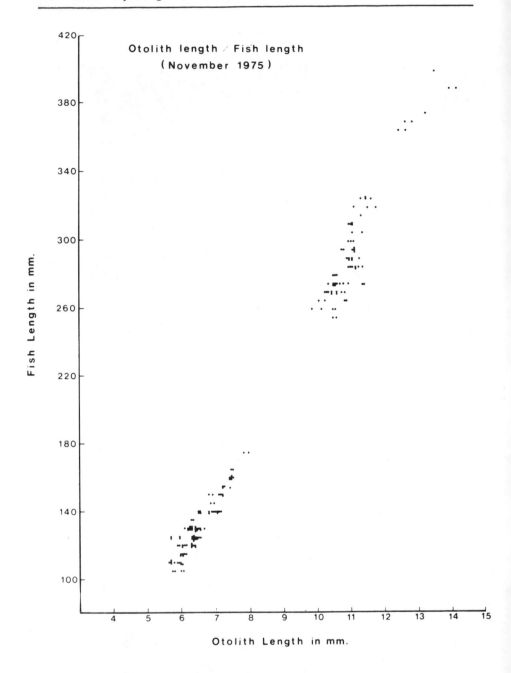

Figure 6. Relationship between otolith length and total body length in samples of saithe caught off Colonsay and Oronsay in November 1975. The two major size groupings apparent on the graph represent fish belonging respectively to the first and second year age groups. Based on data collected by M. Wilkinson.

concerns not only the differences in the overall form of the histograms, but the clearly different positions of the *modal* points of the length distributions in the four sites (Fig. 7). Confronted with these observations the conclusion seems hard to escape that the saithe populations being exploited from the different middens were of different ages, and accordingly that the major fishing activities for this species at the four sites were carried out at different seasons of the year.

In an attempt to provide some kind of 'absolute' calibration for these seasonal indications, observations have been made on the rates of growth of otoliths in modern samples of saithe caught off the coasts of Oronsay and Colonsay at different times of the year. Most of this work has been carried out by Michael Wilkinson in the course of Ph.D. research at the University of Sheffield, and will be published in due course as part of a general study of the fish remains from the Oronsay sites. Clearly, any attempt to make direct correlations between the prehistoric and modern otolith samples must depend on the assumption that the rates of growth of the fish in Mesolithic times were essentially similar to those of the present day. If we proceed on this assumption the conclusion emerges that the Cnoc Sligeach midden was occupied primarily during the mid-summer months (around July-August), Cnoc Coig during the autumn (September-November), and the Priory Midden at some point between the beginning of the winter and the early spring months. As already noted, the otolith samples from Caisteal nan Gillean II appear to reflect occupation over a longer period of the annual cycle, although the well-defined peak representing the second-year fish group would seem to indicate a major emphasis on fishing at this site during the early to mid-summer months (?June-July).

Whether or not the rates of otolith growth during later Mesolithic times were in fact strictly comparable to those of the present day is of course open to debate. If one were to suggest that the increased temperature conditions of the Climatic Optimum period would have been likely to increase the overall rates of growth of the fish, then the seasonal interpretations suggested above would need to be adjusted accordingly, perhaps by shifting the estimated seasons of occupation by as much as 4-6 weeks towards the earlier part of the year (Mellars and Wilkinson, in press). Whether or not adjustments of this kind are in fact necessary is certainly open to question on ecological grounds. The main point to emphasise is that the seasonal interpretations suggested for the different shell middens on the basis of the otolith measurements appear to be in good agreement with a number of other lines of evidence bearing on the seasonal occupation of the sites. In the case of the Cnoc Coig midden, for example, the interpretation of the otoliths in terms of primarily autumn occupation is strongly supported by the large quantities of hazel-nut shells recovered from the site. Similarly the interpretation of the Priory Midden as an essentially

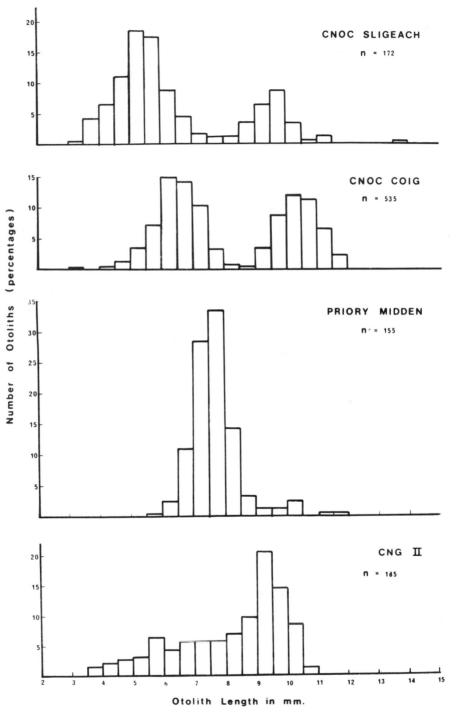

Figure 7. Length distribution of otoliths of saithe in four of the Oronsay middens. The histograms are based in each case on the combined samples of otoliths recovered from all levels in the middens.

winter-season settlement would appear to be supported by a number of observations, including both the relatively sheltered location of the site (in the lee of Beinn Oronsay) and the abnormally low ratios of fish bones to shells recorded throughout the greater part of the occupation sequence (cf. Fig. 4). The latter observation would accord particularly well with occupation during the later stages of the winter or early spring months, when all age groups of saithe are known to retreat into deep water away from the immediately inshore zone (Kennedy 1969: 318-19). Obviously the same argument cannot be applied to the uppermost levels of the Priory Midden in which fish remains are relatively abundant, but even in these levels the almost exclusive representation of fish belonging to the first-year age group would accord much better with the idea of early-winter occupation than with occupation during the summer or autumn months (Kennedy 1969: 318-19).

Until more complete data has been obtained from a number of other sources it would be premature to draw any firm conclusions regarding the overall patterns of seasonal occupation and economic exploitation on Oronsay. In the first place it must be kept in mind that only four out of the six shell middens known to exist on the island have so far been investigated in the course of the current work, and to this extent any attempt to reconstruct total settlement and exploitation patterns must be incomplete. Similarly, we must await the results of further radiocarbon determinations to assess how far the occupation of the different middens can be regarded as essentially synchronous, and how far the different occupations may prove to be – at least in part – successive in time. Lastly, there is an urgent need for information on the seasonal patterns of exploitation of limpets and other marine molluscs which evidently formed one of the staple elements in the Mesolithic economy on the island. Clearly, one should not assume that the collection of shell-fish was necessarily carried out at precisely the same seasons of the year as the exploitation of the fish populations, and indeed it remains a strong possibility that the shell-fish were exploited primarily during the winter and early spring months when most other sources of food were either inaccessible to the human groups or in very short supply. Results of oxygen-isotope measurements on the limpet shells at present being undertaken by Dr N.J. Shackleton should hopefully provide a firm answer to the latter question in the near future.

Methods of exploitation and processing of food resources

Methods of fishing are notoriously difficult to reconstruct from archaeological sources. Fish hooks as such would appear to be totally lacking from the Oronsay middens, but of course it is always possible to envisage other types of equipment which might be employed in line fishery which would leave no obvious archaeological traces. The important point to remember is that there are a number of alternative methods of fishing which are potentially more efficient and more productive than the use of lines, and which might well have yielded the bulk of the fish consumed by the Oronsay communities. The use of nets is one obvious alternative, and in view of the evidence recorded from Mesolithic contexts in other parts of Europe (e.g. Clark 1975: 223-6) this possibility should certainly not be discounted. A second and perhaps more likely alternative is the use of some kind of tidally-regulated fish traps or fish weirs. Numerous ethnographic analogies could be quoted for the use of artificially-constructed fish weirs amongst modern coastal-living groups (e.g. Oswalt 1976: 117-21, 143-5) and the size of the catches produced by these techniques are impressive. Avery (1975), for example, records that the use of stone-built fish weirs along the south-west coast of South Africa regularly yielded catches of between 100 and 500 fish per day, with occasional catches of up to 3,000 fish. Possibly more relevant in the present context is the well-documented use of similar structures (generally known as 'yaires' or 'caraidhs') along many parts of the Scottish coast until comparatively modern times (Grant 1961: 246; Crawford 1961: 110-11). The attraction of this particular explanation in the present case is that it would accord very well with the almost exclusive occurrence of the younger age groups of saithe (less than two years old) among the fish remains from the middens. It is precisely these age-groups of the saithe which frequent the immediately inshore waters throughout the summer, autumn and early winter months, and which would therefore be especially vulnerable to capture by means of traps erected at some point within the intertidal zone (Kennedy 1969: 318-21). Whether or not the rare specimens of much older saithe occasionally encountered in the middens could have been caught by the same techniques, or whether they reflect the use of some other fishing methods (for example spearing from boats; cf. Martin 1716: 144-5) must remain for the present an open question.

Some interesting insights into the way in which the fish were processed on the sites are beginning to emerge from detailed studies of the distribution of the fish remains in the middens. From the large areas excavated at Cnoc Coig, for example, it can be seen that the fish bones tend to be heavily concentrated in particular areas of the site, or at particular stratigraphic horizons, in some cases showing very little admixture with other kinds of food refuse. Such concentrations might conceivably represent periods when fishing was almost the sole subsistence activity carried out from the site, but they seem more likely to result from the systematic use of different areas of the site for the processing of different types of food resources. Similarly there are indications that at some point during the fishing activities – either during the capture of the fish themselves, or alternatively during the subsequent processing of the catches on the site – a separation was made between the very small fish (c. 10-50 gm) belonging to the first-

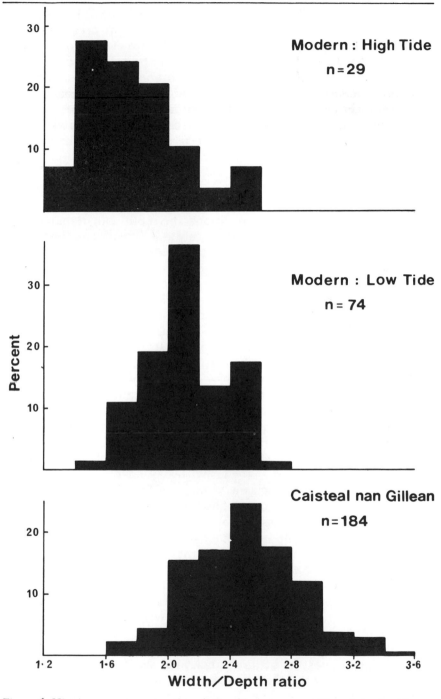

Figure 8. Histograms comparing the relationship between width and depth of limpet shells from the Caisteal nan Gillean II midden with those of modern limpet samples collected from high-tide and low-tide situations along the east coast of Oronsay. Based on data collected by A.P. Fowler (1974).

year age group and the much larger fish (150-400 gm.) belonging to the second year group (Mellars and Wilkinson, in press). A third feature which has been clearly documented in two of the Oronsay sites (Cnoc Coig and Caisteal nan Gillean II) is the occurrence of dense concentrations of bones representing the 'branchial' region of the fish at sharply localised points within the middens. These concentrations almost certainly represent areas where large numbers of fish were gutted, presumably shortly after capture. A detailed analysis of all these aspects of the distributional patterns of fish bones in the middens will be· presented in the forthcoming Ph.D. dissertation of M. Wilkinson.

With regard to the exploitation of shellfish there are perhaps two main points to be made. In the first place it seems unlikely that the heavy predominance of limpets among the molluscan remains from the different middens can be seen entirely as a reflection of the relative abundance of this species around the coastline of Oronsay, and it would seem that some deliberate selection in favour of this resource was practised by the Mesolithic communities on the island. Substantial numbers of both the common periwinkle (*Littorina littorea*) and the dog whelk (*Nucella lapillus*) are present in certain levels of the sites, but there seems little doubt that both of these species would have been accessible to the human groups in larger numbers than their frequencies in the middens would suggest. Two factors may help to explain this apparent preference for limpets. On the one hand both the periwinkle and the dog whelk have a substantially higher shell-weight:meat-weight ratio than limpets, and would therefore involve a higher rate of energy expenditure on the part of the human groups in the collection and transportation' of the resources. Secondly, and perhaps more significantly, the amount of time and effort involved in removing the molluscs from their shells may have militated against the use of winkles and whelks as a major element in the day-to-day food supply. In the case of winkles, for example, it would almost certainly have been necessary to boil the animals before the meat could be removed, while in the case of whelks it is clear from both experiments and from the state of the shells recovered from the middens that it was necessary to go to the lengths of breaking open each shell individually – and presumably picking out the broken shell fragments – to get at the flesh inside. In these circumstances it would not be surprising if periwinkles and whelks were used more to provide an element of variety in the diet than as a staple element in the food supply.

The other interesting feature concerning the patterns of shell-fish exploitation has emerged from an analysis of the shapes of the limpet shells in the middens (Fowler 1974). It is well known that the relationship between the height and length of limpet shells is determined primarily by their position within the intertidal zone, and that limpets inhabiting the lower parts of the tidal range are in general much flatter than those inhabiting the higher parts of the shore (Yonge 1963, 140-1). This has been found to be true for both of the major British species of limpets (*Patella vulgata* and *P. aspera*) and is thought to be related to the varying degrees of exposure to both wave action and dessication experienced in different parts of the tidal range (Ebling *et al.* 1962). The surprising feature which emerged from the measurements of the limpets from the midden sites was that the average height: breadth ratio of the shells was if anything rather less than that of limpets collected from very low-tide situations around the modern coast of Oronsay (Fig. 8). The implication would appear to be that the limpets in the middens were collected almost exclusively from the lower part of the tidal range, and perhaps for the most part from extreme low-tide situations exposed only during periods of spring tides. One possibility is that this phenomenon reflects purely dietary preferences on the part of the Mesolithic groups, since it is claimed by modern occupants of Colonsay that limpets collected from low-tide situations are in fact more tender and in general more palatable than those collected from the higher parts of the shore. Alternatively, of course, it could reflect the results of heavy and continuous human predation on the limpet populations on the island, which might have led rapidly to an over-exploitation of the limpet stocks in the higher and more easily accessible parts of the tidal range.

Stratigraphy and structural features

The excavation of large areas of the Cnoc Coig midden during the course of the last three field seasons (Fig. 3) has thrown valuable light on the overall stratigraphy of the midden deposits, and revealed an interesting series of structural feature associated with different phases in the occupation of the site. In the first place it became clear that the midden was composed essentially of two different kinds of deposits which might be referred to provisionally as 'shell heaps' and 'occupation surfaces'. Detailed analyses of the composition of these deposits are still in progress, but in general terms the 'shell heaps' would appear to consist of roughly dome-shaped accumulations of very loose shells, containing very little intervening matrix and relatively low densities of artefacts (cf. Fig. 9). In the 'occupation surfaces' on the other hand, the ratios of shells to matrix are much lower, the shells tend to be more fragmented, and the densities of most types of artefacts are higher. The relative positions of these two types of deposit fluctuated to some extent during the occupation of the midden, but as a generalisation it can be said that the loose 'shell-heap' accumulations were more frequent towards the seaward edge of the midden while the occupation surfaces were more common on the landward side of the site. At several points the midden deposits were separated by layers of wind-blown sand, most probably derived from

Figure 9. Close-up of midden deposits at Caisteal nan Gillean II, showing the very
loose structure typical of 'shell heap' accumulations and the heavy predominance
of limpets in the midden.

exposed beach deposits associated with an early retreat stage from the
maximum of the postglacial marine transgression (cf. Jardine 1977).
Certainly, the initial occupation of the site can be shown to have been
established on a sand-dune surface, and it would appear that
movements of blown sand were taking place intermittently
throughout the occupation of the site. At their thickest point towards
the eastern edge of the site the midden deposits attained a total
thickness of 65 cm.

The clearest traces of structures were encountered at two points
towards the base of the Cnoc Coig midden during the last season of
excavation (1977). The general features of these two structures were
remarkably similar in all essential respects. In each case the structures
consisted of a roughly circular arrangement of small and closely-
spaced stake holes with an overall diameter of approximately 3.0-3.5
metres, and centred on a very thick and heavily burned hearth.

Immediately surrounding the hearth in each case was a series of pits of varying dimensions, excavated into the pre-midden sand surface and infilled with typical shell-midden material. The interpretation of these pits is particularly difficult. The largest of the pits had a maximum diameter of 45 cm., a depth of approximately 30 cm., and showed evidence of several phases of infilling. For the larger of the pits it would be possible to suggest an interpretation in terms of cooking structures of some kind, possibly intended to hold skin containers which might be used (for example) in the boiling of shell-fish. This interpretation would obviously be more difficult to accept for the smaller pits with diameters of 20 cm. or less, and the explanation of these features remains for the present enigmatic. The character of the structures represented by the outer rings of stake holes must remain equally conjectural. On present evidence we might visualise these as either lightly-constructed tents of some sort, or alternatively as simple wind-break arrangements erected to offer some protection around areas of intensive cooking and food-preparation activities. It is significant to note that in the case of both of these structures the associated hearth deposits could be seen to extend throughout the greater part of the thickness of the midden, clearly indicating a consistent and repeated pattern in the use of these particular areas of the site over a long period of time.

The other well-defined traces of structural features encountered at Cnoc Coig were of a totally different character, and were distributed over larger areas of the site. These features consisted of densely-packed clusters of beach pebbles, usually around 15 cm. in diameter, which could be seen on excavation to extend for depths of up to 20 cm. into the sand deposits which immediately underlay the midden. The most plausible explanation of these 'stone-hole' arrangements is that they represent groups of stones embedded around the bases of wooden posts which were driven only a short distance into the pre-midden surface. The functional interpretation of these features again presents difficulties, but their rather scattered and irregular distribution over large areas of the site, and their consistent association with unusually large, and frequently overlapping, scatters of hearth material would seem to argue against an interpretation as living structures (Fig. 10). A more likely explanation is that they relate to structures associated with the drying, and perhaps smoking, of food resources, such as fish or seal meat. Such an interpretation would seem to accord particularly well with the interpretation of the Cnoc Coig midden as a primarily autumn-season settlement, since it is at this season of the year that we might expect the human groups to have been most concerned with the problems of building up substantial supplies of stored food for use over the ensuing winter months.

Figure 10. Hearth and associated stone arrangements at the base of the Cnoc Coig midden. The scale is one metre.

Conclusion

In retrospect, perhaps the most critical question raised by the Oronsay investigations concerns the overall pattern of seasonal occupation on the island. As we have seen, there is clear evidence from the otolith data that the different middens were occupied at different seasons of the year, and that when viewed as a whole this occupation must have spanned a substantial part of the annual cycle. This in turn raises the difficult and no doubt controversial question of whether Mesolithic communities could have lived on Oronsay throughout the year. There are indications that some kind of regular contact was maintained with groups on the mainland or on the larger islands, but there is at present no way of knowing whether this indicates the regular, annual movements of the entire human group or whether it represents more limited and sporadic trading contacts. Nor do we know whether there were any major gaps in the total occupational sequence represented by the shell midden sites, or whether other types of settlements not marked by shell midden accumulations may be present on the island. If the Oronsay communities did remain on the island throughout the year, what kind of problems would this have raised in terms of the genetic viability of the population over a period of several generations, and how might these problems have been overcome? Equally critical is the question of how the group could have maintained itself in economic terms during the later stages of the winter and the spring months when most of the food resources available on the island – with the notable exception of shellfish – are likely to have been in short supply.

Viewed in a broader context, the Oronsay investigations raise more general questions about the role of shellfish exploitation in Mesolithic economies. As the paper by Bailey in the present volume makes clear, substantial shell-midden accumulations of the kind documented on Oronsay are in fact comparatively rare phenomena, not only in Britain but in Mesolithic Europe as a whole. Obviously, shell middens are only to be expected where the Mesolithic coastline itself is preserved, and to this extent the absence of such sites from the greater part of the southern and eastern coastlines of Britain hardly requires explanation. On the other hand the very sparse representation of middens in the areas of substantial isostatic uplift around the northern and western coasts of Britain evidently cannot be explained in these terms. Particularly striking in this regard is the apparent absence of shell middens from such areas as south-west Scotland, and the larger offshore islands of Jura and Islay, where archaeological exploration has been relatively thorough, and where other evidence for Mesolithic occupation is well documented. Unless we are to suggest that this is entirely an artefact of poor preservation (reflecting, for example, the exploitation of shell middens as sources of fertilizer in areas of acidic soils) the implication would seem to be that in most areas of Britain the exploitation of shellfish formed only a comparatively minor element in the Mesolithic economy. As both Bailey (this volume) and Bonsall (1978) have recently argued, a crucial factor in this context may well have been the relative 'energy budget' involved in the harvesting of shellfish resources; the low calorific content of most species of shellfish, coupled with the high energy cost of transporting the molluscs over large distances would make the exploitation of these resources relatively uneconomical in terms of overall subsistence requirements. Arguing along these lines one would predict that the exploitation of shellfish on a scale sufficient to lead to the formation of substantial midden accumulations would only be likely to occur in two situations: (1) where large quantities of shellfish could be harvested with only a limited amount of movement on the part of the human groups; and (2) where other food resources offering a potentially higher yield of food for a given investment of time and effort were either lacking or in very short supply. When viewed in these terms the strong tendency for shell middens to occur on relatively small islands (e.g. Oronsay, Risga, Portland and several of the Irish sites) makes very good ecological sense; the ability to exploit a large area of coastline within a limited radius of movement would reduce substantially the time and energy costs of shellfish exploitation, while the deficiencies in alternative food supplies may have made the intensive harvesting of these resources – at least in certain contexts – an economic necessity.

Similar reasoning might also be invoked to account for the striking variations documented in the character of artefact assemblages recovered from coastal sites (cf. Meilars 1976). For example, if we are correct in assuming that none of the larger species of land mammals (red deer, boar etc.) were directly available to the Mesolithic communities on Oronsay, then the lack of the normal range of microlithic equipment at these sites might well be explained (Mellars and Payne 1971: 398; Mellars 1976: 399). Conversely, the rich and typical microlithic industries recovered from sites distributed along virtually the whole of the western seaboard of Britain – as well as on the larger islands such as Jura and Islay – might be seen as a direct reflection of the primary economic reliance placed at these sites on the exploitation of terrestrial mammalian resources. What *cannot* be so readily explained in these terms are the mechanisms underlying the initial colonisation of an isolated island habitat like Oronsay, or the occurrence of typical shell midden accumulations at a number of sites on the Scottish mainland (for example in the Oban caves and at a number of localities in the Firth of Forth) where the full range of terrestrial food resources should have been readily available to the Mesolithic groups. A tempting explanation is that these sites, dating from the closing stages of the Mesolithic period and shortly before the appearance of a fully agricultural economy in these areas, reflect either some kind of failure in the normal or 'preferred' range of food resources, or alternatively an increasing pressure on food resources in general as a result of a progressive increase in human population numbers. Whether this will turn out to be an unduly simplistic way of visualising a much more complicated social and economic situation remains to be seen. In any event, it is now becoming clear that the investigation of shell middens should be seen not simply as a rich source of data for economic 'reconstruction' in prehistory, but as potentially relevant to some of the more basic problems concerning the organisation and more long-term development of prehistoric cultural systems.

Acknowledgements

I am particularly indebted to the owner of Oronsay, Lord Strathcona, for permission to excavate the sites, and to the farmer, Mr Andrew McNeill, for his cooperation and interest throughout the excavations. As indicated in the text, the report presented here relies heavily on the research and assistance of a number of people involved in various aspects of the Oronsay project, including Mr D. Bramwell, Dr J. Dickson, Mr A.P. Fowler, Miss J. Goudie, Dr C. Grigson, Dr W.G. Jardine, Dr C. Paul, Mr W. Peacock, Dr N.J. Shackleton, Professor F.W. Shotton, Mr D. Sloan, Dr A. Tricker, Dr V.R. Switsur, Mr A. Wheeler and Mr M. Wilkinson. I am also indebted to my wife for considerable help in analysing the excavated material, and to Mr D. McGilvray, Mr P. McCallister and Mr D. Alexander for assistance in collecting the modern fish samples. Financial support for the investigations was provided by the British Academy, the Association for Cultural Exchange, the Natural Environment Research Council, the Science Research Council, and the Research Fund of Sheffield University.

The present paper is a revised version of a paper originally presented to the meeting of the *Scottish Archaeological Forum* in Aberdeen in April 1977.

References

Anderson, J. 1898. Notes on the contents of a small cave or rock-shelter at Druimvargie, Oban; and of three shell-mounds in Oronsay. *Proceedings of the Society of Antiquaries of Scotland*, 32: 298-313.

Avery, G. 1975. Discussion on the age and use of tidal fish-traps (visvyers). *South African Archaeological Bulletin*, 30: 105-13.

Barry, G. 1808. *History of the Orkney Islands* (2nd edition). London, Longman, Hurst, Rees and Orme.

Bertelsen, E. 1942. Contributions to the biology of the Coalfish (*Gadus virens* L.) in Faroe waters. *Meddelelser fra Kommissionen for Danmarks Fiskeri- og Havundersøgelser (Serie Fiskeri)*, Bind XI, Nr. 2: 1-68.

Bishop, A.H. 1914. An Oronsay shell-mound: a Scottish pre-Neolithic site. *Proceedings of the Society of Antiquaries of Scotland*, 48: 52-108.
Bonsall, J.C. 1978. The coastal factor in the Mesolithic settlement of north-west England. In B. Gramsch (ed.), *Proceedings of the Second International Symposium on the Mesolithic in Europe* (in press).
Clark, G. 1975. *The Earlier Stone Age Settlement of Scandinavia*. London, Cambridge University Press.
Clarke, D.L. 1976. Mesolithic Europe: the economic basis. In G. de G. Sieveking, I.H. Longworth and K.E. Wilson (eds.), *Problems in Economic and Social Archaeology*. London, Duckworth: 449-81.
Crawford, I.A. 1961. A tidal fish pound. *Scottish Studies*, 5: 110-11.
Darling, F.F. and Boyd, J.M. 1969. *The Highlands and Islands*. London and Glasgow, Fontana.
Ebling, F.J., Sloane, J.F., Kitching, J.A. and Davies, H.M. 1962. The ecology of Lough Ine, XII: the distribution and characteristics of *Patella* species. *Journal of Animal Ecology*, 31: 457-70.
Fowler, A.P. 1974. *The Oronsay Middens: A Study of Limpet Shells*. Unpublished B.A. dissertation, University of Sheffield.
Grant, I.F. 1961. *Highland Folk Ways*. London, Routledge and K 'gan Paul.
Grieve, S. 1885. *The Great Auk, or Garefowl*. London, Jack.
Jardine, W.G. 1977. Location and age of Mesolithic coastal occupation sites on Oronsay, Inner Hebrides. *Nature*, 267: 138-40.
Kennedy, M. 1969. *The Sea Angler's Fishes* (2nd. edition). London, Paul.
Mabey, R. 1975. *Food for Free*. London and Glasglow, Fontana.
MacKie, E.W. 1972. Radiocarbon dates for two Mesolithic shell heaps and a Neolithic axe-factory in Scotland. *Proceedings of the Prehistoric Society*, 38: 412-16.
Martin, M. 1716. *A Description of the Western Isles of Scotland* (2nd. edition). Facsimile reprint by James Thin, Edinburgh, 1976.
Mellars, P.A. and Payne, S. 1971. Excavation of two Mesolithic shell middens on the island of Oronsay (Inner Hebrides). *Nature*, 231: 397-8.
Mellars, P.A. and Wilkinson, M.R. (in press). Fish otoliths as an indicator of seasonal occupation in Mesolithic shell middens.
Oswalt, W.H. 1976. *An Anthropological Analysis of Food-getting Technology*. New York and London, Wiley.
Peacock, W.R.B. 1978. Probabilistic sampling in shell middens: a case study from Oronsay, Inner Hebrides. In J. Cherry, C. Gamble and S. Shennan (eds.), *Sampling in Contemporary British Archaeology*. Oxford, British Archaeological Reports (in press).
Shotton, F.W. and Williams, R.E.G. 1973. Birmingham University Radiocarbon dates VII. *Radiocarbon*, 15: 451-68.
Sloan, D. 1976. *The Priory Midden, 1975: A Study in Economic Analysis*. Unpublished B.A. dissertation, University of Sheffield.
Wheeler, A. 1969. *The Fishes of the British Isles and North-west Europe*. London, MacMillan.
Yonge, C.M. 1963. *The Sea Shore*. London and Glasgow, Fontana.

AUTHOR INDEX

Author Index

GENERAL INDEX

General Index